P9-DVJ-381

BP
63
.A4
N27

77711

Religion and politics in the
Middle East.

DATE DUE

BP
63
.A4
N27

77711

Religion and politics
in the Middle East.

THE UNDERSIGNED ASSUMES RESPONSIBILTY FOR THIS BOOK WHILE
CHARGED OUT TO HIM. HE WILL PAY FOR ANY FINES INCURRED OR FOR
LOSS OF, OR DAMAGE TO, THE BOOK

DATE DUE	BORROWER'S NAME & BOX NO.

CORBAN
COLLEGE   WITHDRAWN

5000 Deer Park Drive S.E., Salem, Oregon 9730   /   (503) 581-8600

Also of Interest

Islam: Continuity and Change in the Modern World, John O. Voll

Muslim-Christian Conflicts: Economic, Political, and Social Conflicts, edited by Suad Joseph and Barbara L. K. Pillsbury

A Concise History of the Middle East, Arthur Goldschmidt, Jr.

Local Politics and Development in the Middle East, edited by Louis J. Cantori and Iliya Harik

Rich and Poor Nations in the Middle East, edited by Malcolm H. Kerr and El Sayid Yassin

The Modern Middle East: A Guide to Research Tools in the Social Sciences, Reeva S. Simon

Food, Development, and Politics in the Middle East, Marvin G. Weinbaum

Directions of Change: Modernization Theory, Research, and Realities, edited by Mustafa O. Attir, Burkart Holzner, and Zdenek Suda

Archaeological History of the Ancient Middle East, Jack Finegan

The Government and Politics of the Middle East and North Africa, edited by David E. Long and Bernard Reich

The History of the Sudan from the Coming of Islam to the Present Day, Third Revised Edition, P. M. Holt and M. W. Daly

The Druzes in Israel: A Political Study--Political Innovation and Integration in a Middle Eastern Minority, Gabriel Ben-Dor

The Government and Politics of Israel, Don Peretz

King Faisal and the Modernisation of Saudi Arabia, edited by Willard A. Beling

Yemen: The Politics of the Yemen Arab Republic, Robert W. Stookey

Libya: The Experience of Oil, J. A. Allan

Afghanistan: Key to a Continent, John C. Griffiths

*Available in hardcover and paperback.

Westview Special Studies on the Middle East

Religion and Politics in the Middle East
edited by Michael Curtis

Religion and politics have been intertwined in the Muslim countries of the Middle East from the very beginning of their history; religious values have been central to all Islamic societies. Now, confronted with the challenge of Western ideas and technology, these societies are responding with a fervent Muslim fundamentalism; this "revival" must be seen not so much as a religious renaissance as a restatement of values and concepts that have always existed.

In practical terms, how do these values and concepts translate into the necessities of government? What is the nature of the societies they produce? What are the tensions and conflicts created by the pressure of twentieth-century realities on these traditionalist societies? These and other related topics are discussed in this book by leading Middle East scholars. From the Yemens in the south to Turkey in the north, the focus is on ethnic and religious divisions and on each country's attempt to bridge the gap between modern government and traditionalist practices.

Michael Curtis is professor of political science at Rutgers University. He is the author of *Comparative Government and Politics* and has edited a number of books on the Middle East.

Prepared under the auspices of the
American Academic Association for Peace in the Middle East

AAAPME is an association of academicians teaching in U.S. colleges and universities. The purpose of the association is to study all aspects of the Middle East situation, to utilize the special skills and talents of the academic community to elicit new ideas and approaches for a solution of the Arab-Israeli conflict, and to find a means of reaching a just and lasting peace in the region.

AAAPME publishes a quarterly journal, *Middle East Review,* and periodic studies; organizes academic conferences in cooperation with universities; and conducts panels at professional meetings.

Religion and Politics in the Middle East

edited by Michael Curtis

Westview Press / Boulder, Colorado

Corban College Library
5000 Deer Park Dr. S.E.
Salem, OR 97301

Westview Special Studies on the Middle East

All rights reserved. No part of this publication may be reproduced or transmitted in any form or by any means, electronic or mechanical, including
photocopy, recording, or any information storage and retrieval system, without
permission in writing from the publisher.

Copyright © 1981 by Westview Press, Inc.

Published in 1981 in the United States of America by
    Westview Press, Inc.
    5500 Central Avenue
    Boulder, Colorado 80301
    Frederick A. Praeger, Publisher

Second printing, 1982.

Library of Congress Catalog Card Number: 81-52445
ISBN: 0-86531-065-3

Composition for this book was provided by the editor.
Printed and bound in the United States of America.

רריו

Contents

vii

Contents

BIBLIOGRAPHY

Introduction

Michael Curtis

In John Buchan's adventure story *Greenmantle*, written in 1916, a character observes, "There's a great stirring in Islam, something moving on the face of the waters. They make no secret of it. These religious revivals come in cycles, and one was due about now." Sixty years later the world is now well aware of this stirring, of the revival of power and prestige in the Islamic world, of memories of the Arab past and grandeur, of the revitalization of the religion of Islam and of the rise of fervent fundamentalist Muslim groups using Islamic concepts to attain ends that go further than personnel and family matters.

Many of the 40 existing Muslim countries, with their population of 700 million, have been affected by this revitalization. The extraordinary events in Iran have been a dramatic and extreme illustration of Gibbon's vision of the coming of "the mullah who stands in the pulpit with the Qur'an* in one hand and a drawn sword in the other."[1] A less extreme version has been the imposition of Islamic law in Pakistan by General Zia in 1977 after the downfall of Bhutto. Religious fervor has affected even secular states. Turkey, formally a secular state since the late 1920s, has witnessed the rise of anti-Kemalist religious sentiment. In the Soviet Union, the 50 million Muslims constitute a restless element and the source of possible future fragmentation of the country.

The reassertion of religious values for political ends in the Middle East suggests a need for reconsideration of the process of social change. Social scientists in the post-war period have frequently used the concepts of political development or modernization as devices to explain change and the

---

*For technical reasons connected with the production of this book, we are unable to use diacritical marks and other conventions of Arabic transliteration.

differing characters of political and social systems.
Development, and the concomitant characteristics of industrialization, urbanization, increased communication and
secularism, would lead to the "passing of traditional
society"[2] with its religious and ethnic components.
Development theory suggests the declining relevance of
religion and reduced importance of religious leaders in
political affairs in developed societies where the state
and the exercise of authority derives legitimacy from the
principle of popular sovereignty.

In the contemporary Western societies religion in the
main has indeed declined in significance as a political
factor although even there serious problems such as Northern
Ireland or aid to parochial schools are inflamed by religious
sentiment, and religious revivals have had political import.
But in general religious views and values have been seen as
appropriately pertinent to personal matters. Church and
state have their allotted functions which are distinct and
separate even if the boundaries are uncertain and changing
and even though interaction between the two may be significant.

But ethnic and religious factors have not diminished in
Middle Eastern societies. On the contrary as John Entelis
argues[3], the ethnic factor has reemerged in Middle East
politics with vengeance and violence, and an enduring sense
of ethnic consciousness continues to provide meaning to the
people of the area.

Similarly, religious loyalty for both leaders and masses
remains a powerful emotion, perhaps stronger than the claims
of nationality or the attraction of ideology. Religious
institutions, dogmas and rites have been less challenged in
Islamic than in Western countries. Secular ideologies of the
liberated West have been rejected by many in the Islamic
countries as instruments of foreign domination by infidels.
The acceptance of the "five pillars," the religious duties,
of Islam by the general populace remains strong as do the
basic articles of the faith: the belief in the role and
guidance of Muhammad, the belief in the unity of God, and
in the life after death.

The hold of religion has been apparent in both personal
behavior and political activity. Westerners have been sur-
prised by the opposition of many youth to modernity; young
women have resorted to greater use of the veil or headscarf
covering the hair and ears or to the chador, and young men
have grown beards as a display of religious fervor. Both
sexes have increased attendance at mosques. In Western
societies the place and role of the clergy rests on the
acceptance of traditional behavior[4] which has been weakened
or destroyed by modernization. But Middle Eastern Islamic
clergy have popular support and can form the basis of
opposition to attempts at modernization. Some of those, like
Nasser and Ayub Khan, attempting to speed the modernization
process have felt obliged to use religious symbolism to
gain support.

Moreover, modernization measures have been imposed by elite groups or by individual rulers. They are unlikely to be the outcome of popular pressure or even the consequence of assertion by the middle class. The middle class which in Western societies gained political power after its economic rise has not yet reached a comparable status in the still highly centralized and elitist governmental systems in the Middle East. In these systems no real continuing device of communication on political issues exists between the elite and the populace which thus resorts to occasional riots or mass demonstrations. Nor are there genuine secular avenues of pluralistic expression, opportunities for diversity or provision for legitimate criticism. Not surprisingly the mosque has been an important meeting place for political and social life and exchange of news where political discussion has limited outlets. Hindsight suggests that the West should have been prepared for the popular appeal of the Ayatullah Khumayni in Iran and for his ability to communicate with a considerable part of the people.

The revitalization of Islam has stimulated the growth of fundamentalist Muslim groups. An uneasy and uneven relationship exists between these groups and the political elite in the different systems ranging from the intimate as in Iran and Libya, the tolerant as in Egypt and Turkey to hostility as in Iraq, Algeria, and Syria. Most of these groups have relied on persuasion and propaganda but others, like the attackers of the Great Mosque in Mecca in 1979, have been prepared to use violence.

The essential objectives of these groups, whether conservative or revolutionary, are the elimination of undesirable or immoral behavior such as gambling, drinking alcohol, sexual promiscuity, prostitution, pornography and corruption, the conformity of secular laws with Muslim law, and, at the extreme, the establishment of Islamic governments. The militant fundamentalists who seized the Mecca mosque even demanded the end of soccer, television and the education of women. Common to the militant beliefs of these groups is concern about the process of modernization of Westernization and the accompanying fear that the true values, personal and social, are being lost.

The values and behavior of Islamic societies have naturally been affected by a technologically efficient, politically powerful and militarily strong West. Even the political independence of the Islamic countries and the ending or severe reduction of Western colonial rule, political domination and economic control, has not overcome the past feeling of humiliation, the sense of inadequacy caused by their subordination to the more economically advanced West.

Yet the strength of indigenous values has remained great and the search for an identity of their own has caused these countries to be wary of Western influence in social relations and cultural behavior and even of the very rationale of modern societies based on technology and a high rate of

consumption. Concern over Western influence has meant
reluctance to accept the view that all problems can be
solved, that consumption can continue unrestrained and
that resources can be depleted. These Western views are
seen as a threat to the traditional life and to spirituality,
and challenge the desirability of an agricultural society
and a community bound by other than economic ties.

From the beginning of Islam religion and politics have
been intertwined. In 610 the founder of Islam heard the
Angel Gabriel's voice saying he was the apostle of God and
made known his revelations which became the basis of Qur'an.
But Muhammad was also invited to Medina to restore civil
peace, becoming the political ruler of the community and a
military leader.

At its core Islam implies that its adherents will
facilitate the realization of God's kingdom on earth and
will implement divine law. Government is a religious institution expressing the will of God, the ultimate sovereign and
the source of authority. Legitimacy is equated with actions
in accordance with the law of God as revealed to his prophets.
The duty of these representatives of God is to administer and
to interpret the law. The central purpose of government in
most Muslim political thought is justice which at first meant
maintenance of the Holy Law of Islam and later the maintenance
of the social and political order.

Western political systems, in theory if not always in
practice, embody a distinction between religion and politics;
such a separation is both a limitation on the exercise of
power and a protection of different religions. For those
asserting the political primacy of Islam the Qur'an is seen
as the basis of governmental decision-making, the mosque
as the center of social life, and the religious dignitaries,
the mullahs, as the leaders of the country. The Qur'an deals
with and governs all spheres of life and social behavior, all
aspects of public and private life. The leader of Islamic
communities thus serves both a religious and political function.
In past Arab empires the Caliph was both temporal and
spiritual leader. Those advocating an Islamic system today
hold that the mullahs, as students of the truth, should
administer it or that political rulers be subordinate to them.

The most extreme fulfillment of this view has been in
Iran under the guidance of Khumayni for whom there can be
only one party, the party of God. Political opponents are
viewed as enemies of the faith, warring with God, and, at an
extreme, they can be executed. For Khumayni the supreme
religious authority should oversee the work of the major
political figures to see it is in accordance with the law.
Public policy must ensure the purifying of society.

This view is supported by the 180,000 mullahs and the
even larger number of mosque officials and shrine attendants.
The mullahs will act as the authorities in the judicial system
which will be based on the Sharia, the Islamic law of the
Qur'an. Non-religious figures will no longer be able to be

judges nor will women, the pillars of the Muslim home.
   This extreme Iranian position has illustrated the
differences within Islam between the Sunnis, the majority
of adherents, and the minority Shi'ites who however constitute the majority in Iran itself. The Shi'ites, believing
a religious leader should be the mediator between the human
and the divine and therefore that the clergy should be
politically minded, have been more active than the Sunnis
who hold that individuals can stand directly before God
without the need for intermediaries. The Sunni *ulema* may
have been active in politics in some countries but they have
not taken leadership roles while the Shi'ite leaders, at
least in Iran, have been in the forefront of political
battles.
   Islamic values have not only been expressed in different
ways but have also been expounded by a variety of groups or
individuals. Some, like Jinnah or Bhutto, have been oppor-
tunistic politicians seeking to reinforce their political
position by religious references. Groups such as the Muslim
Brotherhood in Egypt and other countries, the Party for
the Liberation of Islam in Jordan, and the Istiqlal party in
Morocco have tried to challenge the existing structure in
different ways. In Egypt the Muslim Brotherhood has become
the most articulate opposition group in the country. Drawing
strength from both the urban masses and the student population,
the Brotherhood has gone far beyond a role limited to that of
a religious society. Most prominent among the individuals
have been the *ulema*, the preservers of traditional values,
who have been the basis of political leadership in a number
of countries.
   In the most extreme form of Islamic fundamentalism
religion would be the basis for the resolution of social
and political problems as well as for the restoration of
dogma and rites. Though Islam has been given different
expression in different settings and classes, in essence
agreement exists that it is the guardian of morality,
prescribing rules for society as well as for individual
behavior.
   For Islamic societies the problem remains of how to
combine or reconcile Islamic law, *Shari'a*, with the regulation of contemporary public and private matters. However
appropriate they may have been for the 7th century, parts
of the *Shari'a* are difficult to envisage in a modern
context: the justification of polygamy and the generally
inferior position of women, the condition of minorities,
the special taxes paid by non-Muslims, the division of the
world into "Muslim territory" (dar al-Islam) and "the house
of war" (dar al-harb), the call for a *jihad* or holy war
against the infidel, the prohibition of usury, and the
"canonical punishments" (executions, floggings, amputations,
stonings to death) which have occasionally been carried out.
It is not easy to see how these and similar concepts can be
related to contemporary issues, the production and distribution

of resources, coherent decision-making in the state or the
manner of choosing priorities. It became evident on Khumayni's
return to Iran that he had no special political program in any
concrete form.

Islam does not constitute a monolithic entity. Not all
Islamic countries have had their politics dominated by Islamic
values. In Algeria, Syria and Iraq, the regimes in different
ways have resisted the religious challenge to political power.
In Libya Qadhafi has tried to combine or subordinate Islamic
principles with his idiosyncratic concept of *Jamahariyah*
("state of the massdom"). In his *Green Book*, Qadhafi, both
head of state and major theologian, writes that "True Islam
is being revealed: the religion of freedom, progress, equality,
justice." A prominent slogan in contemporary Libya is that
the Qur'an is "the law of our new socialist society." In
Saudi Arabia the royal house remains allied with the orthodox
Islamic school, the *Wahhabiyya*.

Nor have Islamic societies been devoid of internal tension or mutual hatreds. In 1971 the largest Muslim state of
Pakistan disintegrated into two parts. Wars have occurred
or constant tension existed between Algeria, Morocco and
Mauritania, between the two Yemens, between Egypt and Libya,
and between Iran and Iraq. The political systems in Islamic
countries range widely from the Soviet-sponsored and Cuban-
assisted regime of South Yemen to the fundamentalism of Saudi
Arabia.

Islamic revitalization can be related to the extraordinary wealth stemming from the production of oil in Islamic
countries, the common hostility to Israel and to the attempt
to forge an Islamic political position in a social and demo-
graphical context of a larger number of young people and
students.

In less than a decade the world has witnessed the largest
transfer of wealth in its history from the oil consuming to
the oil producing countries. Moreover OPEC, in which Islamic
countries exert major influence, has taken over from Western
companies ownership of the oil fields, control over pricing,
decisions on the level of production and over crude oil
allocation and, increasingly, control over refining and
marketing. The increase in Islamic pride is the consequence
of the dazzling increase in oil revenues and of the subjugation of the oil companies and Western consumers. This pride
has been heightened by the fact that there is no longer any
strong relationship between the amount of oil produced and
the need for income to finance development programs.

But the humiliation of the Arab countries occasioned
by the existence of Israel whose military successes could be
contrasted with the inferiority of Islamic societies still
has not been eliminated. The obsession of some of the Arab
countries with Israel and their ingrained belief that Israel
will eventually suffer the same fate as did the Crusaders
in medieval times has only to a limited degree been tempered
by the example of Sadat in showing that the restoration of

Arab pride did not require the destruction of Israel.

Indeed the preoccupation with Israel led to the convening in 1969 of a Muslim Summit Conference in Rabat. Similar Summit Conferences and meetings of foreign ministers following the initial meeting have led not only to policy resolutions, which are agreed to by consensus of those present but also to the creation of an Islamic Conference Organization and an Islamic Secretariat in Jeddah. It is a remarkable demonstration of the current significance of religion that over 40 Islamic countries, despite the great differences in political regimes, varied stages of economic development and competing national interest, should be united by their common faith. In 1965 Nasser denounced a gathering of Islamic countries proposed by Saudi Arabia as an imperialist meeting "on which they have put a turban." No Islamic country today would openly argue that an organization of Islamic states is incompatible with the contemporary world.

A common faith has also united the Jewish people which throughout history has refused to abandon Zion and has yearned for the reunification of the people and the land where Jewish nationality and spirituality would flourish together. The bible, Jewish worship and historic memories have kept the dream of a Jewish state alive. The remains of stones and structures from the days of the First Temple destroyed in 587 B.C. and the surviving Western Wall of the Second Temple destroyed in 70 B.C. are the physical reminders of the historic bonds with Jerusalem which was the Jewish capital for 850 years and which has contained an almost continuous presence of Jews. In 1922 the League of Nations mandate for Palestine recognized the bonds by speaking of "the historical connection of the Jewish people with Palestine and...the grounds for reconstituting their national home in that country." The land of Israel, as James Parkes has said, "has produced an emotional center which has endured through the whole of the Jewish period of 'exile' and has led to constant returns or attempted returns culminating in our day in the Zionist movement."[5]

Israel today is a parliamentary democracy in which there is no state religion, in which citizens possess freedom of conscience and religion, and in which all religious faiths are permissible. A complex relationship exists between religion and politics. Matters of personal status, including marriage, divorce and inheritance, come under the jurisdiction of each of the religious faiths. The law of return allows the immigration of all Jews though differences might exist on the definition of who is a Jew. Tension exists between advocates or orthodox Judaism and those of a secular disposition in the making of rules pertaining both to individual behavior and political decisions. Not all accept the view that the reestablishment of a Jewish Commonwealth by the ingathering of exiles and the creation of the state of Israel with Jerusalem as its capital is the contemporary implementation of Messianic hopes. Zionism, the national independence movement of the Jewish people, has created the politically independent state of Israel. But for those believing that out of Zion shall come the teachings and out of Jerusalem the words of the Lord, the Jewish task to be holy and to sanctify the name of God implies a Jewish state. The question of whether Israel is to be a Jewish state or a state of Jews remains open.

The same question can be posed of Islamic countries: are they to be countries of Muslims or Muslim states? Bernard Lewis has argued that the Arabs are faced with a choice.[6] They can accept a particular view of modern civilization and merge their culture and identity with it, or they may turn their backs on the West and attempt to return to the lost theocratic ideal or they may reach a harmonious balance between the West and their own inherited tradition. The choice will decide the validity of Buchan's portrait of the prophet preparing to battle to "restore the Khalifate to its old glories and Islam to its old purity."

NOTES

1. Edward Gibbon, *The Decline and Fall of the Roman Empire*, ch. 50.

2. Daniel Lerner, *The Passing of Traditional Society*, Free Press, Glencoe, 1958.

3. John Entelis, "Ethnic Conflict and the Problem of Political Identity in the Middle East," *Polity* (Spring 1979), p. 400.

4. John Kautsky, *The Political Consequences of Modernization*, Wiley, New York, 1972, p. 104.

5. James Parkes, *Whose Land?*, p. 10.

6. Bernard Lewis, *Arabs in History*, Hutchinson, London, 1966.

1
The Return of Islam

Bernard Lewis

In the great medieval French epic of the wars between
Christians and Saracens in Spain, the *Chanson de Roland*,
the Christian poet endeavors to give his readers, or rather
listeners, some idea of the Saracen religion. According to
this vision, the Saracens worshipped a trinity consisting
of three persons, Muhammad, the founder of that religion,
and two others, both of them devils, Apollin and Tervagant.
To us this seems comic, and we are amused by medieval man
unable to conceive of religion or indeed of anything else
except in his own image. Since Christendom worshipped its
founder in association with two other entities, the Saracens
also had to worship their founder, and he too had to be one
of a trinity, with two demons co-opted to make up the number.
In the same spirit one finds special correspondents of the
New York *Times* and of other lesser newspapers describing
the...conflicts in Lebanon in terms of right-wing and left-
wing factions. As medieval Christian man could only conceive of religion in terms of a trinity, so his modern
descendant can only conceive of politics in terms of a
theology or, as we now say, ideology, of left-wing and
right-wing forces and factions.
    This recurring unwillingness to recognize the nature
of Islam or even the fact of Islam as an independent, different, and autonomous religious phenomenon persists and recurs
from medieval to modern times. We see it, for example, in
the nomenclature adopted to designate the Muslims. It was
a long time before Christendom was even willing to give them
a name with a religious meaning. For many centuries both
Eastern and Western Christendom called the disciples of the
Prophet Saracens, a word of uncertain etymology but clearly

The Return of Islam originally appeared in *Commentary* and
was reprinted in *Middle East Review*, Vol. XII, No. 1, Fall, 1979.
It is reprinted by permission of *Commentary* and Bernard Lewis.

of ethnic not religious connotation, since the term is both
pre-Islamic and pre-Christian. In the Iberian peninsula,
where the Muslims whom they met came from Morocco, they
called them Moors, and people of Iberian culture or under
Iberian influences continued to call Muslims Moors, even if
they met them in Ceylon or in the Philippines. In most of
Europe, Muslims were called Turks, after the main Muslim
invaders, and a convert to Islam was said to have "turned
Turk" even if the conversion took place in Marrakesh or in
Delhi. Farther east, Muslims were Tatars, another ethnic
name loosely applied to the Islamized steppe peoples who for
a while dominated Russia.

Even when Europe began to recognize the fact that Islam
was a religious and not an ethnic community, it expressed this
realization in a sequence of false analogies beginning with
the name given to the religion and its followers, Muhammedanism
and Muhammedans. The Muslims do not, and never have, called
themselves Muhammedans nor their religion Muhammedanism,
since Muhammad does not occupy the same place in Islam as
Christ does in Christianity. This misinterpretation of Islam
as a sort of mirror image of Christendom found expression in
a number of different ways--for example, in the false equation
between the Muslim Friday and the Christian Sunday, in the
reference to the Qur'an[1] as the Muslim Bible, in the misleading analogies between the mosque and the church, the
ulema and the priests, and, coming more directly to our
present concern, in the imposition on Muslim history and
institutions of purely Western notions of country and nation
and of what goes on within them. Thus, for example, in
Gibbon's fascinating account of the career of the Prophet,
Muhammad and his contemporaries were inspired by patriotism
and love of liberty, two concepts which somehow seem in-
appropriate to the circumstances of 7th-century Arabia.
For many centuries, Europe called the lands of the Ottoman
Empire Turkey, a name which the inhabitants of those lands
did not apply to their own country until the final triumph
among them of European political ideas with the proclamation
of the Republic in 1923.

Modern Western man, being unable for the most part to
assign a dominant and central place to religion in his own
affairs, found himself unable to conceive that any other
peoples in any other place could have done so, and was
therefore impelled to devise other explanations of what
seemed to him only superficially religious phenomena. We
find, for example, a great deal of attention given by Western
scholarship to the investigation of such meaningless questions
as "Was Muhammad Sincere?" or "Was Muhammad an Enthusiast or
a Deceiver?" We find lengthy explanations by historians
of the "real" underlying significance of the great religious
conflicts within Islam between different sects and schools
in the past, and a similar determination to penetrate to
the "real" meaning of sectarian and communal struggles at
the present time. To the modern Western mind, it is not

conceivable that men would fight and die in such numbers
over mere differences of religion; there have to be some
other "genuine" reasons underneath the religious veil.
We are prepared to allow religiously defined conflicts
to accredited eccentrics like the Northern Irish, but to
admit that an entire civilization can have religion as its
primary loyalty is too much. Even to suggest such a thing
is regarded as offensive by liberal opinion, always ready to
take protective umbrage on behalf of those whom it regards
as its wards. This is reflected in the present inability,
political, journalistic, and scholarly alike, to recognize
the importance of the factor of religion in the current
affairs of the Muslim world and in the consequent recourse
to the language of left-wing and right-wing, progressive and
conservative, and the rest of the Western terminology, the
use of which in explaining Muslim political phenomena is
about as accurate and as enlightening as an account of a
cricket match by a baseball correspondent.

* * *

If, then, we are to understand anything at all about
what is happening in the Muslim world at the present time
and what has happened in the past, there are two essential
points which need to be grasped. One is the universality
of religion as a factor in the lives of the Muslim peoples,
and the other is its centrality.
"Render unto Caesar the things which are Caesar's; and
unto God the things which are God's." That is, of course,
Christian doctrine and practice. It is totally alien to
Islam. The three major Middle Eastern religions are significantly different in their relations with the state and
their attitudes to political power. Judaism was associated
with the state and was then disentangled from it; its new
encounter with the state at the present time raises problems
which are still unresolved. Christianity, during the first
formative centuries of its existence, was separate from
and indeed antagonistic to the state with which it only later
became involved. Islam from the lifetime of its founder *was*
the state, and the identity of religion and government is
indelibly stamped on the memories and awareness of the faithful from their own sacred writings, history, and experience.
The founder of Christianity died on the cross, and his
followers endured as a persecuted minority for centuries,
forming their own society, their own hierarchy, their own
laws in an institution known as the Church--until, with the
conversion of the Roman Emperor Constantine, there began the
parallel processes of the Christianization of Rome and the
Romanization of Christ.
In Islam, the process was quite different. Muhammad
did not die on the cross. As well as a Prophet, he was a
soldier and a statesman, the head of a state and the founder
of an empire, and his followers were sustained by a belief

in the manifestation of divine approval through success
and victory. Islam was associated with power from the very
beginning, from the first formative years of the Prophet and
his immediate successors. This association between religion
and power, community and polity, can already be seen in the
Qur'an itself and in the other early religious texts on
which Muslims base their beliefs. One consequence is that
in Islam religion is not, as it is in Christendom, one sector
or segment of life, regulating some matters while others are
excluded; it is concerned with the whole of life--not a
limited but a total jurisdiction. In such a society the
very idea of the separation of church and state is meaningless, since there are no two entities to be separated. Church
and state, religious and political authority, are one and
the same. In classical Arabic and in the other classical
languages of Islam there are no pairs of terms corresponding
to lay and ecclesiastical, spiritual and temporal, secular
and religious, because these pairs of words express a
Christian dichotomy which has no equivalent in the world of
Islam.[2] It is only in modern times, under Christian influence, that these concepts have begun to appear and that
words have been coined to express them. Their meaning is
still very imperfectly understood and their relevance to
Muslim institutions dubious.

   For the Muslim, religion traditionally was not only
universal but also central in the sense that it constituted
the essential basis and focus of identity and loyalty. It
was religion which distinguished those who belonged to the
group and marked them off from those outside the group. A
Muslim Iraqi would feel far closer bonds with a non-Iraqi
Muslim than with a non-Muslim Iraqi. Muslims of different
countries, speaking different languages, share the same
memories of a common and sacred past, the same awareness
of corporate identity, the same sense of a common predicament
and destiny. It is not nation or country which, as in the
West, forms the historic basis of identity, but the religio-
political community, and the imported Western idea of ethnic
and territorial nationhood remains, like secularism, alien
and incompletely assimilated. The point was made with
remarkable force and clarity by a Grand Vizier of the Ottoman
Empire who, in reply to the exponents of the new-style
patriotism, replied: "The Fatherland of a Muslim is the
place where the Holy Law of Islam prevails." And that was
in 1917.

   In the 18th century, when, under the impact of Austrian
and Russian victories against Turkey and British successes
in India, Muslims began to be aware that they were no longer
the dominant group in the world but were, on the contrary,
threatened in their heartlands by a Europe that was expanding at both ends, the only really vital responses were
religious reform movements, such as the Wahhabis in Arabia
and the reformed Naqshbandi order which spread from India
to other Muslim countries. In the early 19th century, when

the three major European empires ruling over Muslims, those
of Britain, France, and Russia, were advancing in India,
North Africa, and Central Asia, the most significant movements of resistance were again religious--the Indian Wahhabis
led by Sayyid Ahmad Brelwi from 1826 to 1831, the struggle
of Abdal-Qadir in North Africa from 1832-1847, the dogged
resistance of Shamil to the Russians in Dagistan and the
Northern Caucasus from 1830 to 1859. All of them were
crushed, but made a considerable impact at the time.

Then, for a while, Muslims were sufficiently overawed
by the power, wealth, and success of Europe to desire to
emulate European ways. But from the middle of the 19th
century onward came a further wave of European imperial
expansion--the suppression of the Indian mutiny followed by
the disappearance of the last remnants of the Mogul monarchy
in India and the consolidation of the British Empire in that
formerly Muslim realm, the rapid advance of the Russians in
Central Asia, the expansion of the French into Tunisia and
of the British into Egypt, and the growing threat to the
Ottoman Empire itself, all of which brought a response in
the form of a series of pan-Islamic movements.

The unification of Germany and Italy was a source of
inspiration in Muslim lands, particularly in Turkey where
many Turkish leaders thought that their country could play
a role similar to that of Prussia or Savoy in the unification
of Germany and of Italy by serving as the nucleus for the
unification of a much larger entity. But what would that
larger entity be? Not a pan-Turkish entity. Such ideas
were still far away in the future and were not even discussed at that time. The basic political identity and
aspiration were Islamic, and pan-Islamism was the first and
natural response to pan-Germanism and pan-Slavism. It was
not until much later that pan-Turkism and pan-Arabism appeared on the political horizon and, even then, there is
some doubt as to what they really signified.

The end of World War I, the breakup of the Ottoman
Empire, the strains and stresses that followed and the
opportunities which seemed to be offered by the collapse
of Czarism in revolution and civil war also gave rise to
a series of religiously inspired movements--Enver Pasha in
a last throw formed the ambitiously titled Army of Islam,
the objective of which was to liberate the Muslim subject
peoples of the fallen Russian Empire. Some of these movements were linked with the Communists or taken over by the
Communists at a time when the fundamentally anti-Islamic
nature of Communism was not yet understood. Almost all
were expressed in religious rather than in national or even
social terms. Most significant among these movements was
that which has since come to be known as the Turkish
Nationalist Movement. Yet the revolt of the Kemalists in
Anatolia was in its first inspiration as much Islamic as
Turkish. Islamic men of religion formed an impressive
proportion of its early leaders and followers. The language

used at the time, the rhetoric of the Kemalists in this
early stage, speaks of Ottoman Muslims rather than of Turks,
and the movement commanded a great deal of support in the
Islamic world. It was not until after their victory and
after the establishment of the republic that, as a result
of many factors, they began to lay the main stress on nationalist and secular aims.

   During the 20th century, at least in the earlier decades,
such movements of resistance were more commonly expressed in
the fashionable form of political parties and in the fashionable language of political, more or less secular, nationalism.
But neither the party organization nor the nationalist ideology really corresponded to the deeper instincts of the Muslim
masses, which found an outlet in programs and organizations
of a different kind--led by religious leaders and formulated
in religious language and aspiration.

                        * * *

   The most important movement of this type in the 20th
century is the organization known as the Muslim Brothers,
al-Ikhwan al-Muslimun, founded in Egypt by a religious teacher
named Hasan al-Banna. The early history of the movement is
not clearly known, but it appears to have started in the
late 20s and early 30s and to have been concerned in the
first instance mainly with religious and social activities.
The founder, known as the "Supreme Guide," sent missionaries
to preach in mosques and other public places all over Egypt.
The Brothers undertook large-scale educational, social,
charitable, and religious work in town and countryside, and
even engaged in some economic enterprises. They began
political activity in 1936 after the signature of the Anglo-
Egyptian Treaty in that year and, by taking up the cause of
the Palestine Arabs against Zionism and British rule, were
able to extend the range of the movement to other Arab
countries. They sent volunteers to fight with the Arab
armies in the war of 1948, and thereafter seem to have controlled an armed force capable of playing some role in
affairs. As a result, the Egyptian Prime Minister Noqrashi
Pasha dissolved the organization, confiscated its property,
and ordered the arrest of many of its members. He was
assassinated in 1948 by one of the Brothers and shortly after-
ward the Supreme Guide himself was assassinated in circumstances which have never been established. The Brothers,
though illegal, continued to function as a clandestine
organization. In April 1951, they were again legalized in
Egypt, though forbidden to engage in any secret or military
activities. They took part in actions against British
troops in the Suez Canal zone and seem to have played some
role, of what nature is still unknown, in the burning of
Cairo on January 26, 1952. They had close links, dating back
to the war years, with some members of the secret committee
of the "Free Officers" which seized power in Egypt in 1952.

Apart from some general similarities in ideology and aspiration, many of the officers who carried out the coup were either members or at least sympathizers of the Muslim Brothers.

At first, relations between the Brothers and the officers were intimate and friendly, and even when, in January 1953, the military regime dissolved all political parties, the Brothers were exempted, on the grounds that they were a non-political organization. Relations between the new Supreme Guide and the Free Officers deteriorated, however, and before long the Brothers were attacking the new regime for its alleged failures to live up to their Islamic ideals. A period of quiet but sharp conflict followed, in the course of which the Brothers were very active, especially among workers and students and even among the security forces. In January 1954, the government again decreed the dissolution of the Order and the arrest of many of its leaders and followers. Later, there was some reconciliation as a result of which the arrested Brothers were released and the organization allowed to function on a non-political basis. The Anglo-Egyptian agreement of October 1954 stirred up trouble again and was bitterly opposed by the Brothers who insisted that only armed struggle could attain the desired objectives. On October 26, 1954, one of the Brothers just failed to assassinate President Nasser, who retaliated by taking severe repressive measures. More than a thousand were arrested and tried, and six, including some of the intellectual leaders of the movement, were sentenced to death and executed. The Brotherhood was now entirely illegal but nevertheless continued to function and seems to have engaged, from time to time, in conspiracies to overthrow the regime. Many arrests were made and in August 1966 three further executions took place, among them Sayyid Qutb, a leading ideologist of the Brothers. The Order continued to be active, albeit illegal, in some, and more openly in other, Arab countries. It remains a powerful if concealed force at the present day and there are recent signs of a return in Egypt.

The Egyptian Free Officers Movement in 1952 is not the only political movement with which the Muslim Brothers were connected. Another is the Fatah, the largest and most important of the Palestinian guerrilla organizations. Here, too, for obvious reasons, there are some uncertainties regarding the earlier history of the movement, but its past links with the Muslim Brothers seem to be clear. The imagery and symbolism of the Fatah is strikingly Islamic. Yasir Arafat's *nom de guerre*, Abu 'Ammar, the father of 'Ammar, is an allusion to the historic figure of 'Ammar ibn Yasir, the son of Yasir, a companion of the Prophet and a valiant fighter in all his battles. The name Fatah is a technical term meaning a conquest for Islam gained in the Holy War.[3] It is in this sense that Sultan Mehmet II, who conquered Constantinople for Islam, is known as *Fatih*, the Conqueror. The same imagery, incidentally, is carried over into the nomenclature of the Palestine Liberation Army, the brigades of which are named

after the great victories won by Muslim arms in the Battles
of Qadisiyya, Hattin, and Ayn Jalut. To name military units
after victorious battles is by no means unusual. What is
remarkable here is that all three battles were won in holy
wars for Islam against non-Muslims--Qadisiyya against the
Zoroastrian Persians, Hattin against the Crusaders, Ayn Jalut
against the Mongols. In the second and third of these, the
victorious armies were not even Arab; but they were Muslim,
and that is obviously what counts. It is hardly surprising
that the military communiqués of the Fatah begin with the
Muslim invocation, 'In the name of God, the Merciful and the
Compassionate.'

* * *

The Muslim Brothers and their derivatives were in the
main confined to the Arabic-speaking countries. But there
were other parallel movements elsewhere. In Iran this trend
is represented by an organization called the *Fida'iyan-i
Islam*, the Devotees of Islam, a terrorist group which was
active mainly in Tehran between 1943 and 1955 and carried
out a number of political assassinations, the most important
being that of the Prime Minister, General Ali Razmara, in
March 1951. For a while they played some part in Persian
politics, until another, this time unsuccessful, attempt on
the life of a Prime Minister, Hossein Ala, in October 1955
led to their suppression and prosecution and the execution
of some of their leaders. The *Fida'iyan* had links with the
Muslim Brothers in Egypt and elsewhere and exercised very
considerable influence among the masses and, by terror, on
politicians. They even seem to have enjoyed some limited
support from the semi-official religious leadership.
    In addition to these, there were many other religiously
inspired movements in various Islamic countries--the Organization of Algerian Ulema, the Tijaniyya Brotherhood, and,
more recently, the National Salvation party in Turkey, and
one of the most interesting, the Basmachi Movement in Soviet
Central Asia. The word Basmachi, which in Uzbek means
brigand or marauder, is applied by the Soviet authorities
to a succession of religiously inspired revolts against
Russian or Soviet rule which began in January 1919 and continued until 1923 when the movement was decisively defeated,
though activity by small groups of rebels continued for a
number of years after that. The last Basmachi leader,
Ibrahim Beg, withdrew to Afghanistan in 1926 and continued
to raid into Soviet territory from there. He was captured
by Soviet troops and executed in 1931. It is characteristic
of Western attitudes that a search of half-a-dozen major
encyclopedias failed to disclose any article on the
Basmachis--probably the most important movement of opposition
to Soviet rule in Central Asia.[4]
    It is not, however, only in radical and militant opposi-
tion movements that this kind of religious self-identification

and alignment are to be found. Governments--including
avowedly secular and radical governments--have responded
to the same instincts in times of crisis. After the Treaty
of Lausanne, an exchange of population was agreed between
Turkey and Greece under the terms of which members of the
Greek minority in Turkey were to be repatriated to Greece,
and members of the Turkish minority in Greece repatriated
to Turkey. Between 1923 and 1930, a million and a quarter
'Greeks' were sent from Turkey to Greece and a somewhat
smaller number of 'Turks' from Greece to Turkey.
     At first sight, this would seem to be a clear case of
the acceptance to the last degree of the European principle
of nationality--Greeks and Turks unwilling or unable to live
as national minorities among aliens, returned to Greece and
to Turkey, to their own homelands and their own people.
On closer examination, this exchange proves to have a somewhat different character. The words used were indeed Greeks
and Turks--but what precisely did these words mean at that
time and in that place? In the deserted Christian churches
left by the Greeks of Karaman in southern Turkey, the
inscriptions on tombstones are written in Turkish, though
in Greek characters; among the families of the so-called
repatriates, the great majority had little or no knowledge
of Greek but spoke Turkish among themselves, writing it in
Greek characters--just as Jews and Christians in Arabic-
speaking countries for long wrote the common Arabic language
in Hebrew or in Syriac instead of in Arabic characters.
Script all over the Middle East is closely associated with
religion. In the same way, many of the so-called Turks
sent to Turkey from Crete and other places in Greece had
little or no knowledge of Turkish, but habitually spoke
Greek among themselves, frequently writing their Greek
vernacular in the Turco-Arabic script. By any normal Western
definition of nationality, the Greeks of Turkey were not
Greeks, but Turks of the Christian faith, while the so-called
Turks of Greece were for the most part Muslim Greeks. If we
take the terms Greek and Turk in their Western and not in
their Middle Eastern connotation, then the famous exchange
of population between Greece and Turkey was not a repatria-
tion of Greeks to Greece and of Turks to Turkey but a
deportation of Christian Turks from Turkey to Greece and
a deportation of Muslim Greeks from Greece to Turkey. It
was only after their arrival in their putative homelands
that most of them began to learn their presumptive mother
tongues.
     This occurred among two peoples, one of which is
Christian though long subject to Muslim influence, and the
other, though Muslim, the most advanced in secularization
of all the Muslim peoples. Even today, in the secular
republic of Turkey, the word Turk is by common convention
restricted to Muslims. Non-Muslim citizens of the Republic
are called Turkish citizens and enjoy the rights of citizenship, but they do not call themselves Turks nor are they so

called by their neighbors. The identification of Turk
and Muslim remains virtually total. And here it may be
noted that while the non-Muslim resident of the country is
not a Turk, the non-Turkish Muslim immigrant, whether from
the former provinces of the Ottoman Empire or from elsewhere,
very rapidly acquires a Turkish identity.

* * *

With Arabs the situation is somewhat more complex.
In the Arabic-speaking countries there have for long been
substantial minorities of Christians and Jews speaking the
same Arabic language, though in the past writing it in a
different script and often speaking it with a slightly
different dialect. When the idea of Arabism as a common
nationality was first launched in the late 19th and early
20th centuries, Arabic-speaking Christians played a prominent
part in the movement. It was natural that they should be
attracted by a national rather than a religious identity, since
in the one they could claim the equal citizenship to which they
could never aspire in the other. According to this view,
the Arabs were a nation divided into various religions, in
which Christians and even at times Jews might hope to share
in the common Arabism along with the Muslim majority.
From the beginning, Christians played a leading role
among the exponents, ideologists, and leaders of secular
nationalism. As members of non-Muslim communities in a
Muslim state, they occupied a position of stable, privileged,
but nevertheless unmistakable inferiority, and in an age of
change even the rights which that status gave them were
endangered. In a state in which the basis of identity was
not religion and community but language and culture, they
could claim the full membership and equality which was denied
to them under the old dispensation. As Christians, they were
more open to Western ideas, and identified themselves more
readily in national terms. The superior education to which
they had access enabled them to play a leading part in both
intellectual and commercial life. Christians, especially
Lebanese Christians, had a disproportionately important role
in the foundation and development of the newspaper and magazine press in Egypt and in other Arab countries, and Christian
names figure very prominently among the outstanding novelists,
poets, and publicists in the earlier stages of modern Arabic
literature. Even in the nationalist movements, many of the
leaders and spokesmen were members of Christian minorities.
This prominence in cultural and political life was paralleled
by a rapid advance of the Christian minorities in material
wealth.
In recent decades, this prominence has ceased to be
tolerable. Partly through measures of nationalization adopted
by socialist governments, partly through other more direct
means, the economic power of the Christian communities has
been reduced in one country after another and is now being

challenged in its last stronghold, the Lebanon. Christian
predominance in intellectual life has long since been ended,
and a new generation of writers has arisen, the overwhelming
majority of whom are Muslims. There are still Christian
politicians and ideologists, but their role is much cir-
cumscribed in a society increasingly conscious of its Muslim
identity, background, and aspirations. Among the various
organizations making up the Palestine Liberation Organization,
the Fatah is overwhelmingly though not exclusively Muslim.
On the other hand, many of the extremist organizations tend
to be Christian, for in the radical extremism which they
profess Christians still hope to find the acceptance and
equality which eluded them in nationalism.

                              *   *   *

     As the nationalist movement has become genuinely
popular, so it has become less national and more religious--
in other words, less Arab and more Islamic. In moments of
crisis--and these have been many in recent decades--it is
the instinctive communal loyalty which outweighs all others.
A few examples may suffice. On November 2, 1945, demonstrations were held in Egypt on the anniversary of the issue by
the British government of the Balfour Declaration. Though
this was certainly not the intention of the political leaders
who sponsored it, the demonstration soon developed into an
anti-Jewish riot and the anti-Jewish riot into a more general
outbreak in the course of which several churches, Catholic,
Armenian, and Greek Orthodox, were attacked and damaged.
A little later, on January 4-5, 1952, demonstrations were
held in Suez, this time against the British in connection
with continuing occupation of the Canal Zone. The demonstrators looted and fired a Coptic church and killed a number of
Copts. Catholic, Armenian, and Greek Christians had nothing
whatever to do with the Balfour Declaration, and the Copts
are not English; indeed, there is none more Egyptian than
they. One may go further and say that no attack or harm to
the Copts was sought or desired by the nationalist leaders.
Yet, in the moment of truth, the angry mob reacted in-
stinctively to a feeling that the Copts--native Egyptian,
Arabic-speaking, yet Christian--were on the other side, and
treated them accordingly.
     In such incidents they are no doubt local causes which
may help to explain the actions of the mob.[5] But in both
cases, and in others which could be quoted, they reflect a
more fundamental attitude summed up in the tradition ascribed--
probably falsely, but this makes no difference--to the
Prophet, "*Al-Kufru millantun wahida*"--unbelief is one nation
(or one religio-political community). The world is divided
basically into two. One is the community of the Muslims,
the other that of the unbelievers, and the subdivisions
among the latter are of secondary importance.
     The Lebanese civil war in 1958 and the struggle in Iraq

between nationalists and Communists in the spring of 1959
also assumed a strongly religious character. On March 17,
1959, a prayer was recited in Egyptian mosques and published
on the front pages of the Egyptian papers, for those who
had been killed in Mosul:

> God is great! God is great! There is no might and no power
> save in God! May He strengthen the martyrs with His grace
> and ordain them everlasting life in His mercy and abase
> their enemies in shame and ignominy! God is great! God is
> great! There is no victory save in God! Whoever offends,
> God will crush him; whoever exalts himself by wrongdoing,
> God will humble him! Consider not those who are killed in
> the cause of God as dead, but as living, with their Lord
> who sustains them.
>
> O God Almighty, All-powerful! Conquer Thine enemy with
> Thine omnipotence so that he returns to Thee! O God, Al-
> mighty, All powerful, strengthen the community of Thy
> Prophet with Thy favor, and ordain defeat for their
> enemy....In faith we worship Thee, in sincerity we call
> upon Thee, the blood of our martyrs we entrust to Thee,
> O merciful and compassionate One, Who answers the prayers
> of him who prays--our innocent martyrs and pure victims
> for the sake of Thy religion. For the glory of Thy
> religion they shed their blood and died as martyrs: be-
> lieving in Thee, they greeted the day of sacrifice bliss-
> fully. Therefore place them, O God, as companions with
> the upright and the martyrs and the righteous--how good
> these are as companions! (Qur'an, iv, 69.)

The religious passion and fervor are unmistakable and
did not fail to alarm the Christian minorities in Lebanon
and elsewhere as indicating a resurgence of Islamic feeling.
Since then the regimes of the various Muslim states
they become more, not less, self-consciously Islamic both
in the respect they accord to their own religion and in
their treatment of others. This is particularly noticeable
in the so-called radical and revolutionary states which are
intellectually and socially far more conservative than the
politically conservative states, and find themselves obliged
to show greater deference to popular sentiment. The treatment of Christians, though still falling well short of
persecution, has changed for the worse and has led to a
growing number of Christian emigrants, some to Lebanon,
others to countries abroad. A Christian Arab writer has
described the feelings of these emigrants as follows:

> Christians (they say) have no future in a country which
> is becoming all the time more socialist and totalitarian.
> Their children are indoctrinated in the schools, where
> the syllabus is devoted more and more to Islam and their
> faith is in danger. Debarred increasingly from public
> office and from nationalized societies (*sic*, the writer

presumably means companies or corporations), robbed of
the property of their parents and unable to engage in
profitable business in a society where almost everything
is under state control, how can they survive?[6]

An interesting side-effect of these changes is the
evolution of attitudes among the groups who are now called
Arab Americans. These consist overwhelmingly of Christians
of Syrian and Lebanese origin. At the time of their arrival
in the United States, they were, apart from a very small
circle of intellectuals, virtually unaffected by Arab
nationalism, which was in any case still in its infancy even
in their countries of origin. At the time that they left
their homelands and migrated across the ocean, they, like
their neighbors, still thought in unequivocally communal
terms. They were first and foremost Christians, and their
feelings toward their old homeland resembled not those of
American Jews toward Israel but rather those of American
Jews toward the countries in Central and Eastern Europe from
which they had come seeking a better and freer life in America.
For a long time the development of the Palestine conflict left
the American Arab Christians unmoved. Their recent involvement
is a reflection not of their Arabism but of their Americanism,
for in this way they are conforming to a common American
pattern of ethnic identity, loyalty, and lobbying. Recent
developments such as the suppression and expropriation of
Christian schools in Syria, the pressure on Christian communities, and, above all, the current struggle in Lebanon seem
already to be leading to a reassessment of their position
and, among some of them, a return to earlier attitudes.

* * *

The growth of Islam's political effect can be observed
in two respects--in the field of international politics, and
in internal affairs. The attempt to exploit the sentiment
of Islamic brotherhood for international political purposes
dates back to the 1870s, when the Ottoman government under
Sultan Abdulaziz, and then more actively under Sultan
Abdulhamid, tried to mobilize opinion all over the Muslim
world in support of the faltering Ottoman state and to provide
it with the alliances which it needed at this time of weakness and impoverishment. This policy came to be known by the
name of pan-Islamism--a reflection in Islamic terms, as was
noted above, of such European movements as pan-Germanism and
pan-Slavism.
From the beginning, pan-Islamism was of two kinds--one
official and promoted by one or another Islamic government
in pursuit of its own purposes; the other radical, often with
revolutionary social doctrines, and led by a more or less
charismatic religious figure, with or without the sponsor-
ship of a government. The counterpart of Abdulhamid was the
popular activist Jemal al-Din, known as Al-Afghani. Neither

Abdulhamid's official pan-Islamism nor Jemal al-Din's
radical pan-Islamism produced much by way of political
results, though both undoubtedly heightened the common
Muslim sense of identity. This was further helped by the
rapid improvement of communications--the press, the telegraph, and, in more recent times, radio and television.

Radical pan-Islamism of various types appeared during
the interwar period--at first from left-wing and, indeed,
frequently Communist sources, and later from right-wing,
nationalist, and sometimes fascist sources. The most noteworthy example of the latter was the Pan-Islamic activities
of the Mufti of Jerusalem, Haj Amin Al-Husayni, who enjoyed
Nazi sponsorhip and eventually spent the war years in Hitler's
Germany.

The postwar period brought several new forms of pan-
Islamic activity. None came to much until the convening of
the Islamic Congress of Mecca in 1954. From the first, the
most important initiative in the Mecca Congress was that of
the Egyptians whose intentions can already be seen in Nasser's
booklet, *The Philosophy of the Revolution.*

> There remains the Third Circle (the first two were the Arab
> and African circles)--the circle encompassing continents
> and oceans which, as I have said, is the circle of our
> Brethren-in-Islam who, wherever their place under the sun,
> turn with us toward the same Qibla, their lips solemnly
> saying the same prayers.
>
> My faith in the magnitude of the positive effectiveness
> that could result from strengthening the Islamic tie that
> binds all Muslims grew stronger when I accompanied the
> Egyptian mission to Saudi Arabia to offer condolences on
> the death of its great king.
>
> As I stood before the Kaaba, with my thoughts wandering
> round every part of the world which Islam has reached, I
> fully realized the need for a radical change of our
> conception of the Pilgrimage.
>
> I said to myself: The journey to the Kaaba should no
> longer be construed as an admission card to Paradise, or
> as a crude attempt to buy forgiveness of sins after lead-
> ing a dissipated life.
>
> The Pilgrimage should have a potential political power.
> The world press should hasten to follow and feature its
> news not by drawing attractive pen pictures of its rites
> and rituals for the delectation of readers, but by its
> representation as a periodical political conference at
> which the heads of all the Islamic states, leaders of
> opinion, scientists, eminent industrialists, and prom-
> inent businessmen assemble to draw up at this world
> Islamic Parliament the broad lines of the policies to
> be adopted by their respective countries and lay down
> the principles ensuring their close cooperation until
> they have again gathered together in the following
> session.

They assemble demure and devout, but mighty strong;
unambitious of power, but active and full of energy:
submissive to Divine Will, but immutable in difficulties
and implacable with their enemies.

They assemble confirmed believers in the Life to Come,
but equally convinced that they have a place under the
sun which they should occupy in this life.

I remember I expressed some of these views to His
Majesty King Saud.

His Majesty assented saying, "Truly this is the real
purpose of the Pilgrimage."

Truth to tell, I personally cannot think of any other
conception.

As I contemplate the eighty million Muslims in Indonesia,
the fifty million in China, the few millions in Malaya,
Thailand, and Burma, the hundred million in Pakistan, the
well-nigh over a hundred million in the Middle East, the
forty million in the Soviet Union, and the millions of
others in other remote and far-flung corners of the
earth--as I ponder over these hundreds of millions of
Muslims, all welded into a homogeneous whole by the same
Faith, I come out increasingly conscious of the potential
achievements cooperation among all these millions can
accomplish--cooperation naturally not going beyond their
loyalty to their original countries, but which will ensure
for them and their Brethren-in-Islam unlimited power.[7]

Under the skillful and energetic leadership of Anwar
Sadat, who had been appointed Secretary-General, the Islamic
Congress, thus conceived, served as a useful adjunct to
Egyptian policy, along with such parallel organizations as
the Afro-Asian Solidarity Conference and the Arab League.
But it was no doubt this kind of use which also led to its
failure. Like the previous attempts by other Muslim
governments, this new Egyptian-sponsored pan-Islamism was
too obviously related to state purposes and failed to arouse
the necessary response from elsewhere.

But there is, perhaps, a deeper reason for the per-
sistent weakness of official pan-Islamism. In the first
century and a half of the Caliphate, Islam was indeed one
single world state. But at that early date, it ceased
to be so, and was never reunited again. Thus, while the
political experience of Muslims, the shared memories of the
past which they cherish, condition them to a sense of common
social and cultural identity, they do not bring them any
tradition of a single Islamic state, but rather one of
political pluralism combined with socio-cultural unity.

* * *

Attempts at international pan-Islamism have produced
limited results. They have, however, already gone very
much further than anything comparable within the Christian

world, and have occasionally had diplomatic consequences,
as for example when the Arab states as a bloc voted for
Pakistan against India's candidacy for the Security Council--
and this despite India's devoted and selfless service to the
Arab cause. Similar choices may be discerned in the support
given to Muslims in the Philippines, Eritrea, and some African
countries when they find themselves in collision with non-
Muslim majorities or governments. But caution has so far
prevailed concerning the position of Muslims in the Soviet
Union, in Eastern European states, and in China.[8]

Islam has shown its strength much more clearly in the
internal politics of Muslim countries. Here two examples may
serve, both of them in countries under autocratic rule. The
first case was in Tunisia, where in February 1960 President
Bourguiba put forward the interesting idea that the month-
long fast of Ramadan with the resultant loss of work and
production was a luxury that a poor and developing country
could not afford. For a Muslim ruler simply to abolish or
disallow a major prescription of the holy law is unthinkable.
What President Bourguiba did was to try to justify its abolition in terms of the holy law itself. This law allows a Muslim to break the fast if he is on campaign in a holy war,
or *jihad*. Bourguiba argued that a developing country was in
a state of *jihad* and that the struggle to obtain economic
independence by development was comparable with a defensive
war for national independence. In pursuit of this argument
he proposed to abolish the rules whereby restaurants, cafes,
and other public places remained open at night during the
month of Ramadan and to oblige them to keep normal hours.
In support of this new interpretation of the law, he tried to
obtain a *fatwa*, a ruling, from the Mufti of Tunis and other
religious authorities. The religious authorities refused to
give him what he wanted. The great mass of the people observed the fast despite the President's dispensation, and
Bourguiba was finally compelled to beat a more or less
graceful retreat. Even an autocratic socialist head of
state, in pursuit of so worthy an end as economic development, could not set aside a clear ruling of the holy law.

A more striking illustration of the religious limits
of autocracy occurred in Syria in the spring of 1967. On
April 25 of that year, the Syrian official army magazine,
Jaysh al-Sha'b, the Army of the People, published an article
by a young officer named Ibrahim Khalas entitled "The Means
of Creating a New Arab Man." The only way, according to
this article, to build Arab society and civilization was to
create

> a new Arab socialist man, who believes that God, religion,
> feudalism, capitalism, and all the values which prevailed
> in the pre-existing society were no more than mummies in
> the museums of history....There is only one value; absolute
> faith in the new man of destiny...who relies only on him-
> self and on his own contribution to humanity...because he

knows that his inescapable end is death and nothing beyond death...no heaven and no hell....We have no need of men who kneel and beg for grace and pity.

This was the first time that such ideas had been expressed in print in any of the revolutionary and radical Arab states, and the response was immediate and violent. Until that point an apparently cowed population had passively acquiesced in a whole series of radical political and economic changes. The suppression of free speech, the confiscation of property evoked no response--but a denial of God and religion in an officially sponsored journal revealed the limits of acquiescence, the point at which a Muslim people was willing to stand up and be counted.

In the face of rapidly mounting tension and violence, the government took several kinds of action. One was to arrest a number of religious leaders; another was to confiscate copies of the journal containing the offending article and to arrest its author and the members of the editorial board. On May 5, the author and editors were imprisoned and on the following day the semi-official newspaper, *Al-Thawra*, "The Revolution," proclaimed the respect of the Syrian regime for God and religion. On May 7, Radio Damascus announced that

the sinful and insidious article published in the magazine *Jaysh al-Sha'b* came as a link in the chain of an American-Israeli reactionary conspiracy....Investigation by the authorities has proved that the article and its author were merely tools of the CIA which has been able to infiltrate most basely and squalidly and to attain its sinful aims of creating confusion among the ranks of the citizens.

The resistance, it was later announced, had been concerted with the Americans, the British, the Jordanians, the Saudis, the Zionists, and Selim Hatum (a Druse opponent of the regime). On May 11, the author and editors were sentenced by a military court to life imprisonment.

* * *

Even in Nasserist Egypt, Islam continued to provide a main focus of loyalty and morale. Thus, in the manual of orientation of the Supreme Command of the Egyptian forces, issued in 1965, the wars in the Yemen and against Israel are presented in terms of a *jihad* or holy war for God against the unbelievers. In reply to questions from the troops as to whether the classical Islamic obligation of *jihad* has lapsed or is still in force, orientation officers are instructed to reply that the *jihad* for God is still in force at the present time and is to be interpreted in our own day in terms of a striving for social justice and human

betterment. The enemies against whom the *jihad* is to be
waged are those who oppose or resist the achievement of
these aims, that is to say imperialism, Zionism, and the
Arab reactionaries.

> In accordance with this interpretation of the mission of
> Islam and in accordance with this understanding of the
> *jihad* we must always maintain that our military duty in
> the Yemen is a *jihad* for God and our military duty against
> Israel is a *jihad* for God, and for those who fight in this
> war there is the reward of fighters in the holy war for
> God....Our duty is the holy war for God. "Kill them
> wherever you come upon them and drive them from the places
> from which they drove you." (Qur'an, ii, 191.)

     That is to say, the war is a holy war, and the rewards
of martyrdom as specified in scripture await those who are
killed in it. Similar ideas are found in the manual of
orientation issued to Egyptian troops in June 1973, and it
is noteworthy that the operational code name for the crossing
of the Canal was Badr, the name of one of the battles fought
by the Prophet against his infidel opponents. Incidentally,
the enemy named in the manual is not Zionism or even Israel
but simply "the Jews." One of the major contrasts between
Syrian and Egyptian orientation literature is the far
greater stress laid by the Egyptians on religion as contrasted
with the more ideological approach of the Syrians.
     There have been two recent wars in which Muslims fought
against non-Muslims--the Turkish landing in Cyprus and the
subsequent fighting, and the Syrian and Egyptian war against
Israel in October 1973. Both in Egypt and in Turkey, the
language, the rhetoric accompanying the offensives, were
strikingly religious. Popular legend, of the kind that
flourishes in wartime in all societies, also assumed an overwhelmingly religious character, with stories of intervention
by the Prophet and the angels of Allah on the side of the
Muslims--i.e., the Egyptians against their enemies. A writer
who complained of this in the press, pointing out that it
devalued the achievement of the Egyptian armed forces, was
bitterly denounced. Not all the Egyptians are of course
Muslim. An important minority is Christian, and these too
fought in the army and, indeed, number several senior officers
among them. This fact is recognized in the guidance manual
of the army which invokes Christian as well as Muslim religious
beliefs. Yet, at the moment when news got through of the
Israeli crossing to the west bank of the Canal, a rumor
immediately appeared ascribing this penetration to the
treachery of a Coptic officer. There was of course no truth
whatsoever in this story, and the Egyptian government took
immediate steps to discount and deny it. It was probably
not entirely coincidental that a Coptic general was promoted
to an army command at that moment. Even more striking is
the appearance of religious language among the secular Turks

who in the fighting in Cyprus used numerous Islamic terms
to describe themselves, their adversaries, and the struggle
between them.

In recognizing the extent to which communal loyalty
remains a significant force in the life of Muslim countries,
one should not fall into the opposite error of discounting
the degree of effective secularization. Particularly in
the more developed countries, changes which are probably
irreversible have already taken place, especially in the
realms of social and economic life and in the organization
of the law and the judiciary. In some countries, such as
Turkey, Iran, and Egypt, geography and history have combined
to give the inhabitants a special sense of separate identity
and destiny, and have advanced them on the path toward
secular nationhood. But even in these Islam remains a
significant, elsewhere a major, force. In general, the
extent of secularization is less than would at first appear.
In education, for example, ostensibly secular schools and
universities have to an increasing extent been subject to
religious influences. Even in radical states like Syria,
the net effect of secularization seems to be directed
against minority religions much more than against Islam.
A Syrian government report published in October 1967 states
that private schools, meaning for the most part foreign-
based Christian schools, would be obliged to use Ministry of
Education textbooks on Christianity and Islam in which the
teaching of the two religions was unified "in a manner which
would not leave room for confessionalism...incompatible
with the line of thought in our age."

* * *

From the foregoing, certain general conclusions emerge.
Islam is still the most effective form of consensus in
Muslim countries, the basic group identity among the masses.
This will be increasingly effective as the regimes become
more genuinely popular. One can already see the contrast
between the present regimes and those of the small, alienated,
Western-educated elite which governed until a few decades
ago. As regimes come closer to the populace, even if their
verbiage is left-wing and ideological, they become more
Islamic. Under the Ba'thist regime in Syria, more mosques
were built in the three years after the *Jaysh al'Sha'b*
incident than in the previous thirty.

Islam is a very powerful but still an undirected force
in politics. As a possible factor in international politics,
the present prognosis is not very favorable. There have
been many attempts at a pan-Islamic policy, none of which
has made much progress. One reason for their lack of success
is that those who have made the attempt have been so unconvincing. This still leaves the possibility of a more
convincing leadership, and there is ample evidence in
virtually all Muslim countries of the deep yearning for

such a leadership and a readiness to respond to it. The
lack of an educated modern leadership has so far restricted
the scope of Islam and inhibited religious movements from
being serious contenders for power. But it is already very
effective as a limiting factor and may yet become a powerful
domestic political force if the right kind of leadership
emerges.

In the period immediately preceding the outbreak of
the Six-Day War in 1967, an ominous phrase was sometimes
heard, "First the Saturday people, then the Sunday people."
The Saturday people have proved unexpectedly recalcitrant,
and recent events in Lebanon indicate that the priorities
may have been reversed. Fundamentally, the same issue
arises in both Palestine and Lebanon, though the circumstances that complicate the two situations are very different. The basic question is this: Is a resurgent Islam
prepared to tolerate a non-Islamic enclave, whether Jewish
in Israel or Christian in Lebanon, in the heart of the
Islamic world? The current fascination among Muslims with
the history of the Crusades, the vast literature on the
subject, both academic and popular, and the repeated in-
ferences drawn from the final extinction of the Crusading
principalities throw some light on attitudes in this matter.
Islam from its inception is a religion of power, and in the
Muslim world view it is right and proper that power should
be wielded by Muslims and Muslims alone. Others may
receive the tolerance, even the benevolence, of the Muslim
state, provided that they clearly recognize Muslim supremacy.
That Muslims should rule over non-Muslims is right and
normal.[9] That non-Muslims should rule over Muslims is an
offense against the laws of God and nature, and this is
true whether in Kashmir, Palestine, Lebanon, or Cyprus.
Here again, it must be recalled that Islam is not conceived
as a religion in the limited Western sense but as a
community, a loyalty, and a way of life--and that the
Islamic community is still recovering from the traumatic
era when Muslim governments and empires were overthrown
and Muslim peoples forcibly subjected to alien, infidel
rule. Both the Saturday people and the Sunday people
are now suffering the consequences.

NOTES

1. Koran is the more generally used Western transliteration.
2. The modern Arab word for secular is *alamani*, literally
worldly, i.e., pertaining to this world. Probably of Christian
Arab origin, it passed into general use in the 19th century.
3. Another proffered explanation of the name Fatah is that
it represents a reversed acronym for *Harakat Tahrir Falastin*,
movement for the liberation of Palestine.
4. The *Sovyetskaya Entsiklopediya*, on the other hand, devotes
a long article to discrediting them.
5. Local official inquiries decided that these actions had

been instigated by "foreign agents." If so, the agents knew which
themes to evoke, and how to direct the response.

　　6. In *Religion in the Middle East*, edited by A. J. Arberry
(Cambridge, 1969), Volume 1, p. 415.

　　7. Gamal Abdel Nasser, *The Philosophy of the Revolution*,
Cairo, n.d., pp. 67-68.

　　8. A different kind of exception is the refusal of some Arab
and some other Muslim countries to support Turkey on the Cyprus
question. One element in this is residual resentment against
former rulers; another is disapproval of the policies of Westernization and secularization pursued by the Turkish Republic since its
inception.

　　9. The same concept finds expression in the Muslim law of
marriage, which allows a Muslim man to marry a non-Muslim woman, but
categorically forbids a marriage between a non-Muslim man and a
Muslim woman. The rationale is that in a marriage the man is the
dominant, the woman the subordinate, partner--and Islam must prevail.

2
The Anatomy of Islamic Revival: Legitimacy Crisis, Ethnic Conflict, and the Search for Islamic Alternatives

R. Hrair Dekmejian

The recent regeneration of the Islamic ethos appears to have caught the non-Islamic world by surprise. To a Western world preoccupied with growing economic problems and security concerns--inflation, energy, SALT, the Arab-Israeli conflict-- the new challenge of Islam appears disconcerting and even ominous. Few were those, both in the West and in the Communist world, who were able to anticipate an Islamic resurgence in the modern context.[1] Perhaps the conceptual myopia induced by capitalist and Marxist materialism had effectively blind- folded the scholars and statesmen of the non-Islamic world, who tended to disregard or underestimate the regenerative capacity of Islam. This essay is a preliminary attempt to identify some of the characteristics of the contemporary Islamic revival and to discern the possible causal factors responsible for its emergence.

ISLAMIC REVIVAL: THREE BASIC ATTRIBUTES

One of the most significant attributes of contemporary Islamic revivalism is its pervasiveness. The movement of a return to Islamic roots is a trans-national phenomenon; it has been occurring virtually in every Islamic society or community regardless of size or political, economic and cultural environment. Indeed, the quest for a new Islamic identity is discernible not only in the Arab sphere, but also in Nigeria, Turkey, Pakistan and Indonesia. It is manifest not only in countries where Muslims are numerically dominant, but also among Islamic minorities in India, the Philippines, the Soviet Union and the Western countries.

The Anatomy of Islamic Revival: Legitimacy Crisis, Ethnic Conflict and the Search for an Islamic Alternative is reprinted by permission of *The Middle East Journal*, Vol. 34, No. 1, Winter, 1980.

Nor is the Islamic revival limited to particular social
and economic classes or occupations. While much of its
grass roots support has come from the lower and lower middle
classes, there is increasing evidence of widespread emulation
of Islamic lifestyles among the middle and upper middle classes
in such relatively advanced countries as Egypt, Turkey and
Tunisia.

The second unique characteristic of the Islamic rebirth
movement is its polycentrism. Indeed, the merging "trans-
national *ummah*" possesses no single revolutionary or organizational epicenter. The two potential centers which could
provide leadership of the nascent movement—Saudi Arabia and
Egypt—are ruled by conservative elites singularly unwilling
to sponsor a fundamentally anti-*status quo* messianic ideology.
Nor are the prospects bright for the emergence of an Islamic
epicenter through the fusion of the spiritual power of the
Haramayn, augmented by Al-Azhar's religious cadres and
intellectual resources, and financed by Saudi money. Indeed,
at this early stage of its development, the movement even
lacks a leader of charismatic propensity who could provide
some focus in terms of spiritual unity and revolutionary
activity. Nor is there any traditional repository of authority to serve as a symbolic focus; no Sultan-Caliph Abdulhamit II
of a century ago leading the Pan-Islamic movement with the help
of Shaykh Jamal al-Din al-Afghani. The leadership potential
of Ayat Allah Khumayni is limited to the *Ithna'ashari*
("Twelver") sect of Shi'ite Muslims who mostly inhabit Iran
and southern Iraq. Therefore, the return to Islamic roots
has a "nativistic" and "localistic" character; at least in
part it has developed in response to particular conditions
existing in different national environments. In the Iranian
case, for instance, Ayat Allah Ruh Allah Khumayni's Islamic
revolution was largely a reaction to the repressive policies
of a corrupt political order. In contrast, in the Egyptian
case, most Islamic fundamentalists are more likely to press
for social justice for the underprivileged masses. Yet to
the extent that crisis situations in Islamic societies are
similar, the Islamic revival movement may eventually assume
a truly transnational character. It is important to note
that, at the present stage of its development, the cross-
national ties of Islamic revivalism appear to be more
spiritual than organizational.

The third most striking aspect of the phenomenon of
Islamic revivalism is its persistence. The belated discovery of its existence by Western governments and mass media
notwithstanding, the tendency toward Islamic regeneration has
persisted in the last century. Indeed, one may discern a
cyclical pattern of ebb-and-flow between secularist trends
and Islamic tendencies. Thus, the powerful 19th century
impact of European imperialism and Westernization produced
an Islamic reaction ranging from al-Afghani's Pan-Islamism
to Muhammad 'Abduh's attempts to render Islam more applicable
to modernizing environments. The liberal-constitutional period

in Egupt was followed by yet another Islamic revivalist
reaction in the inter-war years in the hands of Muhammad
Husayn Haykal and Hasan al-Banna's Muslim Brotherhood.
The July 1952 Revolution brought in a second secularizing
phase which, after the 1967 war, slowly evolved toward
another phase of Islamic revival. This ongoing dialectic
between secularism and Islam testified to the persistence
of Islam as a social force; it also signifies the continued
failure of the Islamic countries to forge a synthesis--as
a resolution of the conflictual foundations of contemporary
Islamic societies. The fundamental question that begs for
an answer is: Why an Islamic revival in the fourth quarter
of the 20th century? At the present phase of its development, it is foolhardy to identify any precise causal factors.
Nevertheless several general propositions may be advanced
as explanatory hypotheses focusing on developments primarily
in Islam's Middle Eastern epicenter.

A RESPONSE TO CRISIS

At the most general level of analysis, the recent quest
for a return to the Islamic ethos appears to be a natural
response to the successive pathological experiences which
have buffeted Islamic societies in contemporary times.
This protracted crisis milieu included the disorienting
political, economic and social impact of Western and Soviet
imperialism, the imperatives of "pressure cooker" economic
development, the various struggles for independence, the
Arab-Israeli conflict, the Arab loss of Palestine and
Jerusalem, the emergence of Western and Marxist secularist
ideological movements and the ongoing political conflicts
within the Arab sphere and in the larger Islamic context.
Consequently, the catalysts of the crisis environment which
appear to have triggered a return to Islamic roots are multi-
dimensional. Three broad categories of crisis catalysts
are discernible--political, economic, military--each of
which has elicited specific responses from Islam. Each of
these clusters of catalysts warrant detailed explication.

Legitimacy Crisis and Ineffective Rulership

To a significant degree the movement back to Islam
appears to be a reaction to the failure of the elites of
Islamic countries to establish legitimate public order
within viable political communities. In its classic
Weberian formulation, legitimacy involves the transformation
of naked power into authority which is generally accepted
and obeyed without frequent resort to coercion.[2] Thus,
the establishment of a legitimate order is considered one
of the quintessential hallmarks of the modern nation state
which has been manifestly lacking in most of the Third World
countries including those of the Islamic sphere.

The legitimacy crisis in the Islamic countries has its
roots in the failure of political and intellectual elites
to substitute secular ideologies of legitimization and social
cohesion for traditional Islamic legitimacy. In the successor
states of the Ottoman Empire and in Iran, there emerged variants
of "reactive" nationalism, in blind emulation of the European
nationalisms. This mimicry of European precedents included
the borrowing of Western constitutional norms and practices,
often mixed with the authoritarian thought of the German
idealists and in later years with Marxian and other variants
of socialism. Yet after six decades of experimentation, no
ideological synthesis has emerged. Of the four major attempts
to forge a synthesis of political thought as a guide to
political action, two--Ataturkism and Nasirism--appear to
have failed after some temporary success; the third--Ba'thism--
continues its difficult march through the minefields of
Levantine Arab politics. The fourth--Dasturian Socialism--
manifests all the attributes of crisis even before the demise
of the aging Bourguiba.[3]

The Ataturk Model. The earliest attempt to build viable
political community was that of Ataturk on the basis of nativist
Turkish nationalism separated from the Pan-Turanist morass, and
reinforced by strict secularism, Westernization and etatistic
economics. Ataturk's formula for legitimizing the new order
was based on the charisma of his heroism as well as on the
cohesive force of Turkish nationalism--a combination which
became progressively eroded after mid-century under the
challenges of ideological polarization, ethnic separatism
and class warfare. The secularist reforms affected mainly
the military and bureaucratic elites and the intellectuals;
the countryside remained mostly traditional and Islamic in its
orientation, despite the government's antireligious policies.
In retrospect, therefore, Ataturk's unprecedented attempt to
create a new secular foundation for political authority appears
to have been less than a total success, particularly in view
of modern Turkey's protracted domestic turmoil and the re-
emergence of strong pro-Islamic social forces.

The Nasirite Interlude. The second major attempt to
create a modern political order was undertaken by Jamal
'Abd al-Nasir after the 1952 Revolution. Nasir and his
generation of Egyptians grew up at the confluence of four
great intellectual and political cross-currents--Egyptian
nationalism, Islamic fundamentalism, Arabism and Marxism.
In his early years, Nasir had been greatly influenced by
the virulent nationalism of the *Misr al-Fatath* and to a
lesser degree by the Pan-Islamic ideals of the *Ikhwan al-
Muslimin*--the Muslim Brotherhood; once in power, Nasir
was also affected by Arabism and Marxism. Yet unlike
Ataturk, the Nasirite formula for legitimzation did not
rely on a wholesale rejection of the past, but on an
eclectic synthesis of pre-revolutionary political thought

and action. Nasir began as an Egyptian nationalist, only
to make himself the supreme charismatic champion of Pan-
Arabism after the mid-1950s; Nasir's social and economic
policies were guided by Arab Socialism--a mixture of Islamic,
Marxist and etatist principles. Meanwhile, Nasir had rejected the Muslim Brotherhood's "theocratic" ideology without
rejecting Islam. Indeed, the Islamic clerical establishment
was converted into a disciplined arm of the state bureaucracy.
However, regardless of the "mix" of his political formula,
Nasir's legitimacy was basically derived from his personal
charismatic bond with the Arab masses--one based upon the
Egyptian leader's heroic exploits during the 1950s in the
arena of international politics. The reverses of the 1960s--
the Yemen War and the June 1967 defeat--brought the inevitable
erosion of charisma and the progressive atrophy of Nasirism
after the leader's death.

One of Nasir's most significant accomplishments within
the Arab sphere had been the raising of the level of mass
Arab consciousness through the propagation of Arab unity
nationalism (Pan-Arabism). He functioned as the principal
socialization agent of Arabism, who made Arab unity nationalism
a part of the psychological make up of the Arab masses. Hence,
the emergence of a vacuum after his departure, which was
political, spiritual and aspirational. A whole generation
of Arabs had grown up under Nasirism, the aspirations of
which had been unfulfilled. Consequently, the death of the
charismatic was bound to produce a crisis in legitimacy since
the force of charismatic legitimization could not transcend
the deceased leader, and his formula of legitimization (*i.e.*
Nasirism) could not be transferred to a suitable heir for its
continued propagation.

Ba'thism and Bourguibism. As the originators of Pan-
Arabism, the Ba'thists were Nasir's natural rivals, especially
after the breakup of the United Arab Republic in 1961. The
Ba'thist ideological formula projects a notion of Arab unity
based on the glories of the Arab past. While recognizing
Islam's seminal contributions to Arab civilization, the Ba'thist
ideological orientation is essentially secularist and socialist.
What the Ba'th party lacked was the legitimizing force of a
single leader--the halo of charismatic leadership, which Nasir
was reluctant to provide after the Syrian secession from the
UAR. Therefore, the Syrian Ba'thists and their Iraqi rivals
were forced to rely on army support to acquire and retain
power; hence the progressive militarization of the two regimes.
Meanwhile, the Ba'thi regimes pushed ahead with a "legal-
rational" type of legitimizing formula by propagating the
party's commitment to the goals of Pan-Arabism along with
etatistic socialism as a means of realizing social justice
and well being. By all indications, however, the Ba'thist
struggle to establish stable political communities remains
unresolved.

The Tunisian experience in national development is

unique because it combined Habib Bourguiba's charismatic
legitimacy with the legal-rational legitimacy of the Dasturian
Socialist Party based on a mix of socialistic and nationalistic
themes. In contrast to the Nasirite and Ba'thist experiences,
the Tunisian case bore similarities to the Ataturk model; it
possessed the advantages of effective personal leadership and
party leadership which functioned together with relative
success until recent years. However, the fundamental limitation of the Bourguibist model was its localism, e.g. there
was little inclination to export the Tunisian formula via
Pan-Arabism or any other medium.

In most other countries of the Islamic world, the
legitimacy crisis is ever more acute. The formulas of
legitimization have ranged from a mix of traditionalist
Islamic and tribal reinforcements of kingly authority (e.g.
Morocco, Saudi Arabia, imperial Iran, the Gulf states,
Jordan), to using Islam as the state ideology (Khumayni's
Iran, Pakistan), to combining Islam with socialist principles
to support an oligarchy of military men and technocrats (e.g.
Algeria). In two cases--Afghanistan and South Yemen--Marxism
has emerged as the dominant ideology of the ruling elite. In
Libya there is a new experiment to reinforce Mu'ammar Qadhadhafi's
charismatic legitimacy with Islamic and Nasirist maxims within
the framework of direct democracy.[4] With the exception of
Algeria and Libya, there is little evidence of concern among
political elites to develop more effective forms of ideological
constructs to organize popular action and meet the challenges
of modernization.

The Paucity of Social Justice

The crisis of legitimacy--both of political elites and
social systems--has been reinforced by the failure of Middle
Eastern governments to make good on their promises of achieving development and social justice. With the exception of
the wealthy Gulf states, economic problems have increasingly
plagued the Islamic countries. Among the factors responsible
for this economic crisis are elite incompetence and corruption,
inflation, high rates of population growth, as well as the
pervasive lack of developmental ideologies for economic
planning and mass mobilization. Nor are the oil producing
countries free from economic problems, because of the lack of
effective mechanisms of balanced economic development and
income distribution.

In a sense it is ironic that the recent massive infusion
of wealth into the Islamic sphere has been a mixed blessing.
In the international arena oil has brought a significant
increase in the political and economic power of the principal
Islamic oil producing states. Yet the domestic impact of oil
wealth has been overwhelmingly disruptive both for the oil
producing states and their economic clients. The great on-
rush of oil money after 1973 was a primary destabilizing
force in Iran; the Shah's despotic "feudal capitalism"

contributed to its own self destruction by presiding over a
situation of increasing class polarization in the context
of official corruption, inflation, conspicuous consumption
by the Westernized elite side by side with urban and rural
poverty. Nor was the infusion of Arab oil money from the
Arab Gulf states beneficial in promoting stability in such
economically client states as Syria and Egypt. During the
early 1970s, the prospects for receiving large scale economic
aid from the conservative Arab states was partly responsible
for the institution of "open" capitalist economic systems in
these two states and for the concomitant diminution of their
socialist-etatist practices. Consequently both states have
been plagued by instability. In Syria's case the maldistri-
bution of wealth appears to have reinforced ethnic cleavages,
thereby exacerbating the ongoing conflict between the
politically dominant 'Alawis and the economically successful
Christians on the one hand, and the majority Sunni population
on the other. In Egypt, the post-Nasirite policy of *infitah*
has created a new class of millionaires in the midst of
expanding poverty that led to the riots of January 1977.
These disruptive economic developments, which also are
discernible in other developing countries, are further
exacerbated by the inflationary world economy presided
over by the large Western-based multinational corporations.
It is significant that in no less than 13 countries of the
Islamic orbit the *per capita* income is below $800.00.[5]

Burden of Military Defeats

The third factor contributing to the crisis milieu of
the Islamic countries is the persistence of military defeats.
Implicit in their long quest for independence was the aspiration to acquire sufficient military potential to safeguard
their vital territorial interests. However, this deeply felt
aspiration to develop military prowess has not been realized.
With the single exception of Algeria, no Islamic country
acquired independence through a protracted struggle with a
European imperial power. After the achievement of independence, a number of Islamic countries were repeatedly unsuccessful militarily against non-Islamic foes. The successive
defeats of Pakistan by India are a case in point. Yet from
the Pan-Islamic perspective the Arab military failure to
contain Israel was more significant in its general impact.
The effects of the July 1967 war were particulary devastating
due to the magnitude of the Arab defeat and the loss of Arab
Jerusalem--a factor which concerned the whole Islamic community.
Aside from its human and economic costs, these defeats produced
shock waves affecting both Arabs and non-Arab Muslims in
engendering feelings of fear, insecurity and inferiority. The
manifest inability of the Arab states to remove the Israeli
occupation of Arab territory sapped the legitimacy of Arab
ruling elites and their military regimes. Furthermore the
failure of non-Arab Islamic leaders to support the Arab cause

diplomatically and militarily brought an outpouring of
protest from the Islamic faithful in such important countries
as Iran, Turkey and Pakistan.

In searching for the causal factors responsible for the
contemporary revival of Islam, three general catalysts have
been identified. By the late 1960s due to the confluence of
these catalytic factors a multi-dimensional crisis situation
was engulfing the Arab and Islamic countries, which continues
to dominate their social and political life today. Indeed,
it is possible that, in many of the Islamic countries, the
crisis catalysts are only in their early stages of development.

To confront the crisis situation, elites and counter-
elites have proposed and often implemented a variety of
approaches ranging from communist totalitarianism, to socialist-
etatist, mixed capitalist and theocratic systems. Thus, the
Islamic alternative and its variants constitute but one of
these approaches to crisis management.

BACK TO ISLAMIC ROOTS: THE ESCAPE FROM ALIENATION

As a comprehensive system of values and beliefs, Islam
evolved principles and prescriptions that were applied through
the Shari'ah to most aspects of social existence. As such,
it is no mere accident that the three catalytic factors of
the contemporary crisis milieu correspond to three areas of
social activity with respect to which Islam manifests particular
sensitivity and perscriptive relevance.

With respect to the legitimacy crisis and the consequent
failure of national elites to establish viable political communities, Islam offers its own traditional formula of legitimation,
by rejecting the efforts of secular leaders to utilize Western
ideological constructs to promote social cohesion and to guide
political action. The various proponents of a return to
Islamic legitimacy point a critical finger at the non-Islamic
content of such eclectic ideologies as Ataturkism, Nasirism
and Ba'thism, and deplore the emulation of Western and Soviet
models of socio-economic development.

Strongly imbedded in the Islamic conscience is the notion
of social justice (*'adalah*). Gross disparities of wealth and
privilege fly in the face of traditional Islamic maxims of
communal sharing of basic resources. In the context of
increasing class polarization and massive poverty, when
political elites are perceived as the perpetrators of social-
economic injustice, Islam could well become a potent protest
ideology to oppose the "establishment" with religious sanction.
Two recent manifestations of Islamic proletarianist movements
were Khumayni's revolution against the Shah and to a lesser
extent the January 1977 protests in Egypt directed at the
government's lifting of price subsidies for basic commodities.
At the intellectual level, various theorists have proposed
the doctrine of Islamic Socialism to promote a just social-
economic order.[6] In this connection it is instructive to

remember the Quranic maxim which has become a part of the popular conscience--*al'adl asas al-hukm*--justice is the origin of rule.

In assessing the Islamic alternative to the third crisis factor--the persistence of military defeats--one should note Islam's positive attitude toward military prowess. As "the most martial of major world religions," Islam placed religious sanction and blessing upon its armies as the defenders of the faith and state.[7] The use of concepts such as *jihad* (holy war), *ghazi* (victorious warrior), *shahid* (martyred warrior in the name of Islam) and *'izzah* (honor) still evoke great sentiment and devotion among Muslims.[8] As the inheritors of a military tradition, the continuing weakness of today's Islamic armies against non-Muslim states places a heavy burden upon ruling elites, many of whom are military officers. Its proponents see Islam as a powerful mobilizing medium to propel the people against external enemies.

To identify the possible types of Islamic response to societal crisis is not to argue that these Islamic alternatives are necessarily viable; in the long range the new Islamic way may prove to be even less successful in satisfying popular aspirations than the eclectic Western inspired models of political thought and action. The point is that, to an increasing number of alienated Muslims, Islam does appear to provide a practical political alternative as well as a secure spiritual niche and psychological anchor in a turbulent world. Most Westerners fail to realize that the decline of religion in the West has not been matched by a similar decline in the *Dar al-Islam*. Indeed, the self view and attitudes of today's Muslims are determined by two dialectical processes--one historical, the other contemporary. Both deserve examination as explanations for the present phase of Islamic revival.

The Two Dialectics

Clearly the foremost determinant of contemporary Muslim attitudes toward the external world is the way in which Islam theologically orients itself as a source of divine revelation *vis-à-vis* other religions. As a staunchly monotheist faith, Islam considers itself the sole inheritor of a monotheistic prophetic tradition reaching back to the Hebrew prophets and Jesus Christ. By consciously basing itself upon the cumulative process of revelation, the Islamic *weltanschauung* perceives a grand dialectical process of divine design consisting of three epochal stages of revelation, each more perfect than its antecedent. In Hegelian terminology Judaism constitutes the "thesis" which generated Christianity as its "antithesis", leading to the Islamic "synthesis" as the highest stage of divine revelation. To the extent that today's Muslims believe in the inherent superiority of their faith, and its practical relevance, Islam will continue to possess a dynamism which the other religions of the West conspicuously lack.

The second dialectic which has shaped present day Muslim

attitudes is more recent in its inception. It began with
the decline of Islam and the rise of the indigenous nation-
alisms--Turkish, Iranian and Egyptian/Arab. While in each
case, the dialectic passed through somewhat dissimilar phases,
the final syntheses bear the same characteristics.

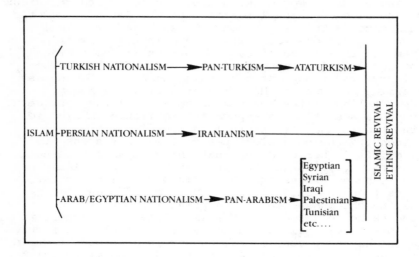

As depicted in the diagram above, the early Turkish
nationalism of Ottomanist reformers (Ahmet Riza) gave way
to the Pan-Turanism of the younger Ittihadists (Ziya Gokalp),
which Ataturk rejected in favor of a new secular Turkish
nationalism, now challenged by Islamic fundamentalism and
ethnic particularism. In Iran, an indigenous Persian nationalism
evolved into an imperial Pan-Iranian ideology under Riza Shah
based on pre-Islamic Aryan themes, which has now been rejected
by Khumayni's Islamic Revolution and resurgent ethnic
separatism.

In the Arab sphere, Egyptian and Arab nationalism
developed separately, only to become united under Nasir's
Pan-Arabism; in the post-Nasir period, Arab national elites
have attempted to propagate their separate nationalisms to
capture popular loyalties, as Ba'thists have tried to sustain
Pan-Arabism without Nasir. It appears that in many cases
the "fall back" of popular loyalties from Nasirist Pan-Arabism
is not to the nation state level, but to Islam and ethnic
particularism.

In all of these cases, Islam constitutes a "fall back"
ideology to capture the alienated, the disoriented and the
angry; in this sense it constitutes a powerful check on mass
alienation and social atomization. Islam can accommodate
the political activist, as well as provide an escape from
politics in the ascetic milieu of the mosque.

Islam vs. Ethnicity

The myopia of many Western scholars toward the latent social and political salience of Islam has been matched by their general disinterest in the political importance of ethnicity in the Islamic world. Despite the massacres and repressions of the past, the Islamic countries remain ethnic "mosaics", with cleavages along sectarian, linguistic, tribal, regional and racial dimensions.

The coincidence of Islamic revival and ethnic consciousness in the context of the present crisis phase of the dialectical process pits Islam against ethnicity in virtually every Islamic country. Assuming that Islamic movements are the wave of the near future, how will Islam deal with ethnic conflicts?

Some proponents of Islamic revival argue that since Islam constitutes the majority faith, it possesses the capacity to absorb and resolve ethnic conflicts on the basis of Muslim unity and brotherhood. This solution has been advocated at various times to counter ethnic separatism in a number of Islamic states, particularly in Pakistan, Iran and Turkey. Since its inception, Islam has been the *raison d'etre* for Pakistan's existence as an independent entity. Despite the secession of East Bengal in 1971, the Pakistani social mosaic--Punjabis, Sindhis, Pathans, Baluchis--is held together precariously by Islam and the Army. It is to be noted that the post-Bhutto period of Pakistani politics has been characterized by a clear movement toward "Islamization" under the regime of General Zia-ul-Haq for the express purpose of preventing the dissolution of the state along ethnic boundaries.

In Iran, Khumayni's clerical regime has based its policies toward Iran's Muslim minorities--*e.g.* Kurds, Arabs, Azeris, Turkomans, Baluchis, etc.--on the imperative of Islamic unity, without much success. In Turkey, Prime Minister Bulent Ecevit's left-of-center regime continued until recently to uphold, however unsuccessfully, Ataturk's secularist doctrines, against growing challenges from Islamic rightists and ethnic separatist movements exacerbating the relations between the politically dominant Turks and the Kurds, Alevis and Lazes.

It is still premature to speculate on the possible consequences of Islamic rebirth movements on the internal and external politics of the Islamic countries.[9] Nevertheless, it should be obvious that the application of Islamic principles to political and economic reconstruction is a most complex and difficult endeavor as reflected by the trials and tribulations of the Khumayni regime in Iran. The creative application of Islamic values and maxims will require the best intellectual efforts of Islamic theorists and political leaders. The likes of Muhammad 'Abduh have not been in abundance in the second half of the 20th century.[10] The tasks of creative Islamic leadership will also include the limitation of excesses against the diverse groups of the "ethnic mosaic"--

the amelioration of ethnic conflicts between Muslims as well as toleration toward Christian and Jewish minorities in Islamic countries.

With respect to the West, the Islamic rebirth movement could constitute a clear political and economic challenge. To a Western world in an "end of ideology" milieu, Islam might appear as a reborn enemy. Nevertheless, it may not be unrealistic to project a future scenario of Islamic-Western accommodation brought about by the powerful mutuality of economic interests, reinforced by their negative perceptions of Soviet goals and aspirations.

NOTES

1. Among the notable exceptions is Bernard Lewis, "The Return of Islam," *Commentary*, 61 (January 1976): 39-49. [Reprinted in this volume. See Chapter 1.]

2. Robert Dahl, *Modern Political Analysis*, (Englewood Cliffs: Prentice-Hall, 1963), p. 19. On Weber's use of legitimacy, see, H. H. Gerth and C. Wright Mills, *From Max Weber--Essays in Sociology*, (New York, 1946).

3. The experience of other Islamic countries is not relevant under this categorization since their dominant elites have either failed or did not attempt to achieve an ideological synthesis as a guide to modernization and as an anchor of elite legitimation.

4. See the *Green Book*, Part One, pp. 55-94.

5. *1977 Statistical Yearbook*, (United Nations: Department of International Economic and Social Affairs, 1978).

6. For example, Muhammad al-Ghazzali, *Our Beginning of Wisdom*, (Washington, D.C., 1953), pp. 130-137.

7. Robert E. Ward and Dankwart A. Rustow (eds.), *Political Modernization in Japan and Turkey*, (Princeton, N.J., 1964), p. 352.

8. Asaf Hussain, *Elites in an Ideological State: The Case of Pakistan*, (London, 1979), p. 127.

9. For an insightful analysis of the linkages between Islam and political values and policy choices, see R. Stephen Humphreys, "Islam and Political Values in Saudi Arabia, Egypt and Syria," *The Middle East Journal*, 33, No. 1 (Winter 1979): 1-19. [Reprinted in this volume. See Chapter 21.]

10. On the "vacuum of Islamic intellectualism," see Fazlur Rahman, "Islamic Modernization: Its Scope, Method and Alternatives," *International Journal of Middle East Studies*, 1, No. 4 (October 1970): 317-333.

3
Islam and Arab Nationalism

Najm A. Bezirgan

A careful reading of the vast literature on Arab
nationalism written in Arabic would clearly show that the
most problematic aspect of the numerous definitions and
formulations of the concept has been its relation to Islam.
It is also clear that the preoccupation of modern Arabic
thought with this relationship has been of long-standing:
it dates at least to the second half of the nineteenth
century.

The *problematic* of this relationship can be seen in
its first form in the writings of Abdul Rahman al-Kawakibi
(1849-1903) who conceived of an Arab nation based on the
idea of separating religion from political hegemony. Al-
Kawakibi, however, wrote in a tradition of religious
thought which included Jamal al-Din al-Afghani (1838-1897),
Muhammad 'Abduh (1849-1905), Rashid Rida (1865-1935), a
tradition that had developed in the wake of two great
religious revivalist movements, the *Wahhabiyya* in the
Arabian peninsula and the *Senusiyya* in North Africa.

The call for an Islamic unification against the
Western incursion is at the very basis of this school of
thought. Yet, because the call was often couched in
political rather than purely religious terms, al-Afghani
and his disciples made a number of contradictory statements
regarding the question of nationalism or patriotism vs.
religion. Thus, in an article published in *Al-'Urwa
Al-Wuthqa*, the journal al-Afghani co-edited with 'Abduh
in Paris, the religious tie among the Muslims is singled
out as the only bond that

Islam and Arab Nationalism is reprinted from *Middle
East Review*, Vol. XI, No. 2, Winter, 1978/79.

has made the Muslims shy away from the consideration of
nationality and refuse any kind of solidarity (asabiyya)
except Islamic solidarity. . .[1]

However,

the Germans differed in regard to Christianity...but
because this secondary difference had an effect on
political unity, the Germans became weak...But when they
...returned to the fundamental principles and observed
national unity in matters of common interest, God returned to them enough power and might to make them the
rulers of Europe.[2]

Muhammad 'Abduh trod in al-Afghani's footsteps and
emphasized the necessity of reforming Islam from within.
But he went a step further in showing his allegiance to
the idea of an Islamic caliphate. He makes it an article
of faith:

For it (the Ottoman state) alone protects the authority
of religion...and religion would have no authority without
it.[3]

Unlike al-Afghani, however, 'Abduh makes no concessions
to nationalism or patriotism as a factor in achieving unity,
although his writings do contain some references to the
necessity of unity between Muslims and non-Muslims who belong to the same nation, i.e., as in Egypt.
Within the same tradition, Rashid Rida represents yet
a third trend. While opposing Ottoman rule, he rejected
any tendency toward establishing separate Arab states based
on non-Islamic solidarity in the Islamic world. But the
Arabs, for him, had a special place within the Islamic nations.
The other Muslims, he held, were pupils of the Arabs. This
opposition to Ottoman rule was counterbalanced in Egypt
by a strong pro-Ottoman movement with comparatively less
interest in religion. The leader of Egypt's Nationalist
Party, Mustafa Kamil, called for support for the Ottoman
state in its struggle against the Western powers. In his
book, *The Eastern Question* (1898) he declares that

the existence of the Sublime State is necessary for the
human race and its continuity is necessary for the safety
of the nations of the West and the East.[4]

Similar ardent support was voiced by other prominent
leaders and by eminent journalists. It was only natural
for these men to see Ottoman and domestic politics as
closely bound in a united front against the British occupation of Egypt, and thus they did not and could not see any
contradiction between patriotism and religion. As Mustafa
Kamil argued, rather rhetorically,

patriotism is the noblest tie between people and the solid
basis on which strong nations are built. The culture and
civilization...(of)...Europe is nothing but the fruit of
patriotism...I see that religion and patriotism are inseparable twins and he whose heart has been taken possession
of by religion loves his fatherland sincerely.[5]

Opposing this reconciliation between religion and
patriotism was the voice of 'Abdulla al-Nadim (1844-1896),
a champion of Egyptian nationalism:

Let the Muslim among you turn to his brother Muslim for the
sake of religious unity, and let the two join the Copt and
the Jew in support of national unity, and let them all be
one man seeking one thing: to preserve Egypt for the
Egyptians.[6]

The first Muslim champion of the idea of Arab nationalism
was certainly al-Kawakibi. In his *Taba'i al-Istibdad (The
Characteristics of Tyranny)*, published in Cairo in 1900,
he advocated, in no uncertain terms, an Arab unity based on
the separation of religion from politics:

Here are the nations of Austria and America who have been
guided by science to find a variety of paths and deep-
rooted foundations for national unity and harmony, but
not administrative unity, for national harmony, but not
sectarian unity. Why is it that we cannot follow one of
these paths?

But this line of thinking is not pursued in his book,
Umm al-Qura, first serialized in Rashid Rida's journal,
al-Manar in 1901-1902. Here al-Kawakibi is more concerned
with wresting Islam from the Turks and restoring it to the
Arabs. Arab hegemony is seen as the only way to salvage
Islam from decay, because the Arabs "are of all nations
the most suitable to be an authority in religion and an
example to the Muslims. The other nations have followed
their guidance from the start and will not refuse to follow
them now."[8]

This emphasis on the role of the Arabs within Islam
can also be found in the writings of Najeeb 'Azouri, a
Christian advocate of Arab nationalism, and a contemporary
of al-Kawakibi. In 1905, 'Azouri published a book in Paris
entitled *Le reveil de la nation arabe*, in which he strongly
argues for the separation of civil and religious powers as
a first step in the direction of establishing an independent
Arab state. Yet this independent state should be headed by a
Sultan who is identified as an Arab Muslim.[9]

Before the appearance of al-Kawakibi and 'Azouri, a
number of secret political organizations were formed by
educated Christians in Beirut and Damascus (or, at least,
led by them) which demanded the complete independence of

the Arab countries from the Ottoman empire. The first and
most radical group was The Beirut Secret Society, which
emerged in 1875. This society demanded independence for
Syria and recognition of Arabic as an official language.
Another, The Society for the Rights of the Arab Nation,
established in Beirut and Damascus in 1881, called for an
Islamic-Christian unity within the framework of an Arab
national unity.[10] Clearly, nevertheless, the nationalist
societies that emerged toward the end of the first decade
of the present century showed more reluctance to establish
a separate Arab identity and renounce the Ottoman caliphate,
partly, perhaps, because of the hopeful political climate
created by the declaration of the second Ottoman constitution
in 1908. The program of *Jam'iyyat al Ikha'al-'Arabi-al-Othmani*
(The Arab-Ottoman Brotherhood Society) founded in Istanbul in
1908 and including prominent Arab intellectuals and military
officers in its ranks, clearly stated that "the Ottoman
fatherland is indivisible" and called for allegiance to the
Ottoman caliphate.[11] The programs of many of the secret
organizations that sprang up in reaction to the obvious mis-
trust of the Arabs by the Turkish leaders of the Unity and
Progress Party indicate no tendency toward abandoning the
feasibility of sharing with the Turks in the Ottoman empire.
The goal of the *al-Jam'iyya al-Qahtaniyya* (a striking Arab
title) which was established in 1909, for example, was to
build an Arabic-Turkish empire similar to the Austro-
Hungarian empire.[12]

In the immediate years before the outbreak of World
War I, a mood of disappointment pervaded the Arab provinces
of the Ottoman empire, but even the most prestigious and
active of the Arab political societies continued to assert
the significance of the Islamic caliphate. Thus the program
of *Jam'iyyat al'Ahd*, established in 1913, with prominent
officers among its members, clearly stated that the Islamic
caliphate was a "sacred trust in the hands of the Ottomans."[13]
The second item in the constitution of *Hizb al-Lamarkaziyya*
(The Decentralization Party), founded in Egypt in 1912,
stated that its purpose was "to demonstrate the advantages
of the decentralized administration to the Ottoman people,
who are composed of different nationalities, languages,
religions and customs..."[14]

Meanwhile, far away in the West, a number of Arab
intellectuals and students living in Paris organized an
Arab conference in June, 1913 to discuss the idea of decentralization. This conference was attended by representatives
from Egypt, Iraq, Lebanon and Syria and the Arab communities
in the United States and Mexico. The conference's resolutions and recommendations were rendered meaningless with the
outbreak of the war, but its ideological significance lay in
its formulation of a new concept of the Arab, based on the
idea of one language and one nation. Also, and for the first
time, the religious factor in the formation of an Arab nation
was publicly denied. "...the religious bond has invariably

failed to bring about political unity," "Abdul Hamid
al-Zahrawi, a member of the conference's executive committee
told a French journalist.[15] And yet, many speakers at the
conference emphasized the need to maintain the unity of the
Ottoman state. One of them, Iskander 'Ammon, put it
succinctly, "...the Arab nation seeks nothing but to change
the form of the corrupt government...and our position would
have been the same even if the ruling body had been from the
heart of the Quraish."[16]

With the defeat of the Ottoman empire and the occupation
of many of the Arab countries by Britain and France, new
definitions of Arab nationalism were advanced by nationalist
writers, and most of these began clearly to take an ideological
turn. Yet the relation of Arab nationalism to Islam remained
at the very center of all discussions. Islam was now given
a new identity. It became an Arab religion, and thus a new
formula was found to show that there was basically no contradiction between Islam and nationalism.

The most outstanding proponent of this new trend was
certainly Sati' al-Husri. In his numerous books, articles
and lectures, al-Husri consistently argued that Islam, as a
religion, is not among the basic component elements of Arab
nationalism but yet cannot be entirely overlooked in the
process of the development of national consciousness. His
argument is based on his concept of religion. To al-Husri,
there are two types of religions in the world. One is the
universal, like Islam and Christianity, which are not the
religions of a particular nation or race but which tend to
link several nations in a bond that is stronger than language
and history. This type of religion, he argues, is opposed to
nationalism. The second type is what he calls "national
religions" such as Judaism, which is the religion of a specific
people. National religions, he maintains, constitute an
integral part of nationalism and cannot be divorced from the
political life of the nation.

With this distinction, al-Husri raises an historical
question. Did the universal religions, he asks, succeed in
establishing a link that is stronger and more comprehensive
than other national links? History, he answers, shows that
they did not, except in a limited sphere and for a very
short period. They could not really blend the different
peoples who embraced them. Christianity, for example, tried
to spread to the entire world but it could not prevent the
division of Christians into different and often hostile
nations. Similarly, Islam united several peoples for a
short period of time.[17] Religious teachings derive their
strength from a specific book which is written in a specific
language that is also used in liturgy and ritual. In fact,
al-Husri claims, religion is based on language. Latin was
spread more by Christianity than by the Roman conquests, and
Arabic more by Islam than by the Islamic administration.
However, he is not always consistent in his exposition of
his "linguistic religion" theory. In an article entitled,

"Arab Nationalism and Islam," he maintains that Islam did
not impose itself on the conquered peoples; many of them
became Arabized without embracing the new religion, and
thus non-Muslim Arab communities emerged.

According to al-Husri, thus, Islam played a very
important role in the evolution and spread of Arab nationalism
because (1) it was the driving force behind the Arab conquests
which spread the Arabic language and, (2) it became the
"protective force" which gave that language a kind of "im-
munity" against the forces of division and disintegration.
Nevertheless, this does not mean that Arab nationalism
remained tied to Islam.[18] Unquestionably, al-Husri's theory,
though less emotional and more historically oriented, does
not differ essentially from the views of the earlier advocates
of Arab nationalism. Al-Husri himself admits this.[19]

Other advocates of the linguistic-historical approach
are no less ambiguous. 'Abdul Rahman al-Bazzaz, another
prolific writer, argues that there is absolutely no contradiction between Arabism and Islam. The two converge on
many points, yet Islam cannot be included as a "necessary"
element in the formation of Arab nationalism. What is
interesting is his view that

> if we equate religion and nationalism, we would exclude
> one-tenth of the Egyptian population, and one-fifth of
> Syria and about one-half of the population of Lebanon
> from Arab nationalism. We would also exclude a sizeable
> proportion of the Iraqis, Palestinians, Jordanians, and
> Sudanese, as well as a great number of Arabs who have
> immigrated to America, Africa and the other continents...[20]

But, on the other hand

> when we lose these millions (of Arabs), the theory (that
> Islam is an essential element) would have us consider...
> every Muslim in Asia, Africa and Europe as brother to
> the Arab Muslim...brothers in the national sense, which
> means that the sons of the same nationality will have
> the same political destiny and one ultimate national
> interest, and requires the establishment of a social
> and political solidarity and association among them...
> Can the advocates of an Islamic nationalism imagine
> the consequences of this type of thinking and...the
> responsibilities and obligations, which are beyond
> our power and resources?[21]

To illustrate why nationalism should not be founded
on one particular religion, al-Bazzaz expands al-Husri's
theory, giving as examples the cases of Israel and Pakistan:

> Israel is a Jewish state, or more precisely "the only
> Jewish state in the world"...This point in itself would
> lead us to say that what applies to Israel cannot be

taken as a criterion because of the differences between
the nature of Judaism on the one hand and the nature of
Islam and Christianity on the other...If we look at
Israel and consider its modern formation, it would become clear to us that the religious spirit undoubtedly
played an active role in the minds and consciousness of
a group of its earlier advocates...But the Jews who
inhabit Israel today are a mixture of races, bloods,
colors and languages. Yet they have maintained a distinctive identity, not because they are the chosen race,
or because of their religious belief, but because, first
and foremost, of their subjugation to religious, social
and political persecution...[22]

Contrary to the claims of some of Israel's leaders,
"Israel is very careful to make Hebrew the basic element
of its nationality...."[23]   And

there are in Israel, a group of Jews who do not believe
in Judaism as a revealed religion; in fact there are
those who do not believe in any religion...on the other
hand there are those who blindly believe in their race
and, like the Nazis, they believe that their nationality
is their religion...nevertheless, we consider all these
peoples Israelis, culturally and mentally, and consequently nationally. In other words, they are Israelis
from the nationalist point of view, irrespective of their
religious faith.[24]

Pakistan, he maintains, was founded in specific
political circumstances. Neither Israel nor Pakistan
provides evidence of the role of religion in the formation
of nationalism.
In the 1950s, with the advent of Nasserism and the
rise of the Ba'th party to power, the question of the
relation between Arab nationalism and Islam became once
again a topic of intense debate. In the early years of
Nasser's rule, there was a distinctive trend toward interpreting Arab nationalism in terms of the political and
economic unity of the Arabs. The idea was advanced and
propagated by the official Egyptian media and by liberal
and progressive intellectuals, but this only lasted until
the end of the 1950s, when a sudden resurgence of emphasis
on the affinity between Islam and Arab nationalism became
the theme of hundreds of books and articles, despite severe
denunciation of this trend by Nasser himself. As the
Egyptian Marxist, Anouar Abdel Malek, puts it, "...the
cultural factor and more specially the religious, was
still alive in Egypt and consequently capable of providing
a theoretical and emotional foundation for Arab nationalism...
(and)...the Islamic or even pan-Islamic trend was solidly
institutionalized in the country in spite of the elimination
of the Muslim Brotherhood."[25] As regards Nasser himself,

it is difficult to trace, in his writings and speeches, a
sustained theory of Arab nationalism. In practice, however,
he wavered between emphasizing a secular and an Islamic
approach to nationalism according to the dictates of the
political realities in the Egypt of his day.

The fundamental ideological principles of the Ba'th
party are more advanced and more elaborate than those of the
other nationalist parties in the Arab countries, but it is
curious that while the party's constitution stresses the
historical continuity of the Arab nation, it makes no mention
of Islam. This does not mean that the party's intellectual
leaders are less concerned with the question of religion than
were the forerunners of the Arab nationalist movements. In
fact, there is a great deal of similarity between the concept of Michel 'Aflaq on this topic and the earlier views
of al-Husri and others. For 'Aflaq, Islam is the beginning
of Arabism. He sees a spiritual affinity between the two; a
view which is also held by an independent Christian nationalist, Qustantin Zuraiq, of the American University of Beirut.
But 'Aflaq is an ideologue par excellence, who is mainly
concerned with establishing historical foundations for Arab
nationalism in order to further the interests of his party.

It is not always easy to understand 'Aflaq's position,
largely because of the mystical-philosophical language he
uses, particularly in his early writings. Thus he said, in
a speech in 1943, on the occasion of the celebration of the
birthday of the Prophet Muhammad:

> The Arabs are unique among the other nations in that their
> national awakening coincided with the birth of a religious
> message, or rather that this message was an expression of
> the national awakening...They did not expand for the sake
> of expansion...but to perform a religious duty which is
> all truth, guidance, mercy, justice and generosity...as
> long as the affinity between Arabism and Islam is strong
> and as long as we see Arabism as a body with Islam as its
> soul, there is no room for fear of the Arabs going to
> extremes in their nationality.[26]

Yet, in the same speech, 'Aflaq also appears to be
following al-Husri's definition of Islam, though not without seeming uncomfortable with it:

> Islam is universal and eternal, but its universality does
> not mean that it can accommodate, at the same time,
> different meanings and different trends...its eternity
> does not mean that it does not change...but despite its
> continuous change, its roots will remain the same...
> (Islam)...is relative to a specific time and space and
> absolute in meaning and action within the limits of this
> time and space.[27]

For the Arabs, 'Aflaq argues, Islam is not an

eschatological belief or a set of moral rules. It is

> the clearest expression of their cosmic consciousness and
> their general outlook...Above all...(Islam)...is the most
> splendid form of their language and literature and the
> largest slice of their national history...[28]

In 1950, 'Aflaq reiterated the significance of Islam
for his movement, but stressed that the State he conceived
for the Arabs was a secular institution, founded on a social
base, or nationalism, and a moral base, or freedom. From
this he concluded that although the State would be secular
by virtue of freeing religion from the yoke of political
life, it would also be the opposite of atheism and corruption.[29]

In his book, *Fi sabil al-ba'th (Toward the Ba'th)*,
two comparatively lengthy articles are devoted to religion.
The first, dated March 1956, appears to be a rebuttal of
the accusation of atheism or Marxism hurled against the
Ba'th by its enemies.

> We consider (atheism) a spurious attitude toward life...
> for life means faith and the atheist is a liar...But we
> look on atheism as a pathological phenomenon that should
> be cured by diagnosing its symptoms.[30]

In the second article, dated April 1956, he completely
rejects the Marxist concept of religion. Any critique of
religion in the Arab world, he maintains, would amount to
challenging what the people consider sacred and invaluable,
and would eventually create a barrier between the party
and the masses.[31]

As is clear from this survey of the literature on the
relation between Arab nationalism and Islam, religion has
always been the idiom in which the overwhelming majority
of the nationalist intellectuals have expressed themselves.
Recent Arabic thought has not known any militant attack
on religion, although religious institutions and the clergy
have been attacked, particularly by the Arab Marxists and
leftists. Among the nationalist thinkers there has, however,
been one notable exception. In 1968, Dr. Nadim al-Bitar,
a Syrian political scientist, published a book entitled,
Min al-Nakba ila al-Thawra, (From the Disaster to Revolution),
in which he launched a violent attack on religious thinking
and institutions. He further elucidated his stand in an
article in the Lebanese periodical, *Mawaqif*, in 1969, in
which he made the following points:

1. Throughout history, no religion has more denied the
    existence of the human intellect and human dignity
    than the monotheistic religions;
2. The evils of religions outweigh their good aspects;
3. The polytheistic religions have been less evil;

4. History has witnessed many religions, whose followers
    have believed that they had the last word on human
    destiny, but all these religions died and there is no
    reason to assume that the present-day religions will
    fare better.[32]

Although Islam is not specifically mentioned, the
implication is quite clear. I know of no violent reaction
to this article, or any condemnation of its author, but it
is my belief that the political climate of the period following the Arab defeat in 1967 had something to do with the
astonishing silence on the part of the traditionalists and
the nationalists.

In his book, al-Bitar argues that both in the past and
at present, Islam has stood against socialism and revolution,
that the religious movements arising in the nineteenth
century were reactionary and that their main purpose was to
halt cultural and social progress. The *Senusiyya*, the
Wahhabiyya and the Muslim Brotherhood movements were, in his
opinion, reactionary political movements which attacked the
Turks, not because they sought freedom and independence, but
because the Turks had deviated from the straight path of
Islam. Al-Bitar also maintains that the victories which
the Arab national movements registered against imperialism
were achieved in the name of the Arabs and not Islam.

Al-Bitar may have some valid points from an historical
point of view, but 'Aflaq was certainly right when he maintained that any attack on religion would create a barrier
between the political leadership at the top and the masses
of people at the bottom. Islam has been a double-edged
sword for the Arab nationalists: they have used Islam as
an effective weapon against Western imperialism and Islam
has also made it easy for them to succeed as the political
leaders of the masses.

NOTES

1. Al-Afghani, *Complete Works*, (Ed. Muhammad Amara), Cairo,
p. 349.
2. *Ibid.*, p. 319.
3. Quoted in Ali al-Muhafada, *Al-Ittijahat al-Fikriyya 'Ind
al'Arab*, Beirut, 1978, p. 120.
4. *Ibid.*, p. 119.
5. *Ibid.*, p. 125.
6. *Ibid.*, p. 127.
7. Al-Kawakibi, *Complete Works*, (Ed. Muhammad Amara), Cairo,
1970, p. 417.
8. *Ibid.*, p. 317.
9. Quoted in Ali al-Muhafada, *op. cit.*, p. 134.
10. *Ibid.*, p. 136.
11. *Ibid.*, p. 139.
12. *Ibid.*, p. 139.

13. *Ibid.*, p. 144.
14. *Ibid.*, p. 144.
15. *Ibid.*, pp. 151-2.
16. *Ibid.*, p. 150.
17. Al-Husr, *Mukhtarat*, Beirut, p. 46.
18. *Ibid.*, p. 131.
19. *Ibid.*, p. 125.
20. Al-Bazzaz, *Hadhihi Qawmiyyatuna*, Cairo, 1963, p. 188.
21. *Ibid.*, p. 188.
22. *Ibid.*, p. 204.
23. *Ibid.*, p. 204.
24. *Ibid.*, p. 206.
25. Anouar Abdel-Malek, *Egypt: Military Society*, (N.Y. Vintage Books), 1968, p. 272.
26. Michel 'Aflaq, *Fi sabil al-ba'th*, Beirut, 1975, p. 128.
27. *Ibid.*, p. 131.
28. *Ibid.*, p. 131.
29. *Ibid.*, p. 166.
30. *Ibid.*, p. 208.
31. *Ibid.*, p. 217.
32. *Mawaqif*, No. 2, 1969.

4
Sources of Arab Nationalism: An Overview

William L. Cleveland

When Sa'ad Zaghlul, Egypt's leading political figure in the early 1920s, was asked his opinion on Arab unity, he is alleged to have replied, "What is the sum of zero plus zero, plus yet another zero?"[1] This attitude on the part of the leader of the state which was the center of both Arabic literary culture and Islamic reformism expresses the factionalism which has tormented inter-Arab political relations in this century. Arab unity, while trumpeted as the objective of Arab nationalist aspirations, has never been achieved. Part of the difficulty in establishing such a political union has been the diverse, and sometimes contradictory, origins of modern Arab nationalism. In part, too, it has been related to the political situation which prevailed in the Eastern Arab states in the years between the two world wars, a situation which gave a defensive and localized coloring to the nationalism then in the process of formation.

This essay attempts to examine the sources of Arab nationalism in the two distinct formative periods of its development--the decade or so preceding World War I and the period between the two world wars--through representatives of various trends. It is intended to show that the concepts formed in the first period fulfilled different needs than were later required, forcing the ideologues of the post-World War I years to build new theories in the face of new circumstances. This, in my opinion, explains much of the uncertainty which is associated with the evolution of Arab nationalism.

The sources of Arab nationalism cannot be identified as having a single, common origin. Both loyalty and

---

Sources of Arab Nationalism: An Overview is reprinted from *Middle East Review*, Vol. XI, No. 3, Spring, 1979.

hostility to the Ottoman Empire, both religious intensity
and rational secularism, helped generate the sentiments
which led to nationalism. It is generally acknowledged that
the three most dominant of these currents in the decade before the outbreak of World War I were Islamism, Ottomanism,
and a growing sense of Turkish and Arab cultural distinctness which developed into two exclusive nationalisms.

By the turn of the century, an active Islamic reformist
movement was underway in the Ottoman Middle East. Although
its center was Egypt, it had its proponents in other major
Arab cities of the Empire. The movement has been termed
the 'defense of an injured self-view' in that it was a response to the political and cultural threat of Christian
Europe.[2] Throughout the second half of the nineteenth
century, the Tanzimat reform program of the modernizing
Ottoman statesmen looked to Western European institutions
as models. From the adoption of constitutionalism and new
commercial codes, to permitting non-Muslims to serve in the
army, the course of reform appeared to undermine the institutions of a divinely ordained society. And, if Westernizing
bureaucrats failed to undermine it from within, the direct
presence of European imperialism would certainly do so from
without. It was as a reaction to these currents that
Islamic reformism was born. Largely an effort to prevent
the encroachment of Europe and the erosion of the Ottoman
Islamic system, the movement sought a revitalization of
Islam both politically and intellectually.

For students of the modern Middle East, the names of
Jamal al-Din al-Afghani (1838-1897) and Muhammad Abduh
(1849-1905) have come to represent a watershed in the re-
direction of Islamic thought. The former, a somewhat
mysterious, itinerant anti-imperialist, saw in the revival
of an Islamic consciousness the catapult with which to
expel the contaminating Western presence from the lands of
Islam. His doctrine mixed various reforming trends, and he
blended them with "religious feeling, national feeling, and
European radicalism."[3] While al-Afghani wrote little, his
presence inspired young Muslims in the various lands where
he resided, and these disciples carried on his program of
activism after his death. Among them, the Egyptian, Muhammad
Abduh is usually recognized as the most significant.[4] After
an early phase of political activism, Abduh adopted a more
restrained approach to Islamic reform than had his mentor.
Working within the established system, he sought a spiritual
purification of Islam which would strip it of its superstitions and lead to a reconciliation of divine revelation
and independent reasoning, thus making the social principles
of the religion compatible with the contemporary demands for
change. In undertaking their reformist activities, both
Abduh and al-Afghani recognized the threat from Western
Europe. But they did not accept the long-term superiority
of European civilization. It was the vigor of their response,
the sense of possibility they had about them, that attracted

young Muslims and gave to Islamic religious sentiment a
politically-charged coloring. This Islamic activism played
a significant part in the early formulations of Arab
nationalism and, as recent events in the Middle East have
shown, continues to be a reservoir from which all classes
of Muslims draw strength in times of uncertainty.

In both British occupied Egypt and the Syrian provinces
of the Ottoman Empire, Islamic reformism and Ottoman patriotism
coalesced into a vision of the independent Ottoman caliphate
as vital to the preservation of Islamic solidarity and the
independence of Islamic territories from European imperialism.
Ottomanism represented an attempt to evolve a sentiment of
Ottoman nationalism which would embrace all the subject peoples
of the multi-national Empire. But repeated Balkan revolts
showed that the union could, at best, apply only to the predominantly Muslim peoples of the Empire, Arabs and Turks.
The sentiment of Ottomanism, with its links to Islamism, was
best expressed by one of its staunchest defenders, the Lebanese
Druze, Amir Shakib Arslan:

> O'Ottomans of the protected kingdom, call upon God for your
> continued existence and for the removal of the [imperial]
> noose from your necks...O'Easterners, call upon God for the
> prosperity of one imperishable state so that the Middle East
> will never fail to have a government equal to those of
> Europe...O'Muslims, call upon God in all regions of the
> caliphate for the preservation of the spark of life of
> Islam.[5]

Although this vision would have to be altered with the
collapse of the Ottoman Empire in World War I, it nevertheless served as the animating force for the majority of
politically aware Arabs until the end of the war. It is
important to realize that the late Ottoman period had an
internal viability. One cannot view it merely as a prelude
to Arab nationalism. Because nationalism was not seen by
the Arab leadership as politically necessary, it was not
debated; and it was for that reason that the Arabs found
themselves without a nationalist ideology in the crucial
decade after the war.

However, it is also true that the debates on Islamic
reform and the nature of Ottomanism did give rise to
sentiments which could later be developed into theories of
nationalism. Two distinct sources of nationalist feeling
can be discerned in the period before World War I, one of
them historically consistent, the other seemingly paradoxical.
Among the Arab Christians of Greater Syria, a sustained
educational effort by European and American missionaries
had produced a small but active new Christian intelligentsia
in the region. One of the more enthusiastic observers of
these activities, George Antonius, has remarked that they
"paved the way, by laying the foundations of a new cultural
system, for the rehabilitation of the Arabic language as a

vehicle of thought."[6] It may be that the success was more
measured than Antonius' assessment would indicate. Nevertheless, it is evident that in the wake of the new educational
institutions came a rediscovery of interest in the classical
literary tradition leading, in turn, to a Christian-dominated
experimentation with new literary forms and to what has been
termed *al-nahdah*, 'the awakening.' In addition to the
aesthetic impulse, Syrian Christians demonstrated a receptivity
to certain European attitudes not shown among Muslims. Syrian
Christian scholars did not need to approach European concepts
through the barrier of divinely revealed Islamic norms--for
them, Europe was "not a threat to ward off, but a model to
copy."[7] Thus, the secular constitutionalism which many
Syrian Christians perceived as the explanation for European
success could, they felt, be transferred to the organization
of their own society. This, in turn, led some of them to
disparage Islamic institutions and to formulate in their
place a doctrine of Arab secularism which viewed Islam as
one of several components of the Arab cultural heritage.
This emphasis on Arab elements external to Islam can be seen
as an effort to end the marginality of Arab-Christians in
Islamic lands; it shows their desire to formulate a type of
society in which a divinely ordained social order is replaced
by a rational, secular one allowing Christian Arabs a full
political role.[8]
    The other formulation of a distinctly Arab component of
cultural identity came from an unexpected source. The Islamic
reformist movement described above raised many questions about
the reasons for the current weakness of the Islamic world.
It was only a matter of time before political rather than
strictly theological answers were found. It was in the works
of the Aleppine journalist and sometime administrator, Abd
al-Rahman al-Kawakibi (1849-1902), that the nationalist
possibilities in Islamic reformism were first expressed. For,
in seeking to solve the problems of Islam in his day, al-
Kawakibi concluded that it was the Turkish management of the
religion which had corrupted it. To al-Kawakibi, the strength
of earlier Islam was its close identification with the Arabs,
most obviously its language, its Prophet, its geographical
origin. This emphasis on the Arab role in Islam led al-
Kawakibi to denigrate the Ottoman-Turkish contribution and
finally to make the step from praising the Arabs' role in
Islam to glorifying the virtues of all Arabs, both Muslim
and Christian, which transcended Islam:

> Let the wise men among us tell the non-Arabs and the
> foreigners who instigate ill-will among us: allow us to
> manage our own affairs, understanding each other with the
> Arabic language, having for each other the compassion of
> brotherhood, consoling each other in adversity, and
> sharing alike in prosperity. Permit us to manage our
> affairs in this world, and make religions rule only the
> next. Let us come together around the same declarations:

Long live the nation! Long live the fatherland! Let us live free and strong.[9]

Hence, in the defense of universalist Islam was found the source of a distinctly Arab cultural and political identity.

However, political action on the basis of al-Kawakibi's doctrines did not develop before World War I. Whatever Islam might show of Arab distinctness, it also showed that when combined with Ottomanism, it touched more deeply the majority of Arabs than did appeals to secular nationalism or political separatism. The pre-war ferment did give birth to various secret societies and loose political organizations. Increasingly active after the Young Turk revolt of 1908, these societies demanded more autonomy for the Arab provinces, especially in matters of education, language, policy and the selection of local officials. Their major achievement was to identify particularly Arab grievances and to cause the Ottoman government to respond to some of their reform proposals. In so doing they may have added to the tensions between a government which saw itself increasingly as Turkish and a minority which frequently asserted its cultural rights as Arabs. Yet, with the exception of certain Christian groups, their objective was not political separation. The name chosen by the most prominent of them, the Ottoman Decentralization Society, shows the desire for accommodation on the part of the Arab leadership, and suggests that Arab opinion, while urging reform and decentralization, favored continued existence within an Ottoman framework.[10]

This was changed by the events of 1914-1918. By treating the Arab provinces as potentially disloyal, the government alienated broad segments of the population from Ottoman policy and stirred vague hopes of an Arab existence separate from the Turks. At the same time, the Arab Revolt, proclaimed in Mecca in 1916, provided a more specific focus for those intent on gaining an independent Arab state. Yet even that Revolt was proclaimed in the name of preserving Islam, not in the name of Arabism or the Arab nation.[11] The titular leader of the Revolt, Hussein, the Sharif of Mecca, sought dynastic security and a permanent power base against his enemies in the Arabian peninsula. British gold and promises of post-war support appeared to offer better chances for Hussein than continued loyalty to the Ottoman government which had appointed him. No matter how much the Revolt has subsequently been sanctified as the cornerstone in the edifice of Arab nationalism, it did not, at the time, mobilize the Arab masses or their local leaders. Direct participation was limited to tribal levies and a few former Ottoman Arab officers. The affair was, to be sure, a revolt, but it was most definitely not a revolution. By rebelling against the Caliph of Islam, Hussein made himself unpopular among the very Arab circles in whose name he claimed to speak.

When the Ottoman Empire surrendered in November 1918,

most of its Arab provinces had been captured by British
forces supported by the levies of Prince Feisal (Hussein's
son) from the Arab Revolt. In what appeared to be the final
sequence in the dismemberment of the Ottoman Empire into its
national components, an independent Syrian kingdom was proclaimed in Damascus, with Feisal as its monarch. Leading
personalities from all over the Arab world, whatever their
wartime loyalties may have been, were attracted to this new
state in which their national destiny appeared to rest.
Yet, in a story that has often been told, the decisions of
the peace conference and the implementation of wartime agreements reversed the process which had led to the creation of
the Syrian Kingdom. When the territories were finally appor-
tioned in 1920 and 1921, France was in possession of Syria,
Britain held the mandates for Palestine (including what was
to be called Transjordan), with its accompanying obligation
to implement the promise of the Balfour Declaration, and
Iraq, as well as continuing to occupy Egypt. The pledges
made to Hussein were sacrificed to inter-allied harmony and
European security. For any student of Arab nationalism,
the sense of bitterness and betrayal which accompanied the
expulsion of Feisal from Damascus, the division of the
former Arab provinces between Britain and France, and the
encouragement of Zionist immigration, on however limited a
scale, must form a constant backdrop to the character of
the national ideology which took shape in the ensuing
decades.[12]

*   *   *

As the first portion of this essay has shown, Islam and
Ottomanism served as the principal factors of political
solidarity among the Arabs before the war. But by the
early 1920s, Ottomanism was irrelevant while Islam was
suffering ever deeper humiliation at the secularizing hands
of Ataturk and through the presence of European occupiers
in the major cities of Arab Islam. It is not surprising,
therefore, that Arab attention was devoted mainly to obtaining political independence from European control, and
not to far-reaching discussions on social reform or the
adoption of particular political systems. To the extent
that this anti-imperialism was pervasive, it is correct to
characterize Arab nationalism as negative during the interwar period. However, even in seeking to organize their
people for resistance to the foreign occupations, the Arab
leadership generated an on-going debate over what special
elements of the Arab heritage could best be used as national
symbols around which to organize the resistance and to shape
the image of the independent Arab State. As Arab intellectuals had not created a clearly defined concept of Arabism
before the war, it is natural that they confronted the
changed circumstances as divided ideologically as they were
politically.

The search to overcome these divisions led to a variety
of proposals, none of which were fully realized, but all of
which have contributed to the formation of Arab nationalism
and continue, in one form or another, to appeal to most
sectors of Arab opinion. In action that tended to crystallize
the mandate boundaries, the special cultural heritages of
certain regions within the Arab world were defined and
political loyalty to them was demanded. The externally
imposed political borders encouraged such localism, especially
in Syria, where the French administration divided the region
into four separate states (Syria, Greater Lebanon, The Jabal
Druze, and the state of the Alawites) based on ethnic or
sectarian concentrations. Representative of this regional
trend in Arab nationalism was Antun Sa'adah (1904-1949), a
Lebanese Christian, who founded the Syrian Social Nationalist
Party in Beirut in the 1930s.[13] Although Sa'adah sought to
overcome the divisions within Greater Syria, he belongs to
the regional current of nationalism for his outspoken belief
that Syria was a distinct and complete entity which should
not be part of a larger Arab nation. In reaching this position, Sa'adah deplored the use of Arab history, religion, and
culture as symbols of a modern, national revival. Instead,
he proposed that Syrian history transcended Arab history and
that Syria, as a distinct nation, was tied to the particular
geographical and historical features which had interacted in
the region from the beginning of human history. Here then,
was one voice, one proposed resolution of the conditions
created by the collapse of the Ottoman Empire and European
occupation.

Further complicating the emergence of a pan-Arab ideology
was the disinterested stance adopted by the majority of
Egyptian intellectuals. Often, in the past quarter century,
the Egyptian and Arab causes have seemed synonymous and of
long standing. However, it was only the comparatively recent policies of the late Gamal Abd al-Nasser which thrust
Egypt into the vortex of pan-Arabism. In the period between
the world wars, Egypt was engaged in its own struggle for
independence from Great Britain, and the foundations of
Egyptian nationhood did not emphasize primarily Arab symbols.
At the same time that Egyptians did not identify with Arabism,
they were not seen as part of any projected Arab nation by
Syrian or Iraqi politicians. Rather than Arabism, Egyptian
patriotism was being focussed on a number of different cultural legacies. Although Islam was at the center of this,
there was also an emergent fascination with the rich pre-
Islamic past. The major symbol of Egyptian territorial
nationalism, the great river which flows through the country,
was eulogized along with the pharaonic civilization to which
it had given birth. No writer of the time captured this
sentiment more aptly than Hafiz Ibrahim, 'the poet of the
Nile.' His Egypt declares:

I am the East's fair crown,

And grace her brow as she with myriad pearls
Adorns my throat. Can any thing be named
Whose loveliness the Western peoples boast
Wherein I have no share?
...Have ye not stood
Beneath the Greater Pyramid, and seen
What I have laboured? Have ye not beheld
Those magic carvings which defeat the art
Of any rival craftsman? Centuries
have not assailed their pigments, though the day
Itself turn color.[14]

In the face of these regional nationalisms, some Arab writers continued to assert the primacy of Islamic bonds in the formation of an Arab political unit. The uncertainty created by Ataturk's abolition of the caliphate and the increasing adoption of secular legislation in the mandated Arab territories made this issue one which aroused much concern. Two of the most prolific writers on the subject were Rashid Rida and his friend Shakib Arslan. Rida (1865-1935), through his Cairo-based journal, *al-Manar*, gained a wide readership for his ideas on Islamic reform. But he was also something of a transitional figure, a man whose starting point for social reform and political organization was Islam, but who, like al-Kawakibi before him, could not but emphasize the close bond between the religion and Arabness:

My Islam is the same in date as my being Arab...I say, I am an Arab Muslim, and I am brother in religion to thousands upon thousands of Muslims, Arabs and non-Arabs, and brother in race to thousands upon thousands of Arabs, Muslims and non-Muslims.[15]

Shakib Arslan (1869-1946) was a Lebanese Druze who passed most of the inter-war period as an exile in Europe. Like Rida and others of his generation, Arslan could never completely forget his earlier loyalties to the Ottoman Empire and to the caliphate which symbolized the binding of Muslims under a single authority. But Arslan's approach to Islamic, and hence Arab, revival was not so concerned with theological points as was Rida's. His was a call for action, and he promulgated a militant Islam charged with political and moral assertiveness. In this, he is reminiscent of al-Afghani.[16] Although he stressed the Arabic core of Islam as the first political unit which should be created, Arslan was not a convincing Arab nationalist. He wrote essentially, and more persuasively, of the spiritual necessity of retaining the Islamic bond among the Arabs, arguing that it, and it alone, would prevent the collapse of the moral quality which gave, in the long run, a superiority to Eastern over European civilization. When Arslan asked, "Should our renaissance be essentially religious?" it was obviously a rhetorical question:

> If Muslims will resolve and strive, taking their inspiration
> from the Qur'an, they can attain the rank of the Europeans,
> the Americans, and the Japanese, in learning science and
> making progress...If we derive our inspiration from the
> Qur'an, we would be better qualified for progress than
> others...With constant discipline, with will and determina-
> tion to march onward, and with correct understanding of
> the essentials of *Iman*--true-faith--taught by the Qur'an,
> let us strive and continue to strive.[17]

In this is manifested the defensiveness so often associated
with Arabic thought over the past century, the assertion
that the imbalance so evident in the relationship between
Europe and the East was not due to any inherent defect in
Islam.   Indeed, Arslan saw that a recognition of true
Islamic principles would lead to a moral regeneration of the
Eastern peoples which, in turn, would be translated into a
political union of Muslims, with an Arab core, millions
strong.   In the face of this numerically and spiritually
superior force, the shallow materialism of European civilization would be overwhelmed.   Because of Arslan's insistence
that activity would produce results, and perhaps because of
his own appealing role as a sharp critic of European imperialism at the core of a European institution, the League of
Nations, his message had a wide appeal and he received much
adulation in certain quarters of the Arabic press in the
late 1920s and 1930s.   Yet, his version of an Arab renaissance
looked to a bygone age for its inspiration and his impact
was greatly diminished by the time of his death.
     The third major expression of Arab political and cultural
identity was formulated by those who rejected regionalism and
Islamic sentiments in favor of secular pan-Arab nationalism.
Their writings have kept alive the idea of a unified Arab
nation bound by ties of Arab culture.   This doctrine received
its clearest exposition from the ideologue and educator,
Sati' al-Husri (1880-1968).   Although al-Husri himself had
been a supporter of the Ottoman cause until the end of World
War I, he adjusted to the changed circumstances by putting
his Ottomanism behind him, joining King Feisal in Syria,
and later in Iraq, and gaining a reputation as the most
outspoken and consistent proponent of what has been termed
a 'pure' theory of Arab nationalism.   What has made al-Husri
particularly significant in the development of Arab nationalist thought is his emphasis on the secular components of the
Arab cultural heritage and his insistence that the consequence
of recognizing these components is to admit the existence of
an Arab nation similar to the nations of Europe which, like
them, ought to be politically unified.
     For al-Husri, the essential factors in establishing
national identity were language and history.   He wrote,
"language is the life and spirit of the nation; it is like

the heart and spine of nationalism, the most important of
its components and characteristics."[18]   If linguistic unity
distinguished the nation, the unity of a shared history
created the special personality of the nation, leading to
"a mutual faith in the awakening and to mutually shared
hopes for the future."[19]

From this general theory, al-Husri elaborated a more
specific doctrine on the existence of an Arab nation. This
nation was principally distinguished by its language and
was thus composed of all who spoke Arabic--a vast region
from Morocco to Iran. Al-Husri found unacceptable the regional stance of Antun Sa'adah or the anti-Arabism proposals
contained in some of the Egyptian Taha Husayn's writings.
For al-Husri, history had shown that shared language and
cultural memories led inexorably to political nationhood
and the power and dignity associated with that status. He
was in the forefront of the pan-Arabists, and the full
extent of his feelings are reflected in this refutation
of Egyptian regionalism:

> Arabism is the strongest and most important of the ties
> which bind Egyptians to each other. This is because all
> Egyptians speak Arabic. We can therefore be certain
> that Egypt is Arab and that its future will be bound by
> the strongest of ties to Arabism.[20]

Nearly a quarter of a century after al-Husri inaugurated
his journalistic campaign on the Arabness of Egypt, that
country and Syria merged to form the United Arab Republic
in 1958. Al-Husri claimed it was the happiest moment of
his life.

Finally, al-Husri's stance on Arab nationalism was
noteworthy for its uncompromising secularism. By refusing
to approach the problem of Arab divisiveness from the
perspective of Islamic civilization under attack, al-Husri
naturally came to conclusions for the solution of that
divisiveness which opposed those reached by Shakib Arslan
and Rashid Rida. Arabic as a national language existed
before Islam, he argued, and the loyalties contained in
that language were the same for all Arabic speakers, be
they Muslim or Christian; those loyalties were to the
Arab nation.

His vision stands in marked contrast to that of Shakib
Arslan: "I believe only in the national tie which is based
on language and history, and I regard the words 'East and
Eastern and West and Western' only as geographical terms."[21]
What al-Husri strove to do in his frequent articles was to
prod his fellow Arabs into an awareness of their Arabism,
their common cultural heritage. If this awareness could
be generated, he felt that the hard political questions of
how actually to achieve political unity would be capable
of solution. Yet, while al-Husri's type of romantic
nationalism came to have a great appeal and to represent

the ideal toward which all Arabs should strive in a common
cause, the reality has been disappointing to those who
have felt as he did.

* * *

In the decades since the collapse of the Ottoman Empire,
there has been tension among the proponents of these various
alternatives to Arab political association. Each doctrine
has contained a bit of the other and few have been as forceful in their disassociation of Islam from Arabism as al-Husri.
Regional pride is a part of any group, but with the creation
of the mandate territories, regional nationalisms--to say
nothing of local administrative machinery--were generated
to the extent that it became virtually impossible to subordinate them fully to the unity that men like al-Husri
so ardently sought. The break-up of the UAR in 1961 may
have represented the final failure of genuine political
commitments--as opposed to propaganda campaigns--to the
ideal of Arab unity. National interest has come to be
defined in the individual terms of each of the several
political states in the region, not by their shared cultural
heritage. Events of the last four years in Lebanon, and of
recent months elsewhere, would indicate that even within the
borders of the Arab states, cultural pluralism, nurtured by
social and economic grievances, has expressed itself more
forcefully than have any sentiments toward unity. Amidst
the sectarian strife, the national uncertainties, and the
ever-intensifying pressure for change, with all its concomitant disequilibriums, a constant practice among Muslims
of all social strata has been a reaching out to Islam. It is
not necessarily a reaffirmation of belief so much as it is
a political Islam of the variety espoused by Shakib Arslan
or, more recently and more forcefully, the Muslim Brotherhood. It is as though, given the apparent failure of pan-
Arabism, there is a turning to the force which was linked
with Arab greatness and respect in the past.
     There certainly appears to be more expression of
this sentiment at the moment than any serious talk about pan-
Arab unity, despite the much-publicized discussion between
Syria and Iraq. Plans for Arab brotherhood and cooperation
may survive, but unification of the cultural Arab nation
into a single political state remains an elusive dream,
espoused by fewer and fewer public figures. Representative
of this trend is the way in which Egypt is turning away
from pan-Arab concerns toward its own internal affairs and
a new affirmation of its own regional ties and symbols.
A poignant example of this was provided by the extensive
participation of the intellectual community in a recent
debate in the pages of *al-Ahram* about the sources of
Egyptian identity. That the debate had to occur at all is
significant. That it included the following remarkable
statement is even more revealing: "Egyptians are not Arabs,

but they cannot disregard the Arab component of their destiny--shared culture and language."[22] Nothing better illustrates the still uncertain identities of the several Arab peoples whose cultural heritage embraces Islam, Arabism, and regional histories of great richness.

NOTES

1. Quoted in Sati al-Husri, *al-'Urubah Awwalan*, Beirut, 1965, p. 60. Throughout this discussion, the focus is on the Eastern Arab World.

2. For elaboration of this theme, see C. Ernest Dawn, *From Ottomanism to Arabism* (Urbana and Chicago: University of Illinois Press, 1973), esp. pp. 184-185. Other useful surveys of this movement are Albert Hourani, *Arabic Thought in the Liberal Age, 1798-1939* (London: Oxford University Press Paperbacks, 1970), Chaps. V, VI, VII; and Majid Khadduri, *Political Trends in the Arab World* (Baltimore: The Johns Hopkins Press, 1970), pp. 55-69.

3. Hourani, *Arabic Thought*, p. 108; for a thorough biography, including a comprehensive bibliography, one should consult Nikki R. Keddie, *Sayyid Jamal ad-Din "al-Afghani"* (Berkeley and Los Angeles: University of California Press, 1972).

4. In addition to the works cited in note 2, Abduh's contribution is examined in Jemal Mohammad Ahmed, *The Intellectual Origins of Egyptian Nationalism* (London: Oxford University Press, 1960); and Charles C. Adams, *Islam and Modernism in Egypt* (London: Oxford University Press, 1933).

5. Shakib Arslan, writing in the Egyptian newspaper, *al-Mu'ayyad*, 11 January, 1912.

6. George Antonius, *The Arab Awakening* (New York: Capricorn Books Ed., 1965), p. 40.

7. Hisham Sharabi, *Arab Intellectuals and the West: The Formative Years, 1875-1914* (Baltimore: The Johns Hopkins Press, 1970), p. 57. See also Robert M. Haddad, *Syrian Christians in Muslim Society: An Interpretation* (Princeton: Princeton University Press, 1970).

8. Haddad, *Syrian Christians*, pp. 5-6; 86-87.

9. Quoted in Khaldun S. al-Husry, *Three Reformers* (Beirut: Khayats, 1966), p. 104. In addition to al-Husry's fine study, an excellent analysis of al-Kawakibi and the developing currents of Arab consciousness is Sylvia Haim, *Arab Nationalism: An Anthology* (Berkeley and Los Angeles: University of California Press, 1964), esp. pp. 15-34.

10. See, Zeine and Zeine, *The Emergence of Arab Nationalism,* (Beirut, 1966); Haim, *Arab Nationalism*, pp. 31-4; and, for an interpretation which gives to the societies a more prominent and activist role, Antonius, *The Arab Awakening*, pp. 101-126.

11. Dawn, *Ottomanism to Arabism*, Chaps. i and iii.

12. The Arab perspective on these developments is eloquently presented by Antonius, *The Arab Awakening:* a useful synthesis is Elizabeth Monroe, *Britain's Moment in the Middle East 1914-1956* (London: Chatto and Windus, 1964), chaps. i and ii.

13. The most thorough treatment of Sa'adah is Labib Zuwiyya-Yamak, (Cambridge, Mass.: Harvard University Press, 1966); a useful summary of his ideas is found in Khadduri, *Political Trends*, pp. 186-194.

14. Quoted in A. J. Arberry, *Aspects of Islamic Civilization* (Ann Arbor: The University of Michigan Press, 1967), p. 363. See also Mounah Kouri, *Poetry and the Making of Modern Egypt* (Leiden: E. J. Brill, 1971); Nadav Safran, *Egypt in Search of Political Community* (Cambridge, Mass.: Harvard University Press, 1961).

15. Quoted in Hourani, *Arabic Thought*, p. 301.

16. Arslan's ideas are summarized in Khadduri, *Political Trends*, pp. 181-182; the present author is currently preparing a manuscript on Arslan, tentatively entitled *Shakib Arslan and the Politics of Islamic Nationalism*.

17. Amir Shakib Arslan, *Our Decline and Its Causes*, trans. by M. A. Shakoor (Lahore: Sh. Muhammad Ashraf, 1944), pp. 134-135.

18. Quoted in William L. Cleveland, *The Making of an Arab Nationalist: Ottomanism and Arabism in the Life and Thought of Sati' al-Husri* (Princeton: Princeton University Press, 1971), p. 100.

19. *Ibid.*, p. 102.

20. *Ibid.*, pp. 137-138.

21. *Ibid.*, p. 161.

22. *The Middle East*, December, 1978, p. 14. The debate was begun in March 1978.

5

The Political Character
of Judaism and Islam:
Some Comparisons

Mervin F. Verbit

Most religions assert that the fundamental goal of
human life is to bring about a qualitative transformation
in the state of the individual. Whether it is the achievement
of eternal salvation through Divine grace, as in Christianity,
or the realization of the merging of one's soul with the All-
Soul of the universe, as in Buddhism, to cite two major
examples, life's purpose is defined in terms of the individual.
Society, in these religions, is the setting for and a reflection
of individual behavior and is important, therefore, as a
determinant and as an indicator of the human condition. However, the social order has no inherent significance of its own
directly implicated in the basic purpose of life. Similarly,
history has no *inherent* meaning in these religions, since for
them the business of life at its core is between each individual and Ultimacy irrespective of the movement of history.
Religions which make the individual the locus of meaning must
be a-societal and a-historical so that each person can face
Ultimacy from the same essential ground, regardless of the
social structure of which he is a part or the historical
conditions which influence what--from this perspective--are
secondary aspects of his life. It is in this sense that a
person can render unto Caesar what is Caesar's without having
to compromise his relationship to God.

By contrast, Judaism and Islam view the social order as
essential. From their perspectives, the fundamental purpose
of human life is to effect a change in the character of
society, and the individual's basic role in life is to be
understood in terms of his contribution toward that end.
Society and history are, thus, inherently meaningful, and
political considerations are necessarily very close to the
core of meaning. In these two religions Caesar *as Caesar*

*The Political Character of Judaism and Islam: Some Compari-
sons* is reprinted from *Middle East Review*, Vol. XI, No. 2,
Winter, 1978/79.

(and not only as man) is to be an agent of God, and what is
Caesar's is, therefore, really God's.

* * *

Judaism asserts that God made humanity that it might
share with Him the completion of creation by fulfilling its
potential for Good. For Judaism, the purpose of human life
is to move toward the perfection of society, which is to say
a world of universal truth, justice, and peace. In order that
man might be creative in this fundamental sense, God endowed
him with the very characteristics which marked God's own
creative activity, thereby making him--alone among the
creatures--"in the image of God." These characteristics,
limited to God and man, are will ("Let there be light...")
and power ("...and there was light"). Mankind has a free
will and control over the world which are qualitatively
different from those of all other creatures. With these two
abilities mankind can enter into partnership with God in the
task of redeeming the promise of creation. The first two
steps toward that end are, inevitably, assurance of the
physical survival of society and assumption of responsibility
for and control over it. Accordingly, the first two commandments given to humanity in the account of creation in Genesis
are (1) "Be fruitful and multiply and replenish the earth"
and (2) "and subdue it and have dominion over...every living
thing...upon the earth." Beyond these two obviously necessary
prerequisites, all people are required to adhere to seven
basic regulations which deal with recognition of the meaning-
fulness of life, with ethical standards, with kindness to
animals, and--significantly--with the development of means
for the collective implementation of moral standards (literally,
the establishment of a legal system). Anyone who follows these
fundamental norms is considered righteous in God's sight.
     Jews, however, have an additional responsibility defined
by their special covenant with God. That covenant was offered
at Sinai to the Israelites as a people and was accepted by
their political representatives (the "elders") and confirmed
in a popular referendum. The essence of the covenant is that
the Jews would be "a kingdom of priests and a holy nation."
The priestliness here is a characteristic of the kingdom and
the holiness, a quality of the nation, not of its individual
members. It is the Jewish people, as a political entity, which
is to serve the priestly role, which is essentially an intermediary role, between God and the political subdivisions of
society. Significantly, Abraham is promised that his descendants would be a blessing "to the families of the earth,"
and Isaiah spoke of Israel's task as being a "light unto the
nations." Abraham's society was organized into family tribes,
and by the time of the Prophets nation-states had emerged as
the major social division. Judaism does not refer to the
Jews' role as being a blessing "to humanity" or "to mankind,"
but speaks rather in terms of the basic political subdivision

of society. Indeed, the terms of the Sinaitic covenant
(which is to say the content of Divine legislation) and
all subsequent Jewish legal development include all categories
of law--civil, criminal, family, economic, political and procedural, as well as ritual and ethical. The Torah was to be
the "Constitution" of the Jewish polity, and it served just
that role in both the autonomous Jewish kingdoms and the semi-
autonomous Jewish communities that followed the destruction
of the independent Jewish commonwealth by the Romans in the
first (and again in the second) century of the Common Era.
The royal acts of Jewish kings and the regulations of medieval
Jewish communities were, in theory if not always in practice,
subject to review by religious leadership--first the Prophets,
later the rabbis--based on Biblical laws. The defining authority
of the rabbinate was, in fact, judicial, as opposed to the
"sacramental" authority of the priesthood in administering the
sacrificial system. The Sanhedrin in its time and the rabbis
of Jewish communities in the medieval period served a function
analogous to that of the Supreme Court, interpreting and applying the Torah as Constitution.

The rabbis were clear that the special role of the Jewish
people was not the result of any inherent quality of the Jews,
but was offered by God out of love. Indeed, there is a *midrash*
(rabbinic legend) that God offered the Torah to the other
nations first and came to the Jews only after the others declined to accept it. The special status of the Jews is
explicitly tied to their acceptance of the Torah and is a
characteristic of the peoplehood, not of the individuals.

It was in order to implement the Sinaitic covenant that
the exodus from Egypt and the settlement of the land of
Israel was necessary. The exodus was not merely a matter of
freedom from slavery, which could have been achieved--and in
other historical cases where slaves were freed was achieved--
without the total emigration of the slaves. However, the
purpose of the exodus was to enable the Jews to establish
an independent society based on a Divine Constitution. The
message which the Biblical account has God relay through
Moses to Pharaoh is not "Let my people go that they may be
free," but rather "Let my people go that they may serve me."
Since political independence requires a geographical base,
the granting of land was an indispensable part of the covenant. The promise of land is given to Abraham in the context
of his descendants' future role in history, and the settlement
in the land is the explicit end (in both senses of the word)
of the journey through the wilderness after the exodus.

In addition to its secular sources and justifications,
therefore, a Jewish sovereign state in the land of Israel is
also a necessary instrument for the fulfillment of Judaism's
definition of history and of the role of the Jews in history.
It is largely because of that definition that Jews, throughout the two millenia of "dispersion" since the destruction
of their state and expulsion from the land, considered themselves (and were considered by their host cultures) to be

refugees always intending to re-establish their sovereign
state in what in Hebrew was always called the Land of
Israel, a land from which they never fully withdrew. (The
only anti-national perspective in Jewish history was the
Reform Jewish response to the "Emancipation" at the turn of
the eighteenth century, and that has long since been abandoned by the Reform Movement itself.)

To summarize, Judaism requires the existence of a Jewish
sovereign state in the Land of Israel, serving to exemplify
the structural arrangements and cultural patterns which will
ultimately enable people, despite the temptations of human
nature and the tensions engendered by human relationships,
to live in truth, justice and peace.

* * *

Islam's political component is also directly implicated
in its fundamental definition of the meaning of life. Islam
asserts that God (*Allah* in Arabic) has revealed Himself
several times in history and that the Scriptures of Judaism
and Christianity are valid accounts of Divine revelations.
Moses and Jesus are among the Prophets of history, a Prophet
being, technically, someone through whom God explicitly
reveals His will to mankind. However, Islam goes beyond
these two religions to assert that God's final, summary, and
therefore conclusive, revelation was made through Muhammad,
who thus became *the* Prophet. The purpose of life is to submit to the content of that revelation, the primary record of
which is the Qu'ran. Islam literally means "submission,"
and "one who submits" is a Muslim. "Mohammedanism" is an
incorrect name for the religion; the Prophet, despite his
crucial role as spokesman, leader, and example, was only the
means toward the end that all humanity submit to God. The
doctrinal declaration of Islam that "There is no god but
God, and Muhammad is His Prophet" defines Islam's central
assertion, then, about the nature of Ultimacy as monotheistic,
and of Ultimacy's relationship to humanity, as delineated in
the Qu'ran.

God's will, according to the Qu'ran, deals not only with
individual behavior, but with social structure as well. Consequently, Islamic law, like Jewish law, has all of the
categories of law found in legal systems of societies--
civil, criminal, family, economic, political and procedural,
as well as the ritual and ethical laws found in more in-
dividualistic religions. Because God's law applies not only
to individuals, but also to national structures, and is intended for the entire world, Islamic thought divides the
world into two realms; the *dar-al-Islam*, or realm of Islam,
in which God's law, as revealed to Muhammad, is accepted and
implemented, and the *dar-al-harb*, or realm of conflict, in
which Islamic law is not accepted. One of the important
duties of the Muslim is *jihad*, literally "holy war," but
extended to any contest designed to bring more of the world

under Divine rule. The need for the political implementation of Divine will is reflected in the Muslim calendar, which begins not with God's revelation to Muhammad, but rather with the Prophet's elevation to leadership in Medina. In effect, Islam begins neither when God makes His will known nor when some people accept it; it begins when there is a polity in which God's will can be implemented. That is the real beginning; the end will be universal application of God's law in the whole world, all of whose states would, ideally, be Islamic in that they "submit" to God. If that goal is militarily unrealizable, active attempts to achieve it may be temporarily postponed, but the goal of worldwide Islamic hegemony remains. Indeed, most Middle Eastern states today are Islamic, not only in that the majority of their populations are Muslims, but more significantly in their structural and ideological identities as political entities. While they vary, of course, in the extent to which they actually apply Muslim law, they all define themselves as polities which submit to that law.

The historical attitude of Muslims to the non-Muslim world follows from fundamental Islamic thought. The Arab conquests imposed Islam by the sword. Only the "Scriptural peoples" (Jews, Christians, Zoroastrians, and later--by special interpretation--certain other groups) were allowed to remain unconverted, with the status of *dhimmis* ("tolerated peoples"), on condition that they accept Islamic rule, pay a special poll tax and suffer "humiliation." "Humiliation" was necessary because it was considered an affront to God to allow those who do not submit to Him (i.e. non-Muslims) to be equal or superior to, or to be more highly favored than those who do. The implementation of "humiliation" varied in Muslim history; in some periods it was largely symbolic, in others it entailed what today would be analogous to civil disabilities or general discriminatory measures, and in still others it meant severe and degrading persecution.

In summary, Islam asserts that God's will is that not only all individuals, but also all states, should be Islamic in identity and in governance and that those non-Muslims who are permitted to live ("tolerated") without accepting Islam must accept civil inferiority. Thus Islam, although in a different context, like Judaism, requires sovereign political instruments for its fulfillment.

* * *

Some of the political similarities between Judaism and Islam are already clear, and others can readily be derived. Both religions are theocracies in the literal meaning of the term. God is seen as the Ruler and Law-giver. Moses and Muhammad have no personal authority on their own; they are both viewed in their respective religions as prophets, teachers, leaders, and judges. They convey, but do not compose, the law. All political

chiefs who follow these initial "founders" are bound by
law; they are regents, not rulers. Israel's kingdom was a
constitutional monarchy; the caliphs were "successors" (to
Muhammad) whose tasks were to implement the Qu'ran and to
expand its sphere of influence.

As we have seen, both religions require sovereign political
entities for their fulfillment. Neither is essentially a personal religion. Both are rooted in a "people" and use that
term in a way that would not fit into descriptions of other
traditions. There is a Jewish people (*am Yisrael*) and a
Muslim people (*umma Muslima*) in a sense in which one cannot
speak of "a Christian people," or "a Buddhist people," for
example.

Because of their structural, political nature, both
Judaism and Islam place primary emphasis on law. The basic
character of a society is defined in and by its law. (The
fundamental importance of Supreme Court decisions in shaping
American society, for example, is proverbial.) The development of law (*din* in both Hebrew and Arabic) is a crucial
process in both religions, and codifications of law by the
Jewish rabbis and the Muslim doctors of law, into the *halacha*
and the *shari'a* respectively, constitute the guidelines for
personal and public behavior. When Egypt recently discussed
its constitution, one of the most hotly debated issues was
whether or not the *shari'a* should become the law of the
land. Similarly, there are many in Israel who would incorporate the *halacha* into public law.

Interestingly, perhaps inevitably, the legal structures
of both religions have the same kinds of sources and processes.
Both give primacy to the Written Law (*Torah she'Bik'tav; Qu'ran*)
and expand the Written Law's meaning in an oral tradition (later
set down in writing) traced through successive generations of
religious leaders back to the original sources (*Torah she B'al
Peh;* the *Sunna* and the *Hadith*). Both vest authority in the
consensus of its scholar-leaders (*chazal;* the *ijma* of the
ulema), and both codify the canons of logic and analogy which
are applicable to the derivation of laws from antecedent
principles (e.g. *kal vachomer; qiyas*). Finally, both deal
with the impact of local custom (*minhag; 'urf*) on law.

* * *

The structural and dynamic similarities in the legal
systems of Judaism and Islam are not consequences of similar
content; the differences between the two legal systems'
specific provisions and underlying principles are substantial
and significant. Rather, their structural and dynamic
characteristics are those of any society's legal system
although their asserted Divine origin makes the "constitutional" document immutable and all that flows from it
sacred.

This is not the only significant political difference
between Judaism and Islam. Judaism claims that only the

Jewish people accepted God's Torah, and therefore only the Jewish people is bound by the Torah. The rest of mankind is subject only to the seven Noachide injunctions, and any non-Jew can please God and fulfill God's design for him by living in accordance with the basic ethical values incorporated in those injunctions. Islam claims that the Qu'ran was given for all nations and that all should be brought to accept its provisions. Consequently, while Judaism accepts converts, it need not and does not actively seek them. Islam, on the other hand, is committed to bring all the world's inhabitants under its rule. Jewish law dictates that non-Jews in the Jewish polity be excluded from certain ritual observances, but they suffer no civil inequality. Islamic law mandates formal civil inferiority for non-Muslims and insists on Muslim sovereignty.

* * *

The conflict between Israel and her Arab neighbors becomes clearer when placed in the context of their religio-ideological backgrounds. The real issue is sovereignty. The Jews insist on their right not only to live on the land, but to have re-established their state on the land from which they had been expelled. The Arabs have proclaimed their willingness to allow Jews to reside there, but only within an Arab-controlled state. Modern Zionism, which is based on the political implications of Judaism, is seen by the Arabs as contrary to the political implications of Islam.
What is especially worth noting is that secularization has not changed the effect of religious ideology very much. Secular Israelis, while rejecting the idea that God and the Jewish people entered into a covenant at Sinai which made the Jews a nation with a historic role and a sovereign polity, nevertheless assert their right of total self-determination as a people. Although they do not assert the concepts of a Divine purpose or a Divine constitution, they still maintain that they have a just and natural right to shape their own lives and policies according to a structure and a law of their own choosing in the land of their own ancestry, the right to which they never yielded and where their physical presence has been continuous. Secular Arabs, while rejecting the idea that God revealed his law to Muhammad for all nations, nevertheless assert their right to complete cultural hegemony in the part of the world whose population is over-whelmingly Arabic. Some Arabs declare that Israel would be acceptable if it were not only "in" but "of" the Middle East. References to Israel as an "imperialistic outpost of European culture" imply that a cultural transformation of Israel, its "orientalization" if you will, would make Israel acceptable to the region.
It is difficult to understand the Arabs' emotional fervor against Israel without reference to the religio-cultural background. Israel's area is tiny, its location--

given contemporary transportation--is not particularly
strategic, its natural resources are negligible in comparison
with those of the Arabs, and its absorption of Jewish refugees
from Arab lands could have been part of one of history's many
population exchanges if the Arabs had allowed more of the
Palestinian refugees to be absorbed in their societies. The
question of pride remains, of course, but that issue is
firmly bound up in precisely the cultural background which
is so consequential. National pride has often been subject
to reinterpretation and rationalization in light of more
tangible interests. For the Arabs, however, national pride
is a fundamental element of their cultural heritage precisely
because of the Islamic insistence on Muslim superiority. The
secularization of culture may de-theologize religious ideologies,
but their residues remain. Even where religious ideology is
ignored or rejected outright, therefore, the Arabs still
desire sovereignty as a manifestation of their hegemony and
Jewish Israelis still desire sovereignty as a requisite for
self-determination and self-protection after a long history
of involuntary dependence on others and the repeated tragedy
to which that dependence exposed them.

       One question remains. In light of the argument presented
here, how is Islamic Egypt's current participation in negotiations whose purpose is the establishment of peaceful relations
with Jewish Israel to be understood? The answer, is, in brief,
that *jihad* need not be fought by arms alone. Economic and
political means can sometimes achieve what military might
cannot. Indeed, some Egyptian spokesmen have expressed the
expectation that peace, by weakening Israel's internal
solidarity, diminishing Israel's ties to World Jewry, exposing Israelis to Arabic culture, and increasing the Arabic
proportion of Israel's population, will generate positive
cultural contact whose enticements will combine with a
changing political balance and thus eventually lead to the
acculturation of the Jews of Israel. On the other hand,
Jewish Israelis are prepared, nay, eager, to assure their
distinctive continuity and to continue to develop their own
culture.

6
Religion and Politics in Egypt

Louis J. Cantori

Faith, as we understand it today, i.e., the pure faith,
free from fanaticism and impurities which were attached to
its substance in periods of decadence - faith which is
remote from irresponsibility and belief in superstitions
and which does not deny man's will and the will of society
to face the unchanging circumstances of life, supported in
this by the brain which God has given him and which distinguishes him from the rest of God's creatures.

* * *

The most dangerous menace to the true essence of this
faith are those who use it to oppose toil, and the pursuit
of knowledge and science. For God in all His glory and
wisdom has placed the pursuit of knowledge on the same
footing as the struggle for His sake and has made it concomitant with faith when He said in the Holy Qur'an:
"God holds in great esteem those of you who believe and
those who have acquired knowledge."

> -President Mohamed Anwar El-Sadat
> *The October Working Paper*
> April, 1974

Contemporary Egypt can be viewed as a microcosm of the
"Islamic Revival" presently manifesting itself in the Islamic
world. As witnessed in the above quotations, even as
recently as 1974 President al-Sadat was setting forth a
liberal national and modernist conception of the essential
compatibility of science and religion. In that year, an
assertive view of this compatibility could be taken, because religion was not perceived as a threatening political
factor. By 1980, while there is no evidence that his
personal, essentially modernist view of religion had

changed, there is ample evidence that religion had in fact
intruded itself into politics.[1] The evidence of this is in
actual events themselves and in President al-Sadat's own
statements, including, "There can be no politics in religion
and no religion in politics."[2]

There are many factors that can be said to be involved
in creating the Islamic revival. A background feature of
the Islamic revival, however, appears to be an emphasis
upon behavior, organization and leadership. Kerr noted in
his study of *Islamic Reform* that contemporary Islam had as
yet seemed to be unable to bridge the polarities of traditional theology on the one hand and somewhat doctrinally
latitudinarian modernism on the other.[3] This theological
failure appears to continue for the most part in the present
"revival."[4] It is as if Muslim populations, not for the
first time, have by their actions moved in advance of formal
theology to arrive at a synthesis in action which awaits
theological justification. Among the specific features which
are contributing to the revival are the recovery of a people's
cultural identity in the working out of a decolonization
process, the role of economically powerful, religiously
motivated leaderships (e.g., Saudi Arabia) in fostering
religious groups within other states and also the change in
leadership generations from those who had been expert in
colonial cultures and therefore effective in defeating
colonialism (Sukarno, Nasir, Nkrumah, etc.) to those who at
present come from rural lower middle class backgrounds with
a more natural understanding and sympathy for popular culture
(Hafiz al-Asad, Saddam Husayn and Anwar al-Sadat).

Viewed from the latter perspective, it can be argued
that the Islamic countries are experiencing the triumph of
popular culture/religion over high or official culture/
religion via this new second generation leadership.[5] It
can be said to follow, therefore, that the Islamic countries
are not so much abandoning modernization as they are attempting to redefine it in popular cultural terms. Looked at
another way, modernization in the Islamic states is not now,
if it ever was, to be understood from a religious point of
view as a secularizing process. Instead, presently the
effort whether very obviously the case, in the current
Islamic revolution in Iran or more subtly in Egypt, is to
"sacralize" modernization. In this sense, Egypt becomes
another instance of the case in which modernity is shaped
to fit tradition.[6]

The political resurgence of Islam suggests immediately
the problem of the relationship of religion to the state.
In what follows, the historical evolution of this relationship is briefly considered. For purposes of deeper analysis
in the post-1970 al-Sadat period, however, the broad brush
of history has to be supplanted by the greater delicacy of
the line of the ink point pen. Thus the major portion of
the present article addresses itself to the relationship of
religion to politics, first in the Nasir period (1952-1970)

nd then in the period of al-Sadat (1970-present).

ELIGION AND STATE IN PRE-REVOLUTIONARY EGYPT

The defensive modernization ambitions of Mohammed Ali
1805-1849) while directed to the strengthening of his army
nd protecting Egypt's borders set up ripple-like movements
hat soon came to affect virtually all elements of Egyptian
ociety. Having come to power with the active assistance
f the *ulama* in 1805, Mohammed Ali then obeyed a classic
ictate of Middle Eastern leadership and turned on them in
rder to free himself from political dependency. This took
he form of subordinating them to himself and the state by
arassing them politically and depriving them of an indepen-
ent economic base by transferring the revenues of religious
haritable property endowments (*awqaf al-khairiya*) from them
o the state. This was accompanied by a relative neglect of
osque maintenance, religious school construction, etc. on
he part of the government. Thus, a religious dualism began
o develop between the favored few *ulama* at the governmental
enter on the one hand who were always prepared to do the
overnment's bidding and to religiously justify its con-
inued efforts at centralizing its political authority, and
he localistic religious leaders and the masses of the popu-
ation on the other hand. This classic Islamic and anthro-
ological distinction between "official" Islam ("big tradi-
ion") and "popular" Islam ("little tradition") had however,
 wider cultural dimension as well.[7]

As a kind of corollary to the preceding dualism there
as a further distinction between the moribund somewhat
olerated and humored "official" religion on the one hand
nd the expansion of modern knowledge on the other. This
orallary had soon began to find governmental organizational
xpression.[8] The *ulama* before 1805 performed not only
eligious activities but educational, legal, economic,
ublis health and social welfare ones as well. As the 19th
entury went on, there soon came to be official government
inisteries to perform these functions. The result was a
hrinkage of societal functions and therefore social impor-
ance for the *ulama*.[9] Even the remaining religious function
as perhaps diminished by the decreasing level of support
or mosque schools (*kuttabs*) and mosque maintenance.

This process was a fairly consistent one through the
9th Century and appears to have continued under the British
ccupation (1882-1922) up to the 1952 Revolution.[10] This
as the case even during the period of liberal nationalism
rom 1924 onwards and was reenforced by two phenomena. The
irst was that the liberal nationalists were basically either
ecularists or modernists in respect to religion. Second,
he palace under first Fu'ad I (1917-1936) and then his
on Faruq (1936-1952) tended to use the "official" *ulama*
o legitimize themselves and compete politically with their

liberal nationalist opponents.

Thus, the overall process before 1952 in respect to
religion and the religious establishment was one of bringing it simultaneously under control of the central government and restricting its operations. Unspoken in this
entire process is the question of how localistic "popular"
religion was faring at the same time. On the one hand,
there is the commentary that the religious brotherhood were
in significant decline by 1950 but there remains the un-
researched question of actual religious activities before
1950 (and after). What does a decline in the organizational
presence of religious brotherhoods at saints' birthdays and
in parades and the scruffy unwashed appearance of their
membership signify? Is it religious decline or is it simply
religious non-visibility?[11] Furthermore, the formidable
appeal of the Muslim Brethern (*Ikhwan al-muslimin*) from the
1930's needs also to be regarded as a vital expression of
"popular" religion.[12]

RELIGION AND STATE UNDER NASIR

The general pattern of the domination of the religious
establishment by central government continued after 1952
with the significant differences that 1) the regime appears
to have been intent upon dominating all aspects of religion
both "official" and "popular" and 2) it was also intent
upon redefining religion along modernist lines. It may
have been the extensive flirtation on the part of the Free
Officers with the Muslim Brethern before 1952 (implying
considerable knowledge of its character) and the later
disillusionment with it that made the new regime especially
sensitive both to the existence and the political possibilities of "popular" Islam.[13] The disillusionment resulted
from the support that the Brethern gave Mohammad Naguib
against Nasir in 1952-54, culminating in their assassination
attempt on the latter in October 1954 and their coup attempt
in 1965. Clearly, in light of this experience the political
potential of "popular" religion was not to be dismissed
lightly.

The attitude towards "official" religion had a similar
political dimension. The pre-1952 religious establishment
tended to be close to the palace and the king. This would
have made it immediately suspect in the eyes of the new
regime and at least one anticipated effort would be that
the master of "His Master's Voice" would now be Nasir.
This is in fact what happened in the personage of Shaykh
al-Azhar (the acknowledged leader of "official" Islam) and
especially with Mahmud Shaltut as Shaykh al-Azhar during
the 1960's. In *fatwas* (religious decrees) ranging from
family planning to the increased societal role of woman,
Egyptians read and discussed Shaykh Shaltut's support of
these and other progressive measures while speculating

that he was compelled to give such support and perhaps really thought differently regarding them.[14]

But the attitude of the regime towards "official" and "popular" Islam was not simply or even perhaps primarily narrowly politically motivated. The regime and especially Nasir himself was essentially religiously sincere and pious. What it wished to see accomplished was the reform of religion along modernist principles. The evidence of this as directed at "official" religion was the "New Law" (*al-qanun al-jadid*) of July 1961 which called for the expansion of the faculties of al-Azhar University from those of Theology, Religious Law, Arabic Language etc. to include medicine, secular law and business.[15] The evidence of the reformist attention given "popular" religion was that the Lenten carnival atmosphere of games, music, comedy and worship at *mawlids* (saints' birthday celebrations) became intellectually elevated by the presence of large scale book expositions by the leading Cairo publishing houses. At the same time, the political distrust of such events was seen in the early 1960's by a heavy police presence and a prohibition of any gathering in the street (as opposed to the *zikrs* [religious dances] taking place in the mosques) of more than five persons.

Perhaps a major result of the combined attention that "official" and "popular" religion received in the Nasir period was the fact of the attention itself. As the government pushed its reform efforts and as it extended its actual control over the religious Sufi brotherhoods it was in effect calling societal attention to religion and in the process perhaps laying the groundwork for its revitalization.

RELIGION AND STATE UNDER AL-SADAT

Under Nasir's direction the state sought inexorably to extend its control over religion. The role of the state and religion under al-Sadat has seen a process in which his basic liberal designs for the society have had an impact in the religious sphere as well. Under al-Sadat both "official" and "popular" religion have shown the effects of his broad political and economic liberalization policies.

Undoubtedly, a major concern on the part of al-Sadat in reference to religion has simply been to use it to increase his own political legitimacy. It is difficult to recall now that the man now called "the master of decisions" based on his decisiveness in war (October 1973) and peace (Jerusalem, November 1977) was called derisively "Sayyid Na'am Na'am" (Mr. Yes-Yes") in the few months before (also decisively) putting down a Nasirist coup attempt in May 1971. Surviving as one of the last of the Free Officers at the center of power had been interpreted negatively as personal weakness. Certainly he was well known for his personal piety as seen dramatically in the *zabeeba* (literally "raisin") or callous on his forehead

from repeated praying. Further to the preceding is that
in spring of 1979 when a combination of his peace treaty and
his hospitality to the ousted Shah of Iran created a right
wing fundamentalist backlash, he was careful to attend the
mawlid (birthday) of Egypt's second most revered saint,
Shaykh Ahmad al-Badawi in Tanta, the rural religious center
of Egypt and did so accompanied by the Shaykh al-Azhar.[16]
    The policy of political liberalization is related to
politics and religion in that it has created both a more
liberal atmosphere for discussion of divergent opinions and
even the opportunity for a degree of freedom in organizing
politically.
    While the regime by the evidence of its own pronounce-
ments remains modernist, the effect of its liberalist policies
seems to be to permit more latitude in the positions of its
religious leaders. The key leader by way of illustration is
the Shaykh al-Azhar. From time to time he has actually taken
positions at variance with government policy e.g. opposition
to family planning and advocating strict adherence to the
religious law (*Shari'a*) including public executions, amputations, etc. At other times, he has simply attempted to follow
relatively minor more traditional policies e.g., such as
insisting that all students at al-Azhar (i.e., the traditional
Faculty of Theology as well as the modern Faculty of Medicine)
should wear caftans and turbans rather than "Western" dress.[17]
The relative independence of policy of al-Azhar is perhaps
assisted by a further factor. The construction budget of
the new campus of the university in Nasir City is underwritten significantly by the Saudi Arabian government as,
it is claimed, is its operating budget. Also to the point,
the location of all of the faculties added since the reform
of 1961 in Nasir City is in itself indicative of the tactical
success of the *ulama* in responding slowly to reform. The
traditional faculties as well as the central administration
of the university remain located in the Sayyidna Husayn area,
just behind the al-Azhar Mosque itself.
    In the 1970's, however, it may be misleading to think
of al-Azhar as a pure bastion of "official" religion. The
Shaykh al-Azhar from 1973-1979 who had previously been Dean
of the Faculty of Theology was alleged to have been a
tasawwuf (*Sufi*) and to have attracted a coterie of Sufis
around him.[18] Thus "popular" Islam can be said to have
captured the citidal of "official" Islam. One indication
of the wider awareness of this phenomenon is a controversy
that developed in the Spring of 1979. Al-Azhar had authorized
the printing of the collected words of a medieval Sufi writer.
The institution was attacked in the People's Assembly by
religious fundamentalists who decried the heterodoxy of the
scholar in question. One conclusion regarding this incident
might be that the safeguarding of a more literal religious
orthodoxy now has moved out of al-Azhar into the wider
society, i.e. away from the establishment *ulama*. In spite
of the tendency for al-Azhar University and its leader, the

Shaykh al-Azhar to diverge at times in policy terms from
the regime, more generally it remains at the moderate
modernist center of religious politics.

A better grasp of the essential moderateness and
modernist character of the regime and its al-Azhar adjunct
can perhaps be seen against the background of the religious
mood in Egypt after 1970. A first major issue that arose
was in regards to the proposed 1971 constitution. Originally, the references to religion were going to remain as
vague as those of the National Charter of 1961. However
in the ensuing controversy in the People's Assembly, the
final version emerged stating that Islam was to be the
religion of the state and the *Shari'a* (religious) law was
to be *a* source of legislation (not *the* source as some
fundamentalists would have desired).[19]

The sharpness of the debate in getting specific references
to Islam inserted in the constitution was matched by inter-
communal (Muslim-Christian) tensions beginning in the latter
half 1972. By that time, the People's Assembly had already
passed a law calling for a life sentence for anyone causing
tensions between Copts and Muslims. In spite of this, at
the end of September, Copts including a bishop were stoned
and a new church set afire.[20] Meanwhile, the activities
of a faith healing Coptic priest in Alexandria had resulted
in a reported 300 conversions from Islam to Christianity.[21]
By the end of December, President al-Sadat accompanied by the
Shaykh al-Azhar felt impelled to visit the Coptic Patriarch
Shenouda III at the main Coptic Cathedral of St. Marks and
the following day in a speech before the People's Assembly
called for an end to sectarian divisions.[22]

In the new government which was formed in March 1973
(in the aftermath of student disturbances in January) with
al-Sadat as president *and* prime minister, al-Sadat appointed
not only a Minister of al-Azhar Affairs as was customary
but he also created a post of Deputy Premier for Religious
Affairs and as Minister of Waqfs. This was an indication
of the importance accorded the religious issues by the regime
and clearly implied the effort by the central government to
reassert its control over religious matters. In addition,
he increased the Coptic representation in the cabinet from
one ministerial post to two. The appointment of the moderate
Abd al-Halim Mahmud as Shaykh al-Azhar the next month seemed
to strengthen this religious policy direction.

If this major policy attention to religion had any
prospects of lessening in the aftermath of the October 1973
war, these were diminished in April 1974 when an organization
called the Islamic Liberation Organization attacked the
Military Engineering College in Cairo with plans to move
from there to a nearby meeting where President al-Sadat
was making a speech and kill him as well. The arrested
leader of the organization had been a long term religious
activist and assassin. The motto of the group suggests its
religious qualities: "Faith, Morals and Virtue". The

organization reportedly had Libyan support and money, a
consistent feature of such groups in Egypt. In June,
90 persons from the I.L.O were arrested for distributing
leaflets calling for the return of the caliphate and by
July the regime claimed it had arrested all.[23]

At the end of April, a new cabinet with al-Sadat remaining as prime minister found the position of Deputy
Premier for Religious Affairs and Waqfs still in existence
and in fact it was not until a year later in April 1975
that this position disappeared in the new cabinet under
Mamduh Salem. The following month (May), the three key
leaders of the I.L.O. were executed.

At the same time as the I.L.O. was organizing and
pursuing its activities, another similar organization had
gotten underway. The organization called *Gama'a al-Takfir
wa al Higra* (The Organization of Atonement and Migration
(i.e., symbolic migration to flee religiously objectional
practices on the model of the Prophet Muhammad's original
Higra of the year 622 A.D. from Mecca to Mdeina) was
founded in 1971 apparently also with Libyan support and
funding. Its leader Shukri Ahmad Mustafa had been previously arrested in 1967 and released in a general amnesty
in 1971. A series of arrests of *al-Takfir* supporters began
at least as early as May 1975 on charges of attempting to
overthrow the government. Shukri Ahmad Mustafa, although
his identity was known, escaped arrest in this crackdown
and subsequent ones in 1976 and early 1977. The end came
in June 1977 with the taking hostage and murder of the
former Minister of Waqfs and al-Azhar Affairs, Muhammad
Husayn al-Dhahabi who had written articles criticizing
the group. Even after Shukri Ahmad Mustafa was arrested
July 8th, bombs continued to explode in Cairo and Mansoura.
The arrests of 620 persons revealed the existence of 50,000
Egyptian Pounds in funds, twenty-five apartments and stores
of weapons and explosives. Even as late as November, however,
further arrests were necessary in order to prevent the
group from being reformed.[24]

Al-Takfir was not an isolated instance of such an
extreme fundamentalist group, however, because at least
two further ones revealed themselves. In October 1977, 104
members of *Jund Allah* ("Soldiers of God") were arrested.
Two days later 80 arrests were made of members of *al-Jihad*
("The Religious Struggle"). The latter organization had
already killed in order to gain weapons and its members were
said to have consisted of many of those released after
arrest in the Military Academy attack by the Islamic Liberation Organization.[25]

Paralleling this entire chain of events was the fate
of potentially the most formidable of the fundamentlist
religious organizations - the Muslim Brethern (*al-Ikhwan
al-Muslimin*). This pre-1952 organization which had had a
charmed existence from 1952 to 1954 until its assassination
attempt upon Nasir also has had a charmed existence since

1970. At the very time as the I.L.O. and the *al-Takfir*
were mounting their activities, the regime had been systema-
tically releasing the members of the Brethern imprisoned
since its 1965 abortive camp attempt. This process is said
to have been completed by March 1975 and a year later in
March 1976 it was seeking permission to organize as a
religious association.[26] This has so far been denied, but
it has been permitted to publish its own magazine, *al-Da'awa*
("The Call" i.e., both to invoke God and in the sense of
missionary activity).

It may very well be that this relative tolerance reflects al-Sadat's own pre-revolutionary partiality to the
Brethern but it may also be that the regime is in fact
engaged in the balancing act of using the Brethern to placate
fundamentalist sentiment by favoring one such relatively
moderate group. In addition, a feature of the continuing
criticism of the political left in Egypt is to accuse it of
irreligion. Thus the fundamentalist "credentials" gained
from the toleration of the Brethern can be used to mobilize
popular sentiment against the left.

The desire to placate religious fundamentalism can be
perhaps illustrated by the strength of religious feeling
that began to well up within the government and in the
People's Assembly on questions of religious law. For
example, in July 1977 the Ministry of Justice was considering proposing legislation that would make apostasy,
applicable only to Muslims, punishable by death. Also being
considered at the same time was a prohibition to the use of
usury, amputation for theft, death by stoning for adultery,
etc. By early September, Pope Shenouda III of the Coptic
Church called for a five day fast of protest against the
proposed laws. In mid-September, the government withdrew
the legislation and President al-Sadat met with the Pope
and the Shaykh al-Azhar to calm religious tensions. Simultaneously, however, there were press reports of gatherings
of 5,000 - 10,000 Muslim Brethern in Cairo and Alexandria
to celebrate the end of Ramadan.[27]

Meanwhile, the general "inward" domestic orientation
of what has been discussed above had begun to be linked
to the foreign policy realm. This has occurred in two ways.
There is first the controversy surrounding al-Sadat's
hospitality to the deposed Shah of Iran. Second, and more
importantly, there is the question of peace with Israel.
Al-Sadat had been careful to get the support of the Shaykh
al-Azhar in December 1977 for his November visit.[28] The
actual conclusion of the peace treaty began to lay him open
to attacks on the question of Jerusalem and once again the
Shaykh al-Azhar endorsed the policy, characterizing it as,
"A blessed Islamic step."[29] More generally however, the
fundamentalist mentality in regards to religion appears to
have resulted in the feeling that the Arab (i.e. "Islamic")
cause has been betrayed.

These issues surfaced dramatically in riots and strikes

on the Asyut and Minya University campuses in March and
April 1979. In a broadcasted dialogue with the faculty of
these universities on April 13th many of these issues were
laid bare. The general context was one of campus excitement
provoked by anger at the peace treaty's selling out of
"Islamic Palestinian Territory" (Wall Poster). Accompanying
this expression of anger from campus Islamic associations
was a whole series of Coptic-Muslim incidents.
     Al-Sadat in his remarks directed himself to first the
role of the Muslim Brethren which had come out against the
treaty and which he described as not only a religious
organization but as "a state within a state" and as such
resembled the communists and therefore could not be tolerated.
He then defended the treaty and went on to say that Egypt
will not have a Khomeini type situation because, in effect,
Egypt is too progressive and advanced. He then went on to
say that religion and politics should not be mixed and that,
"We want a structure which will be principally founded on
our religion - Islam and Christianity."[30]
     Egypt remains, however, beset by heightened religious
sentiment and by continued sectarian conflict. In January
1980 at the time of Orthodox Christmas and afterwards,
killings, acts of arson and other violent acts were directed
against Copts. At the same time, tracts purporting to be
authored by Copts calling for the conversion of Muslims etc.
were being widely circulated. Also, at the same time the
frustrations of economic deprivation and culturally objectionable Western style consumerism continued to aggravate the
situation. Adding to the pressures were the frustrations
of lack of progress on the Peace Treaty connected West
Bank autonomy talks, and the provocative character of
Israeli settlement policy and moves first in the Israeli
parliament and then by Prime Minister Begin himself to
make the Occupied Territory of Jerusalem the capital of
Israel. In addition, there was the additional decision to
grant the Shah of Iran permanent hospitality.
     In a speech on May 14, 1980 commemorating the May 14th,
1971 "Corrective Revolution," President al-Sadat indicated
his further reaction to rising religious sentiment.
Basically, he appeared to once again, as in the case of
Muslim Brethren, be attempting to ride with religious feeling and perhaps coopt it. The organized Coptic opposition
to amending Article 2 of the Constitution to stipulate that
Islamic law shall be the main source of legislation elicited
the response that, "Well, if Article 2 is the reason for all
this, then I tell my Coptic sons who are hearing me now,
and I tell you and our people that since I assumed power in
Egypt, I have been ruling as a Muslim president of an Islamic
state.[31] '[applause]'." His meaning, as he stated it, was
that as a Muslim ruler he had a special responsibility for
the welfare of Jews and Christians. He then further dwelt
on the theme of the ancient character of the Copts as
Egyptians and nationalists.

It is perhaps symptomatic of the extent of religious consciousness in Egypt that al-Sadat felt compelled to assert such a traditional Muslim role for his leadership. Accompanying this statement on religion were the specific political ones, of strengthening his personal authority which made him both President and Prime Minister and which introduced a system of security courts of civilian judges *and* military officers.

Most importantly for the question of religion and politics is the fact that a special decree makes a Deputy Prime Minister responsible for al-Azhar affairs and for local government. It would appear that symbolic and substantive appeals to majority sentiment now will be complimented by strong exeutive authority. As President al-Sadat somewhat forthrightly put it, "The building of democracy is over. What remains is democratic practice and the need for corrections."[32]

CONCLUSION

Egypt can be seen to have pursued a fairly consistent policy in reference to religion from 1952 onwards. It is essentially a modernist one that the militancy of Nasir's foreign policy and the authoritarian character of his regime was able to impose and be relatively free from fundamentalist reaction. A further factor reenforcing this was the theoretical argument that Islam and socialism were compatible. In addition, the reality of the physical austerity (lack of consumer goods etc.) and the relative discipline of socialism created a religious-like atmosphere of collective self-sacrifice.

Modernism in the hands of al-Sadat has had a more difficult time. First, liberalization has resulted in a conspicuous consumption, all the more objectionable due to the extremes of wealth and poverty intrinsic to a Third World society. Second, al-Sadat's foreign policy is perceived by religious fundamentalists as unable to do anything regarding Jerusalem and almost as little regarding the West Bank. Third, until May 1980 at least, the less authoritarian character of the regime has meant a degree of inability to control or repress certain events.

Al-Sadat, like Nasir has been able to keep "official" Islam intact as a political legitimizing factors. Possibly working in his favor is the extent to which "official" Islam has been popularized by a Sufist sentiment which apparently is growing in the country. Working against him is a fundamentalist "popular" Islam which has taken two forms. The first is that of the theologically deviationist sort represented by the al-Takfir and the Islamic Liberation Organization. The second and potentially most dangerous form is that represented by the more religiously orthodox Muslim Brethern. The Muslim Brethern have demonstrated an

assassination and conspiratorial capability in the past.
A possible danger to the regime might be the consequences
of a faltering and failure of the peace effort in respect
to the Palestinians and Jerusalem. Without necessity of
further elaboration, the coincidence of the existing criticism
of the regime's peace policy from both the fundamentalist
religious right and the political left should be noted.
The potential political explosiveness of this coincidence
is obvious.

NOTES

1. For a useful and lucid discussion of the concepts of "modernism",
"fundamentalism" and "secularism" see R. Stephen Humphreys, "Islam and
Political Values in Saudi Arabia, Egypt and Syria," *Middle East Journal*,
33 (Winter 1979), 1-19.

2. In a speech carried by Cairo Domestic Service, August 22, 1979
as reported in U.S. Department of State, *Foreign Broadcast Information
Service*, hereafter cited as *FBIS*.

3. Malcolm Kerr, *Islamic Reform* (Berkeley, Calif.: University of
California, 1966), p. 223.

4. A significant exception to the general absence of a theological
effort to bridge the gap of traditional and modernist theology are the
writings of Dr. Ali Shariarti who has so heavily influenced the Islamic
Revolution in Iran.

5. For a lucid and conceptually suggestive treatment of the concepts of "great" and "little tradition" see Robert Redfield, *Peasant
Society and Culture* (Chicago: University of Chicago Press, 1955), p. 70
ff. For a specific discussion of their application to the Islamic
world, see Gustave von Grunebaum, "The Problem: Unity in Diversity,"
in *Unity and Variety in Muslim Civilization*, ed. G. von Grunebaum
(Chicago: University of Chicago Press, 1955), p. 27 ff.

6. See Lloyd Rudolph and Susanne Rudolph, *The Modernity of
Tradition: Political Development in India* (Chicago: University of
Chicago Press, 1967), especially pp. 3-14. For a similar conclusion
regarding the close relationship of religion and modernization see
Bruce Borthwick, "Religion and Politics in Israel and Egypt," *Middle
East Journal*, 33 (Spring 1979), 145-163.

7. See footnote 5, above.

8. On the theme of the dualism of traditional religion and
modern intellectualism, see Daniel Crecelius, "The course of Secularization in Modern Egypt," in D. E. Smith, ed., *Religion and Political
Modernization* (New Haven, Conn.: Yale University Press, 1974),
pp. 67-94.

9. For this general argument, see Afaff Loutfi El Sayed, "The
Role of the *Ulama* in Egypt During the Early Nineteenth Century" in
P. M. Holt, ed., *Political and Social Change in Modern Egypt* (London:
Oxford University Press, 1968), pp. 279 ff.

10. See Daniel Crecelius, "Nonideological Responses of the
Egyptian Ulama to Modernization," in N. Keddie, ed., *Scholars, Saints,
and Sufis* (Berkeley, Calif.: University of California Press, 1972),
pp. 167-209.

11. On the question of religious brotherhood decline see J. Heyworth-Dunne, *Religious and Political Trends in Modern Egypt* (Washington, D.C.: Privately Printed, 1950), *passim*. On the social role of the brotherhoods, see Michael Gilsenan, *Saint and Sufi in Modern Egypt* (London: Oxford University Press, 1973), pp. 188-207. On the role of Sufi brotherhoods as a manifestation of "popular" religion see Morroe Berger, *Islam in Egypt Today* (Cambridge, England: Cambridge University Press, 1970).

12. The authoritative work on the Brethren is R. P. Mitchell, *The Society of Muslim Brothers* (London: Oxford University Press, 1969).

13. For an example of this early familiarity with the Muslim Brethern, see Anwar el-Sadat, *In Search of Identity* (New York: Harper, 1978), pp. 22-28 and *passim*.

14. This was said at the time in the early 1960's and re-emerged as a defense of Shaykh Shaltut in intellectual discussions during what has been termed de-Nasirfication in the mid-1970's.

15. On the question of the 1961 "New Law" and the resistance of the *ulama* to it, see Crecelius, "Nonideological Response..." and Daniel Crecelius "al-Azhar in the Revolution," *Middle East Journal* (Winter 1966), pp. 31-49.

16. Cairo Domestic Service, May 14, 1979, *FBIS*.

17. In fact, protests developed against wearing such traditional dress and the issue was forgotten.

18. Reference here is to Shaykh Abd al-Halim Mahmud who died in early 1979 and has been replaced by Shaykh Abd al-Rahman al-Baysar. The former had been the Dean of the Faculty of Theology when the present writer had been a student there in the early 1960's.

19. The text of the constitution is in *Middle East Journal*, 26 (Winter 1972), p. 55 ff. and the controversy is detailed in Joseph P. O'Kane, "Islam in the New Egyptian Constitution," *Middle East Journal*, 26 (Spring 1972), pp. 137-148.

20. *Al-Ahram*, August 15, 1972 regarding the law and references to the disturbances. Agence France Presse on the incident at Damanhour on September 30, 1972 as quoted by *Arab Report and Record* (1972), hereafter cited as *ARR*.

21. *Daily Telegraph*, October 15, 1972 as quoted by *ARR* (1972).

22. *Al-Ahram*, December 27 and 28, 1972, respectively.

23. The attack took place on April 18, 1974. *Al-Ahram*, April 21, 1972 contains the organizational details mentioned.

24. The name of the leader was Shukri Ahmad Mustafa. *Al-Ahram*, May 28, 1975 refers to him in connection with the arrest of his followers in Minya. Subsequent details appear in *al-Ahram*, July 8, 1977 and *al-Ahram*, November 8, 1977. Israeli intelligence appears to have assisted the Egyptian authorities in identifying the members of the group. This resulted from the Libyan financing of the group. See the two part article, Sydney Zion and Uri Dann, "Untold Story of the Mideast Talks," *New York Times Magazine*, January 21 and 28, 1979, pp. 32 ff and pp. 33 ff, respectively.

25. *October*, August 28, 1977 (*ARR*, 1977) and *al-Ahram*, August 30, 1977, respectively regarding these two organizations.

26. *Al-Ahram*, March 23, 1975 and March 14, 1975.

27. For the Ministry of Justice proposal, see *al-Ahram*

July 15, 1977 and for the Coptic reactions, *Le Monde*, September 6,
1977 (*ARR*, 1977) and *al-Ahram*, September 22, 1977 regarding the
government's action and President al-Sadat's meeting.   See *al-Nahar*
(Paris), September 26, 1977 (*ARR*, 1977) regarding the reported Muslim
Brethern gatherings.

28.   Agence France Presse, December 19, 1977 (*ARR*, 1977).

29.   *FBIS*, May 19, 1979 as quoted from Cairo Radio.

30.   The entire transcript of this broadcast appears in *FBIS*,
April 13, 1979.

31.   Cairo Domestic Service, May 14, 1980, *FBIS*.

32.   *Ibid*.

7
Nationalism in Twentieth Century Egypt

James P. Jankowski

    Perhaps more than other areas of the world, the Middle
East demonstrates the variability of modern nationalism.
It has its dead nationalisms as well as its unrealized ones,
and the existing states of the region differ tremendously
in the nature and strength of the nationalist sentiment
found animating their emergence and buttressing their continued existence. In general terms, however, three main
variants of nationalism have, over the last century, been
the main competitors for the allegiance of most of the
population of the Middle East. These are a sense of religious
nationalism, in which one's religious community was perceived
to be the object of ultimate loyalty; territorial nationalism,
based on a land and on a sense of the uniqueness of its people
because of their geographical and consequent historical distinctiveness, and linguistic nationalism, derived from a
people's sharing of a common language and the common heritage
that goes with language. Loyalty to the religious community
or *umma*; to a local homeland or *watan*; or to ethnic groups
or *qawm*: these are the three great alternatives between
which the nationalist thought of the Arab population of the
Middle East in particular has revolved. Each of these
variants has had its adherents in Egypt over the past century.

* * *

    Modern nationalist concepts first found expression in
Egypt in the 1860s and 1870s. By then the *de facto* autonomous
state created earlier in the century by Muhammad 'Ali, its
precocious socio-economic growth which was eroding old loyalties
and making necessary new ones, and contact with European ideas

Nationalism in Twentieth Century Egypt is reprinted
from *Middle East Review*, Vol. XII, No. 1, Fall, 1979.

by the educated elite all had developed sufficiently to
generate new ideas of political community. The half-century
from the 1860s to World War I was a fairly unitary period in
Egypt's history in terms of nationalism. While traditional
sentiments of allegiance to one's religious community or
more immediate feelings of loyalty to one's kinship group,
village or quarter are presumed to have been still predominant among the bulk of Egyptians, among leaders of
Egyptian public life and opinion it was doctrines of Egyptian
territorial nationalism or patriotism, of devotion to the
geographically defined Egyptian *watan*, which were most frequently expressed over this half century. Also widespread
through much of the elite were sentiments of Islamic loyalty,
specifically a sense of allegiance to Egypt's technical
sovereign, the Ottoman Empire. Ideas of linguistic Arab
nationalism were virtually non-existent among articulate
Egyptians prior to World War I.[1]

Together with the first intellectuals writing in
partially-nationalist terms in the 1860s and 1870s and with
the impact of the political leaders of the 'Urabi revolt
against Khedival despotism and European encroachment in the
late 1870s and early 1880s, it was orientations towards
Egypt, considered as a separate historical and political
unit, which dominated the public expression of articulate
Egyptians. The most prominent political speculators of this
period, such as Rifa'a Rafi' al-Tahtawi or Shaykh Husayn
al-Marsafi demonstrate, in their writings, an awareness of
the contemporary European terminology of nationalism, a
focus upon Egypt as a distinct land with a distinct history
stretching back in time beyond the Islamic-Arab epoch to
that of Pharaonic Egypt, and a definite tendency to think
of this *watan* of Egypt as a national entity analogous to
the *patrie* of early European nationalism. Similarly, the
'Urabi revolt was, in many respects, an Egyptian patriotic
movement directed against the existing foreign (both Ottoman
and European) domination of Egypt and striving for at least
the autonomy, if not the independence, of Egypt considered
as a separate political unit. The most graphic expression of
this primary orientation towards Egypt found in this first
generation which thought in nationalist terms is the un-
ambiguous slogan of the 'Urabi movement; *Misr lil-Misriyin*,
'Egypt for the Egyptians.'

The same primacy of Egyptian territorial nationalist
conceptions continued to be found in the decades between
the British Occupation of Egypt in 1882 and World War I,
if anything being reinforced by that Occupation. The classic
statements of Egyptian territorial nationalism indeed date
from the period between 1900 and 1914, in the speeches and
writings of the two great tribunes of prewar Egyptian
nationalism, Mustafa Kamil and Ahmad Lutfi al-Sayyid.
Opposed as the ideas of these two were in several respects,
particularly in regard to Egypt's relationship with the
Ottoman Empire, both men were, nevertheless, indisputably

Egyptian territorial nationalists.

References to Egypt as "the world's paradise," "the flower of Islam," "God's heaven on earth" dot the speeches and writings of Mustafa Kamil. His views show a consistent if somewhat simplistic emphasis on the themes of the uniqueness of Egypt, the unity of its population, the majesty of its history. He also expressed a messianic sense of mission parallel to that found in some European nationalisms, a call for Egypt to "become, as she once was, the cradle of moral and cultural greatness, the dispenser of civilization throughout the lands of the East."[2] Both the emotional basis and the almost-mystical tone of the Egyptian nationalism of Mustafa Kamil appear clearly in the following excerpt from a speech of 1907:

> Oh you critics, look at it [Egypt], contemplate it, acquaint yourselves with it. Read the pages of its past, and ask visitors to it from the ends of the earth: has God created any *watan* higher of station, finer of nature, more beautiful of character, more splendid in antiquities, richer in soil, clearer in sky, sweeter in water, more deserving in love and ardor than this glorious homeland?

> The whole world answers you with one voice: Egypt is the world's paradise.... If I had not been born an Egyptian, I would have wished to become one.[3]

The nationalism of Ahmad Lutfi al-Sayyid was more rationalist and pragmatic in its basis, but equally (if not more) Egypt-oriented. Perhaps the most prominent feature of Lutfi's territorial nationalist views was his belief in a distinct Egyptian national character. Basing himself on the belief that "Our nation today does not exist independent of our nation in the past," Lutfi expounded the concept of a unified, homogeneous Egyptian people possessing their own unique characteristics:

> No one has any doubt that we are a nation distinct from any other by virtue of qualities peculiar to us, and which possibly no other nation shares with us. We have our own peculiar color, our own peculiar tastes, and a single, universal language. And we possess a religion which most of us share, ways of performing our activities, and a blood which is virtually one flowing in our veins, while our fatherland has clearly defined natural boundaries which separate us from everyone else.[4]

Thus Egyptian territorial nationalists like Lutfi al-Sayyid, while recognizing language and religion as powerful bonds uniting a people, still elevated neither to the position of sole determinant of national identity. Rather, language and religion were seen as only part of a complex of factors which in their totality produced not a Muslim nation nor yet an Arab one, but the Egyptian nation "distinct from any other."

But Egyptian territorial nationalism was not the only
doctrine of nationalism voiced by articulate Egyptians in
the late nineteenth and early twentieth centuries. Also
widespread was a sense of Islamic political loyalty, more
precisely, allegiance to the main independent Islamic state
in the Middle East and also the state formally sovereign over
Egypt until 1914, The Ottoman Empire. There were various and
frequent expressions of Ottomanism, as the sentiment is called,
in prewar Egypt; it was found in the verse of Egypt's leading
poets, in the prose of Mustafa Kamil and his followers as well
as in the writing of several other political leaders, and
also in considerable Egyptian support for the Ottoman Empire
at times of international crisis, such as the Ottoman-Greek
War of 1897, the dispute between the Ottomans and the British
over their respective jurisdictions in Sinai in 1906, or the
Italo-Ottoman War over Libya in 1911-1912.

There are several qualifications which need to be made
in regard to pre-World War I sentiments of Ottoman loyalty
in Egypt, however. First, for most articulate Egyptians it
was not a case of Islamic/Ottoman loyalties instead of
Egyptian patriotism. Rather, allegiance to the Ottoman Empire
usually coexisted alongside loyalty to Egypt, with no incompatibility between the two being seen. "For every living
nation there are two great obligations; the obligation
towards its religion and its creed, and the obligation towards
its *watan* and the homeland of its fathers," said Mustafa Kamil,
adding that "adherence to religion demands adherence to the
watan...."[5] Secondly, in this blending of nationalist sentiments it was Egyptian territorial nationalism which was
the deeper and more primary with most leaders of articulate
Egyptian opinion. Politicians from Ahmad 'Urabi to Mustafa
Kamil who had contacts with the Ottoman regime by no means
desired the restoration of direct Ottoman rule over Egypt.
Rather, the sense of loyalty to the Ottoman Empire expressed
by many Egyptians seems to have been a sentiment auxiliary
to their Egyptian nationalism, a perception articulated in
particular after the British Occupation of 1882, that a
strengthened *partial* tie with the Ottoman state would be
of instrumental value in their more fundamental goal of
liberating Egypt from European domination. Again, as Mustafa
Kamil wrote: "...our love for Egypt takes precedence over
everything else.... We wish that Egypt be for the Egyptians."[6]
For many of the leaders of Egyptian opinion in this period
it is indeed debatable whether their orientation to the Ottoman Empire should be termed nationalism; perhaps the contemporary sense of Third World solidarity against a common enemy
would be a closer analogue. Finally, there were prominent
Egyptian leaders who explicitly opposed an Ottoman allegiance
by Egyptians. The most important of these was Ahmad Lutfi
al-Sayyid. A secularly-oriented thinker who believed that
there was "no common bond among the Islamic nations,"
Lutfi's position was simply that "we absolutely reject any

attachment to any other homeland but Egypt," he thus enjoined his countrymen to "repudiate today as they have in the past, any accusation of religious bigotry, i.e., "pan-Islamism and fanaticism."[7]

In comparison to the primary sense of Egyptian territorial nationalism and the secondary, more instrumental, attitude of Muslim solidarity with the Ottoman Empire, ideas of Arab linguistic nationalism had virtually no impact in Egypt prior to World War I. An articulate Arab nationalist movement only emerged in the Fertile Crescent just before the war and its doctrines overwhelmingly data from after that conflict; thus there was very little Arab nationalism for Egyptians to interact with up to 1914. But even in relation to what Arab nationalism there was, Egyptian opinion was at best benignly aloof, and at worst suspicious or hostile. As early as 1898, Mustafa Kamil denounced the idea of an Arab Caliphate, with its implicitly anti-Ottoman connotations, as a British plot to sow dissension within the Ottoman Empire, and more than a decade later, after his death, the party he had founded is reported to have rejected a suggestion for cooperation between Egyptian and Arab nationalists.[8] Similarly, Ahmad Lutfi al-Sayyid in 1911 denied the very existence of an Arab problem in the Ottoman Empire, and in 1912 termed both pan-Islamism and "Arab unity" mere "delusions" and "fancies."[9] The only Egyptian leader for whom ideological involvement in pre-World War I Arab nationalism has been documented is the Ottoman Army officer 'Azia 'Ali al-Misri, the founder of one of the main Arab nationalist societies just before the war. But there seem to have been no other Egyptians connected with early Arab nationalism, and Misri was hardly representative of most Egyptian elite opinion; it was his appeal for cooperation which was rejected by the leaders of Mustafa Kamil's party.[10]

* * *

In regard to the development of nationalism in Egypt, the four decades from the outbreak of World War I in 1914 to the consolidation of power of Jamal 'Abd al-Nasir in 1954 divide, without undue strain, into two periods of roughly equal length.[11] In the first of these, from World War I to the mid-1930s, Egyptian territorial nationalism reigned supreme within articulate Egyptian opinion, indeed becoming enshrined in the political institutions of the country as well as in the cultural expression of educated Egyptians. In relation to the other potential foci of national loyalty, this period was marked by the eclipse of sentiments of Islamic political solidarity among the leading segments of Egyptian opinion and by the continued insignificance of Arab linguistic nationalism. The major development of the second period, from the mid-1930s through the early 1950s, concerns this last possible nationalist alternative. Beginning in the 1930s and accelerating thereafter,

a sense of national identity with the surrounding Arab
world developed among significant numbers of Egyptians.
Although in retrospect it appears not to have challenged
the emotional primacy of territorial nationalism among most
articulate Egyptians, it laid the basis for the official
ascendancy of the Arab nationalism in Egypt which was to
occur from 1954 onwards.

    In politics and also in cultural life, sentiments of
Egyptian territorial nationalism were dominant in Egyptian
public life between the two world wars. The Revolution of
1919 against the British Occupation was explicitly and
solely Egyptian nationalist, uniting Egyptians of different
religions in an impressively secular movement, aiming at
the "complete independence" of Egypt and its nineteenth-
century annex, the Sudan, and its leaders eschewed cooperation with other "Easterners" waging parallel struggles for
independence. When Egyptian independence was formally
attained in the early 1920s, the wording of the Constitution
of the new state began with the ringing sentiment "Egypt is
a sovereign state, free and independent" (Article 1) and,
while citing Islam as the religion of the state and Arabic as
its official language (but only in Article 149), made no
mention of political ties or obligations extending beyond
the Nile Valley. The political parties established during
and immediately after the Revolution of 1919 were equally
Egypt-oriented, their programs speaking in terms of Egypt
alone. The pre-eminent party of the period of the parliamentary monarchy, the Wafd, followed a line best summarized
as "little-Egyptism" through most of the interwar period,
its publicists maintaining that Arab problems such as the
war between King Husayn and ibn Sa'ud in the Arabian peninsula
in 1924 were "no affair of Egypt," or that an Islamic issue
such as the possibility of the Caliphate being reinstituted
in Egypt would be only "a new lasso around the neck of
Egypt."[12] The policies followed by Egyptian governments
prior to the late 1930s similarly avoided any official
Egyptian involvement in Islamic or Arab questions.

    The supremacy of Egyptian territorial nationalism
through most of the interwar period was expressed in realms
besides the political. The 1920s were the heyday of
"Pharaonicism;" academic, literary, and artistic schools
of expression which emphasized ancient Egypt's influence
upon contemporary Egypt and which correspondingly denigrated
Egyptian links to peoples and cultures outside the Nile
Valley. In literature, creative artists such as Tawfiq
al-Hakim wrote dramas expounding on the continuity of the
"Egyptian mind" between ancient and modern Egypt, while
literary critics issued manifestos calling for the birth
of a genuinely Egyptian "national literature" emancipated
from what they perceived to be alien Arab-Islamic canons
of poetry and prose. In the visual arts a school of
Pharaonic sculpture flourished in the 1920s, giving rise
to monumental statuary inspired by Pharaonic models, such

as "The Revival of Egypt" which today stands in front of
Cairo University and buildings festooned with lotus and
papyrus (the tomb of Sa'd Zaghlul of the Wafd is a prime
example). In journalistic and academic circles commentators
such as the Copt, Salama Musa, in the 1920s and the Muslim,
Taha Husayn, in the 1930s propounded the radical (and admittedly much-disputed) thesis that the land and people of
Egypt were not essentially part of the "Eastern" world but
rather part of the "Western" universe of discourse which had
begun with Egypt and Greece; Egyptians therefore should orient
themselves towards Europe, not towards Asia.

A good example of the spirit of Egyptian territorial
nationalism of the interwar period is found in the essay
The Policy of Tomorrow written by the Wafdist leader Mirrit
Boutros Ghali in 1937.[13] Few passages state the geo-
historical bases of interwar Egyptianism more clearly than
the following:

> If we look upon the geographical contour of Egypt, we find
> that its frontiers are perfectly defined and that these
> have remained unchanged for some sixty centuries. Nature
> has so arranged, by surrounding Egypt with a desert on all
> sides--East, West and South--that the country has grown
> independently and by itself since the earliest times. A
> unique, permanent form has developed in it, and it has
> preserved its peculiar characteristics up to the present
> day.

Ghali did not go as far as Egyptian nationalists like
Musa or Husayn. He readily admitted that "Egypt was in
fact part of the Islamic world, marked by Oriental characteristics which were conferred upon her by the Arabic
language and the Arabian culture." But what marked the
interwar thinking of Ghali and many other Egyptian territorial nationalists was that these horizontal influences
were trifling in comparison with the more profound vertical
links of Egyptians with their land and their past. While
external influences, and even external obligations, were
accepted--the need for Egypt to be *"what it has always
been, namely a connecting link and a mixing ground for the
civilizations of the Mediterranean world"*--these came nowhere near the emotional commitment which an Egyptian
should have for Egypt itself:

> ...the vortex of Egyptian patriotism and test of Egyptian
> nationalism is nothing but the name of "Egypt" and of
> "Egyptians." In the heart of our national consciousness,
> we recognize that we belong to neither East nor West. We
> admit no doctrine except that of our nationalism...

The main change in relation to nationalist concepts
in Egypt between 1914 and the mid-1930s was the fading of
visible Islamic political loyalties which occurred from

World War I onwards. Externally, World War I and the
subsequent emergence of the new Turkish state was
accompanied by the abolition of the Ottoman Empire and
its Sultan in 1922, the elimination of the Caliphate in
1924, and the sentiment of Ottomanism found in prewar Egypt
was thus abruptly deprived of its central focus. Internally,
the gradual secularization of the Egyptian elite which had
been occurring since the mid-nineteenth century and the
even partial success of Egyptian territorial nationalism in
the creation of the formally-independent parliamentary
monarchy were perhaps the most important factors sapping an
Islamic political orientation by the interwar years. As
already mentioned, the political structure, parties and
policies found in interwar Egypt, at least up to the late
1930s, all demonstrated a general aloofness from Islamic
issues. The main apparent exception--the dabbling of
Egypt's King Fuad in Islamic politics in the mid-1920s in
the hope of obtaining the Caliphate for himself--indeed
confirms the generalization, for Fuad's ambitions and
maneuvers were opposed, on both political and ideological
grounds, by the Wafd and the bulk of Egypt's civilian
political establishment. Identification by Egyptians with
Arab nationalism in particular between 1914 and the 1930s
continued to be insignificant. The oft-quoted remark made
by the Wafdist leader Sa'd Zaghlul in 1925 when asked about
the possibility of cooperation with Arab nationalism--"If
you add a zero to a zero, then another zero, what is the
result?"--accurately captures the dominant attitude towards
Arab nationalism found within the Wafd prior to the late
1930s.[14] While anti-imperialist uprisings in the Arab
world, or what were perceived as Western assaults upon the
integrity of Islam could generate Egyptian protests and
limited financial assistance, they produced no major
Egyptian involvement in these issues until the very end of
the interwar years.

                              * * *

     The collapse of an active Islamic political orientation
in Egypt after World War I should not be taken to mean that
sentiments of Islamic identity were dead in Egypt, however.
Rather, it seems more accurate to say that a certain segment
of the Egyptian elite--the Western-educated, heavily-
Europeanized segment, those who wore frock-coats and fezzes
and who, by upbringing, had little that was still "Muslim"
about them--was temporarily dominant in Egyptian public life.
It was they who drafted the Constitution, formed and led the
political parties and staffed the ministries running the
country in the interwar period, and they followed their
largely-secular inclinations in thinking and working in
terms of Egypt (and their own interest) alone.
     Parallel with this group, however, was another Egypt,
a less-Europeanized, more genuinely Muslim--and Arab--one,

represented by the *'ulama* on one level, and on another by
the burgeoning lower middle class of government functionar-
ies and teachers, educated but less thoroughly Westernized,
closer in thought and lifestyle to the traditional Muslim
and Arab dimensions of Egyptian life. The existence of this
"other Egypt" is seen in various ways in the interwar period:
in protests and demonstrations at the time of external
religious crises such as the Turkish abolition of the Caliphate in 1924; in periodic agitation over perceived Christian
proselytizing in Egypt; in Sa'd Zaghlul's confession of 1926
that the issue of the Caliphate was still "a sensitive one
with the masses."[15] Initially co-opted and controlled by
the Westernized elite, by the middle of the interwar period
this segment of Egyptian opinion was forming its own ostensibly
religious or social, but in actuality inherently political,
organizations: the *Young Men's Muslim Association* in 1927,
the *Muslim Brotherhood* in 1928, the *Young Egypt Society* in
1933. In brief, it was this Egypt which from the 1930s onwards was to challenge the Westernized elite for ascendancy
over Egyptian public life, with one of the major issues being
precisely the insufficient attention paid by the establishment
under the parliamentary monarchy to Islamic customs internally
and to Arab solidarities externally.

Islamic customs internally, Arab solidarity externally:
why the dichotomy? Two factors seem largely responsible for
Arabism's replacement of Islam as the main external focus of
allegiance for part of Egyptian opinion in the interwar
period. The first is the frequently-noted symbiosis between
Islam and Arabism in the thinking of many Arab Muslims. Islam
as an historic religion and the Arabs as an historic people
were born together, and ever since their birth there has
been a considerable overlap between being Muslim and being
Arab to Arabic-speaking Muslims. The other factor is that
an Islamic allegiance lost its central focus in the early
1920s with the end of the Ottoman Empire and that the fiascos
surrounding the attempts to resurrect the Caliphate in the
mid-1920s made meaningful Islamic solidarity appear to be
impossible, or at best very remote (as well as somewhat
disreputable, due to King Fuad's involvement in the issue)
to many Egyptians. On the other hand, at almost the same
time a potentially-promising movement for Arab cooperation/
unity was developing in Western Asia, beginning with the
negotiations for an "Arab alliance," under Iraqi initiative,
from the early 1930s. Thus, with being Muslim and being
Arab as overlapping identities in the first place, and with
the prospects of Islamic unity perceived as highly unlikely
while Arab unity seemed to be entering the realm of the
possible, Egyptians of a Muslim-Arab orientation began to
make an almost unconscious transfer of their outward vision
from Islam to Arabism. The switch in emphasis was greatly
facilitated by Arabism and Islam being seen by many not
as alternatives but as stages, the former being merely a
phase along the road to the latter: "we believe that,

when we work for Arabism, we work for Islam and for the
good of all the world."[16] To use an optical analogy, for
many Egyptians the movement from Islam to Arabism was not
a change of focus: it was to continue to look in the same
place but to see something new there.

But the Islamic-Arabic symbiosis was only one aspect
of the growth of a sense of Arab nationalism in Egypt.
Another, and perhaps equally important factor, was the
growing Egyptian connection with the Arab world, and the
corresponding perception by Egyptians that it was in Egypt's
interest to associate with, or even assume the leadership
of, the neighboring Arabs. A perceived economic interest
probably ranked highest; the belief that the natural markets
of an Egypt desirous of industrialization lay in Arab Asia
and beyond. Political interests were not far behind economic
ones; the attitude that Egypt's Eastern "first line of defense" lay in Arab Asia,[17] or that the hopes which Egyptians
had of becoming a regional power (particularly pronounced
after the signing of the Anglo-Egyptian Treaty of Alliance
of 1936) would be threatened by the creation of an Arab
alliance *sans* Egypt--or by the establishment of a modern
Jewish state in Palestine. Cultural factors also figured,
although less prominently--the combination of Egyptian pride
and sense of *mission civilisatrice* which had developed out
of the leading cultural role in the Arab world that Egypt
had attained by the interwar years. Thus the sense of Arab
identification which began to develop in Egypt from the
1930s onwards drew from two powerful sources; the primarily
cultural one of the relationship between the Arabs and Islam,
and the largely pragmatic economically and politically rooted
one of perceived Egyptian interests in the Arab world. It
seems not unreasonable to speculate that much of Arabism's
power in Egypt came from the combining of these two streams
of inspiration.

Whatever its causes, a considerable growth in Egyptian
identification with and involvement in Arab nationalism is
apparent after 1930. It began in the early 1930s, when
pourparlers over the possibility of an Arab pact or an
alliance among Western Asian Arab states prompted a new
phenomenon in Egypt; press debate over Egypt's relationship
to such plans, and even considerable controversy over the
Egyptian versus the Arab component of the Egyptian "personality." However, the major surge in Arabist sentiment in Egypt
dates from the later 1930s.

For nationalist sentiment to become maninfest and
tangible a referent is often useful: an issue or institution
about which opinion can find expression and, in the process
of expression, feed itself and grow. The Ottoman Empire
had been such a referent for Islamic sentiment prior to
World War I, and its postwar elimination goes a long way to
explaining the eclipse of that sentiment in interwar Egypt.
A similar referent for Arabism in the 1930s and after was
the Palestine issue. The Palestine Arab Revolt of 1936-1939

raised, in a pressing way, several questions which reached
across the spectrum of Egyptian opinion and prodded it to
consider Egypt's relationship to developments in Palestine
and, by extension, also to Egypt's connections with the Arab
world in general. For many Muslim Egyptians the Palestine
problem raised the primarily religious issue of the fate of
the Muslim Holy Places in that land; for more secular Egyptians
the disorders in Palestine and the plans for the partition of
Palestine which these engendered posed questions of a now-
independent and industrializing Egypt's political and economic
interests; and for Egyptians of both inclinations there was
the emotional factor of sympathy with what was the longest
and most intense anti-European revolt in the Arab east in
the interwar period. With these several factors fueling it,
Egyptian involvement in the Palestine problem and, with it,
in the emerging movement for Arab cooperation/unity increased
greatly in the later 1930s. Popular organizations like the
Young Men's Muslim Association or the *Muslim Brotherhood* took
the lead in issuing declarations, in fundraising, in organizing
meetings and demonstrations in support of the Palestinian
Arabs. Within a few years, the leadership of the established
political parties were compelled to make public statements
expressing their solidarity with other Arabs over the Palestine issue. Nor did Egyptian politicians limit themselves to
platitudes: the later 1930s also saw the first Egyptian
governmental involvement in Arab affairs, first with confidential representations to the British about the situation,
then by 1939 with the public participation of the Egyptian
government along with other Arab (and only Arab) governments
in the St. James Conference concerning the Palestine Mandate.[18]
   If the 1930s was the decade of the beginnings of significant Egyptian involvement in Arab affairs, the 1940s was the
decade when that involvement became institutionalized.
Between 1942 and 1944, a Wafdist ministry headed by Mustafa
al-Nahhas took the lead in putting together the League of
Arab States. The League constituted much less than full
Arab unity, indeed in good part being the result of an
Egyptian attempt to forestall the creation of a tighter
Arab union in the Fertile Crescent which might have been a
threat to Egypt's position as the leading state of the Arab
world. Yet Egyptian initiative in its establishment was a
step which would have been inconceivable to Nahhas' predecessor Zaghlul, a generation earlier. In the late 1940s
Egypt and the other states of the League bumbled their way
into the first Arab-Israeli war. Thus, within a decade of
the surfacing of significant Arabist sentiment in Egypt, the
country's leaders felt their interests and ambitions sufficiently engaged in the Fertile Crescent to go to war there.
The defeat of the Arab states in 1948-1949 produced a partial
reaction against an Arab orientation in the early 1950s, with
powerful voices reasserting a sense of Egptian separateness
and isolation as well as questioning the utility of Egypt's
involvement in the Arab world. This proved to be only a

temporary phase, however. By 1954, with the consolidation
of power by Jamal 'Abd al-Nasir, Egypt resumed that march
towards Arab leadership and unity which was to be one of the
most prominent features of its public life through the 1950s
and 1960s.

As with the pre-World War I Islamic/Ottoman orientation
found in Egypt, several qualifications need to be made about
the sense of Arab identification and involvement which
developed in Egypt between the 1930s and the 1950s. Obviously, Egyptian involvement in Arab affairs was, in part,
prompted by political rather than ideological motives. The
rivalry between Nahhas and King Faruq, and the desire of
each to enhance his domestic position by becoming a regional
leader, certainly had a great deal to do with Egyptian sponsor-
ship of the Arab League, and similar instances of political
motivation underlying Arabist policies could be adduced both
before and after World War II. But issues do not become
"political" ones if they are not, to some degree, popular
ones as well. It seems questionable whether Egyptian ministries of the 1930s and 1940s, mainly composed of men of the
older generation who held Egyptian territorial nationalist
views, would have become as involved in Arab affairs if not
for considerable popular sentiment prodding them to adopt
Arabist policies. This is certainly what these leaders
repeatedly told the British in their confidential representations from the 1930s on.

Yet there were also influential Egyptians who never
bought Arabism (at least prior to its becoming an official--
and enforced--ideology under Nasir). Perhaps the most
notable of these was Isma'il Sidqi, Prime Minister of Egypt
from 1930 to 1933 and again in 1946 who, as late as 1950, was
publicly questioning the value of Egypt's involvement in Arab
affairs and writing of the potential benefits of peace and
cooperation with Israel. Other prominent Egyptians who wrote
in anti-Arabist terms in the partial reaction against Arabism
of the early 1950s included Ahmad Lutfi al-Sayyid, still
a believer in exclusive Egyptian nationalism, and (a figure
of some importance in contemporary Egypt) the journalist
Mustafa Amin.[19] Arabism in Egypt before the mid-1950s may
have grown a great deal, but it was still a fragile growth.

Finally, the sense of Arab identification which did
develop in Egypt between the 1930s and the 1950s did not
challenge the deeper sentiment of Egyptian identity felt by
many articulate Egyptians. As with prewar Ottomanism, the
feeling of Arab identity was not a replacement for their
Egyptian identity: it was, rather, a supplement. Like
other supplements, it had a heavily-instrumental aspect:
the promotion of Egyptian self-defense or aggrandizement,
economic advantage, cultural leadership. In this conver-
gence of two loyalties, the Egyptian often continued to be
the more central. There is no better example than the
views expressed by the Secretary-General of the Arab
League, 'Abd al-Rahman 'Azzam, in a famous debate explicitly

concerning Egyptian national identity in 1953.[20] While
arguing strongly for continued Egyptian involvement in and
leadership of the Arab world ("We cannot under any circumstances isolate ourselves from the Arabism of which we are
the heart and the center"), 'Azzam justified this Arabism
primarily on the combined grounds of Egypt's civilizing
mission and its economic-political imperatives. "Egypt is
the first school of humanity, Egypt is God's gift to the
world," he asserted, and asked his audience how Egyptians
could possibly forget their millenial mission; in his view
they could not. Beyond that, Egypt had vital interests in
the Arab world. Terming the Arab area "our living-space,"
'Azzam offered arguments both for the political importance
of the Arabs to Egypt ("We cannot leave Syria to do what
it wants by itself") and its economic importance to Egypt
("industrial development demands that we have a living-
space, and this living-space is our brothers who understand us"). Thus, even for 'Azzam, the Arab world was not
the center of his national consciousness: it was, rather,
closer to an arena, a "circle" in Nasir's terminology of
a year later, in which everlasting Egypt would find its
destiny.

* * *

The complex details of Egypt's championship of Arab
nationalism under Jamal 'Abd al-Nasir have been the subject
of several detailed studies.[21] A brief consideration of
terminology alone is sufficient to indicate the scale of
the formal change in national orientation which occurred
in Egypt in the 1950s and 1960s. The Egyptian Constitution
of 1956 refers to Egypt as "a sovereign independent Arab
state" and to the people of Egypt as "part of the Arab
nation" (Article 1). The country's change of name from
Egypt to the United Arab Republic in 1958, was maintained
throughout the 1960s in spite of the collapse of union with
Syria in 1961. The 1962 Charter of National Action (probably
the most authoritative statement of Nasir's orientation and
goals) early makes references to the "Arab people of Egypt"
and ends with the affirmation that "Ours is an Arab people
and its destiny is tied to the destiny of the unity of the
Arab Nation."[22] All are indicative of an attempt to reorient
Egyptian national allegiances from the narrow confines of
the Nile Valley to the broader linguistic unit of the Arab
world.

But some of the limitation of Arabism as it developed
in Nasir's Egypt need to be pointed out. The first is that,
certainly with Nasir himself, Arabism was an acquired taste
arising out of circumstances rather than an ingrained conviction carried since childhood. As Nasir's *The Philosophy
of the Revolution* recounts the evolution of his views, it
took him some time to become an Arab nationalist. What
began with participation in demonstrations over Palestine

inspired by "the echoes of sentiment" in the late 1930s only
a decade later grew into the intellectual conviction that
"the whole region" was "one complete whole."[23]   Secondly,
as the above references imply, even Nasir's Arabism was not
totally devoid of elements of Egyptian separateness. As
perhaps the best known passage in his *Philosophy* puts is,
the Arab world was only the closest and most important of
three "circles" (Africa and the Islamic World being the
other two) with which Egypt, by geography and history, was
intimately linked.[24]   Although Nasir's tendency to dissolve
Egypt into the "Arab Nation" seems to have developed over time,
it was never complete: even the National Charter of the early
1960s had, in addition to phrases like the "Arab people of
Egypt," references to "the Egyptian people, the creator of
civilization."[25]   On the level of action, the long-debated
question of whether Nasir's Arabist policies were designed
primarily to promote Arab nationalism or primarily to serve
Egyptian national interests is probably a moot point, given
the ambiguity of the evidence about Nasir (many public statements, but no private papers) and the fact that the blending
of ideology and interest to the point where they become
inextricable in an individual's mind is not unknown in Egypt,
as elsewhere. It does seem fair to say, however, that the
sense of Arab nationalism found in Nasir was "far from the
urgency of unity, the Fichtean vocation to national fusion"
found in Arab lands like Syria.[26]

But the most important qualification about Arabism in
Egypt under Nasir is that it may have been much more idiosyncratic than it appeared to be at the time. It certainly
became *de rigueur* to voice sentiments of Arab nationalism
in Egypt in the 1950s and 1960s. Given the rigorous censor-
ship of public expression in Egypt at the time, however,
that in itself is not sufficient to indicate a thorough-
going commitment by Egyptians to Arab nationalism. While
an Egyptian sense of identity with the Arabs had been growing since the 1930s and, in all probability, increased under
Nasir, there is reason to question how many articulate
Egyptians really shared their leader's orientation towards
the Arab world. The most important indication comes from
what has occurred in Egypt since Nasir's death; the reversion
of Egyptian policy and opinion to a more Egyptianist stance
under Anwar al-Sadat.

The drift away from Arab nationalism in the Egypt of
the 1970s is too well-known to need elaboration. The change
of name from the "United Arab Republic" to the "Arab Republic
of Egypt" in the 1971 Constitution was but an early indication of things to come. A retreat from Arabism was
certainly apparent in Egypt's policies in the years which
followed; Sadat's non-pursuance of Nasir's efforts to forge
Arab unity, his emphasis upon Egyptian internal development,
his *de facto* withdrawal of Egypt from the cause of Palestine,
perceived as so vital by other Arabs. In the Egyptian media,
discussions of Arab unity have been replaced by analyses of

"Arab solidarity," with leading publicists taking the
position that Arab unity is "impossible" given contemporary
Arab and world conditions.[27] The converse of this public
withdrawal from Arab unity is the resurfacing of themes of
unadulterated Egyptian territorial nationalism. To read
President Sadat's recent autobiography and his addresses of
the late 1970s is to be thrust back into the mental universe
of Mustafa Kamil or the Wafd. There is the opening invocation of the land of Egypt, its beauty and its perdurance;
the ritual glorification of Egypt's 7000 year-old history
and its role as teacher of the world; the repetitive use of
phrases like "Egypt before anything else."[28] Sadat's
autobiography concludes by emphasizing that "the Egyptian
people differ from many other peoples, even within the Arab
world." Its final sentence refers to Egyptians as "a people
who are working for a modern civilization comparable to the
one they erected thousands of years ago in freedom and
peace."[29] For President Sadat at least, Egyptian patriotism
seems to be fully as powerful an emotion as it had been for
pre-1952 Egyptian leaders.

It also appears that President Sadat's sense of Egyptian
territorial nationalism is not unique to himself. Previously
quiescent Egyptian intellectuals have launched full-scale
attacks on Nasir's Arabism and his attempt to lead the Arab
world, criticizing not only the failure of Nasir's Arab
policies and their ruinous effects upon Egypt, but also
questioning the very desirability of his Arabist vision which
"atrophied the Egyptians politically and undermined their
patriotism to the point where the word 'patriotism' disappeared...."[30] One has only to visit Egypt to sense and to
be told of a considerable Egyptian resentment (which has
definitely been encouraged by official spokesmen) against
other Arabs because of their ingratitude to Egypt after her
expenditure of "the blood of 100,000 Egyptian martyrs and
forty billion Egyptian pounds" for the sake of the Arab
cause over the past thirty years.[31]

But it is important to note that while there has been
a definite swing away from Arab nationalism in Egypt, it
has not resulted in turning the clock back to the 1920s or
earlier in regard to nationalist alternatives. The criticisms
of Nasir's Arabism by some intellectuals have not gone un-
challenged. Other writers defend Nasir and his Arab policies.
What seems to be occurring is a genuine debate rather than
the cloying surface unanimity of the 1960s, a debate in which
an Arab orientation for Egypt still has proponents. Nor
has Egypt's leadership completely withdrawn from a commitment
to interaction with other Arabs. "Arab solidarity" is still
asserted to be a desirable goal for Egypt to pursue, and
President Sadat's utterances continue to refer to Egypt's
"Arab character," to the "Egyptian Arab people," and to
"the great Arab nation" of which Egypt is a part.[32] As in the
Egypt of the recent past, thus, nationalist alternatives
in contemporary Egypt are not mutually exclusive; "In real

life dilemmas need not be resolved, they can be lived...."[33]
While Egyptian territorial nationalism has been the strongest
and most permanent variant of national identity found among
articulate Egyptians in the twentieth century, a new dimension has nonetheless been added to Egyptian nationalist
thought over the past forty years, that of Egypt as part of
the Arab nation, with which it shares both characteristics
and interests. Although this position is not now being
expressed as strongly as it was under Nasir, Arabism has not
been eliminated from Egyptian public life.

NOTES

1. The ideological dimensions of nationalism in pre-World War I
Egypt are dealt with in detail in the following: Jamal M. Ahmed, *The
Intellectual Origins of Egyptian Nationalism* (London, 1960); Jacques
Berque, *Egypt: Imperialism and Revolution* (translated by Jean Stewart:
London, 1972); Albert Hourani, *Arabic Thought in the Liberal Age,
1798-1939* (London, 1962); Mounah A. Khouri, *Poetry and the Making of
Modern Egypt, 1882-1922* (Leiden, 1971); Nadav Safran, *Egypt in Search
of Political Community* (Cambridge, 1961); Charles Wendell, *The Evolution
of the Egyptian National Image: From Its Origins to Ahmad Lutfi
al-Sayyid* (Berkeley, 1972).

2. Cited in Wendell, *op. cit.*, 267.

3. Quoted in Muhammad Muhammad Husayn, *al-Ittijahat al-Wataniyya
fi al-Adab al-Mu'asir* (two volumes: Cairo, 1954), I, 67.

4. Quoted in Wendell, *op. cit.*, 237-239.

5. Cited in Faruq Abu Zayd, *Azmat al-Fikr al-Qawmi fi al-Sihafa
al-Misriyya* (Cairo, 1976), 58-60.

6. Cited in *ibid.*, p. 60.

7. Quotes from Wendell, *op. cit.*, 229, 233, 259.

8. Reported in the memoirs of Kamil's successor as head of the
Watani Party. Muhammad Farid, as excerpted in Muhammad Subayh,
al-Yaqaza (Cairo, 1964), 257.

9. Quoted in Wendell, *op. cit.*, 230.

10. There were also political and financial contacts between
Egypt's *de jure* ruler, Khedive 'Abbas Hilmi, and Arab notables and
nationalists all the way from the 1890's to World War I; but these
involved desires for personal and dynastic aggrandizement which can
hardly be termed "nationalist."

11. Of the many works on Egypt from World War I to the Revolution
of 1952, perhaps the most valuable for nationalist trends are the
following: Berque, *op. cit.*; Leonard Binder, *The Ideological Revolution
in the Middle East* (New York, 1964); Marcel Colombe, *L'Evolution de
l'Egypte* (Paris, 1951); Sylvia G. Haim, *Arab Nationalism; An Anthology*
(Berkeley, 1961); Hourani, *op. cit.*; Safran, *op. cit.*; Afaf Lutfi
al-Sayyid Marsot, *Egypt's Liberal Experiment, 1922-1936* (Berkeley,
1977); and David Semah, *Four Egyptian Literary Critics* (Leiden, 1974).

12. 'Abbas Mahmud al-'Aqqad writing in *al-Balagh*, October 19,
1924, and *ibid.*, May 11, 1926.

13. Mirrit Boutros Ghali, *The Policy of Tomorrow* (translated
by Isma'il R. el Faruqi: Washington, 1953). The following quotations

are taken from pp. 105-111 of this work. (Italics in the original.)

14. Cited in Abu Khaldun Sati'al-Husri, *al-'Uruba Awwalan* (Beirut, 1961), 60.

15. As related by Muhammad Husayn Haykal in his *Mudhakkirat fi al-Siyasa al-Misriyya* (two volumes: Cairo, 1951, 1953), I, 258-259.

16. From a pamphlet of 1942 by Hasan al-Banna of the Muslim Brotherhood as given in his *Majmu'at Rasail al-Imam al-Shahid Hasan al-Banna* (Beirut, 1965), 71.

17. 'Abd al-Qadir al-Mazni writing in *al-Shabab*, Sept. 16, 1936.

18. For further material on the effects of the Palestine issue in interwar Egypt, see my "Egyptian Responses to the Palestine Problem in the Interwar Period, *"International Journal of Middle East Studies,"* forthcoming.

19. This reaction is discussed in Anis Sayigh, *al-Fikra al-'Arabiyya fi Misr* (Beirut, 1959), 254-261.

20. Quoted extensively in Husri, *op. cit.*, 116-126, from which the following passages are taken.

21. In addition to their autobiographical statements and biographies, the following works should be consulted on nationalist trends in Egypt under Nasir and Sadat: Anouar Abdel-Malek, *Egypt: Military Society* (Translated by Charles Lam Markmann: New York, 1968); A. I. Dawisha, *Egypt in the Arab World: The Elements of Foreign Policy* (New York, 1976); Malcolm Kerr, *The Arab Cold War: Gamal 'Abd al-Nasir and His Rivals* (third edition: New York, 1971); Nissim Rejwan, *Nasserist Ideology: Its Exponents and Critics* (New York, 1974); Patrick Seale, *The Struggle for Syria: A Study of Post-War Arab Politics, 1945-1958* (London, 1965); P. J. Vatikiotis, *Nasser and His Generation* (London, 1978).

22. State Information Service, United Arab Republic, *The Charter* (Cairo, n.d.), 3, 9, 103.

23. Gamal Abdel Nasser, *The Philosophy of the Revolution* (Buffalo, 1959), 62-66.

24. *Ibid.*, 58-62.

25. State Information Service, *op. cit.*, 32.

26. Abdel-Malek, *op. cit.*, 249.

27. See 'Ali Hamdi al-Jamal, "Nahnu wa al-Tadamun al-'Arabi" ("We and Arab Solidarity"), *al-Ahram*, Oct. 13, 1978.

28. A speech by President Sadat to the Egyptian National Assembly, April 5, 1979, as given in *al-Ahram*, April 6, 1979.

29. Anwar el-Sadat, *In Search of Identity: An Autobiography* (New York, 1978), 312-313.

30. Louis 'Awad as quoted in Vatikiotis, *op. cit.*, 332.

31. Prime Minster Mustafa Khalil as quoted in *al-Ahram*, April 6, 1979.

32. President Sadat before the National Assembly as quoted in *al-Ahram*, April 6, 1979.

33. Hourani, *op. cit.*, 297.

8
Changing the Law on Personal Status in Egypt Within a Liberal Interpretation of the Shari'a

Mohamed Al-Nowaihi

Let us admit a sad but incontrovertible fact: the status of women in Arab society is one of the lowest in the world as regards their enjoyment of the basic human rights of individual dignity, freedom and equality and the rights springing therefrom in education, work, economic equity and political participation. These rights would enable a woman to lead a life of decency and respect, to be an esteemed member of her family, a useful member of her society and a good citizen of her country, thus benefiting not women alone, but the men and the children as well.

We must not be deceived by certain phenomena. In some Arab capitals women walk about dressed in the latest Western fashions, sometimes vying with Western women in scantiness of attire, as if this were the epitome of emancipation. Yet in most corners of the Arab world women are still forced to wear the veil and are kept in seclusion or confined to virtual house-imprisonment. In some countries the men boast that a woman leaves the house only twice: once when she gets married and moves to the home of her husband and once when she dies and is carried to her grave.

Whenever official propaganda stridently boasts of the political, educational, labor and economic rights granted to women in this or that Arab state, one should inquire how many women do, in fact, enjoy these rights, and how much effort has been expended to make women aware of them and able to exercise them. It is commendable that, in a couple of countries, a woman has reached the high rank of cabinet minister, but how, one must ask, has this affected the lot of the vast majority of women, and how many women have

Changing the Law on Personal Status in Egypt Within a Liberal Interpretation of the Shari'a is reprinted from *Middle East Review*, Vol. XI, No. 4, Summer, 1979.

actually been enabled to exercise the mere right to vote?
In many Arab states, education for females is still
restricted to the elementary or primary school level while
in some, women are prevented from getting any education
whatsoever, even from learning how to read and write. In
most corners of the Arab world, women are denied the right
to work, except for housework and pastoral or agricultural
labor, for which they receive no pay, like serfs. The share
in inheritance allotted to females in the Qur'an, which is
half the share given to males, is frequently withheld or
drastically reduced. In some countries, when a man dies
and leaves ninety date-trees, for example, to be divided
between a son and a daughter, the son does not inherit sixty
and the daughter thirty; he is given eighty-nine trees and
she is given one. Against the Qur'anic edict, this is
justified by what is called *al-khal'* (renunciation). The
girl is asked, "Do you agree to renounce your share in favor
of your brother?" She is left in no doubt as to what would
happen to her if she dares to refuse: the womenfolk tell
her that her corpse will be floating in the nearby river or
the sea in a day or two, or will be consigned to a pit in
the desert. Therefore, she always answers, "Yes." "We
did not rob her of her legal right; she renounced it voluntarily," it is then declared. Indeed, after her complete
renunciation, has not munificence enough been displayed in
giving her the single date tree? In many areas of the Arab
world, including Egypt, a father is loath to let his
daughters inherit their due share after his death. He argues
that the daughters will marry strangers and take that share
out of the family or clan. He avoids this by "writing"
(*Yiktibu*) (deeding) all or nearly all of his property to
his sons -- i.e., he hands over to them a fictitious contract
of sale in which he claims that he has received the price of
the property from his sons.

     In Egypt, a document is given to every non-Muslim woman
who wishes to marry a Muslim. According to Egyptian law, a
contract of marriage between a Muslim man and a non-Muslim
woman cannot be drawn up by the usual *Ma'zun* (the man licensed
by the government to conclude and record marriage contracts)
but must be drawn up by a judge in a court of Personal Status.
The judge cannot draw up this contract until he has advised
both parties of the major edicts, purported to be those of
Islam, on the issue. The contract itself is then drawn up
in Arabic, English and French. The following are its main
provisions:

     1. The husband has the right to take unto himself a
second, third and fourth wife, keeping all at the same time,
despite any opposition the wife may make;
     2. He has the right to divorce his wife whenever he
wishes, whether she agrees or not. He has the right to
prevent her from leaving his house except by permission.
If she deserts his house, he may demand her return and

use legal compulsion (the police) to bring her back.
(Implementation of this use of compulsion was cancelled,
not by a change in the law, but by a ministerial order
issued on February 13, 1967);

3. If divorced, the mother may have custody of her
children, but only with the permission of a judge, and
only up to the age of nine for daughters and seven for
sons, after which the children must be surrendered to
the custody of their father (without any investigation
as to where their best interests may lie);

4. The financial rights and liabilities of both
parties in case of divorce are outlined as regards dowry,
maintenance and sustenance of the children. The divorced
wife is entitled to only one year's maintenance, and the
difference in religion disqualifies each party from
inheriting any of the other's property.

Even this brief summary of the legal, political,
economic, educational and social conditions of women in the
Arab world makes superfluous any comment on the injustice
and inequity meted out to them. Whence did this state of
affairs spring? Until quite recently, most Western writers
had a simplistic answer: from Islam itself. They drew
their arguments from the Muslims themselves, from what
Muslims do and say. Only recently have a number of these
Western writers -- a significant and possibly growing
number -- begun to have second thoughts. They are beginning to see that condemning a religion because of the
practices of those who profess it may be highly unfair,
and accepting the popular interpretation of its original
tenets may be quite wrong, for it is rather the rule
than the exception that those tenets get misunderstood
and misrepresented with the passage of time. They have
therefore gone back to the two fundamental sources of
Islam, the Qur'an and the Tradition of the Prophet
Muhammad, to discover what both these sources say about
the human stature and the legal rights of women. They
have also paid more heed to the more liberal interpretations of modern reformers. One of these Western writers,
Robert N. Bellah, faced with the inequities imposed on
women in the laws on Personal Status in the Arab world
(laws purporting to be derived from the Islamic *shari'a*),
examining whether they really arose from the original
teaching of Islam, declared: "In accord with the way
Islamic law developed, it was the post-Qur'anic and
not the Qur'anic provisions which became the effective
precedents in *shari'a* family law."[1]

Of the Qur'anic provisions, Professor Bellah had
this to say:

The main burden of Qur'anic legislation on family
affairs was to stabilize the nuclear family, limit
pologamy and divorce and protect the interests of wives

and children...and to express the enhanced dignity of the
individual, including women and children, as persons
standing in direct relation to God.[2]

He stresses what he calls "the basic modernity of the
Qur'anic teaching," and goes as far as to say that this
teaching was "universal, progressive, and indeed revolutionary." How then, did this teaching come to be lost
sight of and, in the long history of Islamic law, come to be
positively contravened? Professor Bellah answers, simply,
that the Qur'anic teaching was "too modern to succeed."
I only understood the full import of Professor Bellah's
statement after hearing an illuminating lecture on the
struggle of American women for civil rights by Dr. Elizabeth
Defeis[3] and reading a remarkable address by Jim Robinson of
the American University in Cairo[4] on the rights of American
working women -- many of whom do not know they have these
rights or how to secure them from their employers. It is
the same sad story of the male of the species stubbornly
holding on to his mastery and using all sorts of justifications to maintain it.
In Egypt, the chief justification is the religious one.
The cardinal error is confusion of *al-Shari'a* with *al-Fiqh*.
Al-Shari'a is usually taken to mean Muslim Law, which is does
not mean -- the word simply means "a clear and straight path,"
especially the path to a watering hole.[5] Thus *al-Shari'a* means
"the general Islamic way." *Al-Fiqh* denotes Jurisprudence, but
this is only one part of the *Shari'a*, the human, imperfect,
fallible and changeable part. For, *al-Shari'a* consists of
several elements. The first is the Qur'an, God's revealed
words to His Prophet, together with *al-Sunna*, the Tradition
of the Prophet (i.e., his reported sayings and actions).
These two sources together form the element of *al-nass*, the
text. They contain the fundamental Islamic tenets on creed,
ritual and ethics and are permanent and immutable. But they
also contain a number of provisions on certain mundane
problems that arose during the life of the Prophet, especially
when he established the new Islamic state in Medina. These
mundane provisions, according to the classical Science of
Principles of Jurisprudence itself (*'ilm usul al-fiqh*) are
not immutable. They can be changed, indeed, they must be
changed if circumstances change, and must be modified or
replaced by other provisions, in the light of *al-Maslaha*,
the public good or common weal of the Muslim nation. *Al-
Maslaha* is declared the overriding stipulation for all laws.
Moreover, the provisions contained in both Qur'an and *Sunna*
could not possibly include all the problems that might
arise in human society. The rapid and extensive development
of Muslim society, brought about by the impetus of Islam
itself and the great conquests that resulted, gave birth
to countless new problems. In order to tackle them, there
arose the second element, that of *al-ra'y*, i.e., human
opinion. This is what *al-fiqh*, jurisprudence, mainly

consists of. It contains the opinions of the leading
Imams. But -- and this cannot be too emphatically
stressed -- theirs were only individual opinions, made
to the best of their knowledge and ability, and influenced
by their religious sects and schools and their environmental
and temporal circumstances. They themselves never claimed
infallibility or finality for their pronouncements. They
admitted the possibility of error, saying, always, *wa Allah
a'lam*, (God knows best) and asking for His forgiveness should
they be in error. They allowed every scholar the full right
of *ijtihad* (the right to strive to form his own opinion) and
displayed the most remarkable toleration.

This was the situation in the first five or six centuries of Islam, the age of dynamic growth, tolerance and
breadth of view. But these centuries were followed by six
or seven centuries of decline, when the Muslim world went
into almost total decay, political, economic, cultural and
social. Bigotry, intolerance and obscurantism became rampant.
The door of *ijtihad* was declared shut. No scholar was allowed
to form a new opinion; he was required to adopt the opinion of
one or other of the ancient jurists. It is to this later
period, the "dark ages" as they are termed, that the present
Egyptian laws on Personal Status belong and it is against
this heavy burden of bigotry and suffocation that modern
Egyptian reformers, beginning with the great Egyptian Sheik
Muhammad 'Abduh (d. 1905) have been struggling since the
late decades of the nineteenth century. They have been
campaigning for the reopening of the door of *ijtihad* in
order to be able to go beyond the opinions of the ancient
jurists which -- this must be reiterated -- were mere
fallible human opinions, not meant to be final and immutable;
and in order to be able to form new opinions that may be
more suitable for the vastly changed conditions of modern
times. They want, especially, to change the no longer suitable
provisions of Egypt's laws on Personal Status. For it is
these fossil provisions, governing as they do the relationships of husbands and wives, parents and children, and
affecting every man, woman and child in their daily life
that cause the greatest amount of suffering and the brutaliza-
tion of Egyptian society, affecting not women only, but the
children too, and even the men, were they but to recognize
the heavy price they pay for maintaining their vaunted
masculine superiority through these cruel and inequitable
laws.

The defects of these laws are many, and they include
defects in the provisions on guardianship, custody,
marriageable age, alimony, maintenance, sustenance and
obedience. To dwell only on the two cardinal sins, of
wilful polygamy and a man's unilateral right of divorce:
Egyptian reformers since Muhammad 'Abduh have shown up
the flagrant inequity and the enormity of the damage they
do to individuals and to Egyptian society and the nation
as a whole. Like Muhammad 'Abduh, they have demonstrated

that neither the Qur'an nor the *Sunna* established polygamy
or unilateral divorce as an unconditional right for men to
use at will. Each is heavily weighted with severe limitations and considered in both Qur'an and *Sunna* as evils to
be strenuously shunned and only to be resorted to in cases
of extreme necessity and in order to avoid a greater evil.
There are today few scholars who do not admit this fact,
but Egyptian conservatives are still loath to effect the
required reform by enforceable law. They prefer to leave
it to the conscience of the individual and to depend on
education, religious enlightenment and moral exhortation
to induce men to stop abusing these two privileges.

* * *

New laws on Personal Status have been promulgated in
six Arab states, the Democratic Republic of Yemen, Iraq,
Jordan, Morocco, Syria and Tunisia,[6] placing restrictions
varying in number and extent, on polygamy and unilateral
divorce and specifying penalties, varying in severity, for
their infringement. In the rest of the Arab world these
two privileges are totally unrestricted and left entirely
to the will of the man. When one contemplates this fact,
one is struck by an amazing phenomenon: the situation does
not accord with the adknowledged civilizational development
of the Arab countries. Would one not, for instance, have
expected Egypt to be one of the six countries to change;
indeed, to be the foremost of all the Arab states in the
field of reform? Yet Egypt, whose intellectuals and
scholars were the first to discuss reform and call for it,
remains one of the most backward in this field, with no
restrictions whatever being placed on either of the two
privileges.

The Iraqi Law on Personal Status, issued in 1959,
forbids a man to marry more than one wife except by permission of a judge, who must first ascertain the applicant's
financial ability to support more than one wife and also
verify that there is a legitimate ground for making the new
marriage (financial ability is not enough: the first wife
must be barren, or physically incapacitated and thus unable to cohabit, or otherwise unable to give the husband
his conjugal rights). Moreover, if there is fear that the
husband will not treat each wife with equal justice,
polygamy is not allowed. (This is in implementation of
the proviso in Verse 3 of *Sura* 4). Any man who contracts
a marriage in violation of these requirements faces punishment, either by imprisonment for a term of up to one year,
or by a fine of up to one hundred dinars, or by both
penalties. Divorce must also be by decree of a judge,
or it is legally null and void and the marriage is considered still binding (i.e., the man must go on paying
maintenance to his divorced wife; she still inherits from
him and enjoys all other rights of a wife, except

cohabitation). The Tunisian Law of 1956 is the most far-reaching, however. It does not allow polygamy under any circumstances, and a man who commits it is imprisoned for a term of up to five years and his polygamous marriage is not legally recognized. Divorce can only be effected by decree of a judge, who must first attempt to reconcile the husband and wife (in fulfillment of the Qur'anic injunction in Verse 35 of *Sura* 4). Otherwise, the divorce is not legally recognized and the man must pay financial compensation to the wife, and all her other rights in maintenance and inheritance, etc., are considered still standing.

In Egypt, however, the two Laws of 1920 and 1929 are still operative, placing no kind of restriction or condition or penalty, neither financial nor by imprisonment. Several attempts to reform the laws have been made, but they have all ended in defeat. Thus Egypt -- the country that gave birth to the most ancient civilization in the world; the first country in the East to open its arms to modern civilization; the birthplace of Sheik Muhammad 'Abduh; the land of the great libertarian, republican, democratic, socialist Revolution of 1952 -- is still governed, in matters of Personal Status, by laws enacted in the era of feudo-capitalism, imperialist subjugation, monarchical and Pasha-rule.

* * *

The complex reasons for this state of affairs may be summarized as follows. The revolutionary regime which arose in July 1952 was immediately and continually faced with many obstacles that had to be surmounted and campaigns that had to be undertaken. It had to drive out the dissolute monarchy; abolish the corrupt party system; rehabilitate and re-arm the neglected army; evacuate the colonial army of occupation; curb the worst abuses of the feudo-capitalist order, and lay the foundations of a socialist, or semi-socialist, society. All these political, military and economic struggles engaged most of its energy and diverted it from Egypt's cultural liberation, which it almost totally neglected. There was still another reason. All these campaigns had earned for Egypt the suspicion and hostility of several other Arab countries, and its enemies were eager to use any weapon to discredit Egypt. The revolutionary regime felt extra sensitive to the accusation of religious heresy. It was extraordinarily fearful of allowing any intellectual dispute that might raise that dread accusation. The result was the imposition of restrictions on freedom of discussion which were heavier than those in the preceding regime. For its courage in political and economic reform, it paid the penalty of cowardice in the intellectual arena.

It was not until the early sixties that the government responded to the remonstrances of Egyptian intellectuals who, rejoicing in the 1952 Revolution, welcoming it and

placing their hopes on it for radical intellectual liberation, religious reform, ethical transformation and social
progress, had started a number of campaigns, one of them
being to try to convince the government of the pressing
need to reform the Law on Personal Status. The government
appointed a special committee to review the law, and
Egyptian intellectuals looked eagerly to the committee for
the fulfillment of their hopes. The committee spent years
without producing the expected proposed reforms. When it
finally came out with its proposals, towards the end of
1966, these were found to contain none of the major reforms
advocated for so long. The committee did propose the abolition of the iniquitous *Bayt al-ta'a*, (House of Obedience)
by which a wife who had left her husband could be compulsorily
brought back to him by the police. But apart from a few
other, immaterial, modifications, their proposals preserved
and consecrated the unjust and harmful usages inherited from
the pre-revolutionary era.

The reason for this state of affairs becomes clear when
one studies the composition of the committee. Most of them
were die-hard reactionaries, or at least rigid conservatives
(see *Al-Ahram*, April 9, 1967). A couple of them indeed
supported women's emancipation, but most were against it.
One of them even boasted unashamedly that he was *'aduw li
al-mar' a* (an enemy of women).

One witnessed an astounding phenomenon: a committee
appointed by the revolutionary, emancipatory government to
reform the Law on Personal Status had a majority of members
who did not believe in the emancipation of women. That it
should contain some conservatives one can accept, since all
points of view should be given the right of expression, but
that these formed the overwhelming majority, in revolutionary,
libertarian Egypt, was astounding. And this despite the
fact that among the *'ulama* themselves there is a by no means
negligible number of sheiks with a sufficiency of breadth
of view and liberality of spirit, in the tradition of
Muhammad 'Abduh.

The proverbial straw that broke the back of long-
suffering Egypt was the fact that the only woman selected
to represent Egyptian women on the committee was not chosen
from among the many who support emancipation but from among
those whose attitude to the feminist movement fluctuated
between negligent unconcern and strong, outspoken hostility.
She opposed the view of those few members of the committee
who proposed that a man's right to polygamy should be
restricted -- and it was not even proposed to cancel that
right altogether, as Tunisia had legislated fourteen years
earlier, but that it be restricted within certain limits!
She argued that she was concerned with the interest of the
family above all else. Little wonder, then, that the
conservatives on the committee praised her as *sayyida
'aqila wa muttazina*, a wise and well-balanced lady.

The committee's report was the clearest evidence of

the cardinal error of confusing *al-Shari'a* (the Muslim Path)
with *al-Fiqh* (ancient Jurisprudence). When some of the
committee members were asked why they objected to the condition that divorce must be effected in front of a judge,
they replied that this restriction did not occur in the
sources of Muslim legislation. And yet, the counter-
proposal did not even require the concurrence of a judge,
as in the Tunisian and Iraqi Laws, but only made the modest
requirement that the divorce should take place before a
judge, to enable the judge to attempt the reconciliation
made obligatory by Verse 35 of *Sura* 4.

* * *

The disappointment and bitterness of the Egyptian
intelligentsia was great. They subjected the report to
slashing criticism in the early months of 1967 and called
for a law more courageous in reforming the pernicious abuses
and more in keeping with the liberating spirit of the 1952
Revolution.[7] They kept up their campaign until they began
to see some signs of success -- the news reached them that
the government was on the point of issuing a proposed law
more in line with their demands. But suddenly the disas-
trous war of June 1967 broke out and both government and
intelligentsia became engrossed in other worries. The
abortion of that emancipatory campaign, when it had so
nearly succeeded, was one of the most calamitous results
of that inauspicious Six Day War.
Egyptian intellectuals resumed the campaign in the
early seventies, freshly encouraged by the political and
cabinet change that had then taken place. They were also
encouraged by the fact that the Ministry of Social Affairs
was headed by a woman, one of the best educated and most
courageous proponents of the cause of women's emancipation,
Dr. 'A'isha Ratib. Their optimism was redoubled by the
splendid, though indeed limited, military victory of
October 1973, which gave an enormous uplift to Egypt's
morale and breached the bastion of despondency and defeatism.
On March 26, 1974, the Ministry of Social Affairs published
a proposed new Law on Personal Status. It did not meet
all the reformers' demands, but it was a step forward.
These were its chief proposals:

   1. A husband can effect divorce only in front of a
   judge, who must first attempt to reconcile husband and
   wife. Otherwise, though the divorce will be considered
   legal, the husband will be punished by a term of imprisonment of between one week to three months, or by a fine
   of ten pounds to one hundred pounds.
   2. A husband shall not legally take another wife
   except by permission of the court, and the court shall
   not grant this permission except after an investigation
   to ensure the existence of a legitimate reason and the

husband's ability to provide good treatment and maintenance to each wife. Otherwise, a term of imprisonment
or a fine or both shall be imposed on the husband.
    3. A divorced wife, in addition to the classical
maintenance (which is for a single year's upkeep) shall be
entitled to compensation, to be determined by the judge
according to the husband's circumstances; up to one year's
maintenance for each five years of the marriage, but not
exceeding a maximum of five years' maintenance.

A quick comparison with the Iraqi or the Tunisian Law
promulgated fifteen to eighteen years earlier, will show
the modesty of this proposed law. However, Egyptian reformers were prepared to accept it as better than nothing.
Yet, no sooner was it published than all the forces of
reaction gathered together to attack it virulently. They
resorted to threats of assassination and organized street
demonstrations. And whom did they threaten and against
whom did they direct their screaming marches? Against the
People's Assembly (*Majlis al-Sha'b*), the highest legislative
authority under the Egyptian Constitution. Rapidly did the
government retreat in the face of this vociferous furor.
    And thus, once more, was the revolutionary, republican,
emancipatory, socialist, democratic government of Egypt;
the government that had been bold enough to undertake the
liquidation of the "centers of power" and to embark on the
risky war of October 1973, too weak to withstand the pressure
of the forces of intellectual, religious and social reaction.
    The modest proposed law -- the very minimum that can
serve any useful purpose -- was heard of no more. Instead,
on August 10, 1976, a new proposed law was published. It
would have been farcical if it had not been so tragic.
A husband may divorce his wife at will, without resort to
a court of justice, the only requirement being that he
inform his wife that he has divorced her and not effect
the divorce without her knowledge (as some husbands do in
order to escape from the one year's maintenance obligation).
He may marry a second wife (and a third and a fourth, of
course), the only condition being that he inform the first
wife, who will then have the right to sue for divorce and
will obtain it if the judge concurs, but not otherwise.
In case of either divorce or polygamy there is no punishment
for the man, neither by fine, compensation nor imprisonment.
Punishment is, however, inflicted on the wife who sues for
divorce if she is found to be the offending party in the
conjugal strife, in which case she must pay her husband a
sum of money to be determined according to her financial
circumstances. If the husband is proved to be the one
who has maltreated his spouse, she is entitled to obtain a
divorce, but no compensation. What happens to her after
the divorce, how she will survive at the end of the mandatory year of maintenance, are questions with which the
proposed law does not concern itself.

In the light of this situation, one may well ask
whether Egypt goes one step forward or several steps backward year after year. The answer lies in the fact that the
governmental authority which made this proposed law was
not the Ministry of Social Affairs but the Ministry of
Justice, which wrenched the whole project from the former,
as if punishing it for its ambitious reformatory spirit.

The enormity of the proposed law's cruelty and injustice
is too heinous to contemplate. Since then there has been no
change in legislation and there has been no change in the
climate of opinion, or in the attitude of Egypt's ruling
authorities. The reformists have not given up, however.
They have been using every opportunity to impress the
authorities with the great error, indeed the extreme political
danger, of their lack of courage in face of the forces of
bigotry and reaction. Our revolutionary regime has done
wonders in the military, political and economic spheres,
but it still lags behind considerably in the sphere of intellectual reform. Yet without this reform, all its achievements are evanescent and run the grave risk of being toppled.
Unless a people's outdated intellectual attitudes and frame
of mind is changed; its way of looking at life and reacting
to life's events; its archaic body of preconceptions and
assumptions; its no longer suitable scale of values and
the code of ethics governing its mores -- unless these
issues are freed from the intolerance and moral obtuseness
of centuries of stagnation and obscurantism, all other
emancipatory and progressive acts will be but ramshackle
towers built on shifting sands.

* * *

These arguments have been employed by reformers for
many years. But a new equation has been introduced, that
makes it highly likely that they will be listened to at
last. The magnitude of this new development has dazzled
the entire world, and it is the bold and unprecedented peace
venture undertaken by the President of Egypt to Israel in
November 1977. The President himself lost no time in alert-
ing Egyptians to the fact that this venture was no mere
political gesture; it was the ringing of a bell heralding
the start of a new era, which he called *marhalat al-bina'*
al hadari, the stage of civilizational reconstruction.
He desired peace in order to be able to devote attention
and direct efforts to Egypt's long-neglected reconstruction.
He will allow nothing, he declared in December 1977, to
divert him from that goal. With great irony, he con-
demned that slogan which has been so misused to quell any
call for internal reform: *la sawt ya'lu fawq sawt al-ma'raka,*
no voice to be raised above the voice of the battle.

This was no general and vague declaration of intent:
President Sadat began to spell out the various fields in
which civilizational reconstruction was overdue. In a

public address delivered in Port Said on March 1, 1978
he spoke out in the strongest and most uncompromising terms
ever uttered by a man in so eminent an official position or
anywhere near it. Discussing his project for social security
legislation for all Egyptians, he unexpectedly declared that
the word *fard* (individual) does not mean man alone, but
woman also. Indeed, he said, women may be more in need of
that security, in view of the lamentable behavior of some
men, who abandon a wife after twenty or thirty years of
living together, with no insurance at all to protect her.
He declared his determination to issue a law that ensures,
for women, recognition of their full human stature. Such a
law, he asserted, does not contravene the *Shari'a*, as some,
who attempt to frighten every reformer away claim. *Ghalat!
Ghalat!* (Wrong! Wrong!) he cried out. He warned against
the continuing misuse of religion to inflict injustices that
are far removed from religion; the use of religion as a mask
behind which a man hides his vindictive desire to maintain
his absolute supremacy over women, forcing her into servitude,
making her the creature of his whim, a mere vessel and
purchasable commodity. What kind of atmosphere is this, he
asked, in which to bring up the children, the coming generations of Egypt? "Therefore," he announced:

> I direct my government speedily to issue a Law on Personal
> Status that would ensure security and protection for the
> Egyptian woman. This is what is demanded by religion, both
> Islam and Christianity, in both word and spirit. *El mar' a
> lazim takhud kull huquqha*: Woman must have all her rights.

Was this but a sop thrown to the clamoring feminists?
Anwar al-Sadat's sincerity was all too apparent. His
expressions were too fervent to be false, and if this is
considered a value judgment by those skeptical intellectuals
who have been much too often sold on pipe dreams, objective
reasons also exist to instil confidence and reassurance.
The President's promise was definite and clear-cut, allowing
for no ambiguity. In the directive he issued to his government he even stated a time limit: the required Law on
Personal Status had to be drawn up before the end of the
parliamentary session. Anwar al-Sadat, despite his enthusiastic personality, is not given to reckless pronouncements.
He is known to be a careful thinker who plans his moves with
great caution: "shrewd" and "deep" are adjectives that
have been applied to him. He must have realized the terrible
loss of face, even the political peril, he would be risking
were he to go back on those clear-cut words. He must have
had the fullest determination to fulfill his promise.
It is my belief that President Sadat is unshakably
committed to his policy of peace and of civilizational
development under the aegis of peace. He has several times
declared that he has chosen his destiny (*ikhtart gadari*)
and will not shirk the consequences -- be they what they may.

The reconstruction of Egypt, the liberation of Egyptian
society, the bringing about of the needed progress, cannot
be achieved so long as women are treated so ignobly and
denied their full human dignity. If women are subjugated,
the entire society is kept in slavishness and servitude.
The sons of an enslaved mother imbibe the milk of servility
at her breast. A husband who degrades his wife abases his
own manliness and inflicts an irreparable wound on his own
dignity, no matter how much he tries to hide it by strutting
about and flaunting his masculinity. The whole society
wallows in the mire of abjectness and degradation.

* * *

Will the educated women of Egypt cooperate in Egypt's
reconstruction if they are still denied their basic human
rights? They will not. And without their wholehearted
cooperation, that attempt will end in a fiasco. The educated
women of Egypt are angry and their patience is wearing thin.
To underestimate their potential political power, even under
present circumstances, is a mistake. And that power will,
inevitably, grow by leaps and bounds. As one Egyptian
woman has said:

> The rebuilding of the Egyptian human being is the first
> challenge confronting Egypt now. But the men alone cannot
> meet this challenge; women have a by no means lesser role.
> It is one campaign for the building of a sound and well-
> balanced society. But if we wish woman to participate
> with all her energy and capacity in the battles posed by
> the challenge, we must first accord her equal treatment,
> and we must give her the complete conviction that our
> society believes in her stature and her role in the
> society. We must accord her her rights under the liberal
> *Shari'a.* [8]

The speaker was none other than Mrs. Jehan al-Sadat.
And she was not just "plugging the official line." This
is no recent idea of hers, born of the initiative for peace
and internal reconstruction. She has long been known for
her open and courageous championing of the feminist movement. At a meeting held by the Union of Journalists to
celebrate Woman's Day on March 8, 1974, she declared,
boldly and forthrightly:

> The Revolution has, indeed, recognized the political
> rights and labor rights of the Egyptian woman. That
> recognition, however, was an acknowledgment and not a
> bounteous grant; an acknowledgment that came as the
> fruit of a long struggle waged by the Egyptian woman
> in our contemporary history. But it still remains for
> the Egyptian woman to have all her human rights, her
> rights as a wife and a mother, within the framework

of the liberal Islamic *Shari'a*, in accord with belief in
the divine teaching, and in step with the exigencies of
the modern age.

I believe that the framework of the liberal *Shari'a*
is broad enough to allow woman all her legitimate rights,
in fullest accord with the divine teaching, but not in slavish
confinement within the limitations of ancient Jurisprudence;
in step with the needs of the modern age, which, I believe,
the *Shari'a* is dynamic enough to meet.

POSTSCRIPT: APRIL 1979

The directive issued by President Sadat to his government in 1978 has not yet been implemented. For this, yet
another failure, a plausible excuse may be offered. The
peace negotiations with Israel proved much more difficult
than was expected when the President made his promise, still
in the glow of his historic visit to Jerusalem. However,
there is cause for renewed hope. Following the signing of
the treaty, President Sadat has made several speeches in
which he has answered his Arab critics and explained Egypt's
dire need for peace in order to carry out a multiplicity
of pressing internal reforms. One of the most urgent, he
stated in three of these speeches, is reforming the legal
status of the Egyptian women. In his latest speech, for
instance, at his meeting with the students and faculty of
Ain Shams University in Cairo (as reported in *al-Ahram* the
following day -- April 17, 1979) he declared:

> The rights of women cannot remain suppressed as a result
> of a rigid interpretation of religion. Woman must achieve
> her full rights, if society is to progress on two firm
> feet.

NOTES

1. Robert N. Bellah, in a paper entitled "Islamic Tradition
and the Problems of Modernization," presented at the Seminar on
Tradition and Change in the Middle East, held at Harvard University,
January 16, 1968.
2. *Ibid.*
3. Elizabeth Defeis, in a paper presented at the Open University
Seminar on Law and Change, sponsored by the American University in
Cairo and the National Center for Social and Criminological Research,
Cairo, April 1978.
4. Mr. Robinson is Business Manager of the American University
in Cairo.
5. See the classical lexicon, *al-Qamus al-Muhit*.
6. To these countries must be added Somaliland, which has issued
a reformed Law on Personal Status, restricting polygamy and unilateral divorce.

7. See, for example, how 'Ali Hamdi al Jammal, the editor
of *al-Ahram* described their anger and disappointment, (*al-Ahram*,
April 15, 1967).

8. Mrs. Jehan al-Sadat, in her presentation to the Seminar
on the Civilizational Challenge (nadwat altahaddi al-hadari),
January 16, 1978.

9
Recently Approved Amendments to Egypt's Law on Personal Status

Aziza Hussein

In June, 1979, the first Amendments in 50 years in the
Law on Personal Status in Egypt were approved by the
country's National Assembly, in confirmation of a Presidential
Decree which had passed them on to the Assembly in the form
of a package deal. They were the first such revisions to be
passed in 50 years. The procedure followed in guiding them
through the Assembly was in accordance with the new Egyptian
Constitution and was designed to avoid polemics and fili-
buster during the debate over this very sensitive issue.

The Amendments left unchanged the right of the Egyptian
husband to divorce and to marry more than one wife. However,
they balanced these privileges with responsibilities, within
the religious framework, which had never before been given
legal expression.

The Amendments were carefully formulated to forestall
any unnecessary confrontation with conservative religious
elements. The extreme fundamentalists could not be won
over, anyway, being totally opposed to the very principle of
codification. In their view, the Shari'a (Islamic jurisprudence)--being based on the Holy Qur'an, the Sunna and
the interpretations of the old theological schools--is in
itself sufficient as reference and guide for the judges,
as well as for the individual conscience. Their point of
view is completely at variance with present-day thinking of
social reformers who are concerned about the social and
psychological effects of the old laws on the conditions of
woman and the well-being of the family.

Fundamentalists views apart, all previous efforts to
amend the Law on Personal Status had foundered over the
attempt to curtail, by legal means, the right of the husband
to divorce his wife at will, and to marry more than one
woman. That right was considered to be God-given and as
such should not be restricted or tampered with.

There have always been divergent views on this issue

among the religious authorities, but somehow the conservative
elements had been able to exercise enough influence to keep
the laws unchanged.

The pragmatic approach demonstrated in the Amendments
submitted to the National Assembly in a decree from President
Sadat gained the support of various women's groups, among them
our Cairo Family Planning Association. Two years earlier,
our organization had launched the first systematic effort in
support of amending the Law on Personal Status. It organized
meetings and seminars, making judicious use of the mass media,
and it drafted a comprehensive model for a family code.

It was the first time that this question had been tackled
by a non-governmental organization, on a long-term basis and
with appropriate funding (from IPPF), staffing and expertise.
Equally important, it was the first time that a link had been
forged between the security of the woman within the family,
and family planning as such.

When the long-awaited Amendments were made public, they
were by no means a carbon copy of the code drafted by CFPA.
There were many omissions that, at first glance, caused some
disappointment. Soon, however, this group that had played
a constructive role in campaigning for change, realized that
the Amendments represented good interim legislation, which
addressed itself to some very basic problems without creating
undue friction and confrontation on the social, religious or
political levels.

In fact, President Sadat had even succeeded in winning
over the religious leadership, which spoke up in favor of
the Amendments, in such a manner as to surprise even those
who had themselves campaigned for change. The three most
influential leaders--the Head of Al Azhar Mosque, the Grand
Mufti and the Minister of Wakfs--were jointly interviewed on
television in an hour-long appearance during which they gave
full endorsement to the new legislation, offering religious
justification for the changes.

There were rumblings, of course, from the fundamentalists
and from other traditionalists in the rural areas. Defenders
of male superiority from the lower middle class complained
that man was becoming the victim of discrimination.

These same groups had been equally displeased over the
new legislation which gives women a quota of 30 seats in
the National Assembly--another innovation by President Sadat
in his efforts to improve the status of Egyptian women.

What, then, were the Amendments and what were the
particular issues to which they addressed themselves?

The main grievances against the Personal Status Law
centered on the arbitrary and unilateral rights of the husband to divorce his wife, and his absolute and unquestioned
right to marry more than one wife, as well as the laws re-
lating to parental rights and obligations.

As for the laws regarding legal capacity, property
rights, the right of the wife to retain her maiden name--
those had always been a source of pride to Muslims, since

under Islam, women had been given these rights centuries before they were acquired by women in non-Muslim countries. These laws remain unchanged.

DIVORCE AND CUSTODY

The husband continues to retain the right to divorce his wife without recourse to the courts, the reason given being that a court action would lead to the disclosure of private family affairs and might even result in a scandal which would be harmful to everyone concerned. Of course, religious considerations are also a factor.

The procedures that must be followed, under the new Amendments, place certain restrictions on the man:

1. The husband must register his divorce before witnesses at a Registrar's Office, and his wife must be officially and immediately informed. Failure on his part to inform her make him liable to a penalty. No such restrictions existed before.

2. The divorced wife is entitled to an alimony equivalent to one year's maintenance, plus compensation equivalent to 2 years' maintenance which could be increased by the court in cases of extra damage or the termination of a long marriage. The first installments of these sums are to be paid automatically to the wife, via the Nasser Bank, which is empowered to collect them by various means from the husband. (Under the previous law, the wife was entitled to an alimony equivalent to one year's maintenance.)

3. The husband who divorces his wife must guarantee her a home, if she has custody of his children. He must either find them a home, or move out himself.

4. As for custody, the divorced wife automatically gains custody of her children, to the age of 9 for the boy and 12 for the girl, subject to extensions, by a court decision, to 15 for the boy and until marriage for the girl. The previous law gave the mother custody of her children only to the age of 7 and 9 for the boy and girl respectively, subject to extensions to 9 and 11.

5. As for the wife's right to obtain a divorce, to which she was entitled under the old law by a court decision, on the basis of specific grounds, the new Amendments fix a deadline of 9 months for "court mediation." If attempts by the court to reconcile the couple fail, the divorce is granted without further delay. This has resolved one of the most burning issues and has narrowed the gap between men's and women's rights in divorce.

POLYGAMY

Polygamy has long been a cause of outrage and symbol of degradation for women, especially among the educated class, even though, admittedly, the number of polygamous marriages is negligible in practice. The very existence of the man's right to marry another wife, however, has had a damaging psychological effect on women, especially in the lower socio-economic strata. Moreover, the husband could remarry without having to make this fact known to his wife, before or after his marriage to a second woman.

The Amendments do not restrict a man's right to marry more than one woman, but place practical constraints on the man. The husband now has to notify his wife of his intention to marry another woman. He must also inform his wife-to-be of his present marital status. In fact, secrecy was the major factor in making polygamy relatively easy to practice in certain circumstances. Furthermore, the first wife is entitled to a court divorce within a year of learning of her husband's marriage to another woman. In such a court decision, the second marriage is regarded as damaging to the first wife and entitles her to compensation.

RIGHT TO WORK

Another important and new aspect of the Amendments is the confirmation of the woman's right to work. This right is not contingent anymore on the husband's approval.

In the past, a woman who worked against her husband's wishes was legally placed in the category of *nashez*, meaning "disobedient." As such, she lost her right to maintenance by her husband, who had the right to neglect her. The wife's right to a court divorce was very much jeopardized by the "disobedient" status. The new Amendments have rectified this irregularity in the old law.

10
The Problem of Sovereignty in an Ithna Ashari ("Twelver") Shi'i State

Roger M. Savory

In the West, the struggles between Church and State happened so long ago that many people have forgotten them. But the struggle was real and bloody and went on for centuries. In 1170, Thomas Becket, Archbishop of Canterbury, was murdered in his own cathedral by the agents of the king. Nearly four centuries later, Cardinal Wolsey, the most powerful man in England after the king, had the good fortune to die of natural causes as he traveled back to London to face the King and the block. Henry VIII, determined to smash the power and prosperity of the clergy, dissolved the monasteries and confiscated their wealth. After the king had won his battle with the Church, the people had to win their battle against the king, and that took several more centuries. The struggle between "Church" and "State" in Iran has been going on in an acute form only for some eighty years. To expect instant solutions to the problems is to be unrealistic in the extreme.

In Islam, however, is it not true that there is no division between what in the Western tradition we call "Church" and "State," between *regnum* and *sacerdotium*, the realm of the king and the realm of the priest, as they were termed in medieval Christendom? This is indeed the theory. "In Islam the state provides the frame within which Islam with its demands on the 'community of believers' (the *umma*) and on the individual Muslim must be lived."[1] What distinguishes an Islamic state from, say, a Greek city state, or a modern nation state in the West, is "the religious ordering of state and society."[2] The basis and

The Problem of Sovereignty in an Ithna Ashari ("Twelver") Shi'i State is reprinted from *Middle East Review*, Vol. XI, No. 4, Summer, 1979.

center of the state in Islam is the *shari'a*, the religious
law, which is based in the first instance on the Qur'an,
the revealed Word of God; consequently, the *shari'a* has
assumed the status of a part of divine revelation.

The head of the first Muslim state was the Prophet
Muhammad, who was not only a prophet but the political
leader and law-giver of the first Muslim community at
Medina. He was succeeded as leader of the Islamic state
by a long line of caliphs (Arabic *khalifa*: "successor"),
who were the titular heads of the Islamic state for over
six hundred years until the extinction of the historical
caliphate by the Mongols in 1258 A.D. The classic formulation of the functions of the caliph is that of al-Mawardi
(who died in 1058):

> The defense and maintenance of religion, the decision of
> legal disputes, the protection of the territory of Islam,
> the punishment of wrong-doers, the provision of troops
> for guarding the frontiers, the waging of *jihad* ("holy
> war") against those who refused to accept Islam or submit
> to Muslim rule, the organization and collection of taxes,
> the payment of salaries and the administration of public
> funds, the appointment of competent officials, and lastly,
> personal attention to the details of government."[3]

Ibn Khaldun, writing in the 14th century, agreed:

> The Caliph is the representative of the Prophet, the
> exponent of the divinely-inspired law (*shari'a*), and
> his functions are the protection of religion and the
> government of the world.[4]

By the time that al-Mawardi was writing, however,
and indeed from the middle of the 10th century, this theory
no longer obtained in practice. Temporal rulers styling
themselves "amir" and "sultan" had stripped the Caliph of
most of his political, military and administrative powers,
and left him little beyond a symbolic function as the
Defender of the Faith who legitimized the rule of the amirs
and sultans. The jurists worked hard to clothe what they
called the "emirate by seizure" (*imarat al-istila*) with
the mantle of legality, and eventually, in the words of
Sir Hamilton Gibb, "saved the principle of unity (in the
Islamic state) by the device of a sort of concordat, the
caliph recognizing the governor's sole control of policy
and civil administration of religious affairs."[5]

With the aim of preserving the institution of the
caliphate, and thus the unity of the Islamic state, the
jurists were prepared to go to great lengths to accommodate
juridical theory to political reality. The overriding
consideration was the unity of the state. To preserve
this, the jurists were prepared to condone the usurpation
of the political and military power of the caliphs by amirs

and sultans. To the jurists, anything, even tyranny, was
preferable to anarchy. All based this view on the key
Qur'anic text (IV: 59/62): "O ye who believe! Obey God,
and obey His Messenger, and those who are in authority
among you." The difficulty of identifying "who is in
authority among you" has, of course, caused many problems.

* * *

By the 14th century, therefore, an accommodation between the theory and practice of government in Islamic
states had to a large extent been reached -- *but only in
Sunni states*. Iran is not a Sunni state; it is a Shi'i
state, that is, a state in which the Shi'i form of Islam
is the official religion. Article 1 of the Supplementary
Fundamental Law of 7 October 1907, the second of the two
documents which together make up the Iranian Constitution,
reads: "The official religion of Persia is Islam, according to the orthodox Ja'fari doctrine of the Ithna Ashariyya
(Church of the Twelve Imams), which faith the Shah of
Persia must profess and promote."[6] The major schism in Islam
is between Sunni Muslims, so called because they follow the
sunna or traditional practice of the Prophet Muhammad and
of the early Muslim community, and Shi'i Muslims. In the
world today the ratio of Sunnis to Shi'is is approximately
five to one. Iran, whose population is about 90 percent
Shi'i, is the only state today in which Ithna Ashari Shi'ism
is the official religion. Iran's position in the Middle East
is, therefore, unique in this as in other respects, and one
of Iran's fundamental problems is peculiar to it alone.

This is the problem of sovereignty and legitimacy in
a Shi'i state. By problem of sovereignty, I mean: "Who
is it in the state who has the final authority in decision-
making?" By problem of legitimacy, I mean: "How does that
person or group which possesses sovereignty, that is, the
power to make and carry out decisions, justify the existence
of the state, and what is the basis of his or its claim to
exercise this sovereign power?" No solution to these
fundamental questions of sovereignty and legitimacy has
been reached in the nearly five hundred years since Iran
first became a Shi'i state in 1501. Shi'i jurists have
never attempted to accommodate juridical theory to political
practice as Sunni jurists did in the case of Sunni states.
Indeed, there was no reason why they should, since Shi'i
jurists regard any form of government other than that of
the Hidden Imam as illegitimate.

How was it that these fundamental questions of
sovereignty and legitimacy came to be more acute in a Shi'i
state than in Sunni states? The answer lies in the way in
which Shi'ism developed historically. These fundamental
problems did not originate with Mohammad Reza Shah, or even
with the Pahlavi dynasty, but had their origin nearly 1350
years ago on the death of the Prophet Muhammad in 632 A.D.

Muhammad, as I have already said, was not only a Prophet,
but also the political leader and lawgiver of the first
Muslim community or state. Sunnis believe that he died
without designating a successor, or Caliph. The leaders
of the Muslim community chose one of their number to
succeed him, but not everyone agreed with their choice.
Some maintained that Muhammad, before his death, had
designated 'Ali, his cousin and son-in-law, to succeed him.
Thus was born the Shi'at 'Ali, the "Party of 'Ali," consisting of those who supported the claims of 'Ali to the
caliphate; such persons were termed "Shi'is." It should
be noted that the Shi'i movement was thus from its inception
a party in opposition to the regime in power. Instead of
giving their loyalty to the ruling Sunni Caliph, Shi'is
gave their allegiance to the descendants of 'Ali in the
male line, whom they termed "Imams."

Most of the early Shi'is were Arabs, but the Iranians
soon adopted the movement as an ideal vehicle for the
expression of their protests at being treated as second-
class citizens in a largely Arab empire. To the political
stem of Shi'ism, the Iranians grafted the legend that
Husayn, the younger son of 'Ali, married Shahrbanu, the
daughter of Yazdigird III, the last monarch of the Sasanid
dynasty overthrown by the Arabs. In this way, Shi'ism
was lifted out of its purely Islamic context and linked
with the Iranian historical, traditional and nationalist
sentiments. The son of Husayn and Shahrbanu, 'Ali Zayn
al-'Abidin, "united in his person the double chain of
imamate and Persian royalty."[7]

In 680 A.D., troops of the Sunni Caliph killed the
Third Shi'ite Imam, Husayn, the younger son of 'Ali, on the
field of Karbala in Iraq. By this act they gave the Shi'i
movement a martyr-figure with a powerful and lasting
emotive effect. After Karbala, Shi'ism ceased to be merely
a political movement and became a politico-religious movement which rapidly developed its distinctive theological
doctrines and system of religious law. The most distinctive theological and constitutional characteristic was
the doctrine of the Imamate, the political implications
of which underlie the turmoil in Iran today. The Imams
were credited with special and unique powers, the most
important of which was sinlessness or infallibility, a
doctrine which was developed in order to establish the
superiority of the Shi'i Imams over the Sunni Caliphs.
Infallibility was transmitted to the Imams from the
Prophet by virtue of their having inherited from him the
light of God.

> By becoming a partner in the Prophetic light, the Imam
> ...attained all sorts of transcendental distinctions such
> as the tree of prophethood, and the house of mercy; ...
> the keys of wisdom, the essence of knowledge, and locus
> of apostleship, the frequenting place of angels and

repositories of the secret of God.[8]

For 1300 years since the death of Husayn at Karbala, during the month of Muharram, Shi'is have commemorated his martyrdom with mourning processions which reach their climax on Ashura, the 10th of Muharram. The mourners have slashed themselves with knives, flagellated themselves with chains, and inserted padlocks into the skin of their chests, to demonstrate the overwhelming nature of their grief. At the same time, Muharram is marked by the performance of passion plays in which actors reenact the martyrdom of Husayn.

> What rains down? Blood! Who? The Eye! How? Day and
> Night! Why? From grief! What grief? The grief of the
> Monarch of Karbala! What was his name? Husayn! of Whose
> race? Ali's! Who was his mother? Fatima! Who was his
> grandsire? Mustafa! How was it with him? He fell a
> martyr! Where? In the Plain of Mariya! When? On the
> 10th of Muharram! Secretly? No, in public! Was he slain
> by night? No, by day! At what time? Noontide! Was his
> head severed from the throat? No, from the nape of the
> neck! Was he slain unthirsting? No! Did none give him
> to drink? They did! Who? Shimr! From what source?
> From the source of Death![9]

During the long centuries when Iran was dominated by foreign powers, the performance of the passion plays had a cathartic effect. "Even up to our day, Shi'ism, with its overtones and its aroma of opposition, of martyrdom, and of revolt, is matched quite well with the Persian character -- a character formed in the course of a long history which is very different from the history of other peoples nearby."[10]

In 260/873-4 the Twelfth Imam disappeared from earth and went into occultation. For about seventy years, until 940 A.D., the Hidden Imam was represented on earth by a series of four *vakils*, or deputies; this period is known as the "Lesser Occultation." The last of these four *vakils* died without designating a successor, merely observing that "the matter was now with God." This posed a serious problem for the Shi'i community. Since Shi'is believe that the Imam is the leader of the community, in other words, that government rests in his hands, the question was, "Who was to be the leader of the Shi'i community after the disappearance of the Twelfth Imam?" The consensus of the Shi'i community was that the Hidden Imam should be represented on earth by the Shi'i *mujtahids*, that is, the most eminent theologians and jurists of the time, who hold the title of "Ayatullah," or "Miraculous sign of God." Thus began the period of the "Greater Occultation," which is still in progress. The Hidden Imam became a messianic figure known as the Mahdi or "the Lord of the Age," whose return is expected and will herald the Day of Judgement and usher in an era of justice and equity on earth; various eschatological signs will portend this occurrence.

No problem of sovereignty arose as long as Shi'ism was operating in a Sunni milieu and subject to government by a Sunni ruler. The Sunni ruler was by Shi'i definition a usurper, and Shi'is often operated as an underground movement and were often subject to persecution. Eight centuries of political opposition increased the sense of martyrdom and revolt referred to earlier as characteristic of Shi'ism.

* * *

In 1501 the Safavid dynasty came to power in Iran and the whole scene changed. Shi'ism was proclaimed the official religion of the new state by its first ruler, Shah Isma'il I. But in the absence of the Hidden Imam, did not the government of affairs belong not to the Shah, but to the representatives of the Hidden Imam on earth, namely, the *mujtahids*? And if that was the case, was not the Shah a usurper? In terms of Shi'i theory, he most certainly was! So should he be overthrown? Yes, said some. No, said the majority. Why did they say no? Because they realized that, even if they conceded to the Shah the right to govern, their power in a state in which for the first time 'Twelver' Shi'ism had acquired political power would still be greatly enhanced. Why did Shah Isma'il take a step which was sure to precipitate such a challenge? He had no choice. It was militant Shi'ism which had constituted the dynamic religious ideology which had brought the Safavids to power. Further, there were political advantages: by making Shi'ism the official religion of the Safavid state, Shah Isma'il gave it territorial and political identity and clearly differentiated it from the powerful Sunni states on its borders, namely, the Ottoman empire in the west and the Uzberg state to the east.

Of course, the Safavid shahs, being no mean statesmen, had foreseen that there would be a challenge to their authority by the *mujtahids*. They succeeded in heading off trouble until the end of the 17th century, by a variety of measures which space does not permit me to go into here. The Huguenot jeweller Chardin, who was present at the coronation of Shah Sulayman in 1666, made a brilliantly perceptive analysis of the situation:

> *The clergy, and all the holy men of Iran, consider that*
> *rule by laymen was established by force and usurpation,*
> *and that civil government belongs by right to the sadr*
> *(the head of the religious institution) and to the*
> *Church...*but the more generally held opinion is that
> royalty, albeit in the hands of laymen, derives its
> institution and its authority from God; that the king
> takes the place of God and the prophets in the government of the people; that the *sadr*, and all other
> practitioners of the religious law, should not interfere

with the political institution; that their authority is
subject to that of the king, *even in matters of religion*.
This latter opinion prevails; the former opinion is held
only by the clergy and those whom they supervise; the
king and his ministers close the mouths of the clergy as
it pleases them, and force the clergy to obey them in
everything. In this way, *the spiritual is at the moment
completely subordinate to the temporal*.[11]

With the accession of Shah Sultan Husayn, however, in
1694, the Safavid shahs lost control of the religious
institution. The strikingly enhanced power of the *mujtahids*
were reflected in the creation of a new office, that of
mullabashi, or chief *mulla*. According to Amin Banani,
"some sources suggest a direct religious rule by means of
a concourse of *mujtahids* above the monarch."[11] Some
authorities, among them Browne and Malcolm, have seen in
the dominance of the ruling institution by the *mujtahids*
during the later Safavid period a major cause of the
decline of the state. It is undeniable that it was precisely
during that period that the Safavid state declined not only
in political and military power, but also in economic
prosperity. This certainly holds some lessons for today.

For two hundred years, then, the Safavids avoided any
major confrontation with the *mujtahids*, but, insofar as they
solved the fundamental problems of sovereignty and legitimacy in a Shi'ite state, they solved them on the level of
practical politics only, by a series of pragmatic policies
of considerable ingenuity. The problems have never been
solved to this day on the level either of political theory
or of ideology or of religious law. The dynasties which
succeeded the Safavids did not possess the means of controlling the religious institution which had been available
to the Safavids. The result was that, all through the 19th
century, and right down to recent times, we have had an
ongoing struggle for power between the shah, and the
mujtahids and the *ulama* generally, as to who is going to
rule the state. It was therefore inevitable that, as soon
as the Shah had left Iran, the *ulama* would transfer their
attack to the Bakhtiar administration because it represented
the residual authority of the Shah.

* * *

The overthrow of the Shah, of course, has solved nothing,
but merely released the centrifugal forces which are currently
threatening to tear the country apart. We have the parallel
systems of government of Khumayni and of Bazargan, and we
have the complete breakdown of the rule of law and the sus-
pension of human rights. The 1906-7 Constitution has been
abrogated *de facto*, since Article 35 of the Supplementary
Fundamental Law of 1907 states that:

> The sovereignty is a trust confided (as a Divine gift)
> by the people to the person of the Shah.[12]

We have the referendum of March 30-1, a referendum which
was farcical and meaningless even by the standards of
Iranian elections, in which almost 100 percent of those
who voted are said to have voted for the establishment
of an Islamic republic. It is said that a new Constitution
is being drawn up in secret. Khumayni and his supporters
will undoubtedly try and give constitutional authority to
the *de facto* power which they currently wield. The only
point at issue is whether the Westernized liberal intellectuals of the National Front (at the moment headed by Bazargan),
and the Marxists, will be able to muster sufficient determination and power to stop them.

     The prospects for Bazargan's survival are not bright.
He recently attempted to resign in protest against the continuing execution of Iranians by kangaroo courts, but was
contemptuously told by Khumayni to go back and get on with
the job -- and he did so. In the Iranian context, the loss
of face resulting from this incident means that Bazargan
can no longer be taken seriously. Even if Bazargan were a
stronger leader, however, it is inconceivable that the
present alliance between the liberal intellectuals and the
right-wing religious forces will be more than temporary.
These same forces came together in 1906 and succeeded in
extracting from Muzaffar al-Din Shah the Fundamental Law
which was the first of the two Iranian constitutional documents. The intellectuals on their own could never have
engineered the granting of a constitution; their influence
was not sufficiently strong. To achieve their goal, they
enlisted the support of the *ulama* and the bazaar merchants,
two powerful groups whose outlook and interests were to all
intents and purposes identical. Both these groups were
components of traditional Islamic society, and in no sense
were they reformist, modernizing or progressive. In order
to win the support of these groups, therefore, the intellectuals had to play down and gloss over the fact that the
democratic constitution they envisaged would necessarily
involve a substantial degree of secularization. The moment
that the *ulama* realized what the secularizing aims of the
intellectuals meant in concrete terms, many of them withdrew
their support from the Constitutionalist movement.

     In other words, the aims and objectives of the *ulama*
and of the intellectuals were and are poles apart. In order
to get basic democratic rights written into the Constitution,
the intellectuals had to make massive concessions to the
mujtahids. Only one of the three leading *mujtahids* in Iran
in 1907 was willing to support Article 8 of the Supplementary
Fundamental Law of 7 October, 1907, which read:

> The people of the Persian Empire are to enjoy equal rights
> before the Law.[13]

As a *quid pro quo* for this and similar Articles, the
intellectuals allowed the insertion of Article 2 of the
above Law, which called for the establishment of a Committee
of not less than five *mujtahids* empowered to "carefully
discuss and consider all matters" proposed in the newly-
elected National Consultative Assembly or Majlis, and to
"reject and repudiate, wholly or in part, any such proposal
which is at variance with the Sacred Laws of Islam, so that
it shall not obtain the title of legality."[14]   Clearly this
Article, had it been implemented, would have given the
mujtahids the power of veto over all legislation submitted
to parliament, and I am certain that Khumayni will press
for the inclusion of some such clause in the new Constitution.
     The Constitution of 1906-7, because it contained
inherent contradictions, satisfied neither the *mujtahids*
nor the intellectuals, and proved to be an unworkable
compromise. Within a year, the alliance between these two
groups, whose basic views were poles apart, dissolved.
It is only a matter of time before the present alliance
between Bazargan and Khumayni similarly dissolves, unless,
of course, the intellectuals this time are willing to submit
completely to the wishes of the *mujtahids*.

                              * * *

     To sum up, there is no theoretical basis in a "Twelver"
Shi'i state for an accommodation between the *mujtahids*,
the representatives of the Hidden Imam to whom government
on earth rightfully belongs, and any form of polity whatever, whether it be a monarchy or a republic. After all,
the *mujtahids* could have had a republic in 1924, when one
was offered to the country by Reza Khan. The *mujtahids*
rejected the idea, because they looked at what was happening
in Turkey and did not like what they saw, namely the
secularization of the state under Ataturk. If Khumayni
uses the term "Islamic republic," he does not use "republic"
in the sense in which it is used in the West. He means an
"Islamic state," which is a very different thing. An Islamic
state is one in which sovereignty belongs to God, not to the
people, and one which is based on the religious law of Islam.
     I will conclude by reiterating the central thesis of
this article, namely, that the fundamental problems of
sovereignty and legitimacy in Iran, in a 'Twelver' Shi'i
state, remain to be solved. The attempt by the Pahlavi
shahs to effect a gradual separation of religion from
politics has failed, at least in the short term. No
temporal ruler, whether he be called shah or president,
can ever gain legitimacy in the eyes of the *ulama*, but may
gain *de facto* acceptance as long as in their view he continues to promote the common weal. In the last analysis,
therefore, Iran is ungovernable unless the religious
institution, by which I mean the multifarious members of

the religious classes known loosely as the *ulama*, either
controls the political institution or is controlled by it.
Time alone will tell which it is to be. One thing is
certain: the *mujtahids* will not easily surrender the
dominant political position for which they have been fighting for nearly four centuries.

NOTES

1. E.I.J. Rosenthal, *The Role of the State in Islam: Theory
and the Medieval Practice*, a paper presented to the Colloquium on
Tradition and Change in the Middle East, Harvard 1968, p. 1.
2. *Ibid.*
3. *Encyclopaedia of Islam*, new edition, p. 884.
4. *Ibid.*, p. 855.
5. *"Al-Mawardi's 'Theory of the Caliphate',"* in *Studies on
the Civilization of Islam*, p. 162.
6. E. G. Browne, *The Persian Revolution of 1905-1909*, London
1966, p. 372.
7. V. Minorsky, "The Rupture between Sunni and Shi'ah in
Islam," in *Religion*, vol. II/1935, p. 19.
8. Kulini, *al-Kafi*, quoted in A. A. Sachedina, *Introduction:
The Islamic Messiah, al-Mahdi*, p. 27 of typescript manuscript.
9. An extract from a *marthiya* (elegy) by Qa'ani (d. 1853),
translated by E. G. Browne in *History of Persian Literature*,
vol. iv, Cambridge 1930, pp. 180-1.
10. V. Minorsky, "Iran: Opposition, Martyrdom and Revolt,"
in *Unity and Variety in Muslim Civilization* (ed. Gustave von
Grunebaum), Chicago 1955, p. 201.
11. My translation of Jean Chardin, *Voyages du Chevalier
Chardin*, Amsterdam 1711, vol. vi, pp. 249-50 (emphasis added).
12. E. G. Browne, *The Persian Revolution of 1905-1909*,
London 1966, p. 377.
13. *Id.*, p. 374.
14. *Id.*, p. 373.

11
Khumayni's Islamic Republic

Raymond N. Habiby
Fariborz Ghavidel

The victory in Iran of the Ayatollah Al Ozma Agha
Sayed Ruhallah Khumayni[1] is but a dramatic development in
a movement which, differing in intensity, can be seen in
motion throughout the Muslim world, from North Africa to
South East Asia. This movement of Islamic revival and
renaissance affects a total of 600 million Muslims. It
professes to offer a political, economic and social system
that provides a "better" alternative to both the Western
and the Communist systems; one that Muslims can call their
own, with the hope that it will bring the Islamic nations
a new vitality, a stronger sense of identity and renewed
pride in being Muslims. The West views this revival as a
return to the "archaic 7th century A.D." Its Muslim
proponents believe it will propel the Islamic states into
the twentieth century.

Muslim thinkers have been examining the Islamic way of
life ever since the power of the Muslim states began to
decline, first in India and later in the Ottoman Empire, in
an effort to determine whether this decline and the relative
weakness of the Islamic world came about as the result of
religious, as opposed to economic or political, fragility.
This examination, which began in India in the 17th and 18th
centuries, spread to the rest of the Islamic world and is
still going on. In his book, *The Middle East and the West*,
Bernard Lewis traces the history of this movement which began
in India in the early 17th century with the militant revivalism of the reformed Naqshbandi order. In the Middle
East, the militant puritanical Islamic revivalism of the
Wahhabis of Arabia began when "the Ottoman Empire was
suffering defeat and humiliation at the hands of Christian
enemies...[Wahhabism showed] the way to an activist, militant

---

Khumayni's Islamic Republic is reprinted from *Middle
East Review*, Vol. XI, No. 4, Summer, 1979.

attack on the religious and political order which, so they
believed, had brought Islam to its present parlous condition."[2]
    In those formative years, Muslims did not regard the
encroachments of the West on the Islamic domains as imperialist.
They saw it as an attack by the Christian nations aimed at the
destruction of Islam. Thus, whenever the West pointed to Islam
as the cause of the weakness of the Islamic World, the only
reaction this produced was a Muslim upsurge in Islam's defense.*
The idea of pan-Islamism, in the sense of Muslims uniting
against the common threat posed by the Christian empires
appears to have been born among the Young Turks in the 1860s
and '70s, when intellectuals like Namik Kemal and Ali Suavi
advocated a more militant brand of pan-Islamism as the way to
save the Ottoman Empire.[3] This doctrine found its fieriest
advocate in Jamal al-Din, also known as al-Afghani or al-
Asadabadi (1838/39-1899), who electrified the Muslim world
with his writings and who is still the idol of every movement
of Islamic revival. It is not known whether al-Afghani came
from Afghanistan or from Persia and thus was a Sunni or a
Shi'ite.[4] He wrote in both Arabic and Persian, and his
writings have produced a great deal of intellectual ferment
and debate in the Muslim world. In Egypt, his disciple,
Muhammad Abdu (1849-1905) preached that a Muslim's first
concern must be with Islam, which educates, civilizes and
identifies him and makes him what he is. Muslims, Abdu wrote,
had to cast off the accretions of the post-classical Islamic
age and return to the pure, unadulterated and uncorrupted
faith and practices of the early Islam of the great *salaf*
(ancestors) if Islam was successfully to withstand the
attacks of the West.
    The Islamic revival took an openly militant turn with
the rise of the Senussi order in Libya, the Mehdi uprising
in the Sudan, the *Ma al-Aynaym* in Mauritania and the so-
called "Mad Mullah" of Somaliland. It played a leading
role in the Persian Constitutional Revolution of 1905-6,
which was led by the Shi'a mullahs and, with the demise of
the Ottoman Empire after World War I and the division of
the Islamic world into colonies of the West, gave rise to
movements seeking to drive out the Western Christian
imperialist forces. *Al Ikhwan Al Muslimun* (The Muslim
Brotherhood) developed in Egypt. In India, a movement
arose that led to the creation of Pakistan, and in Iran the
rise of the *Fidai-yan-i-Islam* (Devotees of Islam) opened
the way for the Mussadeq regime of 1951-53. (Iran's prime
minister, Mehdi Bazargan and many of his colleagues either
served in the Mussadeq cabinet or were very close to him.)

---

*Voices like those of Sir Sayyed Ahmad Khan (1817-1898) in
India and Abd al Qayyum Nasiri (1825-1902) in Russia were
raised advocating that Muslims had to model their societies
on those of Britain and Russia if they wanted to modernize
them, but this movement of Westernization made little impact.

attack on the religious and political order which, so they
believed, had brought Islam to its present parlous condition."[2]
     In those formative years, Muslims did not regard the
encroachments of the West on the Islamic domains as imperialist.
They saw it as an attack by the Christian nations aimed at the
destruction of Islam. Thus, whenever the West pointed to Islam
as the cause of the weakness of the Islamic World, the only
reaction this produced was a Muslim upsurge in Islam's defense.*
The idea of pan-Islamism, in the sense of Muslims uniting
against the common threat posed by the Christian empires
appears to have been born among the Young Turks in the 1860s
and '70s, when intellectuals like Namik Kemal and Ali Suavi
advocated a more militant brand of pan-Islamism as the way to
save the Ottoman Empire.[3] This doctrine found its fieriest
advocate in Jamal al-Din, also known as al-Afghani or al-
Asadabadi (1838/39-1899), who electrified the Muslim world
with his writings and who is still the idol of every movement
of Islamic revival. It is not known whether al-Afghani came
from Afghanistan or from Persia and thus was a Sunni or a
Shi'ite.[4] He wrote in both Arabic and Persian, and his
writings have produced a great deal of intellectual ferment
and debate in the Muslim world. In Egypt, his disciple,
Muhammad Abdu (1849-1905) preached that a Muslim's first
concern must be with Islam, which educates, civilizes and
identifies him and makes him what he is. Muslims, Abdu wrote,
had to cast off the accretions of the post-classical Islamic
age and return to the pure, unadulterated and uncorrupted
faith and practices of the early Islam of the great *salaf*
(ancestors) if Islam was successfully to withstand the
attacks of the West.
     The Islamic revival took an openly militant turn with
the rise of the Senussi order in Libya, the Mehdi uprising
in the Sudan, the *Ma al-Aynaym* in Mauritania and the so-
called "Mad Mullah" of Somaliland. It played a leading
role in the Persian Constitutional Revolution of 1905-6,
which was led by the Shi'a mullahs and, with the demise of
the Ottoman Empire after World War I and the division of
the Islamic world into colonies of the West, gave rise to
movements seeking to drive out the Western Christian
imperialist forces. *Al Ikhwan Al Muslimun* (The Muslim
Brotherhood) developed in Egypt. In India, a movement
arose that led to the creation of Pakistan, and in Iran the
rise of the *Fidai-yan-i-Islam* (Devotees of Islam) opened
the way for the Mussadeq regime of 1951-53. (Iran's prime
minister, Mehdi Bazargan and many of his colleagues either
served in the Mussadeq cabinet or were very close to him.)

---

*Voices like those of Sir Sayyed Ahmad Khan (1817-1898) in
India and Abd al Qayyum Nasiri (1825-1902) in Russia were
raised advocating that Muslims had to model their societies
on those of Britain and Russia if they wanted to modernize
them, but this movement of Westernization made little impact.

11
Khumayni's Islamic Republic

Raymond N. Habiby
Fariborz Ghavidel

The victory in Iran of the Ayatollah Al Ozma Agha Sayed Ruhallah Khumayni[1] is but a dramatic development in a movement which, differing in intensity, can be seen in motion throughout the Muslim world, from North Africa to South East Asia. This movement of Islamic revival and renaissance affects a total of 600 million Muslims. It professes to offer a political, economic and social system that provides a "better" alternative to both the Western and the Communist systems; one that Muslims can call their own, with the hope that it will bring the Islamic nations a new vitality, a stronger sense of identity and renewed pride in being Muslims. The West views this revival as a return to the "archaic 7th century A.D." Its Muslim proponents believe it will propel the Islamic states into the twentieth century.

Muslim thinkers have been examining the Islamic way of life ever since the power of the Muslim states began to decline, first in India and later in the Ottoman Empire, in an effort to determine whether this decline and the relative weakness of the Islamic world came about as the result of religious, as opposed to economic or political, fragility. This examination, which began in India in the 17th and 18th centuries, spread to the rest of the Islamic world and is still going on. In his book, *The Middle East and the West*, Bernard Lewis traces the history of this movement which began in India in the early 17th century with the militant revivalism of the reformed Naqshbandi order. In the Middle East, the militant puritanical Islamic revivalism of the Wahhabis of Arabia began when "the Ottoman Empire was suffering defeat and humiliation at the hands of Christian enemies...[Wahhabism showed] the way to an activist, militant

Khumayni's Islamic Republic is reprinted from *Middle East Review*, Vol. XI, No. 4, Summer, 1979.

the religious classes known loosely as the *ulama*, either
controls the political institution or is controlled by it.
Time alone will tell which it is to be. One thing is
certain: the *mujtahids* will not easily surrender the
dominant political position for which they have been fighting for nearly four centuries.

NOTES

1. E.I.J. Rosenthal, *The Role of the State in Islam: Theory
and the Medieval Practice*, a paper presented to the Colloquium on
Tradition and Change in the Middle East, Harvard 1968, p. 1.
    2. *Ibid.*
    3. *Encyclopaedia of Islam*, new edition, p. 884.
    4. *Ibid.*, p. 855.
    5. *"Al-Mawardi's 'Theory of the Caliphate',"* in *Studies on
the Civilization of Islam*, p. 162.
    6. E. G. Browne, *The Persian Revolution of 1905-1909*, London
1966, p. 372.
    7. V. Minorsky, "The Rupture between Sunni and Shi'ah in
Islam," in *Religion*, vol. II/1935, p. 19.
    8. Kulini, *al-Kafi*, quoted in A. A. Sachedina, *Introduction:
The Islamic Messiah, al-Mahdi*, p. 27 of typescript manuscript.
    9. An extract from a *marthiya* (elegy) by Qa'ani (d. 1853),
translated by E. G. Browne in *History of Persian Literature*,
vol. iv, Cambridge 1930, pp. 180-1.
    10. V. Minorsky, "Iran: Opposition, Martyrdom and Revolt,"
in *Unity and Variety in Muslim Civilization* (ed. Gustave von
Grunebaum), Chicago 1955, p. 201.
    11. My translation of Jean Chardin, *Voyages du Chevalier
Chardin*, Amsterdam 1711, vol. vi, pp. 249-50 (emphasis added).
    12. E. G. Browne, *The Persian Revolution of 1905-1909*,
London 1966, p. 377.
    13. *Id.*, p. 374.
    14. *Id.*, p. 373.

As a *quid pro quo* for this and similar Articles, the
intellectuals allowed the insertion of Article 2 of the
above Law, which called for the establishment of a Committee
of not less than five *mujtahids* empowered to "carefully
discuss and consider all matters" proposed in the newly-
elected National Consultative Assembly or Majlis, and to
"reject and repudiate, wholly or in part, any such proposal
which is at variance with the Sacred Laws of Islam, so that
it shall not obtain the title of legality."[14]   Clearly this
Article, had it been implemented, would have given the
mujtahids the power of veto over all legislation submitted
to parliament, and I am certain that Khumayni will press
for the inclusion of some such clause in the new Constitution.
     The Constitution of 1906-7, because it contained
inherent contradictions, satisfied neither the *mujtahids*
nor the intellectuals, and proved to be an unworkable
compromise. Within a year, the alliance between these two
groups, whose basic views were poles apart, dissolved.
It is only a matter of time before the present alliance
between Bazargan and Khumayni similarly dissolves, unless,
of course, the intellectuals this time are willing to submit
completely to the wishes of the *mujtahids*.

* * *

     To sum up, there is no theoretical basis in a "Twelver"
Shi'i state for an accommodation between the *mujtahids*,
the representatives of the Hidden Imam to whom government
on earth rightfully belongs, and any form of polity whatever, whether it be a monarchy or a republic. After all,
the *mujtahids* could have had a republic in 1924, when one
was offered to the country by Reza Khan. The *mujtahids*
rejected the idea, because they looked at what was happening
in Turkey and did not like what they saw, namely the
secularization of the state under Ataturk. If Khumayni
uses the term "Islamic republic," he does not use "republic"
in the sense in which it is used in the West. He means an
"Islamic state," which is a very different thing. An Islamic
state is one in which sovereignty belongs to God, not to the
people, and one which is based on the religious law of Islam.
     I will conclude by reiterating the central thesis of
this article, namely, that the fundamental problems of
sovereignty and legitimacy in Iran, in a 'Twelver' Shi'i
state, remain to be solved. The attempt by the Pahlavi
shahs to effect a gradual separation of religion from
politics has failed, at least in the short term. No
temporal ruler, whether he be called shah or president,
can ever gain legitimacy in the eyes of the *ulama*, but may
gain *de facto* acceptance as long as in their view he continues to promote the common weal. In the last analysis,
therefore, Iran is ungovernable unless the religious
institution, by which I mean the multifarious members of

Many appear content merely to use the vocabulary of Islamic
political theory, like *biat* (contract of investiture), *ijma
al Umma* (community consensus), *mashwara* (consultation),
adalat (justice) and *hurriat* (freedom) in place of providing
practical applications of these concepts.

Nevertheless, Khumayni does deal with some of these
features of the Islamic state, although he tends to slur
over the details about its political processes and functions.
In fact, he appears more to be responding to criticism of
the Islamic state system than to be tackling the subject of
government. His perceptions of this Islamic state are expounded in a book written in Persian entitled *Hukumate Islami*
(The Islamic State), published in the *Nahzate Islami* series
in 1971 (it first appeared in *Najaf al Ashraf*, published in
Iraq, where he was exiled, in 1969).[8]

Primarily, he does not recognize the separation of church
and state. They were not separate in the days of the Imam
'Ali,* he declares--this concept of separation was placed in
the minds of the Muslims by the agents of colonialism to
prevent them from struggling for freedom and independence
(p. 23). The colonialists want to "prevent you from industrializing and will continue to provide you with dependent
industries like assembly plants," he tells his Muslim readers
(p. 25). "This is why they call us political mullahs, but was
not our Prophet also political?" (p. 25).

He defends Islam against the "colonialist propaganda"
that claims Islam fails to provide for a system of government. "We believe in a state, and we know that the Messenger
of God had selected a Caliph," he maintains (p. 21). The
form of government he advocates, however, does not resemble
any contemporary system (p. 52). It will not be an autocracy,
for it will not have a self-appointed or self-proclaimed
autocrat at its head. It will be a constitutional government in the sense that government officials will be bound
to carry out and implement the law (*shari'a*) and decisions
will be taken in accordance with the precepts of the *sunna*
(tradition) and the Holy Qur'an. "Administrators and
executives as such will act in accordance with the provisions
of the Qur'an, and the Islamic government will, thus, be
called the rule of the Almighty" (pp. 52-53).

The government and administration of the Umayyad
(661-750) and Abbasid (750-1258) caliphates are dismissed
as anti-Islamic (p. 39) because they altered the early
Islamic system of government and adopted a monarchical system
similar to that of Rome, the Persian Kingdoms and the

---

*A cousin of the Prophet Muhammad and the husband of
his daughter Fatima. 'Ali is regarded by Shi'ites as
the Prophet's legitimate successor. Those claimed as
successors of the Prophet were called Imams. 'Ali
was succeeded by his sons al-Hasan and al-Husayn.

Khumayni can thus be seen as in the direct line of succession in this movement of Islamic revival. Like Jamal al-Din al-Afghani (presumably a Shi'ite) Khumayni, a senior Shi'ite leader,[5] advocates pan-Islamism, i.e., not simply the revival of Islam in Iran but the revival of Islam in the whole Muslim world. Iran had been evolving as a Shi'ite Iranian state rooted in traditional Persian culture ever since its Safavid dynasty (1501-1736). The same policy had been pursued by the Shah and was symbolized by Iran's national flag, which was the ancient Safavid flag. Khumayni has cast himself in the role of healer of the centuries-old and bloody rift between the Sunni and Shi'ite divisions of Islam. He has already announced that the national flag will now become the flag of Islam.

Iran, a country morbidly fascinated by martyrdom, is the perfect setting for Khumayni, whose personal suffering has won him great respect and the unofficial title of *Imam* (a title borne by the first twelve Shi'ite leaders, most of whom met with violent deaths).[6] Iran also had two well-established and well organized systems of authority, one headed by the Shah and comprising the army, the police, and the notorious SAVAK (secret police), the other comprising the religious establishment of mosques and mullahs (the religious order). Khumayni managed to assume control of the religious establishment early in the battle. He was able to summon thousands of young mullahs and theological students, who made telephone calls, ran duplicating machines, organized meetings in mosques and prepared banners, and who "were more radical and far more attuned to reborn Islamic militancy than were the ayatollahs."[7] The Shah's governmental structure collapsed, but the religious establishment continued to function, and became the sole government of Iran. This helps to explain how an exiled Iranian, living first in Iraq and then in France, managed to wield such immense power and achieve victory.

In the Muslim view, Islam is the universal religion of God on earth and an Islamic government can only represent the direct government of God. The state is God's state. He commands and Muslims submit to His will. Thus a Muslim's central political obligation is based on the religious dicta of the Qur'an. Present-day Muslim reformists present an idyllic portrait of the early Islamic state and insist that it can be resuscitated in the modern world under the law of Qur'an, which was given by God and which contains all the principles needed to govern the Muslim *Umma* (community). So long as Muslims abide by the law, they are with God and in God's care. He will grant them power, freedom, happiness and success. Those who are not with God are punished on earth as in heaven. On earth, this punishment may take the form of having to endure foreign rule, decadence and poverty. However, they speak of the Islamic state and the *shari'a*, but fail to provide adequate details about the nature, structure and political processes and function of the state.

Pharoahs of Egypt.   "This anti-Islamic form of government
has continued to the present day," he asserts (p. 39).
Islam does not recognize the Institution of the monarch and
the concept of princely rule" (pp. 13-55).   "Our only basis
of reference is the time of the Prophet and the Imam 'Ali."[9]
     Khumayni does not speak of an Islamic state, but of an
Islamic republic.   The word "republic" was not used in the
early days (*sadr*) of Islam.   Since he is a Shi'ite, he is
probably referring to the state created by the first four
Orthodox Caliphs, who were selected for life by the *biat*.
Translated into modern terminology, this means that the
first four Caliphs were elected presidents for life.   Yet,
in a press interview with *Le Monde* (May 6, 1978) Khumayni
showed a willingness to accept the Iranian constitution of
1906--if and when it was amended "to serve the cause of
Islam."   "We will choose qualified persons from among those
who are well acquainted with Islamic ideas and concepts of
government," he declared in this interview.[10]   These ideas
are elaborated in his book, *Hukumate Islami*.   The Islamic
umma needs a government that is honest, not corrupt, and
powerful and competent," he writes (p. 50).   Government is
necessary in order to guard against moral corruption and the
disintegration of the Islamic ways of life and Islamic principles (p. 51) and because of the needs of national defense
and the permanent protection of the Islamic state (p. 37).
"We need to develop institutions of government and a bureaucratic organization to enforce Islamic law.   They are essential
in perpetuating Islamic law and in maintaining social order"
(p. 30).   "Without them one can expect anarchy" (p. 29).
     The government he appears to be advocating is one that
will comprise an executive, a legislature, a judiciary, a
bureaucracy, a political party and the Islamic law.   In
Islam, he writes, the *Amir al-Mu'mineen* (Commander of the
Faithful) heads the executive branch (p. 28).   Khumayni also
refers to him as Caliph (p. 21).   As the executive, the Caliph,
he maintains, "is selected to enforce the laws that were handed
down by God to the Messenger" (p. 22).   "He is not selected to
create laws, as this has already been done by the Prophet and
is collected in books" (p. 21).   "He is to carry out and enforce the Islamic laws and to ensure their fullest implementation.   It is the execution and the implementation of the
law, not the creation of law which will advance the cause of
man and guarantee him justice, happiness and prosperity" (pp. 21
and 27).
     The need for an executive branch is also stressed, for
without one it is impossible to carry out all the provisions
of the *Shari'a*, he declares (p. 33).   The essence of the executive system is the *vilayet* (trusteeship) system (p. 22).
Islamic government equates leadership with duty and service
rather than privilege.   It entails the duty to carry out the
administrative tasks set forth in the holy *shari'a* (p. 64).
The ruler must therefore possess superior knowledge of the
laws pertaining to social justice; he must be familiar with
the Islamic concepts of the administration of the state

and the science of management (p. 60); he should also
know how to perform his functions lawfully, no matter how
small these may be (p. 59); he should disassociate himself
from the luxuries of life and lead a humble existence (p. 55)
and he should have good moral and ethical qualities and must
not be touched by sin, since he will be responsible for the
collection and expenditure of state revenues and will be
dealing with all budgetary affairs (pp. 60 and 61).

The head of the government must also meet two fundamental requirements: he must have a thorough knowledge of
Islamic law and he must be just and well versed in Islamic
jurisprudence (p. 58).

Khumayni rejects the idea of social superiority or
status for those in special positions. This idea, he writes,
does not exist in Islam. Superiority must be expressed in
superior intellect and morality (p. 64). For this reason
government should lead to social justice and not to social
privilege or social prominence and wealth (p. 85). He advocates a system of succession based on the competence of the
leader and the service he has rendered to the people and not
on a system of favoritism or a self-imposed autocracy (p. 55).

Regarding the legislative branch, "the main difference
between the Islamic republic and a constitutional monarchy
or a republic is that the representatives of the people do
not assemble to pass laws or to make laws. Such power in
Islam is in the hands of the Almighty. No other law is
legitimate. The Almighty is the sole legislative power.
Therefore, in Islam legislative assemblies and law-making
bodies are replaced by consultative assemblies which shall
meet to plan social service projects, with Islamic law as
the determining source" (p. 53). The law is the *sunna*
and the *sunna* and in Islamic society absolute *ijma* (consensus)
exists in this respect. That is why the Islamic government
will prevent passage of anti-Islamic laws by sham and
illegitimate so-called "national assemblies" (p. 53). In
the judicial branch, "in order to maintain Islamic laws and
perpetuate the essence of law, it is essential that an
Islamic government have a judicial arm as prescribed by the
shari'a. It will, together with the executive, protect
Islam against anarchy and abuse" (p. 62). As to political
parties, he declares, "all factions should become one and
develop a united front. One Front. One Party. The Party
of God" (*hizb Allah*).[11]

The Islamic laws of the state are to be applicable
at all times and are not limited by either time or space.
They are basic to all forms of social organization (p. 28).
The Qur'an and the *sunna* embody all the laws and systems
required for the well-being and the prosperity of human
beings (p. 33). The "law" provides for all of a human
being's needs (p. 33). It provides the rules governing
social relationships, such as with neighbors, children,
fellow citizens and also marital relations. It provides
the laws of war and of peace, of relations with other

nations, of commerce, industry, agriculture and a penal code (p. 32).

According to Khumayni, the difference between the laws of Islam and the laws of Western society are these: Islamic law does not regulate the sale of liquor, of interest-bearing bank loans, or of prostitution. This is not because Islamic law is incomplete, as some claim, but because these activities were declared illegal (*haram*) in Islam, and therefore they are not subject to regulation (p. 13). Imported laws have been the source of the problems of Islamic society, he maintains. "I am shocked to read about those who claim that the laws of Islam are crude and harsh, and that they reflect the violent nature of Arab society. The imported laws provide that a person be shot by a firing squad if he smuggles in heroin, but this violent punishment is necessitated by the permissiveness of the imported laws. They claim that the firing squad is not a violent punishment in heroin smuggling cases, yet to them eighty lashes administered for drunkenness is regarded as violent" (p. 15). He cannot, he writes, see how the sale of liquor to corrupt the mind and the maintenance of prostitution can be regarded as acceptable while the smuggling of drugs, an activity that can be traced to drink, is regarded as evil. "It is acceptable and non-violent for the 'powerful boss' to shed the blood of thousands in Vietnam, yet Islamic law, which sets guidelines for the fight against corruption and defends freedom is not acceptable" (p. 17).

The sources of revenue in Islam, he writes, are the *khoms* (a tithe of one-fifth of income) and the *zakat* (alms giving), which are paid into the *bait mal al muslimun* (state treasury). These are collected for the administration of the Islamic society and the well being of its citizens, and are sufficient for the administration of a large government apparatus (p. 34). The state budget must be spent on social services such as health, education and development, and also on defense. However, no member of the ruling class should acquire an advantage over other citizens by securing special benefits from the state revenues (pp. 35-6).

In a November 1978 speech[12] Khumayni declared that the Islamic Republic, and the kind of laws it would have, "will be up to the people of Iran." The referendum on the Islamic Republic was held March 31-April 1. Khumayni has made it clear, however, that what he plans is a step-by-step procedure. "...the ideal is the creation of the Islamic state," he has declared, but the first concern was the destruction of the Shah's regime, to be followed by the creation of a regime which "answers the essential needs of the people."[13] The government of Mehdi Bazargan thus appears to be a provisional government whose task is to prepare the groundwork for the Islamic Republic.

It would be wrong to dismiss the wave of Islamic revival now sweeping through the Islamic world as a reactionary religious movement. Rather, it should be seen as an effort,

on the part of an important segment of mankind, to deal with
its world on its own terms. Unfortunately, however, because
there are so many Muslim states, this Islamic revival may
become a game played by these states to prove which is the
most Islamic.

If there is going to be a conflict of ideologies in
the Islamic world, it will be between the forces of Islam,
Marxism and nationalism. And the West appears to have no
ideology, at this stage, to offer in their place.

* * *

Khumayni On The Shah

The Shah could not head an Islamic state because he was
the very essence of obscurantism, was oriented toward the
past and carried out the policy of the imperialists in order
to keep Iran a backward state.[14] His subjugation to foreign
powers compromised the progress of the Iranian people and his
claim that he was leading Iran to the "frontier of a great
civilization" was a lie and only an excuse to undermine the
country's independence.[15]

Khumayni's movement also gave other reasons for the
uprising. These were spelled out in a *Statement* issued in
March 1977:[16]

1. The Shah is a King, and of kings the Qur'an says:
"Kings when they enter a country despoil it and make the
noblest of its people the meanest." (S.XXVII v. 34), (p. 1).
2. Shah-in-Shah (King of Kings), the title given to
himself by the Shah, is an Islamic title belonging to God
alone. According to the Prophet Muhammad: "The curse of
Allah will be upon one who calls himself King of Kings and
upon one who calls another man by such a title" (p. ii).
3. The Shah uses the title *Khodayagan Aryamehr*,
which means 'God-like.' Can a real Muslim call himself
God-like? (p. 3).
4. The Shah, and his father before him, plotted to
destroy the anti-colonialist and revolutionary ideals of
Islam. Like his father, the Shah is a loyal follower of
Muawiya and Yazid[17] (p. 3).
5. The Shah follows in the footsteps of Muawiya and
Yazid, his ancestral teachers. He proclaims Islam yet
he donated petroleum to the Israeli aggressor, so that
Zionist phantom jets are free to drop bombs on Muslim
Arabs (p. 4).
6. The Shah exiled the Ayatollah Khumayni (p. 4).
7. He granted the development contract for Dasht Ghazvin
(an agricultural area) to Israel. The food produced is
shipped to Israel to feed Israeli soldiers so that they can
slaughter homeless Palestinian revolutionaries and Muslim
Arabs (p. 4.).
8. He placed the fate of the people in the hands of

American and Zionist spies and military advisors (p. 6).

9. He spent money on his coronation, goes on skiing trips to Switzerland, changes his clothes every day, buys fur coats; he and his wife take milk baths to soften their skins while many Iranians are freezing, starving and destitute (p. 14).

10. He purchased arms from the U.S. to "blow up the innocent hearts of revolutionaries in Zofar and Palestine" (p. 16) and thousands of Iranians (p. 15).

The *Statement* also quotes from a speech delivered by the Imam 'Ali at the Battle of Saffain. (From *Nahgul Balaghah*):

> *Aim at the center...Satan is hidden there. He is hidden deep inside the enemy's chief and his clowns, who claim to be Muslims* (p. iv).

Why Muslims Must Be Revolutionaries

The *Statement* issued in March 1977 also gives the reasons why Iranians who believe in Islam have to be revolutionaries. These are:

1. The Islam of the Prophet Muhammad is the only true Islam. The true Islam is a revolutionary Islam... The Islam which the Prophet Muhammad brought is revolutionary; the Iranian Muslims are joining this revolution precisely for this reason (p. 5).

2. A true Muslim can be nothing else but a revolutionary. A Muslim is either a revolutionary or he is not a Muslim (p. 6).

3. This war (against the Shah) is a sacred war, and in response to God's commandment (p. 7).

4. This is a battle between truth (*hagh*) and falsehood (*batil*), (p. 12).

5. Allah has given the Muslims assurance of victory (p. 5), and Islam is providing, again, light and warmth to the spirits of every free and dignified man and woman; is giving them hope and encouragement (p. 10).

6. The Islam of the colonialists--those who claim that Islam is for the next world--allows the colonialists to loot all the wealth, resources and productivity of the Muslim nations (pp. 4 and 5).

Views On Marxism

On Iranian Marxists and communists, Khumayni is quoted in the May 6, 1978 *Le Monde* interview as having this to say: "...the Islamic concept based on the unity (oneness) of God is the antithesis of Marxism," and therefore the term "Islamic Marxist"* is an absurdity. He denied

*The Shah labelled the opposition "Islamic Marxists."

that an alliance between the Muslim masses and the communist
elements ever existed, and averred that he had instructed
his followers to "shun any organic collaboration" with them
and had commanded them not to cooperate with Marxists even
in the overthrow of the Shah, since "we are opposed to their
ideology and know they will stab us in the back if they come
to power, and will establish a dictatorial regime which is
contrary to the spirit of Islam."

In his Islamic society, nevertheless, "the Marxists
will be free to express themselves, because Islam answers
the need of the people and is capable of counteracting the
Marxist ideology." Marxists will not, however, "be free
to conspire." (According to *Newsweek*, the Tudeh communist
party is to be banned.)[18]

The question was also dealt with in the *Statement* of
March, 1977. Here, the "great unity between the Muslim
revolutionaries and the Marxist revolutionaries in the
common struggle against the criminal enemy" was cited. While
the Shah termed the Islamic movement (*Mujahidin-e-Khalgh*)
"black revolutionary and Islamic Marxist," it stated, a person
can only be either a Marxist or a Muslim. He cannot be both
simultaneously," it declared (p. 2). "There is no doubt that
Islam and Marxism differ in many areas...yet a Marxist who is
slaughtered for the cause of the people...is following precisely the advice 'Ali gave to his two sons: *Be the enemy
of the oppressor, and the supporter of the oppressed*"
(p. 10).

On International Relations

During the Second World War, Khumayni developed a program
of action on three issues: Liberty, Independence and Resistance to Foreign Domination.[19] It now appears that he
envisages a pan-Islamic nationalist policy for Iran, whereby
the country will ally itself with the neutralist states and
gradually normalize relations with the U.S., the Soviet Union
and Britain. Iran has already announced that it will no
longer act as the policeman of the Persian Gulf and that it
would withdraw its forces from Oman and Zofar and its contingent now serving with the U.N. forces in southern Lebanon.
It will probably withdraw its garrisons from the islands of
the Hormuz Straits at the entrance to the Persian Gulf and
leave the Central Treaty Organization (CENTO).

In its new Muslim role Iran's relations with Israel
come to an end. Iran gave as its reason for its decision to
pull its U.N. contingent out of southern Lebanon the fact
that it has now become a confrontation state against Israel,
and as already announced, no longer sells its oil to Israel
(and South Africa). Khumayni is particularly embittered
against Israel which, he has declared, "usurped the land
of a Muslim people and committed innumerable crimes. The
Shah, by maintaining diplomatic relations with Israel and
extending economic aid to it was acting against the interests

of Islam and Muslims."[20]   He called on all Muslims to join
in the fight against all their enemies, including Israel
and vowed to persist in the same path.   Concerning the
Israeli action of March, 1978 in Southern Lebanon, where
the population is mainly Shi'ite, he declared that he wanted
the people of Iran and all the Shi'is of the world to help
their southern Lebanese brothers, but that only governments
have the means at their disposal to put pressure on Israel
in order to compel it to withdraw.[21]   One of Khumayni's first
acts was to recall the Iranian mission in Israel.   His
followers ransacked the Israeli Mission in Tehran and proclaimed it the Embassy of the PLO.   Iran's first foreign
visitor was Yasser Arafat, who was given a hero's welcome.
In Khumayni's announced path of pan-Islamism, closer cooperation between Iran and the PLO can be expected, and Iran may
join the Arabs in the event of a new Arab-Israeli war.

Oil Policy

Iran needs its oil and must sell oil in order to acquire
foreign exchange.   Oil is to be sold to all countries except
Israel and South Africa, it has been announced, but oil, and
gas, will be developed primarily to fill Iran's own needs
and not necessarily those of the rest of the world.[22]   It
is not likely that production will be permitted to reach the
pre-revolutionary level, but it will be sold to the highest
bidder at the highest possible prices, and the present oil
consortium of foreign companies will be phased out.

Political, Social, and Economic Issues

Political and religious freedom is promised to all (so
long as no one attempts to undermine the Islamic Republic)
except the Tudeh party.   In Iran's present transitional
stage, however, it is difficult to see how this promise
will be effected.   Khumayni had, also, criticized the Shah
for "granting freedom."   Freedom, he declared, "is not
something to be awarded...Freedom is an inalienable right
which belongs to the people.   The law (*shari'a*) has given
the people freedom."[23]

On The Status Of Women

Personal status for Muslims is to be ruled by Islamic
law.[24]   "Islam has always been opposed to the concept of
women as (an) object and has restored her dignity.   Women
are equal to men and like (man) is free to choose her destiny
and her activities...we wish to liberate women from the
corruption that is menacing them."[25]

On Industrialization

Khumayni has said that he does not oppose the

industrialization of Iran, but its industries must be
nationalized and integrated into the economy, in a harmonious
balance with agriculture. Industry should not consist of
assembly plants that are dependent on the foreigner.[26]
His three-point program for reform was presented in a 1978
speech:[27]

> 1. *In the Agricultural Sector:* "We will create the
> conditions to enable the Iranian farmers to live on a par
> with their fellow countrymen."
> 2. *In the Industrial Sector:* "We will take steps to
> enable us to respond to domestic needs independent of
> assistance from abroad and the colonialist nations, so that
> we will not need their assistance. We will improve the
> life of our workers to enable them to enjoy a better
> standard of living."
> 3. *On Mineral Resources:* "We will adopt a policy that
> will take into consideration the needs of the world but
> will also protect an independent Iran and the way in which
> the people benefit from these resources."

Khumayni appears to be in full agreement with al-Afghani
on the issue of Islam and industrialization. According to
al-Afghani, it was Islam that inspired a philosophic spirit
and science among the Muslims:

> Those who forbid science and knowledge in the belief
> that they are safeguarding the Islamic religion are really
> the enemies of that religion...there is no incompatibility
> between science and knowledge and the foundation of Islamic
> faith.[28]

In his book, *Hukumate Islami*, Khumayni is critical of
those nations that have achieved such great technological
advancement that they have conquered outer space, and yet
these so-called advanced nations have failed to cope with
their social problems. This is because they lack the
ethical and moral power to do so, despite their immense
material power. Technological advancement should be balanced
by the moral and ethical values of the Holy Qur'an; this
advancement must serve mankind, not produce destruction,
he declares (p. 20).

NOTES

1. This spelling is used in all the English translations of the
publications of the Liberation Movement of Iran.
2. Bernard Lewis, *The Middle East and the West*, (University
of Indiana Press, 1965), p. 99. See also, Fazlur Rahman, *Islam*,
(Anchor Books, 1968), among others.
3. The best study of this period is by Sarif Mardin, *The*

Genesis of Young Ottoman Thought: A Study in the Modernization of Turkish Political Ideas, (Princeton University Press, 1962).

4. Nikki R. Keddie insists, in *An Islamic Response to Imperialism: Political and Religious Writings of Sayyid Jamal-al-Din "Al Afghani,"* (University of California Press, 1968), that al-Afghani was born in Iran and was a Shi'ite.

5. Khumayni is one of the four senior Ayatollahs in the Shi'ite Imami sect of Iran. The other three are: Kazim Shariatmadary of Qum; Hazarat Shirazi of Mashad; Mahmoud Taleghani of Tehran. Khumayni was attached to the holy city of Qum, to which he has returned, leaving Taleghani in charge of Tehran.

6. From an article by R. W. Apple Jr., in *The New York Times, Week in Review,* Section 4, p. 1E, January 28, 1979. Shi'ism highly values the *shehada* (martyrdom) and the Shi'ites punish themselves ritually for their ancient failure to help al-Husayn at Karbala.

7. *Ibid.*

8. Ayatollah Khumayni, *Hukumate Islami* (The Islamic State), (*Nahzate Islami* Series No. 2, No place of publication, 1971). The quotations in this article were translated by the authors from the Persian text, and the relevant pages are given in parenthesis.

9. From a press interview with the correspondent of *Le Monde,* translated into English and published as a pamphlet by The Liberation Movement of Iran Abroad, P.O. Box A, Belleville, Ill. The interview appeared in *Le Monde* on May 6, 1978.

10. *Ibid.,* p. 12.

11. *Kammimeh Khabarnameh* (speech delivered by the Ayatollah Khumayni on the occasion of the death of the martyrs of Yazd and other cities in Iran), published by the National Front of Iran (*Jabha Melli Iran*), *Najaf,* No. 17, June 1978, p. 13.

12. *Iran Times,* No. 37, Friday, November 24, 1978, p. 6.

13. *Ibid.,* p. 11.

14. *Ibid.,* p. 7.

15. *Ibid.*

16. *The Statement of O.M.K.I., in Response to the Recent Accusations of the Iranian Regime,* (Liberation Movement of Iran Abroad, Belleville, Ill., March 1977); henceforth referred to as the *Statement.*

17. *Ibid.* Muawiya and Yazid, founders of the Umayyad dynasty, cursed by Shi'ites for being responsible for the deaths of 'Ali and al-Husayn.'

18. *Newsweek,* February 12, 1979.

19. *Newsweek, op cit.*

20. *Le Monde, op cit.*

21. *Ibid.*

22. *Newsweek, op cit.*

23. *Zamimeh Khabarnameh, op cit.,* p. 18.

24. *Ibid.*

25. *Le Monde, op cit.*

12
Sectarianism and the Iraqi State

Yosef Gotlieb

Iraq, whose name derives from the Arabic for rootedness, is a country that has been in perpetual turmoil since its inception. Nearly two score changes in government have taken place in that country since its admission to the League of Nations in 1932, and virtually none of these changes has been the result of democratic election or popular mandate.

Many of the conflicts that have wracked Iraq have been of a patently sectarian nature, and those which were not obviously inter-sectarian had inter-communal causes or consequences that penetrated deep into this highly heterogenous nation. Iraq is a cauldron of diverse ethnicities, linguistic groups and religions. Its heterogeneity, often subsumed beneath the Arab identity that its leaders project, belies much of the economic, as well as sociopolitical phenomena of the Iraqi state. One might describe Iraq as a society in search of an identity, a nation in perpetual revolution owing to an unrelenting and violent dialectic between the ruling elites that have taken power in the country and the numerous subnational groups that have responded to the imposition of centralizing national symbols and legitimizing creeds.

The modern Iraqi state was born in the First World War era. Occupied by the British in 1914, who stationed troops in what was then known as Mesopotamia so that British oil interests and the strategic land route to India could be protected, Iraq was fashioned out of the former Ottoman *vilayets* (provinces) of Baghdad and Basra. After the War, following the emergence of a dispute between the British, who had been awarded Iraq as a mandate, and Turkey, the International Court, acting at the behest of the League of Nations, adjudicated clashing claims to the oil-rich Mosul area, which had also been a *vilayet* under the Ottomans. Awarded to the British, Mosul became the third piece of the nascent Iraqi state, as part of a state-building process

which has been described as artificial and wholly arbitrary
by a number of Middle East historians.[1]

The populations of these three disparate sections of
Iraq have, historically, had very little to do with one
another.[2]   Although the overwhelming majority of Iraqis
are Muslims, even this religious common denominator serves
poorly as a cement for national integration.   The country's
Muslims are about evenly split between the Shi'a and Sunni
branches of Islam.   The Sunnis, however, are found within
both the Arab and non-Arab, specifically Kurdish, communities.
The Shi'ites, therefore, form the largest single communal
grouping in the country.   They are also the least educated,
most impoverished and neglected sector of the Iraqi Muslims.
Concentrated for the most part in the Basra region, the
southlands of the Iraqi state, the Shi'ites are especially
to be found in the areas around the shrine cities of Najaf
and Karbala, the holy cities of Shi'ism, where the martyrs
Ali and Hussein, victims of the first political schism of
Islam, fell in battle and, according to Islamic tradition,
are buried.

The religious question in Iraq is directly tied to the
ethnic situation and, ultimately, to the political affairs
of the nation in both the domestic and international spheres.
The Shi'ite community, for example, includes a large number
of ethnic Persians, among whom are a number of the Shi'ite
ulema (religious leaders) of Iraq.   One of the reasons put
forward by the Iraqi authorities for their 1980 war with
Iran was the alleged agitation of Persian shi'ite *ulema*
in Iraq for an Iranian-style Islamic Revolution.   In the
months preceding the War, some thirty-five thousand ethnic
Persians were removed from their residences by the Iraqi
Government and deported across the border to Iran.   In 1974,
at a time when Iraqi-Iranian hostilities were high, sixty
thousand ethnic Persians had been similarly deported.[3]
Deportation, the suppression of the Shi'ite *ulema* and the
death, under suspicious circumstances, of a prominent Imam
in southern Iraq, preceded the deterioration of relations
between Iraq and Iran that resulted in the 1980 War.

The relationship between intra-Muslim interactions and
the various forms of Iraqi nationalism is intriguing.   While
the dominating Sunni elites have persistently attempted to
impose a pan-Arab regime of a Ba'thist, Nasserite or similar
bent, the Shi'ites have always seemed to favor a patriotism
wholly based on the Iraqi state.[4]   The reason for this
divergence of nationalist outlook is to be found, at least
in part, in the differences between the perceived self-
interest of the Sunni and Shi'ite communities: the former
would be strengthened by almost any form of pan-Arab unity.
The original pan-Arab scheme popular under the period of
the Hashemite monarchy in Iraq (1921-1958) entailed the
proposed unification of Transjordan, Iraq, and parts of
Syria under a Greater Crescent federative state led by a
Hashemite monarch.   Subsequent Nasserite proposals for a

unitary state composed of the United Arab Republic (Egypt
and Syria) and Iraq, and Ba'thist formulas for unification
with Syria and Jordan all involved Iraq's inclusion in a
state where the Sunnis would form a large majority. Obviously, the Sunni community viewed these scenarios as quite
acceptable, while the Shi'ites as a bloc opposed any plan
whereby they would constitute a small minority in a dominantly
Sunni state.

THE ETHNIC MANIFESTATION OF RELIGIOUS TENSION

Aside from the overtly religious tensions that underlie
Iraqi national life, inter-ethnic hostilities, along with
concomitant linguistic differences, serve as an undergrid
of unrest. Iraq is at least twenty-five percent non-Arab.
Of the estimated thirteen million inhabitants of the country,
perhaps four million or more are Kurds. The Iraqi Kurds are
part of a Middle Eastern people, numbering between fourteen
to eighteen million, who live on a contiguous swath of land
that has been divided between, and is presently ruled by
Iraq, Iran, Turkey, Syria and the Soviet Union. The Kurds
are an Indo-European people, ethnically unique, and unrelated
racially or linguistically to the Arabs. During the past
hundred years, Kurdish rebellions have taken place throughout
the Middle East in pursuit of national rights, autonomy or
secession. The Iraqi state, owing to the ad hoc manner in
which the Mosul province was acquired and to the large concentration of Kurds resident there, has been a frequent site
of Kurdish insurrection.
Another large ethnic minority in Iraq are the Turcomans,
a Turkic people with kin on the Iranian side of the border.
Primarily inhabiting the Mosul area, the Turcomans are to be
found wedged between the Arabs and Kurds of that district.
As a result of their geographic location, the Turcomans have,
on occasion, been the victims of Arab-Kurdish hostility.
Iraq, though it has never been considered a unique
nation-state, is composed of territory formerly known as
Mesopotamia, "the land between the two rivers" (the Tigris
and the Euphrates). Since the birth of Islam, the area has
represented the limits of Arabization. The Persians, while
accepting Islam following the Arab conquest of Persia after
the death of the Prophet Muhammad, refused to subjugate their
ancient culture and language to the desert Arab warriors who
brought the message of Islam. The differentiation of *dar
al-Islam* (the domain of Islam) from *dar al-Arabiyyah* (the
domain of the Arabs) resulted from the stubborn refusal of
the Persians to submit to Arabic language and folkways.
Consequently, there is a traditional enmity between the
Iranians and Arabs which has been reflected in a number of
ways by the relations between the Arabs and Iranians of
Mesopotamia and its tangents.
Before the state of Israel's independence in 1948, the

Jews constituted the second largest ethnic group in Iraq
after the Kurds. Though a Jew served as the first Iraqi
Minister of Finance, the usual tensions and discrimination
historically faced by Jews in the Middle East was part of
Jewish existence before and during the Ottoman rule over
Baghdad, Basra and Mosul, and also during the period following Iraqi independence. As a result of the partition plan
adopted by the United Nations in 1947, which led, *ipso facto*,
to the establishment of the State of Israel, Iraqi Jewry
began emigrating to Israel in an exodus which left fewer than
five thousand Jews in Iraq by the end of 1951. At present,
no more than five hundred Jews remain in Iraq. The emigration to Israel of the Jewish population followed a series
of pogroms and repressive measures adopted in 1934, 1936 and
1941 and which led to considerable loss of life and property.
    Aside from the Arabs, Kurds, Jews, Turcomans and Per-
sians, a number of small ethnic groups are also to be found
in Iraq. Among these are a number of Christian communities,
including Armenians, Assyrians and Indians. All of these
groups are associated with unique linguistic and cultural
matrices, Arabic having become the ascendant culture in Iraq
only after the proclamation of the Hashemite Kingdom under
King Faisal in 1921. While Winston Churchill, who in his
capacity as British Colonial Secretary was instrumental in
the formation of Iraq,[5] would later boast that he created
Iraq "one day in Cairo," the importation of Faisal, a leader
of the Arab Revolt, and someone who was strongly identified
with Arab nationalism set the way for the Arabization of
Iraqi society. As a result, the several millions of non-
Arabs in Iraq have been de facto second-class citizens of
the Iraqi state.
    The sectarian unrest that is virtually synonymous with
Iraq began concurrently with the formation of the State.
When it was announced that the League of Nations had given
Britain possession of the country, serious riots broke out
throughout the tribal areas of Basra and Mosul. The riots
were not, however, a manifestation of Iraqi nationalist
fervor,[6] as some have asserted, since there had not been an
Iraqi nation before then, but they did represent widespread
discontent with the replacement of one form of foreign rule
(Ottoman suzerainty) by another (the British mandate).
Further, the introduction of the Sunni Arab monarchy of the
Hashemites exacerbated tensions in the country, especially
between Shi'ite and Sunni, and Arab and non-Arab. Through
the deployment of British troops, Faisal's installation as
King of Iraq was secured, and "legitimized" through a single-
question referendum which affirmed his rule by what appeared
to be an impressive 96 percent of the Iraqi voting populace.
In the words of Lady Gertrude Bell, who belonged to the
British colony in Iraq that virtually ran the country, the
wheels of the election machinery were "very well greased"
by British baksheesh.[7] Moreover, the election was boycotted
en bloc by the Kurds and other national minorities who would

not acquiesce to the imposition of an Arab crown on the mandatory regime.

Between 1921-23, Kurdish revolts spread throughout Iraqi Kurdistan under the leadership of Sheik Mahmoud Barzanji of Suliemaniya.[8] Sheik Mahmoud was appointed Governor of the Suliemaniya district by the British in the summer of 1923, whereupon he seized the opportunity to revolt against Faisal. Mahmoud was subdued only after the intervention of British troops and the Royal Air Force. Again appointed Governor by the British, owing to his standing as the strong-man of the area, Sheik Mahmoud launched a second insurrection in the summer of 1924, followed by a third revolt in 1927. In 1929, following another Kurdish boycott of national elections, when Kurdish representatives failed to secure autonomy for the Kurdish areas from the Iraqi Chamber of Deputies, further unrest kept Iraqi Kurdistan festering. Sheik Mahmoud fled to Iranian Kurdistan where he proclaimed a Kurdish state, one which was not realized.

In opposition to the settlement of Turkish Assyrians in Iraqi Kurdistan, further bloodshed took place as Sheik Ahmed Barzani led the Kurds of the Barzan region in revolt against the newly independent Arab government in 1932-33. Continuous Kurdish opposition manifested itself throughout the 1930s under Sheik Ahmed and his younger brother, Mullah Mustafa Barzani, who later was to be identified as the preeminent Kurdish leader of the century. Severe repression against the Kurds, and especially against their leaders, was pervasive throughout the 1930s and the first part of the Second World War. Only after the British occupation of the country in 1943, following the establishment of a short-lived pro-Axis Government in Baghdad, did the Kurdish community receive some measure of relief.

Kurdish nationalism, generated in the first decades of the present century, rapidly became highly organized and sophisticated. For the most part, this nationalism has been leftist in outlook. In the mid-forties, the Iraqi Communist Party (ICP) splintered into two parts, the ICP proper and the Kurdish Communist Party which, while refraining from advocating Kurdish independence or autonomy did, however, champion the cause of Kurdish civil and national minority rights as an integral part of their program. After World War II, Mullah Mustafa Barzani led another Kurdish uprising against the Arab authorities, and the use of artillery, armor and air power were required to suppress it. The deployment of the Kurdish *Pesh Mergas* ("Those Who face Death") forces made Kurdish nationalism a most formidable foe of the Iraqi regime.

Despite their lack of heavy arms and supplies, the *Pesh Mergas* have remained an intractable force in the mountainous recesses of Iraqi and Iranian Kurdistan since their formation. In 1946, after it became obvious that they would be overrun, the Kurdish forces retrenched in Mehabad, in Iranian Kurdistan, where, under Soviet tutelage, a Kurdish Republic was proclaimed and survived for some months. Following the collapse of the

Kurdish Republic, the Kurdish nationalists faced a period
of dire suppression and eclipse, and the Barzani leadership
was forced into exile in the Soviet Union. A clandestine
United Democratic Kurdish Party (UDPK) developed and, with
the overthrow of King Faisal II as part of the Republican
Revolution of 1958, the UDPK, with Mullah Mustafa Barzani
at its helm, shared power with the army officers who took
control of Iraq. The Kurdish Communist Party and the Iraqi
Communist Party reintegrated, the latter advocating Kurdish
national rights within a single Iraqi state and the UDPK
favoring various versions of autonomy.

By November 1960, relations between the Republican
military dictators and the Kurds had again deteriorated,
and Mullah Mustafa Barzani prepared for revolt against the
regime in Baghdad. Throughout the 1960s, four Iraqi governmental offensives were launched against the Kurds, who remained, for the most part, concentrated in the mountain fast-
ness of Kurdistan. All of the numerous Iraqi regimes that
seized control of the country and attempted to manage it saw
the Kurdish question as among the most serious of their
problems and elevated the suppression of the Kurdish revolt
to the status of a national imperative. They feared that
any gains made by the Kurds could lead to the disintegration
of the whole Iraqi state, since other minorities were likely
to follow the Kurdish lead and pursue greater autonomy.
Additionally, Iraqi oil reserves are to be found beneath
Kurdistan, and the increasing dependency of the Iraqi central
treasury upon oil revenues required that authority be reimposed
on the Kurdish districts. During the four wars against the
Kurds in the 1960s, napalm, strafing, and bombardment were
employed by the Iraqi military forces. The various offensives
have been described by some, I believe without exaggeration,
as genocidal in scope. Each offensive began and ended with
a new set of agreements between the Kurds and the Iraqis, all
of which were terminated in betrayal and treachery by the
central regime in Baghdad.

In January 1970 one of the agreements was reaffirmed by
Ahmad Hassan al-Bakr, then President of Iraq. The agreement
called for the granting of autonomy and virtually all national
minority rights to the Kurds. After waiting until 1974 for
these reforms to be implemented, the Iraqi Kurds, under the
leadership of Mullah Mustafa Barzani and the *Pesh Mergas* of
the Kurdish Democratic Party (KDP) entered a new phase in
their campaign with another revolt in that year. Increasing
gains, as a result of which the Kurds kept the large contin-
gents of Iraqi forces at bay, appeared to be leading to a
Kurdish military victory that would guarantee their demands.
As victory approached, an agreement struck between Saddam
Hussein (then Vice President, and currently President of Iraq)
and the Shah of Iran ended Iranian support for the Kurdish
campaign. The Iranian assistance was essential for the continued Kurdish effort against Baghdad, and when the Shah and
the Iraqis settled a dispute over the Shaat al-Arab estuary

in March 1975, the Kurdish struggle was dealt a lethal blow.
It is the reintroduction of this same dispute over the Shaat
al-Arab that precipitated the Iraqi-Iranian War in 1980.
The Kurdish regions in both Iraq and Iran have been hard hit
by the fighting, and have responded with verbal and military
attacks of their own against both governments.

The Kurds are the largest of Iraq's national groups,
but they are not alone in suffering persecution at the hands
of the Baghdad Government. Despite assurances issued to the
League of Nations as a condition of admission to that organization in 1932, the Iraqis began their first years of independent statehood with a massacre of the Assyrian community
when, in 1933, at least twenty Assyrian villages were razed
by Iraqi military forces after a minor dispute between border
guards and an Assyrian delegation returning from Syria in
search of a haven for their community escalated into a full-
fledged pogrom. Colonel Bekr Sidqi, who later became Prime
Minister of Iraq, was promoted to the rank of General, owing
to his "heroic" leadership in the Assyrian massacres.[9] He
was responsible for plans toward a "final solution" of the
Assyrian problem, and while he was not successful in effecting
a complete genocide, he did succeed in generally eliminating
the Assyrian presence from Iraq through forced emigration.

The Yazidis, a small and often misunderstood sect in-
correctly referred to as "devil-worshipers" were also victims
of Bekr Sidqi's punitive campaigns against the smaller
minorities in Iraq. Like the Assyrians and Armenians, they
had been accustomed to the communal autonomy afforded them by
the Ottoman *millet* system, by which the various minority
communities maintained responsibility for their communal
affairs as autonomous parts of the sultan's realm. These
communities found it most difficult to resign themselves to
life as minorities in an authoritarian and highly centralized
Arab state.

While there have been relative lulls in the unrest, the
tensions between the various ethnic and national groups in
Iraq have always erupted with ferocity. In political life,
the highly totalitarian character of Iraq's ruling regimes
has led to the sublimation of ethnic and other sectarian
questions through proscribed or banned political parties.
The minorities have always been involved at the highest
levels in the Iraqi Communist Party, for example, and frequently accommodations with the Communists have had as much
to do with inter-ethnic politics as with anything else. A
series of riots which took place in Kirkuk during July 1959
exemplifies the ethnic dimension in Iraqi politics.[10] In
the course of protests initiated by the Iraqi communists,
who were at the time in good standing with General Abdul
Karim Kassem, the Iraqi dictator and initiator of the 1959
Republican Revolution, a free-for-all developed between the
Turcoman residents of Kirkuk proper, the Kurdish inhabitants
of nearby villages, and the Arab government's local military
detachments. The most vulnerable of the three groups, the

Turcomans, paid dearly in both life and property losses as
the riots proceeded through five days of savagery. The
Communists later regretted that "excesses" had been committed
by individuals operating under their leadership. However,
it has been difficult to ascertain whether the Communists
were operating as upholders of a particular brand of ideology,
or as frustrated ethnics whose anger and rage were misdirected
against other minorities.[11]

Further exemplifying the ethnic factor in Iraqi politics
is the participation of Kurdish parties, reportedly including
the Kurdish Democratic Party of Iraq, which is headed by two
sons of the late Mullah Mustafa Barzani, in a recently constituted National Assembly.[12] The presence of the Kurdish
parties in this largely cosmetic, though nonetheless official
Iraqi institution at a time when the Kurdish parties continue
to decrie the ruling Ba'th indicates the power of this submerged nationality in Iraqi public affairs.

As Michael C. Hudson has written, "Subnational and supranational loyalties of a primordial character are not only
incompatible with one another but also appear to have greater
salience than affinities with [the Iraqi] state or regime."[13]
The unrelenting assertion of these subnational, e.g., Kurdish,
Turcoman, etc., identities, and of supranational identifica-
tions such as pan-Arabism continue to work against the integration of the diverse Iraqi citizenry into a cogent nation-
state. The effectiveness of pan-Arab legitimizing creeds,
enforced by authoritarian police-state agencies, has proven
incapable thus far of suppressing sectarian unrest in the
Iraqi state. Unless and until a process of power-sharing
between all the various sectors of the Iraqi state is
achieved, either through an Iraqi federation of autonomous
entities or through some other political system, Iraq will
continue to be embroiled in impassioned manifestations of
sectarian discontent. The imposition of a pan-Arab or
similarly exclusivist ideology appears to be unacceptable
to much of the highly heterogeneous Iraqi citizenry. No
matter how enriched the Baghdad regime becomes from the
infusion of oil revenues, unless all sectors of Iraqi
society share equitably in decisions pertaining to allocation and policy, Iraq will continue to be locked into a
cycle of unremitting sectarian turmoil.

NOTES

1. See, e.g., Michael C. Hudson, *Arab Politics: The Search
for Legitimacy*, (New Haven and London: Yale University Press,
1977), pp. 268-269, and A. H. Hourani, *Minorities in the Arab World*,
(London, New York and Toronto: Oxford University Press, 1947), p. 94.

2. See Joseph J. Malone, *The Arab Lands of Western Asia*
(Englewood Cliffs, New Jersey: Prentice Hall, 1973), p. 78.

3. *The Washington Post*, Friday, April 11, 1980, p. A18.

4. Hourani, *op cit.*, p. 94.

5. See Jon Kimche, *The Second Arab Awakening: The Middle East 1914-1970* (New York, Chicago, San Francisco: Holt, Rinehart and Winston, 1970), p. 142, and George Antonius, *The Arab Awakening* (New York: Paragon Books, 1979), pp. 316-19, and p. 324.

6. Hudson, *op cit.*, p. 271.

7. See George Lenczoweki, *The Middle East in World Affairs*, fourth edition, (Ithaca, New York and London: Cornell University Press, 1980), p. 263.

8. For an account of the Kurdish national campaign in Iraq see "Unremitting Passion: The Kurdish National Movement" in Yosef Gotlieb's *Redefining the Middle East: The Question of Self-Determination*, forthcoming.

9. See Lenczowski, *op cit.*, p. 266.

10. Malone, *op cit.*, p. 98.

11. See Lenczowski, *op cit.*, p. 294.

12. *The New York Times*, November 6, 1980, p. 12.

13. Hudson, *op cit.*, p. 268.

13
Religion and Politics in Israel

Daniel J. Elazar
Janet Aviad

Israel is formally a secular democratic state. That
is to say, Israel has no established religion nor any provisions in its laws requiring a particular religious affiliation, belief, or commitment--Jewish or other--as a prerequisite
for holding office (a requirement which is quite common in
other Middle Eastern constitutions, most of which provide that
only Muslims can hold public office or at least certain
offices). On the other hand, there is a close interconnection
between religious communities and the state, including state
support of all recognized religions except those which explicitly
reject such support and a special status by consensus for the
majority religious community.
Any religious community can apply for and receive official
recognition in Israel and receive state support. Israel's
Ministry of *Religions* is just that, not of one religion only.
It is a ministry which serves Jews, Muslims, Druze, various
Christian denominations and others.
According to the laws of the state, the recognized
religions in Israel are granted their status by the Knesset
which gives their officials authority, under Israeli law, in
matters of personal status (marriage, divorce, etc.), and in
other matters pertaining to the governance of their respective
religious communities. In fact, one can say that as a matter
of constitutional principle, no Israeli Knesset could possibly
interfere with those prerogatives in any systematic way; there
would be a unified front on the part of all the religious
communities in Israel to prevent this. Indeed, those people
who actively adhere to their religions--Jewish, Muslim, and
others--would not recognize the Knesset as a source of
authority for their religious communities but only as the
regularizer of that authority within the context of the state.
For them, the real source of authority is the religious or
Divine source, i.e., the Jewish rabbinate obtains its authority
through Jewish religious law and the Muslim imams obtain theirs
through Muslim religious law. In this sense there is a

rootedness of religion in the larger constitutional fabric
of the state which no regime could possibly conceive of
seriously disrupting.

In addition, religion functions as a legitimizing device
in Israel no less than in other Middle Eastern countries;
this is what is meant when people talk about Israel as a
Jewish state and, of course, the majority of Israelis, as
Jews, very much want Israel to be a Jewish state. Virtually
all Israelis recognize this connection between Israel and
Judaism as well as Jewishness. It is well known that many
of the original founders of Israel were secularists. They
saw Israel as a Jewish state in the strictly or almost
strictly national sense of the term "Jewish"--though one
finds ambivalence in their thinking on the subject. Their
approach to Jewishness has failed to become dominant, however
much it has served to loosen the bonds of religion with regard
to the behavior of Israel's Jews.

THE JEWISH RELIGIOUS SITUATION IN ISRAEL

The Jewish religious situation in Israel is one that
defies conventional definition and is characterized by continued flux. The Jews in Israel reflect all the ambivalence
of modern society with regard to the relationship between
religion and society, if perhaps less with regard to religion
and politics. In this respect, it is possible to discern a
measure of modernization (in the sociological sense) that is
taking place among Jews in Israel, albeit in the Islamic world.
This is partly because, for the majority of the Jews in Israel
or their parents who came from elsewhere, Israel itself has
not been a strong element in the modernization process which
started earlier. More significantly, the Jewish religion is
only partly rooted in pre-modern patterns. In many ways, the
Jewish people was modern before modernity. Jewish religious
tradition is also associated with patterns which are also
quite at home in modern society, so there has not been the
kind of undiluted confrontation between traditional religion
and modernization that has been true in some other cases.
One sees this even in the way that the ultra-Orthodox Jews
in Israel fit into modern economic and political life. There
have been some elements of confrontation, but for the most
part, there is not the same problem of confrontation and
contradiction that there is in the Islamic world, for example.

To the outside observer, the impression might be of two
tight camps--the religious and the non-religious--whose lines
are set. Actually, the situation is much looser, and more
complex. Among the Israelis who call themselves religious,
there is great diversity in attitudes towards the state and
the modern world. Among the Israelis who call themselves
non-religious, there are large groups which are extremely
close to the tradition and there are groups which have
espoused a humanist secular outlook and have minimal contact

with the tradition. The word *dati* meaning "religious" is used narrowly referring to one who observes the religious law but it by no means describes the extent of religious observance or commitment in the state. It is assumed that one who is observant also accepts the traditional Jewish world-view and understands himself as bound by God's revelation as recorded in the Bible and developed by rabbinic authorities whose word is authoritative. Thus, the meaning of the word "religious," as used in Israel, is not identical with the same word in the broader American sense which suggests someone who is spiritual and might or might not believe in God. The difference in the use of the word is very important, since its opposite, "non-religious," also does not imply the same thing in Hebrew as it does in English. To be "non-religious" in Israel does not necessarily mean that one does not believe in God or even that one does not observe any of the religious traditions, but rather that one is not totally observant. Everyone who is not strictly halachic is included in the category "non-religious," although many do accept many traditional views and preserve substantial elements of Jewish tradition in their own lives and in the lives of their families.

Another usage has developed in Israel to distinguish between groups within the general "non-religious" category. That usage is the word "traditional" which refers to people who are selectively observant and who do not declare themselves to be atheists or agnostics. Only the latter, who are termed secularists, are considered to be non-religious and many of them selectively maintain Jewish religious practices, particularly in their homes. The criterion accepted by the public for determining one's "religious" commitment is the traditional Jewish criterion of performing *mitzvot* (Divine commandments). The presuppositions underlying such performance, that is belief, are not defined. While there are quite a few studies and polls of the former, very little research has been done on the latter.

It is quite clear that Jewish behavior, in the sense of traditional acts as well as traditional responses to symbols of Judaism, is common among vast numbers of the population which do not define themselves as "religious." Among this large "traditional" group there is a measure of traditionalist commitment. One can speak with certainty of the fact that this large portion of the population exists, and that within this group, Judaism is a positive value. However, it is not a value accepted as authoritative and obligatory in the traditional sense, but is rather a value which demands selective and sporadic acts of commitment.

The fact that these various types of religious commitment exist side by side in Israel must be remembered when considering their viability and strength. The general social-cultural context is a supportive force in the survival of Jewish traditionalism. In the Diaspora no such supportive context exists. Therefore, in the Diaspora, a vague commitment can be watered down and emptied of substance; whereas

in Israel it may be strengthened. Thus, because the atmosphere
of the Sabbath descends upon the entire country, observance
seems appropriate, even when limited to certain aspects and
not all. Because the entire country prepares for holidays
and observes them in some ways continuous with the tradition,
it is fitting and easy for some observance to take place in
the home. Another factor strengthening the "traditionalist"
is the reality of a living Orthodox community, which is a
reminder and a goad to those inclining towards tradition anyway and a justification of Israel as a Jewish state for many
ostensible "secularists" as well.

Underlying all religious commitment in Israel is the
inherent interweaving of the religious and national moments
in Judaism. The two are inseparable, which means that the
national and religious dimensions in Israel are necessarily
intertwined. Thus, national holidays are either traditional
Jewish holidays or incorporate traditional elements in themselves so that they become semi-religious holidays. Every
people or nation sanctified events and individuals and places
which have critical associations in their history. In Israel
this process of sanctification is heightened by the power of
the Jewish symbols which are used in the process of sanctification. Every society, traditional or modern, has certain
rituals which increase group loyalty and integration. Religion
is obviously a source of group cohesion and solidarity. In
Israel, Judaism or precipitates from Jewish history fulfill
this function in what from the earliest days has been the
religion of the nation. This religion of Israel, as a nation,
is one which is linked to a force beyond the nation itself.
This means that the events, people, and places sanctified by
the State of Israel somehow become part of the ancient national-
religious tradition. For some Israelis, the religious and
traditional groups, Israel is a nation under God. For others,
the reference to God has dropped; however, the idea that the
state must be directed towards a goal beyond itself remains.
In both cases, the religious elements are interwoven with
national elements.

Therefore, it is difficult in Israel to distinguish
between a pure national Israeli identity and a Jewish identity.
National historical consciousness does not exist without
reference to the religious historical past. Continuity with
Jewish national culture implies continuity with the religious
tradition in some form. The sources to be confronted are
religious sources. The consciousness and sensibility are
religious. No matter where one stands himself as far as
commitment to Judaism is concerned, in Israel he must understand the religious past and its continuities today.

RELIGION IN ISRAEL AND THE UNITED STATES: FUNDAMENTAL
DIFFERENCES

It should be obvious that the relationship between

religion and state in Israel is radically different than
that in the United States. The formal and sharp separation
of church and state and the maintenance of neutrality toward
religions in the public realm is the product of the specific
experience of the United States, where free church Protestants
were influential in determining that there would be no established church and that all religions would be organized
as voluntary denominations. Both Judaism and Catholicism
had to accommodate to the Protestant pattern of religious
organization and the Protestant definition of church-state
relations.

The United States is a pluralistic society in which
the individual, exercising free choice, is of central concern. The individual affiliates voluntarily with any number
of groups, one of which may be a religious denomination.
The religious denominations compete for members, as it were,
with each other and with whatever causes or ideologies are
popular in the general society. In this effort to attract
members and hold them, religious organizations may place
heavy emphasis upon the benefits which the individual will
derive from his or her participation. Such participation
is described as bringing a measure of personal happiness,
moral improvement, and good for the family. Joining a
religious institution, church or synagogue, is considered by
most to be part of the American way of life. It is a positive
value for the individual, the community, and the country.
Religion is perceived in America as a beneficial force, and
at the same time, a force which does not demand too much in
terms of obligations, moral or ideological.

Given the religious situation in America, it is not
surprising that many Americans find it difficult to understand the religious situation in Israel and, indeed, the
Middle East generally. If one attempts to transfer the
American model of church-state relations to Israel, or if
one attempts to understand Israeli Judaism through the eyes
of the Reform or Conservative American Jewish models, one is
likely to become confused. First, while there is no established church religion in Israel, Judaism, Islam and all
other major religious groups are state-supported. Second,
Jews in Israel who are deemed "religious" are orthodox and
live according to the very demanding way of life of traditional Judaism. The synagogue plays a very minor role in
Israeli Judaism, since it does not serve as the center for
non-ritual functions. In Israel the entire country is Jewish
space, and the synagogue is a place where one prays.

In Israel, Judaism is a very live force which drives
and divides people, and which in many ways legitimates the
state. In both respects, it is closer to the traditional
conception of Judaism than the American model. Americans,
in trying to understand the complexities of religion and
state in Israel, must abandon American conceptions of the
proper relationship of religion to state and must attempt

to understand the religious situation of Israel from within.
This means understanding the general situation in such matters
in the Middle East, the context of the religious-national
tradition of Judaism (which is in the classic Middle Eastern
mold), and the specific historical and social conditions of
Israel.

Historical Background: The Positions of the Religious Camp

The State of Israel was established after a break of
twenty centuries during which Jewish law, although used in
the governance of diaspora communities, was not applied to the
operation of a state. Furthermore, the situation of a modern
Jewish state is different from that of any earlier Jewish
polity. Technological change and secularization have brought
unprecedented changes in all spheres of life. Internal changes
have occurred which have broken the religious unity of the
Jewish people. Whereas in earlier periods when Jews ruled
themselves there was a fundamental agreement upon national
self-definition and structures of life, today no such consensus exists. This implies that there are various visions
of national purpose, various interpretations of how one should
live in Israel, and various views as to the cultural shape
which the homeland should have. Finally, the state includes
non-Jewish citizens who are guaranteed equal rights as individuals, full religious liberty, and a measure of cultural
autonomy. Consequently, the state itself was established as
a secular polity but, in the Middle Eastern pattern, one
which expresses its neutrality by supporting all religions
on an equal basis.

A majority of the leaders of the modern Zionist movement
were not traditional Jews. While they might have wanted to
maintain certain continuities with Jewish tradition, they did
not accept the authority of the religious law and did not
accept the values and goal of life as they were defined by
the Orthodoxy they knew in Western or Eastern Europe. Rather,
they wanted to construct a new Jewish society and a new
Hebrew man whose formation would be based upon general
Western values and humanist ideals, which would include
experiences and opportunities outside the purview and bounds
of the Orthodox way of life. Nevertheless, the Zionist
pioneer did not reject Judaism altogether. The situation
and the relationship were much more complicated than a brutal
amputation of the past and of the Jewish heritage he had
received from his fathers.

The Zionist movement, after all, arose out of the
failures of Jewish assimilation in Europe. When it had
become clear that emancipation and assimilation would not
bring redemption to the Jews in Europe, the Zionist movement
emerged to bring that redemption through a return to the
homeland and the construction of an autonomous Jewish entity
there. Many of the early leaders of Zionism were assimilated
Jews who had little relationship to Jewish culture. Others,

who were concerned about the continuity of the national
culture, were opposed to its religious character. Therefore,
the Zionist movement presented a revolutionary alternative
to European Jewish life whose ideals threatened the religious
way of life and the religious establishment in Europe.

Among the socialist pioneers in particular were a group
of militant secularists. People of enormous idealism and
burning conviction, they came to Palestine to establish a
Jewish homeland where they could realize their ideals and
values while constructing a home for a reconstructed Jewish
people. Part of the reconstruction for them involved a
thoroughly secular Jewish state.

Religious Jews were inherently committed to end the
exile and return to Zion as part of the process of redemption.
However, could one participate in the effort to end exile
when the leaders of the effort were non-Orthodox Jews?
And could one participate in the effort to end exile when
it might be against the will of the nations of the world and
against the will of God himself? The tradition had warned
Jews against rebelling against the foreign powers and against
"pushing the end."

Even those religious Jews sympathetic toward the Zionist
effort recognized that the Zionist movement was led by non-
traditional Jews, and that the ideals of the movement were
not those which Orthodox Judaism envisioned for a national
homeland. According to the religious view, a Jewish homeland
implied a Torah-society--a society which governed itself
according to the *Halachah* and whose culture messianic period.
All Jews, religious or non-religious, who participated in the
Zionist enterprise, were, even if unintentionally, agents
in God's scheme to initiate the redemptive process in Israel.
According to the Rav Kook, settling the land through an ingathering of the exiles were commandments of such import,
especially at this historic moment of the beginning of the
redemption, that their fulfillment overrode hesitations
regarding cooperation with secular Jews in the effort.

The theological grounding which existed, in addition
to the particular historical situation of the Jews at the
turn of the century, led a significant number of moderate
Orthodox rabbis to support the Zionist movement and to form
their own party within that movement. Accepting the Zionist
principle of acting to achieve a political goal, the return
to the land of Israel, they wanted to exercise pressure within
the Zionist movement as religious Jews. Therefore, in 1902,
under the leadership of Rabbi Isaac Joseph Reines, these
rabbis formed the Mizrahi party. (Mizrahi is a play on words
meaning "of the east" and also an abbreviation of *Merkaz
Ruhani*, which means spiritual center.) From the beginning,
the goal of the religious Zionists was two-fold: to influence
the Zionist organization in a religious direction, as they
defined that direction, namely in terms of the *Halachah*, and
to influence Orthodox Jews to support Zionism. This they
could do only by legitimating the movement in the eyes of

the Orthodox public which still included a majority of
world Jewry. The manifest goal of Mizrahi, one which
could draw such masses to its ranks, was "the land of
Israel for the people of Israel according to the Torah
of Israel." The linkage of the Zionist movement to
Orthodox Judaism and the construction of a Jewish
settlement according to the Torah of Israel could only
be accomplished if Orthodox Jews joined in the Zionist
enterprise and attempted to influence it.

Turning to both the Zionist Congress and his
Orthodox brothers, Rabbi Samuel Mohlever, a great
supporter of Zionism, stated the Mizrahi position:

> It is essential that the Congress unite all "Sons of
> Zion" who are true to our cause to work in complete
> harmony and fraternity, even if there be among them
> differences of opinion regarding religion. Our
> attitude towards those among us who do not observe
> the religious precepts must be, as it were, as if
> fire had taken hold of our homes, imperiling our per-
> sons and our property. Under such circumstances would
> we not receive anyone gladly and with love who, though
> irreligious in our eyes, came to rescue us? Is this
> not our present plight, my brethren? A great fire,
> a great conflagration, is raging in our midst and we
> are all threatened....If brethren put out their
> hands to us in aid, doing all in their power to
> deliver us from our dire straits, are there such
> among us who would spurn them? If all factions
> really understand this...this covenant of brothers
> will surely stand. All Sons of Zion must be
> completely convinced and must believe with a perfect
> faith that the resettlement of our country--i.e.
> the purchase of land and building of houses, the
> planting of orchards and the cultivation of the
> soil--is one of the fundamental commandments of our
> Torah....Whoever assists us and does not hold this
> faith is comparable to one who contributes to a
> cause in which he does not really believe. The basis
> of Hibbat Zion is the Torah, as it has been handed
> down to us from generation to generation, with
> neither supplement nor subtraction. I do not intend
> this as an admonition to any individual...I am never-
> theless stating in a general way that the Torah,
> which is the Source of our life, must be the founda-
> tion of our regeneration in the land of our fathers
> (Hertzberg, pp. 402-403).

As long as the aim of the Zionist movement was
almost exclusively political, the disagreements between religious and non-religious Zionists over

religious and cultural matters could be ignored. But
when the Zionists focused upon the cultural program of
the national renaissance, the issue could not be avoided
and ideological battles were fought out between segments
within the movement. Despite the conflicts, the religious
Zionists remained within the Zionist movement. Here, the
unifying tendency embodied in the ideal of Love of Israel
predominated over the centrifugal tendencies emerging from
sharp ideological conflicts. As Rabbi T.J. Reiner stated,

> There is no greater sacrilege than to allege that Zionism
> is part and parcel of secularism for the truth is that
> it is precisely the holiness of the land that induces
> the secularists to participate in the movement...it is
> in this that we may see the greatness of Zionism, for
> it has succeeded in uniting people of diverse views,
> and directing them toward a noble aim--the saving of
> the people--and this is its glory (Abramov, p. 71).

Many Orthodox Jews could not accept what they regarded as the illegitimate compromising postures of the
Mizrahi organization. Following the Tenth Zionist
Congress, in which a cultural program for the Zionist
movement was approved, the anti-Zionists organized
Agudat Yisrael (1912), a party whose explicit goal was
to oppose all Zionist activities in Europe and Palestine
and to deny the basic claim that the Zionist movement
represented and embodied the will of the Jewish people.
Agudat Yisrael claimed that it represented the Jewish
people, and that those who abnegated the tradition had
left their people.
The theological grounding of Agudah's position was
old and firm. "Forcing the end" had long been a suspected effort and one to be feared by Jews who had a
sense of history. Flowing from this stance was the
notion that Torah-true Jews ought dedicate themselves
to the traditional act of fulfilling the Torah in exile
and waiting for redemption, which could come only at
God's beckoning and in his own good time. There were
Agudah rabbis who favored and sanctioned *aliyah* (immigration) to the land of Israel, but only within the framework of a Torah-true community. There could be no possibility of cooperating with non-observant Jews and certainly not of living with them in the same community.
The Agudah rabbis feared the inroads which the
Zionists were making in Palestine, and this fear increased following the Balfour Declaration (1917). The
declaration introduced the support of a major power in
building a Jewish homeland. It also made the entire
project very real and imminent. The Ashkenazic Orthodox
community in Palestine, often known as the Old Yishuv,

which was centered mainly in Jerusalem, had in the
interim developed its links with Agudath Israel as the
Palestinian branch. Its members determined to block
Zionist efforts wherever possible and to separate themselves from all religious Jews who supported the Zionists.

However, the separation could not be clear-cut, since
the institutions of the Old Yishuv needed money to survive,
and the control of such funds was delegated by the British
to the Zionist-sponsored *Vaad Leumi* (National Council)
composed of non-religious and religious Zionists. Throughout the 1920s, great efforts were made by Chaim Weizmann
and others to bring the Orthodox anti-Zionists into the
Vaad Leumi in order to gain unity of the Jews in Palestine
and in order to increase the religious legitimation of
the Zionist organization. However, these efforts came to
naught. In the end, the Zionist agreed to fund *yeshivot*
(religious schools) without getting the active cooperation
of the anti-Zionists, but in this way securing a truce
between the two groups.

It must be recognized that the battle between the
religious and non-religious camps in Palestine was a
principled one over the nature of the society to be constructed in the Jewish national home. Those Orthodox
who took a radical anti-Zionist stance were those who
have been fending off changes in their way of life and
beliefs since the beginning of the enlightenment and
emancipation. Ever since the modern period began, these
people felt they were witnessing the breakdown of traditional Jewish life. They were determined to resist
the continuation of this process. In their view, Zionism
was a secular movement and therefore a profanization.
It was led by non-observant men and women, usurpers of
God's power, who were leading Jews astray. The use of
Hebrew as a spoken language was an example of profanization; secular studies in the Zionist schools were
another; granting of women the right to vote in Zionist
institutions another. The greater the influx of Zionists
into Palestine, the greater the defensiveness of the
Ashkenazic Old Yishuv. This defensiveness and opposition was expressed geographically in the determination
to live in separate neighborhoods which were to be as
self-sufficient as possible.

Needless to say, the anti-Zionist Orthodox totally
rejected the Mizrahi, seeing them as traitors to the
Torah who were doubly dangerous because they purported
to be otherwise. Although the position of Agudath Israel
has undergone radical changes since the early 1920s,
differences as to the meaning and valuation of the
Zionist enterprise continue to be manifest today in the
battle between the two party groupings in the Religious
Camp: the National Religious Party (Mafdal), built

around the Mizrahi, and the Agudath Israel.

In the early 1930s the relationship of the religious population towards the non-religious underwent a significant change. Throughout the Mandate period, the religious Zionists had participated in Zionist activities and were integrated into the new Yishuv. The Mizrahi organization had brought to Israel many Orthodox settlers and had developed the concept of the integration of Torah and Labour, which permitted the religious immigrants to engage in agricultural work and thereby become part of the major developing thrust of the new Jewish society. Whereas previously Orthodox Jews had lived almost exclusively in cities engaging in petty crafts, artisanry, business, the movement of Torah and Work projected a new ideal in tune with the general Zionist focus upon the value of physical labor and agricultural settlement. Out of the Mizrahi there developed a new party, HaPoel HaMizrahi (Mizrahi Labor) for those who chose the way of life of agricultural pioneering and who had specific interests which could be furthered by this organization. HaPoel HaMizrahi joined the Histadrut (the Zionist Labor Federation and bastion of Labor Zionism) in labor activities. The religious Zionists succeeded in establishing a number of important kibbutzim (collective agricultural settlements) and moshavim (cooperative agricultural settlements), based upon the concept that an integrated religious life included both labor and study.

Throughout the 1930s Agudat Yisrael in Palestine had maintained its posture of aloofness and separation. However, in the 1930s, this stance underwent great changes, although not without an internal struggle. The immediate cause of the change was the influx of Orthodox immigrants from Central Europe, who were more moderate in their approach to modernization and Zionism than were the old settlers. Second, the burning threat of Nazism forced Agudah leaders to consider ways of cooperating with the Zionists in order to bring Jews out of Europe. Some of the Palestinian old-time Agudah leaders remained firm in their position of negation of Zionism and continued to block all changes. Others, however, began to alter their position as the situation seemed to demand.

An example of the inner division and conflict within Agudath Israel may be seen in the battle over the establishment of the Horev school in Jerusalem. Agudah members from Germany had immigrated in sufficient numbers in the early thirties to wish to establish a school for their children which would follow their own educational principles. Influenced by Samson Raphael Hirsch, the German Orthodox wanted to build a school which would include high level general studies as well

as Torah studies, would offer the same education to
girls, and would conduct its program in Hebrew. The
school was established in 1934, and immediately became
a target of attack from the Old Jerusalem Orthodox
who objected to the innovations in mixed education,
in Hebrew, and in secular subjects. However, the
German Jews did not yield. In fact, their position
gained strength as more Agudah members arrived in the
country and the conflicting approaches within Agudah
became more evident. The official formal indication
of the change in approach was the agreement of Agudat
Yisrael to cooperate with the World Zionist Organization,
which came into effect in 1934. Agudat Yisrael was
reorganized in Palestine under the leadership of Rabbi
I.M. Levin. The reorganization recognized the various
trends within Agudah, and more important, effectively
renounced the separatist policy of the Old Yishuv.

Agudat Yisrael began urging its members to abandon
Europe and settle in Palestine during the late 1930s.
Following the war, when the need for an independent
Jewish state was so painfully evident, Agudat Yisrael
entered into an agreement with David Ben-Gurion, backing
the establishment of the state. This agreement succeeded
in establishing unity among all elements of the Jewish
population on the eve of the proclamation of the state.
The nature of the agreement is very important, since it
set out the basic lines which have been followed ever
since and have enabled the religious parties to remain
within the government. In a letter to Rabbi I.M. Levin,
Ben-Gurion, as head of the Jewish Agency, offered certain
conditions which would guarantee certain demands of the
Orthodox in the future Jewish state. The conditions
enumerated were actually continuations of practices
embodied in legislation or which had become customary
during the Mandatory period. Thus, it was agreed that
the Sabbath would be the official day of rest in the
Jewish state, that *Kashrut* laws (dietary laws) would be
maintained in all public institutions in the state, that
religious school systems would be maintained and funded
by the state, public transportation would not operate
for the country as a whole on Sabbaths and holy days,
and that matters of personal status, primarily marriage
and divorce, would be controlled exclusively by religious
law. On the other hand, the religious camp conceded that
the state radio would continue to operate on Sabbaths
and holidays and local practices with regard to public
transportation would be maintained.

These conditions constitute the famous "status quo"
which the Israeli government and the religious parties
have continued to support. It is certain that Ben-Gurion,
in agreeing to these conditions, sought to avoid conflicts

within the Jewish population. He also sought to gain
for himself the support of a sizeable and constant
element of that population, namely, the religious
community, Ben-Gurion felt that he had provided a
national minimum in the area of religion, which would
guarantee that observant traditional Jews and secular
Jews could live as they desired without coercing each
other or violating each other's principles in any
intolerable way. At the same time, this minimum guaranteed the Jewish character of the Jewish state. Both
religious parties accepted the arrangement and represented their constituencies in the provisional government formed by Ben-Gurion in 1948.

However, there is a great difference in both the
mode of participation and in the ideology underlying
the participation of Agudat Yisrael-rooted and the
Mizrahi-rooted parties in the state. In the manifesto
of Agudat Yisrael, written in 1912, it was stated that
"The Jewish people stands outside the framework of the
political peoples of the world, and differs essentially
from them: the Sovereign of the Jewish people is the
Almighty; The Torah is the Law that governs them; and
the Holy Land has been at all times destined for the
Jewish people. It is the Torah which governs all
actions of Agudat Yisrael." By entering into the state
framework, Agudat Yisrael effectively modified its
manifesto. At the same time, because its participation
remains partial, Agudat Yisrael remains loyal to the
major aspects of its original position. In the view
of the ultra-Orthodox, a total Halachic way of life can
best be maintained by withdrawal from those areas con-
taminated by modern secular ideas, values, and sensibilities. These include most areas of life within a
modern state. Therefore, the participation of Agudat
Yisrael is partial, limited to those areas which have
specific reference to religious activities or religious
spheres.

Given this reservation about the nature of a Jewish
State which is not an *halachic* entity, it is not surprising that Agudat Yisrael has sought and has received
exemption from military service for its young people;
that is to say, male yeshivah students and all women
who chose exemption. It is not clear, according to
the *Halachah*, that males ought go be exempt, and
various opinions exist. Agudat Yisrael persuaded Ben-
Gurion, by the claim that yeshivah students were needed
desperately in the effort to rebuild the *yeshivot* which
had been destroyed in Europe. Ben-Gurion, sympathetic
to the overall goal and knowing that the total number of
boys involved was no more than 1,000 at the time, granted
the military exemption. Today, that exemption extends

to more than 10,000 *yeshivah* students, and is still
respected by the Israeli government. What is important
to recognize is that the very seeking of the military
exemption reflects more than a fear of a *halachic*
violation which could be incurred during military service.
Rather, rejection of the armed forces reflects suspicion
of and withdrawal from the state and its political
efforts, as well as withdrawal from secular elements of
the society as represented by the army.

In contrast to the refusal of Agudat Yisrael to
permit military service, the Mizrahi and its successor,
the National Religious Party (NRP), have regarded self-
defense in the armed forces as an act of devotion to the
state and the Land. While the state is religiously
neutral or even negative in the view of Agudat Yisrael,
in the view of the religious Zionists the state is a
positive *religious* value. The establishment of an
independent Jewish polity in the land of Israel is a
step in the messianic process, which cannot be reversed.
It follows, obviously, that military service is of
positive religious values as is the army itself.

Historical Background: The Positions of the Secular Camps

In understanding the status quo agreement and the
entire position of Judaism in Israel, one must consider
why the Zionist movement and later the state whose
majority is not religious in the accepted Israeli sense
of Orthodox, have legitimated and established religious
institutions in Israel and have sanctioned the presence
and influence of the religious in Israeli society.
One must ask why the non-religious population has
agreed or acquiesced, as the case may be, to the
pressures of the religious. One must ask why there
has not been a real *Kulturkampf*, as is so often
suggested will occur, against the powers of "religious
coercion." To understand the answer to this question,
one must examine some aspects of the Zionist revolution:
the aspects of genuine continuity.

Jews who defined themselves as socialist Zionists
brought with them from Europe a combination of rationalist
and socialist ideals, the former determining a rejection
of the traditional understanding of revelation, history,
and messianism; the latter providing a humanist surrogate
for them. However, within the workers' movement there
were several approaches to religion and tradition which
must be distinguished from each other. First, there was
the negative approach of that group which rejected
religion and tradition totally. For these radical
Zionists, Judaism represented a survival from more

primitive times, and was now a brake upon the progress
of the Jewish people. It was considered necessary, in
the view of these radical Zionists, to break loose from
the entire religious framework before the work of national
and individual reconstruction could begin. This approach
flourished for a generation or so in certain prominent
circles and then began to decline. While spokesmen for
it can still be found, it is no longer a significant
force in the country.

Another approach was an ambivalent one, far more
complicated than the abrogation of religious practices
or the denial of religious concepts would seem to indicate. It is this approach which shall concern us because
it remains characteristic of the leadership of Israel and
prevalent among the secular population. The roots of
the ambivalence of the socialist Zionists towards
religion and tradition lie first in their deep attachment
towards their immediate past, a sense of warmth and
nostalgia to what had been received at home. These
sentiments operated to moderate a staunchly negative
ideological stance against Judaism. Far more significant
than this rather passive, relfexive, appreciation was an
active sense that they, in some way, as pioneers in *Eretz
Yisrael*, were actualizing selected but core elements of
the Jewish tradition. They saw themselves as builders
of a Jewish society and culture which would be freer,
more healthy, and within a more universal framework
than had been possible within the fettered conditions of
exile. Finally, they considered themselves, as a group,
to be a vital link in the historical continuity of the
Jewish people, identified themselves romantically with
the ongoing historical spirit of Israel, and invoked
history and destiny when speaking of the meaning of
the Zionist activity.

The sense of participation in a redemptive process,
the longing to establish a utopian society, and the
sense of being actors in a drama which had world-historic
significance linked even the secular *halutzim* (pioneers)
with traditional religious ideals, ideas, and attitudes.

The religious equivalences must not disguise the
secular grounding of the workers' movement and the
secular approach of some of its leaders to the Jewish
tradition. While there was a deeply felt need to maintain historical continuity and even to receive legitimation from Jewish history, there was also a conscious
attempt to dismiss the religious base of the Jewish
tradition as meaningless or irrelevant.

The context of the national settlement facilitated
and made real the transition from a religious to a
national self-definition. Here the sense that the
sacred was a social force, whose manifestations are

confined to society itself, could be experienced easily
and naturally. Zionism as an experience and as a project
could be considered a mode of Jewish being which needed
no external legitimation because it was indeed the
natural fulfillment of the Jewish struggle for survival.
Some socialist Zionists might have appreciated the
tradition while feeling free to abandon its religious
framework or use it selectively, finding in their own
national self-definition a sufficient substitute for
the national-religious self-definition of their fathers.
It is the apparent self-evidence of this transition from
religious to national categories within the Zionist
framework which may account for the almost total lack
of interest in religious questions on the part of the
halutzim.

The Jewish people thus became the carrier of
sanctity, the representative of the sacred, and particular cultural values, previously religious values also,
were now sanctified because of their association with
the nation. During the period of the second aliyah a
process of selection took place in which certain values
from the religious tradition were sorted out to be
retained in the new Hebrew culture. Those selected
were chosen because they could be interpreted as meaningful to the national or socialist vision of the
pioneers. Thus, the Bible retained its sacred quality
but was interpreted in terms of its national value.
The Bible was understood as a Jewish cultural monument,
a link to Jewish history, the legitimator or Jewish
claims to the land of Israel, and as a source of universalist humanist ideals. It was emptied of its explicit
meaning as the record of Israel's breakthrough to
transcendence and became the treasure of Israel's
national past.

An inescapable ambivalence towards Judaism derived
from these developments is characteristic of Israeli
society today. Within Israel large groups of the population feel very positively towards the Jewish tradition
and select elements from it which they observe within
their own familiaries. While not accepting the entire
world view and structure of Judaism, they want to maintain ties to the tradition which was once identified
with Jewish national religious culture; they want to
preserve elements and aspects of that tradition as part
of Israeli culture and as values in Israeli society.

There is no clear consistency in the process of
selection from the tradition on the part of either the
Zionist pioneers or contemporary "non-religious" Israelis.
Various customs, ideals, attitudes, and values are maintained often for reasons which are not conscious and in
ways which are not explicit. This is indeed the hold

of a living and dynamic tradition upon its descendents and the path through which it evolves in new situations. The result in Israel today is continuity despite rebellion. Both the pioneers of the early aliyot and the citizens of today feel the pull of ancient and submerged loyalties towards the Jewish tradition.

The citizen of contemporary Israel who may be defined as a *maseroti* (traditionalist) may not be concerned with definitions or justifications of the Zionist revolution in terms of Jewish tradition. He is concerned, however, with the character of the Jewish State and its legitimation. More and more in recent years he has come to recognize that both depend upon some link to the Jewish tradition. Judaism is somehow constitutive of Jewish identity and the State of Israel is identified as a Jewish State. This recognition has grasped the non-believer -- even the rabid anti-believer -- and has been the source of much inner anguish. It is this essential core character of Judaism which inclines the non-religious within the Israeli population towards sympathy with the Orthodox, no matter how annoying the former find what they perceive as the rigid demands of the latter upon the general society. And it is also this recognition of the significance of Judaism in national life which supports the positive ties towards the tradition of those who are not non-religious but who are also not Orthodox, namely the traditionalist parts of the population.

RELIGION AND POLITICS

The hope of the religious population in Israel is that the entire population will eventually become Orthodox and that the state will conform in its laws and actual behavior with the demands of the religious tradition. However, the Orthodox groups have had to compromise in actuality and to operate with the reality of a non-halachic state governed by a leadership which is not Orthodox. Both religious parties, the NRP and Agudat Yisrael, have attempted to influence government policy in two areas. First, they have worked to establish by law their own institutions and separate services. Second, they have defined certain areas in the public realm which would be governed by religious law, and have established this fact through government legislation.

On the institutional plane, this means that the Orthodox have constructed their own school systems and have gained government support for its separate existence. The NRP-backed religious school system is part of the state system and receives its funding from state

taxes. The extreme Orthodox do not want their schools
to be part of the state system, so have gained recognition and funding for their independent schools. The
rabbinate and law courts are under the control of the
Orthodox and are free of government interference except
insofar as the latter are subject to the review of the
Israeli Supreme Court. Religious law dictates that all
public institutions be kosher, that certain restrictions
of the Sabbath be imposed upon the entire population,
that marriage and divorce be regulated by the *halachah*.
The imposition of religious traditions in these areas
has been accepted by Israelis, religious and non-
religious. The acquiescence of large parts of the non-
religious population together with the efforts of the
religious parties has resulted in the obvious continuity
between the modern state and Jewish tradition. While
Israel has no established church and all religions are
equal before the law, the state is not exactly neutral
nor secular, and is not divorced from the symbols nor
the institutions of Judaism.

This is not to say that the state is a religious
entity nor that it fulfills the ideals of Judaism. In
fact, there are Israelis who argue from a religious point
of view, that the Jewish symbols and the public celebrations of Jewish rituals are mere window dressing for a
basically secular state and society. Thus, to call
Israel a Jewish state, in any religious sense, is a
distortion. From the ideologically secularist perspective,
it may be argued that the religious presence is hypocritical and offensive. In either case, it is clear
that the relation between Judaism and society in Israel
is complex and not easily analyzed.

The religious parties exist because of the intense
politization of public life in Israel and the heavy
involvement of government in almost all spheres of public
activity. Thus, a major segment of the religious leadership is convinced that it must remain in politics simply
in order to guard the Jewish character of the state and
the religious institutions which exist rather than withdraw and permit these areas to be secularized. The
power of the religious lies in the coalition government
system of Israel. The majority party in that coalition,
from the rise of the state in 1948 until the election of
1977, was the Labor Party. This party never emerged
from an election with enough votes to form a government
alone, and was forced to reach a party agreement with
other smaller parties in order to form a coalition
government. Every coalition has sought to include the
religious parties, which together have secured between
10-15 percent of the vote in every election. In fact,
every coalition has included the Mafdal, meaning that

the latter received support for its special interests,
namely religious affairs, while the dominant coalition
partner received the support of the religious in
economic and foreign policy matters.

The major religious party is the Mafdal (NRP)
(Mifleget Datit Leumit) established by the union of
Mizrahi and Poalei Mizrahi after 1956. The second
religious party is Agudat Yisrael, and there is a small
third party, Poalei Agudat Yisrael, the labor branch of
the second. The strength of the Mafdal has been around
8-10 percent, while the strength of Agudat Yisrael and
Poalei Agudat Yisrael together has been between 3 and
5 percent. Both electorates have remained fairly
stable. The two parties are often at odds, reflecting
the fact that the Mafdal has chosen to be a coalition
partner and consequently accepts the concomitant
responsibility to maintain coalition loyalty while Agudah
maintains its independence so as to be able to remain
consistent with its religious principles at all costs.
The Mafdal has held the Ministry of Religious Affairs
and the Ministry of the Interior almost constantly. In
the recent election of 1977, it was also given the
Education portfolio which its leaders had long desired.

Both religious parties have dedicated themselves
to preserving the status quo arrangement. However, the
NRP has adopted a "go-slow" policy in certain areas
where Agudat Yisrael has pushed for immediate and total
action, often seeking to embarass the NRP in its conciliatory approach. Sensitive to charges of seeking to
coerce the non-religious population in religious matters,
the Mafdal has been willing to compromise. Thus, instead
of a comprehensive national Sabbath observance law which
would include the banning of all business activities, the
compromise evolved permits local buses to run and certain
businesses to open in specific localities and under
specific conditions. In the area of *Kashrut*, the Mafdal
attempted to pass a law banning pig breeding in the state
for many years. It was only when a coalitional balance
permitted, in 1962, that such a law was passed.

The Agudah, however, has greater opportunity to
make demands upon the government, not having any cabinet
seats to lose. Anxious to demonstrate that the Mafdal
is compromising, Agudah sometimes proposes bills just
to embarass the Mafdal. It is clear to Agudah that
its bills have no chance of being accepted, but the
symbolic protest is made through the presentation of the
bill, and the embarassment of the Mafdal accomplished.
Thus, Agudah proposed that all flights of El-Al, the
national airline, be stopped on the Sabbath and that
no airplanes from foreign fleets be allowed to land on
Israel or take off. The Minister of Transportation

explained that both proposals were impossible given
the conditions of international commercial aviation.
The Mafdal was forced to abstain from voting, not being
able to vote against the government of which it was a
part. The excuse offered by the Mafdal is one that
has been repeated often:

> It was with pain that we abstained from voting on
> Rabbi Porush's motion dealing with Sabbath violation
> by El Al. It was not because we underrate the
> gravity of these violations, or ignore their impor-
> tance. The contrary is true. We regard this as a
> grave desecration of the Sabbath, which is one of
> the sublime and holy symbols of our entire nation.
> If we had known that by voting for the motion, we
> would assure its passage, we would not have hesi-
> tated to raise our hands and would have been pre-
> pared to jeopardize our participation in the
> government. Unfortunately, voting for the motion
> would have been an empty demonstration and, to the
> best of our judgement, the loss would have exceeded
> the gain. Our record in the struggle for religious
> interests is well known; our achievements in this
> sphere are considerable. We shall continue our
> struggle for a complete and comprehensive Sabbath
> throughout Israel, and we do not despair of success.

The image conveyed to many through such a statement
is that the Mafdal is prepared to compromise on principle
in order to remain within the coalition, and this is
precisely the point which Agudah wants to make. However,
it ought to be pointed out that the ability to compromise
and yet stand firm at certain points is what has enabled
the Mafdal to achieve the gains it has. When the dominant
party is more dependent on the religious partner in the
coalition, more can be demanded. When the opposite is
true, little can be demanded.

In the past, the Mafdal concentrated its efforts
within the rather confined areas of its specific religious
interests. Its thrust was mainly defensive: to protect
gains rather than to seek new ones. Recognizing the
reality of the non-religious character of the majority
of the population, their larger goal was seen as the
distant end of a long process of change. In the interim,
the immediate goal of guaranteeing the maximal influence
of religious precepts upon the public life and the maximal
support for separate religious institutions was pursued.
This has required a posture of adaptation, compromise,
and adjustment rather than aloofness, intransigence and
inflexibility. Thus,

those religious Jews in Israel, and they are in the
vast majority, who participate in the political life
of the state as presently constituted, cannot avoid
the uneasy feeling that in its present form, the State
of Israel is hardly an authentic embodiment of Jewish
national life. It is acceptable as a transitional
phenemenon. In all probability this transition is a
long one involving many generations. One can reconcile
oneself with it only if the State refrains from measures
which commit it officially to the secular view of
Jewish nationalism (Goldmann, p. 12).

The religious parties are convinced that a withdrawal
from the political sphere would not create a neutral state.
Rather, it would produce a secular society, whose state-
funded institutions would have an inherent advantage over
religious institutions, and whose secular way of life and
world-view would compete in the marketplace with religion
and inevitably dominate. The American experience, where
religion and state are separated completely in principle,
witnesses to the necessary diminution of the significance
and role of religion. This may be sufficient in the case
of Christianity, where religion makes relatively few practical
demands on a daily basis, but, in the case of Judaism where
the scope of religion is total, the withdrawal of the state
from the public sphere would mean a serious threat to the
Jewish character of the society.

In recent years, the NRP has flexed itself outside the
more traditional concerns of the religious party and has
attempted to influence foreign policy in connection with
the peace settlement and territories. The Young Guard,
which has emerged within the Mafdal, has taken the territories issue as central to their concerns, and has fought
hard against government concessions. Whether the Young
Guard will have the strength to oppose a peace settlement
which conceded territories, and therefore, would pull the
Mafdal out of the government coalition, has yet to be seen.
However, it is certain that the religious party has made
itself very visible and has made its voice heard in this
issue. Altogether, the Young Guard has attempted to change
the image of the Mafdal to that of an energetic, independent,
and principled party. At this writing, it has begun to
develop proposals in the economic sphere as well, in response
to the weakness of the present government in that sphere.
Should this new direction develop, the Mafdal might begin
to be transformed into an Israeli paralleled of the broad-
based Christian Democratic parties of Europe but this would
require a sea-change in its internal character and orientation.

The Provision of Religious Services

In order to provide services to the Jewish and non-
Jewish populations, the State of Israel has established a

Ministry of Religions on the state level, whose head is a
cabinet minister. It is responsible for the government's
role in the provision of religious services to all recognized religious groups. All recognized non-Jewish communities conduct their own law courts for religious matters,
maintain their own religious schools, and conduct their own
marriages, divorces, and burials. The Israeli government
guarantees their freedom in all these areas, and attempts
to facilitate relations between all religious communities.

An extensive statewide and local structure provides
services for the Jewish sector of the population. Its
officials are appointed by the Ministry of Religions or
elected by bodies outside the Ministry but funded by it in
all or part. The highest governing Jewish religious body
is the Supreme Rabbinic Council, which was established during
the Mandate period and continued by the State. The Council
consists of eight rabbis, half Sephardim and half Ashkenazim,
two of whom are the chief rabbis of the country. These men
meet to deal with religious questions which reach the state
plane and hand down decisions. When there is a question
which involves state legislation, it is renewed by the
Knesset which does not always accept their decision. There
have even been occasions when the decisions of the chief
rabbis or the rabbinical council have not been accepted by
the religious parties. Agudat Yisrael has never recognized
the Rabbinical Council and the Chief Rabbinate altogether.
It has established its own independent council of sages which
rules on problems which arise within the ultra orthodox
community. The Supreme Rabbinical Council is authoritative
for the Sephardic religious community and the Ashkenazim
who identify themselves with the NRP or who do not identify
themselves with the ultra orthodox. Likewise, with the
chief rabbinate where the withdrawal of the ultra orthodox has seriously weakened the power of these rabbis from
the inception of the office during the mandate. The Sephardic chief rabbi, the *Rishon LeZion*, is accepted as the highest
authority among the Sephardim in Israel. His office is the
oldest rabbinic office in the country, dating back to Ottoman
times. It preceded the Ashkenazic position, which was created
by the British, by several centuries. Rav Kook was the first
Ashkenazic chief rabbi.

On the local plane there are chief rabbis in every major
city, as well as local rabbinic courts. There are also local
religious councils which are responsible for administering
all religious services in the various localities. Thus, the
country is divided into special districts generally following
municipal boundaries in which religious services are provided by special authorities specific to each. On the local
as on the state plane, the ultra orthodox do not accept the
authority of the religious councils and turn to their own
councils and courts. The Conservative and Reform Jews,
because they do not want to be recognized as separate
religious bodies (that is to say, outside of the Jewish

fold), do not have their own courts and utilize the Orthodox mechanisms when necessary.

Conflicts in Religious and Non-Religious Viewpoints

The existing arrangements belie certain real tensions between the religious and non-religious sectors of the population over the place of religion in the state. These tensions emerge in several ways. There are often intellectual arguments over the place of Judaism generally, usually regarding a specific issue of public conflict but generalized to the entire relationship of Judaism to the State of Israel. These intellectual battles remain in journals and newspapers, indicating a problem or reacting to one, but not in themselves leading to practical action. There have been occasions, however, when the conflict between religious and non-religious elements, which is usually quiescent but always potential, emerges in a case of public debate or even street violence. The instances where heated differences of opinion break into actual violence seem to be cases where a change in the strategic balance of power appears to be in the making and the status quo appears to be getting upset. Thus, if there is an agreement as to which streets in Jerusalem should be closed on the Sabbath to preserve the rights of the Orthodox, and the Orthodox community attempts to expand the number of streets or enter a new area of the city and close it on the Sabbath, non-Orthodox elements may become incensed and resort to verbal arguments and then non-verbal expressions, all of which are returned in kind. The point is that people on both sides accept the status quo, grudgingly or willing. When it appears that that status quo is being altered, the principle of non-coercion arises, the fears of being pushed around by one group or another emerge, and violence may result.

There also have been a number of legal cases tried in the Israeli court system or debated in the Knesset which test the long-range issues involved in the current religion-state arrangement. The first such raised in the Knesset was the question of a written constitution for the state, which was taken up in 1949. Proponents of a written constitution argued that a new state needed such a document to guarantee individual rights and democratic governmental arrangements, and that certain values of the Zionist revolution and halutzic realization should be recorded in this document to perpetuate the original vision. The Orthodox were among the strongest opponents of the Constitution (although far from the only ones). They did not want the values of secular Zionism immortalized in a constitution for the Jewish State. As long as no explicit public document existed declaring the secular nature of the state, the religious could participate in the functioning of the government. However, if a constitution were to explicate norms and values of a secular nature, the religious would be

forced to denounce the document and the government which
approved it. Moreover, it was not just the secular character of the document which aroused opposition, but also the
assumption underlying the writing of such a document. For
the Orthodox, the Torah of Israel is the eternal basis of
the Jewish people, which eventually would be recognized
as such by all, while the Jewish state could enact secular
legislation--technically as an interim measure--a full-
blown constitution was another matter.

In the debate, it was not simply the religious parties
which countered the pro-constitution forces. Various
ideological groups also opposed a written constitution for
their own reasons. Hashomer Hatzair, for instance, opposed
any document which would not declare the foundation of the
Jewish State to be a radical socialist one. Finally, Ben-
Gurion himself opposed the proposed constitution, because
he felt a fight in its favor was premature. He was not
prepared to wage a war on its behalf, nor has anyone else
after him. A compromise solution emerged whereby the Knesset
was empowered to enact "basic laws" of a constitutional
character piecemeal which would ultimately form a complete
constitution. Six such laws have been enacted to date, none
touching on questions of religious principle. This leaves
the issue of religious or secular authority unresolved in
a sense, but permits various factions to live together on a
day to day basis in which the secular authority does make
the decisions.

Another conflict which gave expression to the debate
within Israel over national self-definition is the "who is
a Jew" controversy. As in many European countries, every
Israeli is registered at birth with the Ministry of the
Interior. Every Israeli possesses an identity card on
which religion and nationality are recorded. For Jews,
normally they are recorded as Jewish in both categories.
The question is what defines a Jew as Jew and whether the
category "Jew" can refer to nationality and religion or
the reverse. These issues have been tested in several
cases in the Israeli courts and have aroused intense interest
and concern, not only in Israel but through out the world.
The matter is a weighty one because it epitomizes the most
basic question of who defines Judaism and being a Jew in
the modern Jewish state. The religious leadership consistently has demanded that the only criteria admissable in
these matters are halachic criteria, and that these halachic
criteria be applied totally and without exceptions, although
they have not always pressed the issue.

The most famous test case in this area resulted in a
non-*halachic* decision, but one which the Orthodox accepted.
This case, that of Brother Daniel, rests upon the meaning
of the Law of Return, which recognizes anyone who is Jewish
as an *oleh*, i.e., someone who has "returned" (literally,
ascended) to Israel. This is a privileged status. For those
possessing it citizenship is automatic. The *oleh* is entitled

to certain material benefits from the government or the
Jewish Agency. A Jew who declares himself Jewish can become a citizen under the Law of Return, which implicitly
recognizes Israel as the state of the Jewish people, whereas
the non-Jew must pass through normal procedures for citizenship. Thus, the Law of Return guarantees all Jews (except
those being sought as criminals by foreign countries) the
right to enter and be citizens of Israel, and to receive
national services from the moment of entry as an *oleh* into
the country.

In 1962, a Polish monk, Brother Daniel, applied for
entry into Israel as an *oleh*, according to the Law of Return,
on the grounds that he was Jewish. Daniel had been born
Oswald Rufeisen in Poland to Jewish parents and had been
hidden by them in a monastery during the Holocaust, where
he converted to Catholicism. In explaining his case and
request to the Polish government, when he pplied for a pass-
port, Daniel wrote,

> I, the undersigned, the Rev. Oswald Rufeisen, known in the
> monastic order as Brother Daniel, hereby respectfully apply
> for permission to travel to Israel for permanent residence,
> and also for a passport. I base this application on the
> ground of my belonging to the Jewish people, to which I
> continue to belong, although I embraced the Catholic
> faith in 1942, and joined a monastic order in 1945....

Daniel was claiming that because his mother had been a Jew,
and he considered himself a Jew nationally, although he had
become a Christian, he was entitled to be registered as a
Jew in his identity card and was eligible for the privileges
of an *oleh*. The attorney for the State, opposing Brother
Daniel, claimed that one who converted to another religion
may not be considered a Jew and was not entitled to claim the
Law of Return or the privileges of an *oleh*. The court,
on the one hand, recognized the *halachic* position claimed
by Daniel. Under the *Halachah*, one born of a Jewish mother
remains Jewish for certain purposes, no matter what. On
the other hand, the court departed from this strict interpretation of the *Halachah*. The majority opinion distinguished
here between the *Halachah* and the law of the state, in this
case, the Law of Return. The Court stated that the law "has
a secular meaning, that is as it is usually understood by
the man in the street--I emphasize, as it is understood by
the plain and simple Jew...A Jew who has become a Christian
is not a Jew." That majority opinion of the court rested
upon the notion that a Jew is what is understood by the
simple Jew on the street. This was a rejection of the
formalistic halachic view, according to which Daniel could
have been registered as a Jew because he was born of a
Jewish mother. In the eyes of the court, the national
history of the Jewish people demonstrated that one cannot
be a Jew in nationality and a Christian in religion.

Religious conversion to Christianity implied, according to the judges, that Daniel had indeed rejected his Jewish national past. The decision was that he could become a citizen of the Jewish state only by going through the normal procedures of naturalization and citizenship (which he subsequently did).

Secular versus religious authority in matters of Jewish self-definition has been tested on other occasions, always causing complicated and emotional debate within the country. The cabinet crisis of 1958 is another example of such a test case, this time raised over the issue of how one registers children of mixed marriage in the national registry. It was asked whether the simple declaration of both parents that they consider the child Jewish and want him registered as such would be sufficient to have the government of Israel indeed recognize this child as Jewish. The Interior Minister declared that he would accept the subjective self-definition, and not insist on *halachic* standards. This meant that a person could intend or will his child Jewish if one parent were Jewish, and that the *halachic* criteria of either the mother's being Jewish or conversion to Judaism were over-ridden. The Mafdal resigned from the Cabinet because of this decision, causing Ben-Gurion to revoke the decision temporarily, and deal with the question of how to register the children of mixed marriages, which is really the question of who is a Jew. After gathering the scholars' opinions, the government in accordance with their views, ruled in favor of halachic criteria and against the Minister of the Interior, who subsequently revoked his directive. This immediate crisis was settled. However, the basic problem was not solved but postponed.

The religious definition of who is a Jew has been accepted by the government. However, because some secularist Jews in the country feel "coerced", new cases have arisen and undoubtedly will arise in the future, testing the *halachic* definition. The Eitani case again tested the definition in a way similar to Brother Daniel. Ruth Eitani has been born of a Jewish father and non-Jewish mother. During the Holocaust, the mother identified herself with the Jewish father and suffered the entire Holocaust period with the family. Ruth went through the war and immigrated to Israel, fought in the Haganah, raised a family, and became active in politics. It became known that her mother was not Jewish, had never converted herself or the children, and that therefore, halachically, Ruth Eitani and her own children had to be converted. This, despite her self-identification as a Jew, the action she had taken on behalf of the Jewish people, and her having received Israeli citizenship as a Jew, on the basis of her honest self-representation as such. The issues on both sides, the *halachic* and non-*halachic*, were fought out again in the Eitani case. Finally, Ruth Eitani and her children did undergo formal conversion.

The Shalit case was another which arose to challenge

the registration of Jews in Israel. Benjamin Shalit, a
naval officer, had married a non-Jewish woman. Shalit sought
to have his children be registered as Jews in nationality and
nothing in religion, thus asserting a new conception: a Jew
by nationality who rejects any religious profession. The
government repeated the decisions of 1960 in the "who is a
Jew" case. Despite any subjective profession on the part
of an individual, objective criteria determined one's status
as a Jew. One born a Jew was a Jew in both religious and
national terms in the eyes of the state. And one born a non-
Jew could become a Jew, even nationally, only through a
religious conversion.

None of the legal cases or Knesset debates has altered
the government commitment to the status quo, which supports
the *halachic* interpretation in personal matters: status,
divorce, marriage. It appears that the majority of the
population has either agreed with this policy or acquiesced
to it. The reason behind the agreement or acquiescence has
been suggested above: a sense that the religious definition
protects the Jewish character of the state and a desire to
maintain the unity of the Jewish people, religious or non-
religious, Diaspora Jew or Israeli.

Religious Pluralism

There is one point of potential conflict which involves
Jews from the Diaspora as well as Israelis. This is the
issue of religious pluralism within the Jewish people. When
Israelis of all stripes define "religious" they mean one group
or another within Orthodoxy. Moreover, the only religious
parties in the country are Orthodox, and control of publicly
supplied religious services is in the hands of the Orthodox
exclusively.

It is hardly surprising that this monopoly of the Orthodox exists in Israel. Virtually all of the religious Jews
who came to Palestine were Orthodox, and those among them
who knew anything about non-Orthodox religious options,
opposed them firmly. The few Reform or Conservative Jews
who came to Palestine, even when they established a congregation, were too few in numbers to have any impact upon the
country. It is only in recent years, when centers of both
movements have been built in Jerusalem, and when enough
congregations have been founded throughout the country that
their presence is beginning to be felt, have the Reform and
Conservative Jews in Israel been able to raise claims against
the Orthodox monopoly.

The Conservative and Reform rabbis in Israel have re-
quested the right to perform marriages in Israel. They have
been denied this right. In the Diaspora, most Orthodox Jews
recognize the marriages, divorces, and conversions of the
Reform and Conservative rabbinate, out of necessity. No
split within the Jewish people had occurred because the
Orthodox consider a marriage or divorce performed by a

certain rabbi to be invalid halachically. Precisely in
order to avoid such a rift, the Orthodox have ignored the
issue. In Israel, however, the Orthodox rabbinate has
refused to follow the *halachah* and therefore cannot be
called "religious." The existence of over 30 Reform and
Conservative congregations in Israel as well as other institutions has not changed the basic stance of the Orthodox
who regard themselves as the only legitimate representative
of Jewish religious practice and do not recognize the claims
of others.

CHANGING ATTITUDES TOWARD RELIGION AND STATE

The attitude of the non-religious public towards Judaism
and religious Jews has been changing in the past 12-15 years.
This is not to say that there has been a general return to
Judaism, but rather, a reawakening of interest in Judaism
and Jewish sources among groups who in earlier periods displayed no such interest. On the basis of the studies and
writings available, we can only conjecture as to their
causes.
First, one can point to the almost natural diminution
of the force of a nationalist ideology, Zionism in this case
and its inability to replace religion either for the individual
or the community. Nationalism does not provide the answers
for the ultimate questions of meaning which arise at critical
moments, such as when a nation faces war or an individual
faces death, birth, or other crises. Such moments occurred
in Israel in 1967 and 1973. Both wars caused a heightened
awareness of the particular religious and cultural elements
which sustain the life of the nation whether or not they
recognize similar rights for Conservative or Reform rabbis.
In matters of conversion, *Israeli law* does not reject non-
Orthodox conversion outside of Israel. The threat of the
religious parties is that they will present a bill asking
the Knesset to deny recognition of Reform and Conservative
conversions. In the U.S., as a result of the vast increase
in intermarraige, the number of such conversions has risen
dramatically. Most of these are performed by non-Orthodox
rabbis. If the Israeli government refuses to recognize such
conversions, it refuses to recognize as Jews thousands of
converts and their children who are recognized as Jews in
the U.S. This would spell a rift in the Jewish people.
Thus far the government has held by a ruling that anyone
who comes with a conversion certificate from a Jewish
community, as long as he or she does not claim to be a
member of another religion, will be recognized as a Jew.
The Knesset has refused to get involved in questions of
religious pluralism and legitimation in the Diaspora, so
that any conversion is a conversion.
The matter goes further because by accepting *de facto*
the conversions of non-Orthodox diaspora rabbis, the Knesset
also accepts the rabbis themselves as legitimate *de facto*.

The religious parties in Israel are determined to avoid
recognizing the non-Orthodox movements, claiming that they,
the nation, is conscious of them. People were propelled
into reflection about the nature and significance of the
Jewish state, and obviously, about their own lives in it.
Although there are no empirical studies about changes
in national consciousness in Israel after the Six Day War,
it is certain that the past 12 years have wakened self-
questioning and reconsideration of principles among many
sectors of the population. This was quite evident in the
kibbutz movement because of the high degree of articulation
of some young members of the movement. In the movement's
magazine *Shdemot* one can see the unearthing of the most
profound religious and ethical questions, and the effort of
non-Orthodox Israelis to resolve them with reference to
traditional sources. It is quite likely that the movement
and wrestling found in the kibbutzim is present among many
other less articulate groups. Until more empirical studies
have been done, we can content ourselves only with the indication that a change in Israel has been occurring since the
Six Day War, one of whose results is a more positive attitude
towards Judaism than existed in earlier periods in the life
of the State. For a very few, this has meant a return to
traditional forms and Orthodoxy. For many more it has meant
a searching for ways to express growing interest, openness,
and positive sentiments.
Another aspect of these processes since the 1967 war
is a growing acknowledgement among virtually all sectors of
the Jewish population that the state cannot survive if it is
not a Jewish state and that the Jewish character of the state
is preserved most fully by those recognized as the authentic
guardians and continuators of Judaism, the Orthodox. Therefore, there is a clear desire not to alienate the religious
elements of the population. Here the need to have God and
the Covenant as parts of the political order is not a product
of sheer instrumental calculation, as was Napoleon's concordat
with the Church. Rather, one finds in Israel among many of
the non-religious a non-manipulative desire to maintain contact with the traditional world as part of the complicated
constellation of historically determined attitudes towards
the substance of Jewish belonging and national meaning. Thus,
the mutual needs of the religious and non-religious, those
of political power and those of spiritual ideals, lie beneath
and undergird the existing inter-relationships of religion
and politics in Israel today.

Five Sets of Relationships

Relations between religion and politics in Israel can
be divided into five categories. First, there is what might
be termed the politics of establishment religion, the religion of the religious establishment that controls those
organs that are recognized as authoritative by the state.

For the most part this is the religion represented by the
National Religious Party, which has been a coalition partner
in every lasting government since the state was established.
For two generations, it has exercised a predominant, though
by no means exclusive, influence over the public expression
of religion in Israel. This is the relationship that has
been studied and written about almost as if it were the
only one.

On the other hand, there is the popular religion of
the broad public, basically a modernized folk religion
which is very widespread in Israel. Even though only a
quarter of Israelis define themselves as "religious" (which
in the Israeli context means Orthodox), probably the largest
single body of Israelis--the estimates are round 40 to 50
percent--define themselves as "traditional." In the Israeli
context, "traditional" is an umbrella term used by people
who are highly observant by any western standards to those
who simply maintain certain home customs but consider themselves believers. Even among the 25 percent who define
themselves as "secular," many retain a very substantial element of folk religion in their own lives--Sabbath observance
in the home, avoidance of overt mixing of meat and milk,
and the like--though they will define themselves as secular
because, for them, these represent a comfortable kind of
folk religion, rather than manifestations of religious belief.

Popular religion in Israel is a combination of residual
folk traditions, of commonly accepted ritual practices, of
elements of an emerging civil religion (a third category
discussed below) and of certain infusion of Hasidic mystical
modes into the folk and establishment religion. One can
find parallel phenomena in other Middle Eastern countries
and probably in many other countries outside the Middle East
as well.

Popular religion is well rooted in Israel, in almost
every quarter. It is undergoing radical change, principally
because of the process of detraditionalization taking place
among so many of the 55 percent or so of Israelis who come
from Afro-Asian backgrounds. On the other hand, most of
the Jews who came from European backgrounds started that
process a generation or two earlier and many are now being
retraditionalized in certain ways. That process is also
introducing changes, best reflected in the emerging civil
religion of Israel.

The civil religion is the third element in the process
of rapid development in Israel today. In a sense, civil
religion enhances the point of intersection between establishment religion and popular religion. The transformation
mentioned above from use of the term "Rock of Israel" to the
reading of the Psalms in a neo-traditional manner in the
Knesset, reflects that civil religion, one which is grounded
in traditional Judaism but which is not traditional Judaism.

Israel's civil religion reflects the re-emergence in
new ways of the civil religion which existed in Israel prior

to the destruction of the Second Commonwealth and the great
Jewish dispersion (Elazar, 1978). In this respect it is
different from the Talmudic or Pharisaic Judaism embodied
by Israel's establishment religion and which has been the
dominant mode of Jewish religious expression for at least
1600 years. It is, in essence, a new Sadduceanism based on
the centrality of Jewish public life in the expression of
Judaism. The evolving civil religion in Israel seeks to
sacralize expressions of Jewish moralistic nationalism
connected with the state and to infuse into those expressions
traditional religious forms.

Fourth, there is extremist religion, so-called because
it is more extreme in its expression of classical Talmudic
Judaism than establishment religion. These are the people
who make the headlines by throwing stones at autos that
travel through or near their neighborhoods on the Sabbath,
who protest the immodesty of Jewish women dressed in modern
fashion, and in their most extreme expression, reject the
state. As small as they are in numbers, consisting of at
most a few tens of thousands, by the broadest definition,
they are really a state within a state, and it is accepted
that they will be. They maintain their own schools, institutions, rabbinical courts (apart from the establishment
rabbinical courts used by the rest of the population), and
the like. There are points of intersection between them and
the larger polity, but generally the policy is to try to
leave them alone, to give them the same state support as
every other group, but in order to get them to leave the
state alone. This is an uneasy relationship that leads to
sporadic conflict when the intersection between the two
groups occurs around certain critical issues, but this
should not obscure the degree of routine cooperation that
exists between them at other times.

Finally, there is an emergent non-establishment Judaism
in the form of the *M'sorati* (Conservative) and Reform
movements which, taken together, are approaching 50 congregations in strength. With *M'sorati* congregations now being
formed in all parts of the country and the first Reform
rabbi recently ordained in Israel, it is reasonable to
conclude that these non-establishment movements are in the
country to stay. While they remain formally unrecognized,
there are increasing contacts between them and the authorities in the course of daily activities and, in some respects,
they have gained a certain tacit recognition. For example,
the Ministry of Education has supported the establishment of
a *M'sorati* school within the framework of the state educational
system, various congregations have obtained land for buildings
from the municipal authorities, and occasionally non-
Orthodox rabbis have been authorized to perform marriages.

CONCLUSION

What are we to conclude from all this? It is vitally
important to understand that the government of Israel does
not control or seek to control the religious establishment
in the state although the two are clearly and continually
engaged with each other. Rather, the various religious
communities and groups utilize state instrumentalities to
further their own ends and to relate to other groups as parts
of the compound or federation of communities that form Israel
as a state.

What of the future? The shift toward greater concern
for Jewish tradition on the part of pace-setting elements
of Israeli society is a reflection of at least two factors:
the perennial search for meaning (the "wrestling with God"
which is embedded in the very meaning of the Hebrew word,
Israel) which is characteristic of Jews, including Israeli
Jews and the concern for the Jewish future of Israel. These
factors are mutually reinforcing and both are appropriate
in a world where religious concern seems to be on the rise.
One unexpected response to this may be developing with regard to establishment religion in Israel. Until recently,
the National Religious Party was only concerned with maintaining its position as a balance wheel in coalition politics,
so that it could protect the religious camp within Israel as
a compound republic. It had no aspirations to seek power
beyond that. With the failure of the Labor Party to keep
its monopoly as government coalition leader and the subsequent failure of the Likud in the last several years,
there has been a new development within the NRP, in which
the younger guard sees its party as having a role to play
beyond simply being the balance wheel. Traditionally, the
NRP followed the lead of its dominant coalition partner
in economic, foreign affairs and defense policies. In the
last two years, there has been a move on the part of the
young guard toward taking the party into policy initiatives
in spheres in which it was never active before, not only
toward defining NRP policies on their own, but in leading
the coalition as well. This is in response to the failure
of the Likud to define policies clearly, or of Labor to
define alternative policies.

There is a growing sentiment today within the NRP to
open up the party and to move it in the direction of the
European Christian Democratic parties--in other words, to
make it a broader based party that can compete for control
of the government as the major party in a coalition. This
sentiment is still very tentative. It will probably run
into very great problems because of the character of at least
two factors: the Orthodoxy of establishment religion in
Israel and the character of the NRP as its principal spokesman. Were this to come about in the Israeli context, it
would probably take the form of a confederation or federation
of "religious" and "traditional" parties similar to the

Labor Alignment or the Likud, rather than an enlarged NRP
pure and simple. All of this represents a development
that has not yet attracted any public attention but, if
it is pursued, is likely to affect the shaping of Israel's
politics over the next few years, and perhaps the state for
the coming generation and longer.

Just as it is very difficult to define or delimit
Judaism in Israel, it would seem well nigh impossible to
predict its future. The words *dati* or *hiloni* are useful
only as labels, which often hide as much as they reveal.
While those who call themselves *dati* may be assumed to
believe and practice Judaism, it is not certain that those
who are called or call themselves *hiloni* do not believe
and do not practice. Similarly, while the State of Israel
is officially secular, since it is a Jewish state the meaning
of secular in its context is not clear. As indicated, the
national and religious are tied together inextricably in
Judaism. From the early period of the Zionist movement
until today, the "non-religious" Zionists have never been
able to govern without religious groups. Therefore, God
and the Covenant have always been, somehow, a part of the
government as they are somehow a part of the state, making
the religious condition of Israel extremely complicated and
one which even challenges comprehension.

Two elements must be understood if one is to grasp the
fundamentals of the complex religious situation in Israel.
Alongside or beneath the enlightenment ideals of pioneer
Zionism, which have left so visible a mark upon the society
of present day Israel, was a deep sense of and concern for
Jewish identity. This sense may have been obscure but was
substantial, and was experienced by all Zionists. The
second element was another sense, felt by some Zionists,
that Judaism could not be dispensed with in a Jewish state.
Judaism is constitutive of Jewish identity even for the
unbeliever--even for the rabid anti-believer--and here lies
one of the sources of much inner Jewish anguish and conflict
for the last two centuries. It is this recognition,
conscious or unconscious, of the essential constitutive
character of Judaism which inclined the secular Zionists
towards cooperation with the Orthodox, no matter how annoying they found their demands. Moreover, it was this
essential character of Judaism for Jewishness in the long
run which has been recognized as particularly important to
the first element, Jewish identity, and therefore, for
Jewish survival. The relationship of religion and politics
in Israel reflects all of this.

BIBLIOGRAPHY

Abramov, Zalman, *Perpetual Dilemma, Jewish Religion in the
     State*, Fairleigh Dickinson, 1976.

Canaani, David, *Haaliyah Hashniyah ha-Ovedet ve-Yasasah
    La-Dat ve-la-Masoret*. Sifriat Hapoalim, 1976.
Elazar, Daniel, "The New Sadducees," *Midstream*, September
    1978, pp. 20-5.
Friedman, Menahem, *Dat ve-Hevrah*, Yad Ben-Avi, 1977.
Goldmann, Eliezer. "Religious Issues in Israel's Political
    Life," Jerusalem, World Zionist Organization, 1964,
    pp. 84-94.
Hertzberg, Arthur, *The Zionist Idea*, Doubleday, 1959.
Liebman, Charles and Don-Yehiyah, Eliezer. "Hafradah ben
    dat v-medinah: Sismah ve-tokhen," *Molad*, nos. 25-26,
    1972.
Steinsalz, Adin. "Religion in the State of Israel,"
    Judaism, vol. 22, no. 2, 1973, pp. 140-150.

14
Religion and Its Role in
National Integration in Israel

Emanuel Gutmann

Religion plays a many-faceted and ambiguous role in
the integrative process in the Israeli Jewish community.
Very broadly viewed, it has a dual and contradictory function.
In one sense it is a source of disaffection, dissension and
conflict. But to the extent that it provides a common primordial sentiment, it preserves common attachments and loyalties
and thus serves as a fusionary element. Judaism, as one
observer put it, has, contrary to many other religions,
hardly ever departed from its path as a mono-ethnic religion,
and this has strengthened the ethno-national coherence among
Jews, both in practice and in purpose.[1] In functional terms
it may be said that religion is generally considered to have
served as the main integrative factor preserving the unity
of the dispersed, preemancipation Jewish people,[2] and that
if one wishes to speak of a unity of a "community of fate,"
it is of the fate of co-religionists.

However, in terms of modern national ideology, based
on the secular conception of national Jewish identity, one
would have to reverse the above formula and say that the
Jews have always been a mono-religious people.[3] This may
be considered to be the prevailing view in Israel, i.e., a
part of the Zionist belief system, and it implies that most
Israelis today accept the notion that being Jewish (including
Israeli Jewish) has at least something to do with the Jewish
religion.[4] Only a tiny minority claim that in the totality
of Judaism, religion has--or ought to have--no part at all.

However, this formulation makes it necessary to redefine
the role of religious elements in present-day Judaism, and
there are widely divergent points of view on this issue, in
Israel and in the diaspora. There are those (a few in Israel,
and more abroad) who reject outright the major premise of the

Religion and Its Role in National Integration in Israel
is reprinted from *Middle East Review*, Vol. XII, No. 1, Fall, 1979.

nationalist formulation, either from a fundamentalist-
Orthodox standpoint, which pursues the pre-modern conception
of a religious, or ethno-religious congregation; or from a
diametrically opposite view; the assimilationist assertion
that Jews are members of a "church" (or churches) bound, it
may be, by sentiments of solidarity with coreligionists in
other countries, but abjuring all ethnic ties.

It is possibly one of the paradoxes of Jewish history
that with the advent of emancipation for the Jewish communities in the West in the eighteenth and nineteenth centuries
that coincided with the secularization of their host societies
and the general decline of religious belief, the Jews were
redefined, as a religious congregation in the strict sense
of the term. The rise of competing "trends" and movements
within Judaism which made for religious diversity produced,
in combination with the widespread assimilatory tendencies
in the respective countries, a very considerable centrifugal
momentum. Consequently, the effectiveness of religion as
an integrative factor declined drastically. However, this
was at least partly counterbalanced by the anti-assimilatory
barriers exercised by their gentile surroundings and, on
another level, by the continued cohesiveness of the Jewish
communities in most of the Eastern--i.e., Oriental--countries.

With the beginning of the modern Jewish national movement,
toward the end of the nineteenth century, the situation became
rather more complex. Zionism, based on the conception of the
Jews as a national entity rejected, and was as such rejected,
by the assimilationist tendencies prevailing in Western nation-
states, and found itself in radical dissension with Jewish
orthodoxy and fundamentalism, which repudiated any possibility
of a Jewish variant of modern secular nationalism.

Consequently, and as a result of the rather extreme
secular and laicist attitudes of a substantial part of the
early Zionist leadership, and their often rather clamorous,
manipulative adoptions of religious sentiments, rituals and
symbols to serve profane purposes and actions--religion became
a factor of conflict within Judaism, and with obvious disintegrative effects. Later, and more markedly since Israel's
independence, although there has prevailed a widespread
consensus about the role of common religious attachments
as a sort of all-embracing "umbrella" providing one element
of national unity, religion has increasingly become a more
contentious subject. The use of state authority by the
religious establishment has contributed to formal integration
on the legal level, but at the same time has not been able
to contain the widening cleavage between the religious and
the non-religious sectors of the population.

* * *

The single, most important element in the integrative
functioning of religion is the "establishment" of the "church"
as part of the governmental institutions. The integrative

function has thus neither been left to fortuitous, uncontrolled developments nor to fluctuating power relations and the impact of spiritual activities, but has been formally institutionalized. Religious communities (and not only the Jewish) are formally recognized by the State. The rabbinate is a wing of the government, religious courts are part of the judicial system and religious law in matters of "personal status" (i.e., in family and domestic relations) is part of the law of the land. It is this so-called non-separation that is at the hearth of church-state relations.[5] However controversial, a substantial majority of Israelis are at least reconciled to this system, precisely because of its reputed integrative effect.

At the cost of possible politicization of religion, in the sense of outside, secular, and at least conceivably even laicist and anti-religious control and interference, religious norms in their orthodox interpretation are being enforced with the sanction of the civil authorities. Rightly or wrongly, the imposition of religious marriage and divorce on all Israelis is generally considered to be the single most effective measure to preserve the unity of the Jewish people in Israel and throughout the world, whereas the introduction of civil marriage (and for that matter, of religious but non-orthodox marriage) would jeopardize this unity irreversibly. How significant this unity is in the eyes of the Israeli public can be gathered from its views, as expressed to pollsters, and by the fact that most Israelis are willing to go along with this situation, even at the price of a feeling of discomfort and uneasiness because of the hardships it can create and what at least some consider as the indignities to which a few unfortunates are exposed by the system.

However, given the prevailing social and ideological cleavages in the Israeli public and, in particular, in its attitudes on religious matters, what can be said about the existing system is that, at best (which is a good deal), it provides the formal premise for national-behavioral unity in a number of small yet crucial ways. One of these is the country-of-origin aspect of this system. Slight differences in ritual, such as in the prayerbook, the conduct of synagogue services and various dietary laws, had developed in the various countries of dispersion over the centuries. When the British Mandatory Government of Palestine gave the rabbinate its first formal status, it was established on a dual basis, i.e., in all its bodies there must be parity between Ashkenazi and Sephardi/Oriental rabbis and also in the case of all other dignitaries. Thus, on the council of the Chief Rabbinate there are two co-equal Chief Rabbis. Attempts to abolish this duality in the name of "national integration" have not been successful; those who resist this change do so, when they feel the need to have recourse to ideological arguments, in the name of pluralism.

In this, as in many of its activities, and because of the very fact of its basis in governmental authority, the

religious establishment is hardly conducive to national
integration in the sense of promoting consensus or
diminishing the effect of cleavages. Moreover, the
effectiveness of this system in the wider sense is, to say
the least, controversial, and at times may actually be
counterproductive from the point of view of its own expectations.

Another example of a practice aiming at behavioral
uniformity is the strict surveillance of the rabbinate over
the observance of *kashrut* in all public institutions, including the army, and in all organizations and firms open
to the public. Even if this aspect of orthodoxy is less
weighty from the national-existential viewpoint, it can be
more meaningful in everyday life. Here again the Israeli
public, in spite of frequent expressions of dissatisfaction,
is willing, by and large, to accept the existing arrangements
for the sake of unity, even if it actually means adopting the
norms of the minority as guidelines for the behavior of the
majority. But it is difficult to see in this any substantial
integrative achievement and, not surprisingly, many Israelis
regard the situation as no more than the result of internal
power politics, or more specifically, the outcome of coalition
bargaining that puts the votes of the religious parties at a
premium.

The same applies to public Sabbath observance and, in
particular, to the stoppage of practically all public transportation on the Sabbath. This is the result of coalition
agreements alone; it was not a legally established practice,
as were some of the laws (on *kashrut*, etc.) previously
mentioned, but its origins are of little importance to that
part of the Israeli public that finds it unduly restricting.
To the non-religious section of the Israeli public it is
seen, above all, as religious coercion, and this feeling is
at least partly derived from the belief that this kind of
interdiction does not contribute to social integration. And
for that matter, it does not even operate effectively in the
view of those who do observe the Sabbath.

Quite different kinds of problems are presented by the
status of the various non-Orthodox trends in Judaism. Although
it would appear at first sight that what is involved here is,
perhaps, religious integration, in the Israeli context these
problems have very serious connotations for national integration. Partly because of the claim to exclusivity by the
"right faith," common to so many religions, but also for the
avowed purpose of disallowing what is seen as religious
dissension in order to prevent the cleavages and conflicts
deriving from it, the "established" Jewish "church" is
Orthodoxy, to the exclusion of all others, not only the
Conservative, Reform and Progressive movements, but also of
such communities as the Karaites, Samaritans and Falashas.
Freedom of religion and of worship is, of course, guaranteed,
and also operates in practice, and the Supreme Court has
actually ruled that freedom of religion and ritual must be

allowed and supported by the authorities even if this comes at the price of religious dissension.[6] This is not, however, what is at stake here. The relevant issue is that what must be considered the benefits of establishment, both the material and the legal, are preserved for the orthodox "church" alone, as the only fully recognized Jewish "religious community." Thus the other trends do not receive (unimportant exceptions excepted) any governmental financial support, and their religious dignitaries are prohibited from performing marriages or sitting in religious courts. Moreover, the marriages and divorces performed abroad by rabbis of these trends are not recognized in Israel. The inequity of this treatment can be seen in proper perspective when it is compared with the treatment received by those ultra-orthodox groups and congregations who do not "recognize" the established orthodoxy, but are nonetheless fully supported and recognized by the religious establishment--to the extent that they are interested at all in such support and recognition.

The other, much more salient aspect of this situation from the integrative vantage point is, of course, that as long and so far as the determination of "Who is a Jew?" is in the hands of orthodoxy, all these groups cannot be integrated into the Jewish-Israeli community. This point is yet far from being settled with any finality, and the tug-of-war over it continues. The rabbinate and the religious sector have not had it all their own way by any means, but full social integration into the national community has, to varying degrees, not yet been made possible for members of these non-establishment religious groups.

* * *

But Man lives not by law and regulations alone, and national integration is not achieved solely by these means. The world of symbols, of ritual and myth has important functions in the lives of individuals and collectives, as creators of group identity, as instigators of group cohesion (and dissensus) and as providers of legitimacy. Because of the peculiarities of Jewish history, there was no symbolism other than religious before secularization began, and all material and spiritual aspects of life were conceived as part of the religious order.[7] The new Israeli state made widespread use of traditional religious symbolism for its own ceremonial and the like purposes, analogous in a way to what Bellah has called "civil religion" in the United States.[8] The reasons for this usage stem both from the feelings of collective filial piety and the appeal these symbols have to the most solid common denominator of the highly heterogeneous Jewish-Israeli population. Zionism, independence and statehood are looked upon (at least by the non-orthodox majority) as the most significant *caesura* in Jewish history, demanding innovative symbols to match a revolutionary ideology. But, at the same time, they are also conceived of as stages in the

eternal existence of the Jewish people, a concept which
demands the reception of old values and symbols, even if in
a new and transformed shape or form. In this process, as
often as not, the original or traditional forms have been
cast aside and the innate contents or values (which, at least
partly, depend on the ideological stand of the people involved), discarded. But at least one observer has seen
indications that the traditional religious context or meaning
of some of these symbols has recently been reasserting itself,
and that other traditional symbols are steadily penetrating
into national life without first being secularized.[9] This
tendency to make use of religious symbols for non-religious
purposes cannot be viewed by intransigently religious people
as anything else than a profanation or, at best, as an invalid
surrogate, and hence arouses in them uneasiness if not outright repugnance. But among the overwhelming majority of
Israelis, religious or otherwise, the integrative effect of
these symbols appears to have been quite substantial.

Undoubtedly the most controversial use (or misuse, as
some would have it) of religious symbols, feelings and attachments is connected with the ongoing public debate on foreign
and security policy, or more specifically, the future of the
West Bank and Jerusalem and other areas controlled by Israel
since 1967. The special significance of holy places and
heavenly promises to the Children of Israel regarding their
land are well known, as is the recourse to them as the source
for the rightfulness of Jewish settlement in the country.
What is new today is the interpretation of the national
interest in accordance with what the people who invoke it
consider to be Divine guidance (as interpreted by their
spiritual leaders), and their insistence that this must take
precedence over the rule of law and governmental authority.

But none of this is entirely new. After all, use of
symbols for political purposes, even when taken in their
full religious context, has been made before. Also, the
more orthodox wing in Israeli politics has always accepted
the guidance of its Council of Sages for all major political
decisions (such as whether to participate in elections, join
the cabinet, on important policy decisions, etc.) and even
the less extreme orthodox party *Mafdal* has, at times,
allowed its ministers to receive orders from the rabbinate.
Outstanding in the case of *Gush Emunim*, however, is that
while the majority of its members and followers are religious,
this group also has non-religious participants and adherents,
who accept its politics and its activities but apparently
disregard the religious aspects involved. Yet the image of
Gush is that of a highly motivated group of politico-
religious zealots who, despite their prominence, remain a
small minority in the religious community. And it would be
incorrect to view *Gush Emunim* as an extremist group in the
religious camp which causes the clash with the non-religious
majority. The issues at stake are political, and both the
religious and the non-religious in Israel are deeply divided

over them.

* * *

It may be a gross over-simplification to speak of two
population sectors, the religious and the non-religious,
in Israel (just as it is erroneous to reduce all social
problems to the Ashkenazi-Sephardi cleavage), for in both
sectors, the religious and the non-religious, there are
ample internal divisions, fissions and dissensions. Nevertheless, it is a fact that the religious population is becoming more and more isolated from the non-religious,
primarily as a consequence of policies deliberately followed
with this aim in mind. As a result, the cleavage between
these two separate segments of the population is ever
widening.
      These developments can readily be shown in many ways.
In the first place, there is a growing tendency toward
physical segregation, i.e., an increasing percentage of
religious people congregate together, so that the phenomenon
of strictly religious neighborhoods is on the increase in
almost every Israeli city and town. Although the ultra-
orthodox have always preferred to live in secluded quarters
(in Jerusalem, B'nai Beraq, etc.) and there is a network of
religious kibbutzim (every kibbutz is organizationally
affiliated with a specific kibbutz movement in accordance
with the ideology of its members), this tendency of the
general religious public to herd together is new. Again,
though statistics are not available, it appears to be a
fact that the percentage of "intermarriages" between
religious and non-religious families is comparatively small,
and this has not been on the increase recently.
      School segregation, from kindergarten through high-
school and even to university, is very far advanced. The
government school system is divided into two trends, the
state (i.e., non-religious) and the state-religious trends,
and to these must be added the "independent," (i.e., non-
state) schools controlled by *Agudat Israel*, the ultra-
orthodox wing of the religious camp. Some one third of all
elementary school children attend religious schools. There
has been a slight drop in this percentage, but almost all
children from religious homes attend these schools, and the
wall-of-separation between the various schools is actually
growing. (Ironically, the Zionist Organization too, has a
separate department of religious education for the Jewish
communities outside Israel.)
      In the field of labor, although they collaborate with
Histadrut within the framework of their trade union departments and in the provision of social services, there are
two separate religious labor federations, each affiliated
with a religious political party. A good many religious
workers belong to Histadrut and the possible merger of the
larger of the religious unions with Histadrut is being

mooted, but, so far, the advantages of separate existence appear to be decisive to the religious unions.

The army presents a very special case. Its integrative role has often been described and praised (and in the main, rightly so), for it is the first meeting ground and the provider of a common experience for the diverse elements of the population. Much attention is paid to make army service as compatible with the demands of religious observance as is feasible, so as to obviate any possible argument against army service for religious people alongside everyone else. The chief army chaplain has the rank of general. There is a large staff of rabbis and religious supervisors at all command levels. The army mess is strictly *kosher*, and applicable to all ranks are strict standing orders (in times of non-emergency situations) concerning Sabbath observance.

The exemption (upon request) from military service offered to girls from religious homes (about one third of all girls are thus exempted, not a few on false pretences) as well as to students in the ultra-orthodox *yeshivot* (higher institutions of religious learning) not only actually creates a clear separation between those who serve in the army and those who do not, but also makes for strained relations between the non-religious public and the ultra-orthodox. Most non-extreme orthodox religious people themselves strongly object to this exemption. On a completely different level, the practice has recently begun to become widespread for some *yeshiva* graduates who do not seek exemptions and are reputed to make excellent fighters to form their own subunits, thus initiating a divisionary practice in the army as well.

Religion plays a major role in nation-building and national integration in Israel, despite all the problems involved. Partly by accident of numbers (electoral strength) and the play of party politics based on it, and partly as a result of ideologically determined and also calculated political conceptions, religion is one of the major elements of everyday politics. Thus, in addition to a process of politicization of religion, very strong tendencies introduce religious matters and interests into politics, thereby levelling religion with other aspects of public life. And, parallel with its integrative function, religion also serves as one more cleavage in Israeli society, with all the political implications of such a situation.

NOTES

1. Benjamin Akzin, *State and Nation* (London: Hutchinson, 1965), p. 48.

2. Ben Halpern, *The Idea of the Jewish State* (Cambridge: Harvard University Press, 1961), pp. 4-6. It should perhaps be stressed that in a functional analysis such as this, religion and religious symbols are not simply viewed as manipulative devices

or as "an essential piece of equipment." See Kenneth Minogne, *Nationalism* (New York: Basic Books, 1967), p. 116. Religious matters are of course constantly being put to political usages, for which neutral terms, such as "cultural engineering" may be more appropriate. See e.g., Ali A. Mazrui, *Cultural Engineering and Nation-Building in East Africa* (Evanston: Northwestern University Press, 1972). On the use of religious dispositions by African and Asian nationalists, see Elie Kedourie, "Introduction" to *Nationalism in Asia and Africa* (New York: Meridian, 1970): pp. 69-77.

3. There is much truth in the claim that "it becomes impossible to determine the direction of the casual relationship between people and religion. Both possessed each other." Anthony D. Smith, "Nationalism and Religion. The Role of Religious Reform in the Genesis of Arab and Jewish Nationalism." *Archives des Sciences Sociales des Religions*, no. 35, 1973, p. 29.

4. Charles S. Liebman, "Religion and Political Integration in Israel," *The Jewish Journal of Sociology.* Vol. 17(1), 1975, p. 23.

5. For full details of this situation, see S. Zalman Abramov, *Perpetual Dilemma, Jewish Religion in the Jewish State* (Rutherford, Madison, Teaneck: Fairleigh Dickinson University Press, 1976).

6. Israel Peretz and Others vs. The Local Council of the Township of Kfar Shmaryahu, *Supreme Court Judgements* 16 (1962):21 Off.

7. Charles S. Liebman, *op. cit.*, p. 18.

8. R. N. Bellah, "Civil Religion in America," *Daedalus* 96 (1967), pp. 1-21. This is not the place to pursue this topic in detail, but for more reasons than one, the use of the civil religion analogy has to be pursued with care.

9. Charles S. Liebman, *op. cit.*, pp. 19-20.

15
Gush Emunin:
Politics, Religion,
and Ideology in Israel

Kevin A. Avruch

In the period following the Yom Kippur War, a new
movement began to gain increasing popular support in Israel.
Called *Gush Emunim* (The Bloc of the Faithful) this movement
presented an irredentist stance vis-à-vis the West Bank
(Judea and Samaria) and other "administered territories"
(the Sinai, the Gaza Strip, the Golan Heights). The focus
of Gush's activities was the establishment of Jewish settlements in the territories beyond the "Green Line." The
settlements were founded with volunteer labor and without
the consent of the (then) Labor Government.[1]

To the political opponents of Gush, these settlements
were illegal; a blatant act of defiance against the Government. Many demanded their removal; if necessary by force.
The Gush response was to reject all the *political* arguments.
In its view, each settlement was but a further move toward
the integration of *Eretz Yisrael* (The Land of Israel) into
a Third Jewish Commonwealth. The leaders and supporters of
Gush saw themselves as standing "above party politics" and,
if necessary, above the parliamentary process. They claimed,
for their movement, a legitimacy based on *religious* (i.e.,
nonpolitical) values, the ultimate value being that of
Messianic Redemption. In this light, the advent of the
Jewish State was, to them, less the result of the triumph
of a particular "movement of national liberation" (i.e.
Zionism) than the beginning of a divinely inspired and
ordained redemptive process. And this process depended,
among other things, on the territorial integrity of *Eretz
Yisrael.*[2] Failure to settle The Land, or withdrawal from
presently occupied territories was viewed as only secondarily

Gush Emunin: Politics, Religion, and Ideology in Israel
is reprinted from *Middle East Review*, Vol. XI, No. 2, Winter,
1978/79.

a military-political "blunder." This failure--or with-
drawal--would constitute man's (or his government's) direct
contravention of God's will: it would cause the interrup-
tion, or worse, the cessation, of the redemptive process.
     When, on May 17, 1977, the right-of-center Likud Party
headed by Menachem Begin came to power, the new Prime Minister chose the Gush settlement of Kaddum as the site for his
first post-election speech. There he proclaimed Judea and
Samaria to be "a part" of Israel. By July, the Government
had announced plans for the creation of sixteen new towns on
the West Bank. Of these, seven were listed as projects
planned by Gush Emunim. Two related transformations had
occurred: "political" and "religious" legitimacy, hitherto
separate, appeared to have united, in the form of a Likud
Government fostering a Gush Emunim program. And Zionism, it
was claimed, had undergone a major and inevitable reorienta-
tion finding, at last, its "true expression."
     An examination of the roots of the Gush Emunim movement
shows that these transformations did not come about *de novo*
with the replacement of a left-wing by a right-wing government. They are rooted in the development of Zionist ideology
and in its transformations after statehood. The rise of
Gush is connected with the rise of certain movements and
with ideological change in the context of ongoing social
change. Insofar as "social change" means "modernization,"
a social movement whose ideology is based on religious or
traditional values and symbols must "secularize" this
ideology if it is to remain viable.[3] Where, however, the
original movement--in this instance, Zionism--was based,
from its beginning, on a more complex ideology, fusing
religious-traditional and secular-modern values and symbols,
does the course of ideological change clearly lie in the
direction of secularization? This question will be discussed
later.

THE EMERGENCE OF GUSH

     The rise of Gush Emunim dates to the days following the
Six Day War. At issue was the disposition of the territories
occupied in the course of that war. Formerly Jordanian-held
East Jerusalem and some of the city's hinterland were annexed,
but the Government balked at annexing the other areas. Instead, an "Open Bridges Policy" was instituted for the West
Bank. This kept the area tied to Jordan in several ways.
     In reaction to this policy, a movement called *HaTnuah
L'Eretz Yisrael HaShlema* (The Whole Land of Israel Movement)
arose that demanded immediate annexation of the territories,
and its supporters represented most shades of religiosity and
political orientation in Israel, including *Mapam* on the left.
In time, the religious, Orthodox components of this movement
became increasingly conspicuous in it. Chief among these was
a Land of Israel faction, composed of relatively young people

concentrated in the *HaPoel HaMizrahi* (Religious Worker)
segment of the National Religious Party (NRP). This faction
had thought to find, in the NRP, the political leverage that
the Land of Israel Movement lacked in the Labor parties.
In the NRP, the "Youth Faction" kept pressing their elders
to make settlement of *Eretz Yisrael* (The Land of Israel)
the *sine qua non* of the NRP's participation in any Labor-led
coalition government. The NRP elders, however, treated the
issue with caution, and their public statements on it were
ambiguous.

In the aftermath of the war of October 1973, the Youth
Faction hardened its stand on the territories. They despaired
of the NRP leadership, which seemed to follow Labor and, even
worse, which failed to defend Likud when Labor portrayed Likud
to the 1973 electorate as the "War Party." For those reasons,
(among others) the leaders of the Youth Faction began to
dissociate themselves from the NRP and to organize a movement
that would be above party politics. Based on the issue of
settlement, this movement would, in addition, owe no responsibility to the ideological or organizational demands of any
given party.

But in claiming to stand above parties on the issue of
settlement, this movement first had to validate its right to
talk down to the parties. This right could not be based on
values of political legitimacy unless the movement was itself
to become another political party--and this its leaders wished
to avoid. Therefore, the movement and its issue were linked
to values of a "higher order," i.e., to religion. They were
linked to the very bedrock of religion: to Redemption, the
End of Days, the Coming of the Messiah. In February 1974,
this new movement, Gush Emunim, was officially named and
founded at Kfar Etzion. Several hundred people attended the
event. Two years later, Gush organized a two-day march
through Samaria in which some 20,000 Israelis participated.

Gush is linked to the "bedrock of religion" through
the writings and teachings of Rav Avraham Yitzhak Kook (1865-
1935) as interpreted by his son, Rav Zvi Yehuda Kook (b. 1891).[4]
Rav. A. Y. Kook, the first Ashkenazi Chief Rabbi of Mandatory
Palestine, was the founder of *Merkaz HaRav Yeshiva* (The
Rabbi's Center) in Jerusalem in 1924. Headed by his son,
the Yeshiva is today the spiritual and ideological center
of the Gush Emunim movement. It was here that many of the
activists and leaders of Gush received their religious training from the 1950s onward, and the Rabbis Kook (father and
son) are considered the spiritual founders of the movement.

In the early twentieth century, Rav A. Y. Kook had
defended Zionism against its Orthodox critics by portraying
the emergence of the Zionist movement as a sign of the beginning of Divine Redemption. He held that the Jewish people's
tie to The Land of Israel was part of the "very essence" of
their nationhood, and that Jewish resettlement of The Land
was both an indicator of, and a spur to, the redemptive
process. From these premises he was able to argue that all

Zionists, be they secular or even anti-religious, insofar
as they were engaged in reclaiming The Land--and whether
they knew it or not--were acting as agents of the Divine
Will. He therefore enjoined pious Jews to work *with* secular
Zionism and not against it. Calling the secularists wrong
in separating the "religious" from the "political-national"
concepts of Judaism and the Jew, he believed that the intrinsic
holiness of *Eretz Yisrael* and the unfolding sacredness of
ge'ulah (Redemption) would, in time, correct this secular
misconception. At the *Merkaz HaRav Yeshiva* he instilled,
in hundreds of students, this fervent "religious Zionism."

The Rabbis Kook taught a religious Zionism that
possessed a dynamism lacking in secular Zionism. Because
this religious Zionism is based on the *process* of Redemption,
it comes with an explicit theory of change. Among other
things, this theory relates political and social change,
e.g., the isolation of Israel in the international arena,
the alleged decline of Zionist commitment among Israeli
youth, and so on, to ideological change. As the redemptive
process continues, the theory holds, certain transformations
of Zionism necessarily occur. Secularists would come to see
the error of their separation of "political-national" from
"religious" conceptions of Judaism and the Jew; religious
legitimacy would replace the "mere" political legitimacy of
the Zionist movement and, thus, Zionism would find its
"true expression" at last.

For the Rabbis Kook, a crisis of ideological secular
Zionism was to be expected as part of the workings of the
process of Redemption. However, a process of a different
sort was also at work. For the Rabbis, what was of importance was the dynamism of Redemption. But what was also
occurring was that the dynamism of the nationalist movement
was facing the crisis of its routinization.

IDEOLOGICAL CRISIS AND CHANGE

Charisma, in the Weberian sense of that which is
aussertaglich, can be applied to movements as well as to
individuals.[5] Zionism (in both its secular and religious
forms) developed into a movement whose appeal, authority,
and mission were imbued with charismatic qualities (as were
individual Zionist leaders, beginning with Herzl). The
charismatic character of Zionism became especially clear
when the magnitude of the European Holocaust became known,
and in the critical days immediately preceding and following
the establishment of the State. With the establishment of
the State, Zionism began to face a long period of heightening
ideological crisis. In part, this crisis focused on the
tension between the encroaching routinization of Zionism's
charisma and the demands placed on Zionism that it continue
to design a modern state (and people) and chart the course
of this state toward, in the words of Ben-Gurion, "the

fulfillment of its historic mission in redeeming mankind."[6]

What, the question came to be asked, was Zionism's role to be after the creation of the State of Israel? If the sole aim of Jewish nationalism lay in the establishment of a Jewish State, then once the State was established, Zionism's "task" must surely be over and done with: routinization (or the coming of "normalcy," in the Zionist's own parlance) ought to be welcomed. However, it was welcomed neither by the secular Left nor by the religious Right, and their method of countering routinization was to deny that the "task" of the Zionist movement was over. In pursuit of the continued task; the staunchly secular Ben-Gurion could speak rhetorically of "mission" and "Redemption," but the parties of the Israeli Left could never quite bring themselves to institutionalize this rhetoric into a party platform or an ideology: there were, after all, problems of consistency and dissonance. Consequently, with Ben-Gurion, they made another "impossible" (i.e., Messianic) task the primary focus of Zionist attention. This was *kibbutz galuyot*, the "ingathering of the exiles," with the goal of the complete dissolution of the Jewish Diaspora. The State was to become the means to this end.

Kibbutz galuyot might have served the function of re-sisting the routinization of Zionism but for one key problem. The Jewish Diaspora, especially in the democratic West, stubbornly resisted its own dissolution. Even those in the Diaspora who considered themselves staunch Zionists regarded *kibbutz galuyot* with what can only be termed "ambivalence." Zionism—far from being revitalized—suddenly lay in danger of fragmentation into "Israeli" and "Diaspora" varieties, each hostile, wary, or merely uncomfortable with the other. As the dream of the Ingathering of the Exiles remained unful-filled, the debate in Israel about the demise of Zionism intensified.

In this debate, the religious Right, unlike the secular Left, held one important advantage: it could use such terms as Mission and Redemption unselfconsciously; after all, these constituted the basic charter of religious Zionism. Never-theless, the religious Right did not make consistent or effective use of the terms in the years preceding the Six Day War. In part this was because the Left still claimed the monopoly on such Zionist symbols of the Good as *halutziut* (the pioneering spirit), *avoda atzmit* (self labor), and *hagshama* (self-realization through immigration to Israel). More importantly, however, it was because the Left had forced the religious Right into seeking the legitimate access of power and decision-making through the vehicle of the party, i.e., on inherently political grounds. Thus, the religious Right came to fight its quotidian battles in the political arena, and these battles, even in the service of *halakha* (Rabbinic law), brought to the religious parties the same taint that accrued to all parties in the political arena. Israelis, even religious Israelis, were coolly skeptical when it was a minister with portfolio who spoke

of Mission, Redemption, and the End of Days. They were
even more skeptical when the individual was not a minister,
spoke like a prophet but was suspected of eyeing a portfolio.

While the religious Right fought constant holding
actions with the aim of conserving the *status quo* in matters
of religion (especially those concerning personal status) it
was unable to make effective and unselfconscious use of its
basic Zionist charter: the notion of Redemption. But it
did not, for twenty years, fight its holding actions in vain.
The crisis of ideological Zionism, the routinization of the
movement in the face of demands that it remain charismatic,
did not abate (if anything, the institutionalization of
ideology into parties--by which the Left kept legitimate
power inherently "political"--hastened routinization at the
expense of sustaining charisma). The Left's program of
kibbutz galuyot continued to fail and, in time, the lack of
Zionist commitment among Israeli youth became yet another
topic of apprehensive debate. Through all this, the religious
Right could wait: for if Zionism was in trouble, it was
the predominant concept of secular, Left-Zionism that
suffered the most. Holding actions were being fought on
levels higher than that of the jurisprudence of personal
status.

The swift military victory of June, 1967 was followed
in Israel by a period of elation, relief, and hope. The
hope focused on the chances for peace with Arab neighbors;
chances that were thought to be good. This bright period
was short-lived. Although the war was followed by an economic
boom and increased immigration from the West, Israel became
increasingly isolated in the international arena and warfare, now in the form of terror-raids and Israeli reprisals
continued. Western immigration began to decline after 1972
and this period also saw the beginning of a significant
emigration of Israelis *to* the Diaspora. As the scene
darkened and the debate on the "deterioration" of Zionism
continued, The Land of Israel Movement took shape and was
able to attract non-Orthodox as well as Orthodox support.
Soon, "settlement of the Land" replaced *kibbutz galuyot* as
the major future-oriented task facing Zionism and Zionists.
The Land, which had once shared primacy in the Zionist
movement with other nationalist goals--sovereignty and
the revival of the Hebrew language (culture)--now came to
embody the reactive thrust of Zionist charisma in its
entirety.[7] Out of all this, and after the near-disaster
of the Yom Kippur War, the movement called Gush Emunim
crystallized. It was, in a sense, eminently adapted to
appeal to Israelis for several reasons, and primarily
the following:

• Gush maintained that Zionism would change, in
accordance with the redemptive process. What, in Zionism,
the secularists bemoaned and saw as symptoms of its continuing demise, the religious (following the Kooks)

regarded as a "natural" development toward its true expression.

* The concept of the territorial integrity of *Eretz Yisrael* was central to the Kooks' dynamic of Redemption: as "The Land" was put forward as the premiere symbol of Zionism, according to Gush it was the Kooks' religious ideology, based upon Redemption, that best adapted to capitalize on (and encourage) the symbolic shift.

* Rav A. Y. Kook had conceived his Zionism as divorced from the arena of party politics; he has stood aloof from all parties, religious as well as secular. By following the Kooks, Gush was able to justify its own aloofness from parties and its formal dissociation from them. Here, at last, was a segment of the religious Right that was effectively and unself-consciously able to use the notions of mission and Redemption unhampered by portfolios, or the lack of them. Here, finally, was a segment of the religious Right that was able to seek and claim legitimacy in values other than political.

* By focusing on the issue of settlement, Gush was able to coopt some of the key symbols formerly monopolized by the secular Left. Primary among these was the idea of *halutziut*, (the pioneering spirit). The new *halutzim* (pioneers), Gush claimed, were those willing to settle those areas now occupied by the Israeli Army.

* Rav A. Y. Kook's mystical ideas regarding the intrinsic holiness of *Eretz Yisrael* and the unfolding sacredness of Redemption were amenable to interpretation by Gush as a mandate for its fight against the moral impurities of the times.[8] The battle against the secular Left thus became a battle against *hityavnut* (Hellenization). With the Left cast as the Hellenizers and Gush Emunim as the Maccabees, this battle ultimately became a conflict—as sociologist Janet O'Dea puts it—against "the fears of the possibly unsettling or disintegrative effects of"—nothing less than—"Western culture."[9]

As previously mentioned, proponents of one theory of modernization argue that social movements whose ideology is based on traditional values must, in the face of modernization, secularize their ideology if they are to remain viable. But in Zionism we have the case of a social movement whose overarching ideology was a fusion, or integration, of both secular-modern and religious-traditional elements. It was, moreover, the secular-modern elements (such as class, party and State) that predominated until the establishment of the State and beyond. Leaders representing these elements were prominent among those who shaped the institutions of Israel, and who held the monopoly on Zionist symbols of the Good. Those representing the religious-traditional elements were forced into fighting holding actions aimed at conserving the *status quo*. Social change in Israel (the ongoing modernization of the society)

should, therefore, have presented few, if any, problems to
a transcendent Zionist ideology that was, in its predominant
expression, already "modern." To face the needs of modernization, the secularization of the Zionist ideology had, it
appeared, a fine and felicitous headstart.

The real situation was, however, far more complex.
Modernization encountered another process: the routinization
of the Zionist movement. This routinization was resisted by
both the religious and the secular sections of Zionism, the
Right and the Left, and their resistance plunged Zionism--
the movement and the ideology--into crisis. The secular
Left and the religious Right confronted this crisis in different ways. The Left pushed forward the program of the Ingathering of the Exiles. (The religious Right, it should be
noted, did not oppose this program. The Ingathering of the
Exiles is part of the eschatology of the End of Days, and
if the Left had succeeded, therefore, its very success would
have provided further evidence of the correctness of Rav A. Y.
Kook's characterization of Zionism and the State of Israel as
representing the beginning stages of Redemption.) But as it
became apparent that the program would fail, the onus of
its failure fell on the Left--and on the predominant conception
of Zionism that had guided the Zionist movement and the State.

Added to this crisis of ideology were the continuing
social and psychological crises of a state and its people
living under siege. After 1967, and particularly after 1973,
a segment of the religious Right was able to appear with an
explanation for *all* the crises that beset the State, its
people, and Zionism. Religious-traditional elements had
always been a part of the overarching Zionist ideology, but
they had appeared to be a subordinate and disappearing part.
Putting forward the integrity of the Whole Land of Israel as
its goal, but formally divorced from political parties, Gush
Emunim now offered a formula for the continued viability of
the Zionist enterprise. In the face of any, and all, "social
change," Zionism must resist further secularization and, in
fact, "return" to its only "true and possible expression":
the expression of the Divine Will.

Gush has, it appears, been trying to *traditionalize*
Zionist ideology in response to modernization. In a sense,
the most traditional elements of Zionism have been mobilized
and put into service; and it is in this sense that Gush
chose very carefully to label its most insidious enemy, not
Labor, the Left, or the hostile Arab regimes, but Hellenism.
For, in keeping with the traditional Jewish *weltanschauung*,
it is, in the final analysis, Hellenism and Hellenization
against which Gush does battle.

One crucial question remains, however. In whose
"service" are these traditional elements being put? Is it
in the service of a "revitalized" Zionism, of the Jewish
State, or of a new religious-political movement that calls
itself "The Bloc of the Faithful" and denies its own
political existence?

NOTES

1. In some cases the settlements pre-date the actual formation
of Gush (e.g., Kiryat Arba, in Hebron). These were in the main
associated with the Whole Land of Israel Movement. Today, however,
these settlements are fully identified with the efforts of Gush
Emunim.

2. What exactly constitutes "Eretz Yisrael" is a matter of
some controversy; a maximalist Biblical interpretation (e.g.,
Genesis 15:18) puts the borders as extending from the Nile to the
Euphrates.

3. On social movements see, e.g., R. Heberle, *Social Movements*
(N.Y.: Appleton-Century-Crofts, 1951), and W. R. Cameron, *Modern
Social Movements* (N.Y.: Random House, 1969). For a view of seculari-
zation see K. Markides, "Social Change and the Rise and Decline of
Social Movements: The Case of Cyprus," in *American Ethnologist*,
1:309-330, 1974.

4. Some of Rav A.Y. Kook's writings are included in *Orot*
(Lights), Jerusalem, 1950 (2nd edition).

5. Cf. M. N. Zald and R. Ash, "Social Movements Organizations:
Growth, Decay, and Change," in *Social Forces*, 44:327-340, 1966.

6. Quoted in D. Leon and Y. Adin's *The Voices of Jewish
Emancipation* (Jerusalem: The Zionist Library, 1972), p. 58.

7. Cf. Ben Halpern, *The Idea of the Jewish State* (Cambridge:
Harvard University Press, 1961), pp. 25ff.

8. Including the several scandals that wracked Labor's camp
in the months preceding the elections of May, 1977.

9. See Janet O'Dea, "Gush Emunim: Roots and Ambiguities,"
Forum 2 (25):46, 1976.

16
The Lebanese Identity

Kamal S. Salibi

The earliest evidence of a sense of Lebanese identity
is to be found in the writings of some Lebanese historians
of the first half of the nineteenth century. By that time
the Shihabs, a Sunnite Muslim family from the southern Anti-
Lebanon who had inherited the emirate over the Druzes and
Christians of the southern Lebanon in 1697, and had become
converted to Christianity according to the Maronite (Uniate
Catholic) rite in the second half of the eighteenth century,
had succeeded in extending their sway, *de facto*, over the
whole of Mount Lebanon, from the mainly Christian hinterland
of Tripoli in the north to the Druze-Christian hinterland
of Sidon in the south. A Lebanese entity had thus emerged,
separate and distinct from the rest of Syria, bringing the
Maronites and Druzes of the country, along with its other
Christian and Muslim sects, under one government.

The emirate inherited and expanded by the Shihabs had
a long history behind it. It had developed in earlier Ottoman times out of feudal privileges enjoyed by the Druze
chieftains of the southern Lebanon since the thirteenth and
fourteenth centuries, when the Mamluk rulers of Egypt and
Syria, to secure the loyalty of the warlike Druzes, recognized hereditary feudal tenure in the Druze mountain
(feudalism in the Islamic states was not, as a rule,
hereditary). The Ottomans, who conquered Syria from the
Mamluks in 1516, permitted the Druze chieftains to maintain
their privileges under a paramount emir (first recognized
in 1591) who was charged with the maintenance of order, the

The Lebanese Identity originally appeared in *The Journal
of Contemporary History*, January, 1971, and was excerpted in
Middle East Review, Vol. IX, No. 1, Fall, 1976. It is reprinted by permission of *The Journal of Contemporary
History*, as excerpted.

dispensation of justice, and the collection and remittance
of the revenue. This gave the southern Lebanon a relative
security; and, in time, Christians (mainly Maronites) from
the northern Lebanon came to settle there under the protection of the Druze emirs. In the course of the seventeenth
and eighteenth centuries the emirate of the southern Lebanon,
while it continued to enjoy its political privileges, became
further differentiated from its surroundings as a result of
its peculiar economic and social development. The silk
production which its emirs encouraged and protected provided
a regular (though modest) basis for its economy, enabling its
thrifty and industrious peasants, particularly the Christian
newcomers who were the main silk producers, to buy land and
become peasant smallholders of a kind almost unknown elsewhere in the region. Silk brokers and other entrepreneurs,
again mostly Christians, gradually emerged in the larger
villages and towns as a small middle class which grew in size,
wealth, and influence as commercial relations with Europe
developed, and as Christian merchant families left the
troubled Syrian interior for the less troubled realm of the
emirate. Backed by the growing Christian middle class and
by the peasant smallholders, the Shihab emirs, in the course
of the eighteenth century, trespassed on the traditional
privileges of the mainly Druze feudal chiefs to extend their
own power. The destruction of feudal privileges reached its
climax under the forceful and ambitious emir Bashir II
(1788-1840), who succeeded in establishing a firm control
over an expanded Shihab realm and ruled it in the manner of
an enlightened despot.

The involvement of Bashir II in the struggle between
Muhammad Ali Pasha of Egypt (backed by the French), and the
Ottomans (backed by the British), brought about his downfall
in 1840. In the following year, a co-ordinated opposition
of Druze and Christian feudal chiefs, encouraged by the
Ottomans and the British, brought an end to the Lebanese
emirate. The idea of a separate and distinct Lebanese
entity, however, remained alive among the Christian middle
class and freeholding peasantry--more particularly among the
Maronites who enjoyed French protection. It was, indeed,
during the period of division and anarchy following the end
of the emirate that a Maronite scholar, Tannus al-Shidyaq
(d. 1861), wrote the first coherent history of Mount Lebanon,
depicting the country as a feudal association of Maronites,
Druzes, Melchites, Sunnites, and Shi'ites under the leadership of the Shihab emirs.

Shidyaq began his career as a clerk and political agent
in the service of the Shihabs, then turned to commerce and
teaching after their downfall. The mere publication of his
history (entitled *Akhbar al-a yan fi Jabal Lubnan*, or History
of the Notables of Mount Lebanon) in 1859 shows how the idea
of Lebanon survived the emirate. By the time the book
appeared, however, its feudal conception of Lebanon,
reflecting the brief but dramatic resurgence of feudal

power in the country after 1841, was becoming outmoded.
In 1861, following two decades of intermittent civil war
between peasants and feudal chiefs, and between Maronites
and Druzes, a new settlement was worked out for the country,
giving it the *de jure* status of a Mutesarrifate (autonomous
province) within the Ottoman Empire. The arrangement was
made as a result of French military intervention, and it
was guaranteed by the European Powers: France, Russia,
Austria, Prussia (later Germany), and Sardinia (later Italy).
The Mutesarrifate comprised Mount Lebanon to the exclusion
of Tripoli, Beirut, and Sidon and the valley of the Biqa
(the fertile alluvial plain between the Lebanon and the Anti-
Lebanon). It was to be governed by a non-Lebanese Ottoman
Christian mutesarrif assisted by an elected administrative
council and a locally recruited civil service and gendarmerie.
No feudal prerogatives were to be recognized. The Mutesarrifate
was to have its own budget derived from local taxation and
subsidized, when necessary, by the Ottoman state. Only revenue
in excess of the Lebanese budget was to be returned to the
Ottoman treasury. Citizens of the Mutesarrifate were exempt
from Ottoman military service.

The establishment of the Mutesarrifate of Mount Lebanon
gave the Lebanese identity, for the first time, a legal definition. To be Lebanese was to enjoy citizenship in the Mutesarrifate, and the various privileges that went with it. The
rapid development of Mount Lebanon after 1861, moreover, gave
the Lebanese a pride in their identity and a sense of national
achievement. Under the enlightened government of the
mutesarrifs, Lebanese initiative flourished in an atmosphere
of relative freedom; so did the educational and cultural
activities of Roman Catholic and Protestant missionaries,
which were a major factor in the general development. The
country appeared as a model Ottoman province--a fact which
was reflected by the common saying, still remembered and
repeated: 'Happy is he who has a shed to keep one goat in
Mount Lebanon.'

It was among the Maronites, by far the largest community
in the Mutesarrifate, that the sense of Lebanese identity
developed most strongly. While the majority of the Maronites
saw in the Mutesarrifate a Maronite national homeland, an
imaginative minority among them, composed mostly of leaders
associated with the government, saw in it a free association
of communities which the Maronites, as the major community,
were called upon to lead. To these Maronite leaders, the
Mutesarrifate was not an end in itself, but a step towards
full Lebanese statehood. While admitting that the arrangements made in 1861 were in keeping with the Lebanese social
and economic development as it then stood, they insisted
that these arrangements were seriously restrictive of further
development. The territorial limits of the Mutesarrifate,
which deprived the country of ports for its commerce and
suitable land for its agriculture, were to them particularly
unsatisfactory. Lebanon, they maintained, could not develop

to its full potential unless its territory was enlarged
to include the coastal cities of Tripoli, Beirut, Sidon,
and Tyre, along with the Biqa and the plain of Akkar, to
the north of Tripoli.   In a book published in Paris in 1902
under the title *La Question du Liban*, a Maronite lawyer
associated with the government of the Mutesarrifate, Bulus
Nujaym (*pseudonym* M. Jouplain), eloquently put forth the
arguments for the expansion of Lebanon and called upon
France, traditional friend of the Lebanese, to help them
achieve full statehood and, ultimately, independence.   The
arguments of Nujaym were repeated and developed in the years
that followed by a number of other Christian Lebanese
nationalists who organized themselves in committees and,
from the safety of Egypt or France, solicited international
support for their cause.

A great opportunity for the fulfillment of the Lebanese
nationalist demands came in 1918, with the victory of the
Allies in the first world war and the collapse of the Ottoman Empire.   By special agreement between the Allies, the
French occupied Beirut and the coastal zone, then received
from the League of Nations a Mandate over the territory of
present-day Lebanon and Syria.   On 1 September 1920, the
French High Commissioner, General Henri Gouraud, proclaimed
in Beirut the State of Greater Lebanon with its present
boundaries.   On 23 May 1926, with the promulgation of the
Lebanese Constitution, this state became the Lebanese
Republic.

The establishment of Greater Lebanon certainly satisfied
the demands of the Christian Lebanese nationalists, but it
also brought with it a serious problem.   Under the Mutesarrifate, the Maronites, with their keen sense of Lebanese
identity, were an overwhelming majority, and their sense of
national identity appears to have been more or less shared
by the Druzes and the Christian minority groups.   In Greater
Lebanon, however, the Maronites became the largest single
community, and the Christian communities together formed only
a small majority.   In the coastal cities which were incorporated in the new state, the majority was Sunnite Muslim.
Tyre and its hinterland were predominantly Shiite Muslim;
and Sunnite and Shiite Muslims also predominated in the Biqa
and other annexed territories.   Of these two communities,
which now ranked second and third in number after the
Maronites, the Sunnites had pronounced pan-Arab sympathies,
and their leaders clamored for union with Syria, which was
predominantly Sunnite.   The Shiites, who had hardly any
co-religionists in Syria, were happy enough to be included
in Lebanon; their traditional wariness of the Sunnites,
however, made them hesitant to declare their Lebanese
sympathies openly, and some among them even professed a
dissimulating pan-Arabism.   The Druzes, also anxious to
keep the goodwill of the Sunnites, remained reserved.   It
soon became clear that the Christian Lebanese had to face
the pan-Arabism of the Sunnites with little active help

from either the Shiites or the Druzes. Even the Christian
ranks were soon divided over the issue. While most of the
Greek Orthodox supported the Lebanese idea, some among
them saw in the conflict between Lebanese nationalism and
pan-Arabism an opportunity to challenge the established
Maronite leadership by professing pan-Arabism, or the
intermediary position of Syrian nationalism--in a Greater
Syria, they felt, the Greek Orthodox rather than the
Maronites would be the major Christian community sharing
power with the Sunnites, as there were hardly any Maronites
outside Lebanon. With the Greek Orthodox thus divided, the
Maronites and other Catholic communities remained the only
solid Lebanese nationalist block. It was largely left to
them to develop a workable formula for the country.

The initial formula for Lebanon was worked out by a
group of leaders among whom the most prominent was the banker
and intellectual Michel Chiha (d. 1954), a Roman Catholic
and a second generation Lebanese of Assyrian extraction whose
family came originally from Iraq. Chiha (writing in French)
depicted Lebanon as an association of Christian and Muslim
communities living together in a spirit of cooperation and
mutual respect. The country, he maintained, had a character
all its own, recognizable in all the stages of its history.
It was, in essence, a Mediterranean country, whose people
had been active in the Mediterranean world since ancient
times. The Phoenicians, with whom the history of the country
begins, were traders who established a commercial empire in
the Mediterranean, bringing wealth to their cities from over-
seas. The modern Lebanese, like them, were destined for
trade; their country, situated at the cross-roads between East
and West, was ideally suited for the purpose. In addition to
being traders, the Phoenicians had been cultural intermediaries
in the ancient world; among other things, they had developed
the modern alphabet from older Oriental scripts and transmitted
it to the Greeks, who in turn passed it on to the Romans. Like
their Phoenician forefathers, the modern Lebanese were called
upon to play the role of cultural intermediaries, explaining
to the West the heritage of the East, and introducing the
East to the modern material and spiritual civilization of the
West. The Lebanese, according to Chiha, were well-prepared
for this role, as they alone had a complete understanding of
both the East and the West.

To Chiha, the viability of the Lebanese system depended
on the maintenance of traditional relationships. The Constitution which he helped to draft (he was, in 1926, the
secretary of the drafting committee) established a legal
framework for these traditional relationships but did not
fix them permanently, leaving them to develop by spontaneous
give-and-take; and develop they did. In 1926, the Sunnite
Muslims were still clamoring for union with Syria, and few
Sunnite leaders dared defy their co-religionists by participating in Lebanese politics. The choice of a Maronite for
first President would have confirmed their worst suspicions

that Lebanon was meant to be a Maronite national homeland.
Hence a Greek Orthodox, Charles Dabbas, was chosen as first
President. With no Muslims available to form the first
cabinets, the premiership was assigned to Maronites. The
first Sunnite Muslim to show readiness to share in the
management of affairs, Muhammad al-Jisr, was elected President
of the Chamber of Deputies. Later, when more Muslims became
eager to share in Lebanese politics, the Presidency of the
Republic was reserved for the Maronites (starting in 1934)
and the Premiership for the Sunnite Muslims (1937). Still
later, the Presidency of the Chamber of Deputies was reserved
for the Shiites (1947). Shortly before the political independence of Lebanon from the French Mandate in 1943, a
gentleman's agreement was worked out between the Christian
and Muslim leaders establishing a fixed ratio of six Christians
to five Muslims in the membership of the Chamber of Deputies,
which is hence always a multiple of eleven. It was also
agreed then that key security positions (like the Army command
and the Directorate of General Security) would be reserved
for Christians. The Muslims promised loyalty to Lebanon
as an independent state, and agreed to cease their demands
for the dissolution of Lebanon in a larger Arab entity; the
Christians promised to regard Lebanon as a member of the Arab
family of nations and to follow a national policy that does
not run contrary to the general Arab interest. The gentleman's agreement of 1943 is known in Lebanon as the National
Pact, and it remains unwritten. After the crisis of 1958,*
the National Pact was supplemented by another agreement,
again unwritten, to divide administrative posts equally
between Christians and Muslims and as equitably as possible
among the sects, in order to ensure the maintenance of the
national unity of the Lebanese people...As the term of the
Maronite President of the Republic near[ed] its end, Sunnites,
Shiites, and Druzes join[ed] the Greek Orthodox and others in
searching for a suitable Maronite to succeed him. Members
of the Chamber of Deputies divid[ed] along political lines,
with little regard to sect, to elect a Shiite President for
the Chamber, or to choose a Sunnite Premier to form the
Cabinet. Leading army officers of all sects accept[ed] a
Maronite as their commander. Any defiance of the system
[was] regarded as sedition.

*During the middle of May 1958 rioting broke out in protest
against the possible revision of the Lebanese Constitution
that would permit President Chamoun to take office for a
second six-year term, thus extending the tenure of Lebanon's
pro-Western government. Radio Cairo and Radio Damascus
urged the Lebanese to sustain the revolt and demanded
President Chamoun's resignation. Syrian aid to anti-
government forces in Lebanon led to a Lebanese complaint to
the U.N. and a request by Lebanon for U.S. intervention.
President Eisenhower dispatched U.S. troops to Lebanon
following the *coup* in Iraq of July 14. (Ed.)

        While the Chiha formula for government, as supplemented
by subsequent conventions,...proved eminently workable, the
Chiha image of Lebanese identity has proved less so. Most
Christian Lebanese, anxious to dissociate themselves from
Arabism and its Islamic connections, were pleased to be told
that their country was the legitimate heir to the Phoenician
tradition. Christian writers like the poets Charles Corm
(writing in French, d. 1963) and Said Aql (writing in Arabic),
tried hard to build up the Phoenicianist image of Lebanon.
Lebanon, they maintained, had become culturally connected
with Arabism by sheer accident, and it was time to set
things right by picking up where the Phoenicians had left
off and forgetting the unfortunate interval. Said Aql
was particularly vocal in preaching a Phoenician Renaissance.
Although himself a master of classical Arabic style, he urged
the abandonment of classical Arabic, together with the Arabic
script, and proceeded, with little success, to write prose
and poetry in the Lebanese vernacular, using an adapted Latin
script. In addition to providing grounds for dissociating
Lebanon from Arabism, the Phoenicianist idea appealed to the
predominantly Christian middle class by promoting the image
of the Lebanese as traders. It also presented the Lebanese
emigrant as a Phoenician adventurer setting out for the unknown, thereby consoling the Christians, somewhat, for the
fact that their numbers were being steadily reduced in the
country by emigration to North America, South America, and
more recently Australia. However, while the general run of
Christians gave their enthusiastic support to Phoenicianism,
most Muslims dismissed it as nonsense and ridiculed the
extravagant claims of Corm, Aql, and their followers. The
Sunnites were particularly vehement in their rejection of
the Phoenicianist formula, which they denounced outright
as part of a French imperialist conspiracy against Arab
nationalism. Even when they agreed to accept Lebanon as a
separate entity under the terms of the National Pact, the
country remained to them Arab and its people not a separate
Lebanese nation, but part of a larger Arab nation. Sunnite
writers like Muhammad Jamil Bayhum (a Beirut notable who
was associated with Sharif Faysal's Arab movement in 1918)
and Umar Farrukh (a professor of Islamics at a leading
Muslim college in Beirut), insisted that Lebanon, in its
history and culture, was inseparable from the main current
of Arabism. They admitted that the modern Lebanese could
legitimately take pride in the achievement of their
Phoenician predecessors. But the Phoenicians, they insisted, were Canaanites who came originally from the Arabian
peninsula: they could hence be claimed, in a way, as Arabs.
While this last claim was clearly untenable, it could not
be denied that there was much truth in the Sunnite position.
Lebanon was undoubtedly Arabic in speech and traditional
culture. Its history in Islamic times, until certainly the
seventeenth century, could be clearly separated from the
history of Syria (if not from Arab and Islamic history in

general) only by lame artifice. No theory of Lebanese
nationality could be valid if it did not take into consideration the fundamental historical and cultural connection between Lebanon and Arabism. The fact remained, however, that Arab nationalism had a distinct Islamic (more
particularly Sunnite) flavor, which made it in general
unacceptable to the Christians. Moreover, the Arab
nationalist formula for Lebanon which the Sunnites urged,
if carried to its logical conclusion, could hardly be
counted upon as a guarantee for the continued existence
and safety of Lebanon as a separate entity. In 1958, when
Egypt and Syria joined to form the short-lived United
Arab Republic...Lebanon was thrown into a crisis verging
on civil war as its Arab nationalists clamored for the
country to join the union. Since the Arab-Israeli war of
June 1967, Lebanese Arab nationalists...urged permission for
Palestinian guerrilla organizations to operate freely in
Lebanon, thereby compromising the sovereignty of the country
and exposing it to Israeli retaliation. If the Phoenicianist
formula for Lebanon, intellectually untenable because it
ignores the country's Arab heritage,...proved unworkable
because it [was] rejected by the Muslims, the Arab nationalist
formula, apart from being unacceptable to most Christians,...
proved dangerous to the sovereignty of the country by calling
it in question at intervals of alarming frequency. As an
alternative to Phoenicianism, Lebanese nationalists have tried
to promote the image of Lebanon as a refuge and a haven for
freedom. This image had first emerged as a distinct thesis in
the early years of the French Mandate, in the work of the
Jesuit missionary and Orientalist Henri Lammens (d. 1937)
who lived and taught in Beirut. In his classic *La Syrie;
precis historique* (Beirut 1921), Lammens depicted Lebanon,
historically, as a haven for the persecuted and oppressed
of Syria: 'à tous ceux que révolte la tyrannie des pachas,
la Montagne s'ouvrait' (*ibid.*, II, 63). The Lammens image
of what he called *l'asile du Liban* was a powerful one, and
certainly more suitable than Phoenicianism as justification
for a Lebanese national identity. It was acceptable not
only to the Christians, but also to the Shiites and Druzes
who were historically acquainted with persecution. It
was hardly complimentary, however, to the Sunnite Muslims
who were presumed to have been, historically, the persecutors
and oppressors. In recent years, as many Sunnites and others
[left] Syria and Iraq to seek political refuge in Lebanon,
the idea of *l'asile du Liban*...gain[ed] recognition and
[became] more widely accepted. Lebanese Sunnites, nevertheless, remain[ed] disinclined to subscribe to it as an
acceptable theoretical basis for a Lebanese nationalism.

   Despite its historical validity and broad appeal, the
l'asile du Liban formula fails as a foundation for a theory
of Lebanese nationality; and its failure, like that of
Phoenicianism, drives home the fact that no intellectual
justification for a separate and distinct Lebanese identity

can be successful if it leaves out the Muslims, more particularly the Sunnites. There remains, however, the question:
is any such justification necessary? During the fifty years
that have elapsed since the establishment of the State of
Greater Lebanon, the practice of Lebanese nationality has
been clearly ahead of the theory. The Lebanese, despite
persisting differences which often seem grave, have actually
become more and more of a distinct people, recognizing themselves as such and being recognized by others as such, simply
by the process of living together and sharing in a common
national life. The steady growth of the Lebanese middle
class, which has come to include an increasing proportion
of Muslims and Druzes, has broadened the meeting-ground for
the various Lebanese communities, all of which have developed
vested interests in the country. The recurring internal and
regional crises which, on the surface, have so frequently
made the Lebanese system seem precarious and its continued
existence questionable, have, at a deeper level, served to
sharpen the sense of Lebanese nationality by forcing the
Lebanese, time and again, to redefine their internal and
external relationships, thereby gaining a deeper understanding
of their national life. Developments in the region have also
helped. The contrast between the democracy and liberalism of
Lebanon (which the sectarian division of the country helps
to secure) and the authoritarianism which continues to gain
ground in the Arab world, is making the image of Lebanon as
a separate entity more and more distinct; so is the relative
prosperity and stability of the country in contrast to its
neighbors. While the search for a historical and philosophical
basis for Lebanese nationality continues, it is, in the main,
by the day-to-day process of being Lebanese that the people
of Lebanon are becoming more and more of a nation. Considering the increasing facility with which fundamental problems
are being handled, and in spite of the dangers which so
frequently threaten the Lebanese system, one would not expect
the process to be easily reversed.

17
Ethnic Conflict and the Reemergence of Radical Christian Nationalism in Lebanon

John P. Entelis

In the aftermath of the devastating Lebanese civil war
of 1975-76[1] political commentators and scholarly analysts
have been quick to provide numerous possible explanations
as to the root causes of Lebanon's most violent and bloody
domestic conflict since the Druze-Maronite massacres of the
early 1860s.   Most explanations tend to focus on the
system's inability to respond effectively to the enormous
social and political forces unleashed by social mobilization[2] or modernization.   Such rapid modernization has inevitably generated an expansion of the political arena and
a concomitant enlargement of the socio-political elite.
Simultaneously, broad scale social mobilization, which has
characterized Lebanese society in the past decade and a
half, has increased intra-elite conflict, stimulated the
rise of powerful often disruptive new ideologies, and
aroused the mass public into a renewed sense of political
consciousness.   Lebanon's neo-feudal administrative structure
and archaic political order proved incapable of responding
to these multifaceted developments.

In addition, insenitive government officials and self-
serving political leaders turned their heads away from the
vast social inequalities that rapid yet uneven economic
growth had created.   As "objective structural changes"
were being buffeted by rapid inflation, social ferment, and
unsettled urban masses, wide-spread corruption, nepotism,
and favoritism pervaded virtually every aspect of the system,
further weakening the country's political legitimacy.
Finally, of course, the "catastrophic deterioration in

*Ethnic Conflict and the Reemergence of Radical Christian
Nationalism in Lebanon* is reprinted by permission of the
Journal of South Asian and Middle Eastern Studies, Spring,
1979.

Lebanon's regional position,"[3] made the country vulnerable
to incessant physical attacks from within and without.
As it became more squarely enmeshed in the Arab-Israeli
conflict it rapidly demonstrated that it lacked both sufficient
military capability and political will to respond effectively
or credibly to this threat.

Both the domestic and regionally-related concomitants of
Lebanon's political and social disintegration are often
directed at the country's much maligned confessional system
of rule, a system in which almost all significant political
and administrative positions in state and government are
distributed according to a rather mechanistic procedure of
proportional representation based on religious affiliation
as determined by a 1932 French-sponsored census.[4]   Given
the severity of existing ethnic and communal cleavages and
the fragmented nature of Lebanese political culture confessionalism appeared appropriate to meet the several demands
of social stability, political democracy, and economic
development.   Moreover, despite its formalization as the
modus operandi of the Lebanese political system in the early
1940s in the form of the so-called National Pact (*mithaq
al-watani*),[5] confessionalism could trace its roots to mid-
nineteenth century feudal Lebanon[6] and, more generally, to
the whole pattern of Middle Eastern social organization as
it developed over the centuries including its important
millet component which evolved during the period of Ottoman
rule.

Yet neither its relative effectiveness as a pragmatic
regulator of inter-communal tensions nor its quasi-legitimiza-
tion as a historical principle could sufficiently "salvage"
confessionalism during a period of rapid social mobilization,
accelerated political demands, and disruptive regional
conflicts.   Indeed, as both the internal and external "loads"
on the system increased, as clearly was the case in the late
1960s and early 1970s, confessionalism came to be regarded
as a major obstacle to the very political stability and social
harmony that its creation was supposed to engender.   Instead,
confessionalism fostered immobilism in government, postponed
needed social reforms, perpetuated archaic and inefficient
bureaucratic practices, encouraged corruption and favoritism
in high places, and, in general, retarded the process of
rationalization in government and administration.   In other
words, while the breakdown of the Lebanese polity in 1975-76
could be traced to incompetent and venal political leaders
its roots were essentially systemic: that is, "the Lebanese
confessional solution was no longer adequate to the loads and
demands of the present situation."[7]

While much of this argumentation is valid, it tends to
overstress the malfunctioning of the *mechanism* of confessionalism while neglecting the fundamentality of primordial
attachments in a multiethnic society.   In other words,
while confessionalism may have failed to create sufficiently
flexible and adaptive structural mechanisms to mediate and

control inter-ethnic divisions during periods of severe
societal stress, this institutional breakdown was only a
byproduct or consequence of a more basic conceptual dilemma;
namely, the refusal of a significant number of indigenous
elites of transnationalist persuasion to recognize and, over
time, internalize the legitimacy of Lebanon's ethnic reality.

Thus emerge two diametrically opposed perspectives regarding the causes of and possible remedies for Lebanon's
political disintegration. For those who attack confessionalism
and its ethnic-centered underpinnings, ethno-confessional
identities and interests are but "masks" for more profound
class conflicts; indeed ethnicity itself is viewed as an
expression of socio-political retardation, unenlightenment,
or ignorance.[8] More ideologically-inclined analysts deny
the relevance of ethnicity altogether considering it instead
as an unfortunate vestige of underdeveloped and unmobilized
society which, in any case, is but a temporary phenomenon
that will sooner or later disappear. Finally, to most
ideologues, regardless of political predisposition, ethnicity
is to be dismissed and cast-off in the process of rationalization and secularization "because ethnic identity is too dense
and inarticulate to be a product of reason. It confines men
within parochial networks of relations."[9]

Such is the view of many analysts of Third World political
development who relate political conflict of societies in the
process of modernization to class or ideological-nationalist
considerations of which ethnic attachments constitute but
contributory rather than causal factors. The reality of
course is that in Lebanon, as throughout the Middle Eastern
world today, inter-ethnic confrontation challenges the unifying impact of nationalism and supranationalism which have yet
to reduce effectively primordial sentiments and develop a
common purpose.[10] Indeed rather than being doomed to
extinction by the forces of change and modernization,
ethnicity in Lebanon continues to reveal remarkable adaptive-
ness, resiliency, and "modern" tendencies. This is so because
of all the groups that individuals attach themselves to,
ethnic groups seem the most encompassing and enduring. The
primacy of ethnic association is also part of a broader
phenomenon evident among people in most Third World states
who remain strongly bound up by what Clifford Geertz has
called the "gross actualities of blood, race, language,
locality, religion, or tradition."[11]

As used here and borrowing from Enloe, ethnicity has
both a communal and a personal dimension. Specifically,
ethnicity refers to a

> peculiar bond among persons that causes them to consider
> themselves a group distinguishable from others. The content
> of the bond is shared culture. Culture, in turn, is a
> pattern of fundamental beliefs and values differentiating
> right from wrong, defining rules for interaction, setting
> priorities, expectations, and goals. Cultural bonds grow

out of men's recognition of the distinctiveness of their
own standards of behavior and prizing of those standards
to the extent that they feel most comfortable and secure
when among persons sharing them. On the personal level,
ethnicity equips an individual with a sense of belonging;
it positions him in society. As social relations become
complex and impersonal, ethnic identity may be grasped
tenaciously. It is a familiar and reassuring anchor in
a climate of turbulence and uncertainty.[12]

While virtually no state in the modern period can
escape the reality of primordial attachments, that is,
attachments that stem from certain "givens" of social
existence, Lebanon, as a severely fragmented polyethnic
society, highlights, in its political history, the persistence of primordial ties in local and national politics.
Moreover, although an impressive modernization has generated
a noticeable degree of class mobility and status differentiation, "membership in a given class still does not provide
the average Lebanese with a sense of identity."[13] Despite
its size and influence, Lebanon's middle class, for example,
remains diffuse and amorphous as a social group. Simply
put, "class consciousness is not as intense or meaningful
as kinship or confessional consciousness, and it is doubt-
ful whether the emergence of a more cohesive middle class
could dilute the sense of identity associated with primordial
affinities."[14]

More than ever before ethnicity continues to be a crucial
"fact of life" in Lebanon which cannot be wished out of
existence however much political ideologues may consider
the lifting of ethnic and primordial ties to the level of
political supremacy as pathological or irrational. In fact,
the consistent inability of ideological politics to take
hold in the over thirty years of Lebanese independence is
in great part due to the unwillingness of critically-situated
political elites, mostly of authoritarian persuasion, and
their Palestinian supporters residing in the country to
recognize the legitimacy of ethnic sentiments and associations not as symbols of feudal communal ties and archaic
political practices but as the basis of a modernist
"ideology" consistent with the multi-ethnic and multiconfessional character of the society.[15] Instead, there
has been a constant determination by selected indigenous
and exogenous forces to impose a unitary nationalist framework that would deny and, in fact, eliminate the subnational
attributes of Lebanese citizens. This reflects a critical
inability to recognize in political terms "the legitimate
existence of groups who find their security in preserving
their own culture and political position within the state
confines."[16] Those advocating an imposed political inte-
grationism have tended to subdue and blur differences rather
than accept them and build on a social ground of reality.
The result has been civil war and political decay often

conceptualized in such false and misleading dichotomies
as revolutionism versus reactionism, populism versus
elitism, socialism versus capitalism, Arab nationalism
versus Lebanese parochialism, etc.

A consensual acceptance of the principle of multiethnic
pluralism as operationalized under confessionalism has never
fully existed since the country's formal creation as Greater
Lebanon on September 1, 1920.   Prior to that time the Ottoman-
regulated *mutasarrifiyah* (governorate) of the *sanjaq* (administrative district) of Lebanon had been relatively successful
in stabilizing the hitherto precarious and turbulent political
life of Mount Lebanon.   Characterized by a relatively high
degree of social cohesion and an accepted predominance of
Maronite rule Lebanon, in the 1864-1920 period, was able
to enjoy an extended era of systemic harmony.   However, the
incorporation of Sidon, Tripoli, the Biqa, and Beirut with
their overwhelming Muslim populations into the new state
of Greater Lebanon weakened what in the preceding fifty
years had developed into a cohesive "national" unit in the
Mountain under the recognized leadership of the Maronite
Patriarch.   In addition the rise of an Arab nationalist
consciousness in the post-Ottoman period worked to disrupt
the system's internal social harmony.

The principle of confessional allotment of seats within
a given administrative or electoral district that the
Reglement Organique of 1861 established was an appropriate
governing instrument so long as no broader or extra-territorial
nationalist ideology competed for the loyalties of the Mountain's subjects.   Now, with a large Muslim population incorporated virtually against its will into a predominantly
Maronite state, at a time when the concept of pan-Arab unity
was beginning to emerge, existing communal cleavages were
exacerbated while new levels of para-nationalist conflicts
emerged.   Inevitably, there developed divergent perspectives
as to the nature of Lebanese nationhood with consequent
strains on the system's stability.   As Zuwiyya Yamak observes:
"The most immediate and urgent problem that faced the nascent
state of Greater Lebanon in the 1920s was that of fusing
its mosaic population into a politically viable and socially
cohesive entity."[17]

The core of the ethnic dilemma confronting Lebanon today
is thus traceable to this early period when competing ideological perspectives concerning the country's national identity
began to take form.   Arab nationalists, for example, have
traditionally viewed Lebanon as an integral part of the Arab
world ethnically, culturally, historically, and geographically.
For the more extremist among them, Lebanon can have no separate
political identity except within a well-defined Arab framework.[18]   More moderate pan-Arabists concede to Lebanon a
certain ethnic and communal distinctiveness without, however,
denying its essential Arab character.

Syrian nationalists also deny Lebanon's separate political
existence, regarding it as a geographical and political anomaly.

Only within its "proper" environmental context as historically
developed can Lebanon have any viable meaning. Thus, pan-
Syrians, especially the Syrian Social Nationalist Party, seek
Lebanon's reintegration as a subordinate unit into the
Syrian "nation."

Lebanese nationalists, on the other hand, regard Lebanon
as possessing certain fundamental attributes which differentiate it from the rest of the Arab world and justify its
independent status. Citing the Mountain's historical development, the unique mosaic pattern of its population, and its
traditional role as a bridgehead between East and West
Lebanese nationalists defend the state's separate existence.
Some of the more zealous elements among them deny *any* Arab
character to Lebanon preferring to associate its historical
development to Phoenician or other Mediterranean-inspired
ancestral roots. More moderate groups, however, are willing
to accept a Muslim-Christian symbiosis so long as it does not
imply a renunciation of Lebanese sovereignty.

Finally, there are those among both Christians and Muslims
who seek to transform Lebanon either into a national homeland
for Levantine Christians or have it included as part of a
larger pan-Islamic federation. Until the recent civil war
at least neither "pure" Christian nationalism nor Islamic
fundamentalism found much support among Lebanese nationals.

Two important factors have determined *Sunnite attitudes
towards Lebanese nationhood*: first has been the psychological
frustration arising from loss of prestige and recognition.
Having once held a privileged position under the Ottoman
Empire, Sunnites resented their minority status in Greater
Lebanon. Their historically-dominant place in the Islamic
world was abruptly altered in 1920 when the Sunnites suddenly
found themselves in an inferior position, treated almost as
second class citizens. Even after nearly sixty years of
incorporation within the Lebanese state this psychological
crisis continues to determine the attitudinal response of
Sunnites to their social and political environment.

The second determining factor influencing Sunnite
attitudes is the concept of *'urubah* or Arabism. *'Urubah*
is a semi-mystical term denoting the essence of being an
Arab--"the sense of belonging to the Arab nation, the
possession of Arabic as mother tongue, the fact of having
been born an Arab in an Arab land, being a Muslim."[19]
Implicit in the feeling and awareness of Arabism is unity
or *wihdah*. *Wihdah* involves political unity, "but also the
aspiration for a more profound unity transcending the
merely political or economic."[20] Moreover, Arabism posits
the indivisibility of the Arab nation; the longing for
wihdah reflects the will to restore to wholeness what has
been violated by history, adversity, and accident.

Both *'urubah* and *wihdah* constitute the fundamental
components of Arab nationalism (*al-qawmiyyah al-'arabiyyah*).
This "nationalist" feeling has a profound psycho-ideological
meaning to all Arabs and especially Sunni Muslims, while

identification with Lebanese nationhood implies, in great
part, a denunciation of *'urubah* thereby severing the Muslim
from the Arab *ummah* or Nation.

Besides ideological and psychological dissatisfactions
there exist concrete socio-economic and political grievances
further alienating an already disaffected community. Compared
to Maronites and Christians in general, the Sunnites are an
economically less-advanced subnational group who, rightly or
wrongly, blame their current status on the policies of
Lebanon's Western-oriented, predominantly Christian elite.[21]
It is thus not surprising that to this day the Sunnite masses
display only a tenuous loyalty to Lebanon, its institutions,
and national symbols.

The major determining factor conditioning the *Christians'
image of Lebanese nationhood* has been the constant identification of Lebanon as a place of refuge, a territorial enclave
serving to protect oriental Christians from Muslim attempts
to subjugate and disperse them. According to the Christian
frame of reference only in Lebanon can minority religious
sects of the Middle East find protection, free of intimida-
tion and persecution; this is the role Lebanon has traditionally played and one it should continue playing in the
future.

As a minority people living in an Islamic state, usually
on the fringes of its social life, sharing neither its
responsibilities nor its rights, it is understandable that
a "persecutionist" mentality would eventually develop among
them. This, in essence, was the major unifying link among
Lebanon's numerous Christian sects. And, although no homogeneous nationalist attitude predominated among all of them,
the Maronite community, as the largest and most powerful
confessional group manifesting certain clearly identifiable
patterns of community consciousness, initiated and inspired
a generally acceptable nationalist ideology among the
Christians and, to a much lesser extent of course, the
Druze peoples of the Mountain.

The Maronite community has a historical self-conscious-
ness and a keen sense of a common destiny. Unlike other
confessional groups it views Lebanon as its one and only
homeland. As Iliya Harik informs us the Maronite people
are a national group reflecting "distinctive ethnic characteristics, a single religion, and a long history; for
centuries they lived in one compact area and once had a
distinct language (of which they kept some vestiges in their
religious books) and memories up to the recent past."[22]
They are also unique among the Christians of the Arabic-
speaking world in that they are the only one of the many
sects who can be considered a compact minority. Other
Christian sects are spread out over larger areas and nowhere do they form groups more compact than a few villages.
This difference is what makes the Maronites so self-conscious
of their identity as a separate people.

Although the roots of Maronite nationalism may be found

in the sixteenth century its essence emerged in the early
and mid-seventeenth century under the intellectual stimulus
of the Maronite hierarchy. Throughout its development it
was closely related to the idea of Western especially French
protection and association. Trained abroad in Catholic
schools, clerical and lay Maronite elites transported Western
ideas and influences back to Lebanon which, for better or
worse, determined the community's nationalist orientation
as it related to non-Maronite Christians and Muslims. It was
thus not surprising to have Maronites view Lebanon "not so
much as the western frontier of the Arab East but as the
eastern frontier of the Christian West...."[23]
     This Maronite nationalism, apart from the psychological
satisfaction it might have given the Maronite community, may
have had a political rationale so long as Lebanon remained
a relatively homogeneous social entity. But once this
homogeneity was fractured, as it was in 1920, Maronite
nationalism had little *raison d'etre*. Moreover, after independence had been achieved and Western hegemony over the
Arab world destroyed, the concept of promoting Lebanon as
a national home for Levantine Christians became an untenable
formulation. The appearance in 1945 of a publication entitled
*S.O.S.: The Lebanon, the "Christian National Home" of the
Near East*[24] was probably the last open attempt to assert
the supremacy of the Maronite nationalist ideology at least
until the outbreak of sectarian conflict in 1975.
     Two ideological offshoots of Maronite nationalism are
the concepts of Phoenicianism and Mediterraneanism. The
notion of tracing Lebanon's origin to ancient Phoenicia was
first introduced in the writings of Tahhus al-Shidyaq, a
secular Maronite writer of the middle nineteenth century.
Later it was used by Christian writers to emphasize the non-
Arab character of Lebanon.[25] Mediterraneanism was similar
in its intent since it sought to link Lebanon's physical and
cultural origins to the Mediterranean basin, again as a means
of distinguishing Lebanon from its Arab milieu. Both concepts found limited support among organized groups although
much of their implications have been accepted by more militant Lebanese Maronites. These two intellectual movements,
which found their greatest strength in the 1930s and 1940s,
were directed at countering the Arab nationalist idea and
Syrian nationalism and had few positive attributes with which
to create a viable Lebanese nationalist ideology which could
give Lebanese a coherent world view of themselves and their
society.
     Lebanonism or Lebanese nationalism, especially as pro-
pounded by Lebanon's powerful, predominantly Christian
political party, al-Kataib,[26] has attempted to fill this ideological void by presenting a broadly interconfessional (although with unmistakably strong Maronite roots) interpretation
of Lebanese nationhood. It is not that the Kataib was the
progenitor of the Lebanese nationalist concept in its modern
form--Michel Chiha was probably the most original thinker on

subject[27]--but, rather, that it was the Kataib, as the largest and best organized political group in Lebanon, which adopted, refined, and then propagated Lebanonism as its primary ideological doctrine.[28]

How can these competing ideological orientations concerning the nature of Lebanese nationhood be reconciled so as to enable a communally segmented society to develop socially, economically, and politically within an essentially democratic framework? The *mithaq al-watani* managed to resolve only part of this identity dilemma. It was, in fact, a pragmatic arrangement which, by establishing coexistence rather than conflict as the basis of relations between the religious communities, discouraged the rise of "irrational" confessionalism and, consequently, prevented the possible dissolution of the state. Nevertheless, the *mithaq* was not meant as a long-term formula for national unity; rather it was a temporary accommodative measure by which conflict could be minimized. By identifying what Lebanon was not--neither fully part of the Western world nor fully part of the Arab world--it consecrated the notion of a negative consensus; that is, national concurrence on what the state should *not* be.

While the *mithaq* was an effective political measure it was manifestly unable to resolve the more serious national and communal cleavages which arose in the decades following independence. If Lebanon was not to be dissolved some form of national identity had to be created which could bring together culturally and socially discrete groups. Since basic loyalty to the national community is far weaker than the traditional set of loyalties, the problem then becomes whether, and how, a sense of joint citizenship and of Lebanese nationhood, based on common values, can be created, strong enough to counterbalance the centrifugal forces in the communities. This problem, of course, is not unique to Lebanon. Throughout most of the developing world the basic problem facing the young nation-state involves the need to induce loyalty to the nation and to ensure that loyalties to subnational groups do not lead to disintegration of the state. The political actors must share a consensus on the "rules of the game," a consensus that will mitigate intense group conflict and encourage citizens to support the national regime.

In Lebanon, however, the dichotomy between the need for unity and the fissiparous impact of communal and ethnic consciousness is compounded by a further problem: the strong psychological attachment of a significant number of Lebanese Muslims to a pan-Arab nationalist identity. Thus, among the Muslim masses essentially two sets of loyalties prevail: primordial loyalties which find practical expression in the concepts of *ummah*, *'urubah*, and *wihdah*. Communal attachments serve not only parochial needs but may also serve the daily demands of support, stability, and services which communal chieftains can provide. By so doing the dependence upon the central authorities is minimized, further weakening the link

between individual and state, and lessening the chances of
creating a unified national state. Transnational attachments
satisfy psychological needs since they stress the Arab and
Islamic components of the Muslim's identity. For most Maronite
Christians, however, Lebanon remains the superordinate political symbol to which they identify.

There are four possible ways this dilemma may be resolved.
First, there is the *assimilationist* pattern of revolutionary-
socialist Arab states which entails the elimination of the
distinctive cultural traits of minority communities and the
substitution of some kind of overarching Arab nationalist
culture. *Separatism* as advocated by an increasing number of
dissatisfied Christian elements, especially Maronite, constitutes a second alternative. Even before the outbreak of
sectarian violence in 1975, these groups privately called
for the separation of predominantly Christian Mount Lebanon
from the remaining parts of Lebanon and the subsequent creation
of an autonomous, Western-inspired, Western-supported, and
Christian-dominated state. Towards this end the Maronite
patriarch and his close supporters, both lay and clerical,
have threatened to revive the independence of the former
sanjaq of Mount Lebanon. A third option is a policy of
segregation. Among many of Lebanon's traditional *zu'ama*
(feudal chieftains or local bosses) remains a strong desire
to avoid any form of meaningful integration or, on the other
hand, the dismemberment of the state, both of which would
eliminate their political dominance over a traditional
clientele group.

A final alternative is a *pluralistic* pattern of vertical
integration wherein national rather than trans-national
loyalties would be established without eliminating subnational cultures. In the latter, the primary effort would
be directed at creating a sense of territorial nationality
overshadowing but not necessarily destroying subordinate
parochial loyalties, and a definition of national community
which will not only identify the Lebanese to himself but
also provide canons of behavior for responding to his environment. The task thus becomes to accommodate the particularism
of sect with a definition of community that is compatible
with the dictates of the modern world. This implies that
political unity and cultural diversity can simultaneously
be established as the foundation for a modern state. The
first alternative is advocated by Arab nationalists, the
second and third by neo-feudal elements, and the last by
the Kataib and its like-minded allies.

The problem of creating a viable political community
is essentially a problem of consensus. Consensus is viewed
in a pragmatic way by the Kataib; that is, a basic consensus
can only be established by maximizing integrative values
through the interplay of individual and group interests
rather than by avoiding conflict and competition either
through coercion or exhortation. Thus, the establishment
of a viable national identity must fuse together culturally

disparate groups into a single territorial unit while
concurrently preserving a plural society in which each
group's self-conscious cultural qualities are allowed free
expression.

For the better part of its nearly forty-five year history
the Kataib has been involved in concerted efforts at creating
a genuine pluralistic democracy in Lebanon. In addition, of
all the organized political groups in the state the Kataib has
been unique, at least until the late 1960s, in adopting an
instrumental approach to the problems of development and
social change. It has not tried, for example, to destroy
or control parochial loyalties and structures in the name
of abstract socialist or trans-nationalist ideologies;
instead, it has attempted to generate spontaneous popular
support by adopting pragmatic policies that appeal to traditional sentiments and interests. The result has been an
adaptive interaction between modernity and tradition that
fuses parochial and universal elements.

This has not always been its orientation however. From
its founding in 1936 to the early 1950s the Kataib was
dedicated to narrow sectarian interests.[29] Although its
organizational apparatus, paramilitary structure, and human
formation were formally directed at preserving the territorial
integrity and political sovereignty of an independent
Lebanon,[30] at heart the emphasis was on stabilizing political
life in the country in order to better protect and promote
Christian and especially Maronite interests. Nowhere in
their official pronouncements or public statements could one
find a concern for structural change, social rectification,
or political development. Its chauvinistic nationalism found
support among schoolboys, university and college students,
young men of the lower middle class, apprentices, young
employees, and minor officials who eventually came to constitute the majority of the movement's early membership.

In the decade following independence, when the practical
implications of the National Pact were being worked out, the
Christian community's largest and most "modernist" political
party began to shed some of the more "irrational" and militant
elements of its nationalist ideology. In other words, working
within a relatively stable domestic and regional political
environment in which the competing perspectives on Lebanese
nationhood were gradually and peacefully being reconciled,
the Kataib began to assume a more "conciliatory" political
posture.

This process was accelerated in the aftermath of the
1958 civil war[31] and continued ten years thereafter notwithstanding the turbulence of the Nasser era when pan-Arabist
and other trans-nationalist sentiments were particularly
strong throughout the Arab world including Lebanon.[32] Thus
by the 1960s the Kataib emerged as a modernizing party
dedicated to national integration and social reform. Indeed,
the Christian Kataib was in the forefront of the national
"dialogue" that was taking place at the political, economic,

and even social levels between Lebanese Christians and
Muslims. While the national identity dilemma was by no
means fully resolved Christians increasingly began to feel
that their Muslim compatriots were staking real and enduring
claims in Lebanon as Lebanon. More than any other period,
the years between the end of the 1958 hostilities and the
outbreak of the 1967 Arab-Israeli war confirmed K. Salibi's
observations regarding the emergence of a viable Lebanese
national identity. He writes:

> The Lebanese, despite persisting differences which often
> seem grave, have . . . become more and more of a distinct
> people, recognizing themselves as such and being recognized
> by others as such, simply by the process of living together
> and sharing in a common national life. The steady growth
> of the Lebanese middle class, which has come to include an
> increasing proportion of Muslims and Druzes, has broadened
> the meeting-ground for the various Lebanese communities,
> all of which have developed vested interests in the
> country.[33]

It seems uncertain how far these positive trends might
have developed if the June 1967 Six Day War had not broken
out, which introduced an added and potentially destructive
dimension to the system's always fragile equilibrium. What
now seems certain is that the rise of a Palestinian nationalist
consciousness in the form of a revolutionary resistance movement among Lebanon's 350,000 Palestinian refugees reinforced
by the overt support of many of Lebanon's disaffected Muslim
masses, students, leftist intellectuals, and radical political
groups brought into serious question the legitimacy of the
confessional principle and, with it, the durability of the
Muslim-Christian "entente."

While the Palestinian presence in Lebanon and its
radical politicization in the post-1967 period did not *cause*
the breakdown of the confessional system, upon which the
Christian-Muslim entente was based, it did create a number
of psychological and structural conditions which ineluctably
led to a militant, indeed violent, disavowal of the pluralist
formula by large segments of Muslim elites and masses and
smaller but not inconsequential groups of non-Maronite
Christian elites.

The most ominous consequence of the presence of a
massive and mobilized Palestinian guerrilla movement in
Lebanon was the virtual undermining of Lebanese territorial
integrity and national independence. Not only had the state
become physically porous as both Palestinian guerrillas and
Israeli armed forces crossed Lebanon's southern and southeastern frontiers with brazen indifference to Lebanese
international legal rights but the country also became
increasingly exposed to a multitude of supranationalist
revolutionary ideologies that attracted the attention of
many disillusioned groups in the state including Lebanese

Muslims. In addition to the serious permeability of the
Lebanese state in ideological and territorial terms there
also existed a large and continually swelling foreign
population of Syrians, Iraqis, Jordanians, etc. which further
compromised Lebanon's national sovereignty. Thus, in defining the nature of inter-ethnic relations in the state in
the post-1967 period the whole of the Lebanese, Syrian,
Jordanian, and Israeli-Palestinian regional area would
more appropriately constitute the effective delimitation of
the Lebanese political process. From this perspective
Lebanese Christians and especially the Maronites represent
a permanent, miniscule, and enfeebled minority.[34] The
degree to which their political rights and communal liberties
could be guaranteed within a pluralistic Lebanese framework
were, in effect, a function of existing Muslim attitudes
and practices within this expanded regional area. That is,
in order to feel secure in their position as a distinct
ethno-confessional community with its numerous sectarian
sub-affiliations Lebanese Christians looked to their Muslim
compatriots in the country for a reaffirmation of the
legitimacy of their separate existence, the viability of
the confessional arrangement, and the durability of the
Christian-Muslim entente. As "Lebanese first" it was hoped,
and expected, that Lebanese Muslims would act as that necessary
link or buffer between "regional" Muslims and Lebanese Christians in any conflict involving non-Lebanese elements that
threatened the operation of the multiethnic formula with
its democratic derivative. Unfortunately, and mainly owing
to the Palestinian guerrilla presence in Lebanon, this
proved not to be the case.
     Since the Six Day War and particularly after the collapse
of the 1969 Cairo accords regulating Palestinian guerrilla
activity in the country,[35] Lebanon had become the object
of fierce attacks as refugee camps were turned into armed
fortresses from which armed attacks against Israel were
being undertaken. As a result much of South Lebanon, where
most Palestinian-Israeli military engagements were taking
place, found itself depopulated and devastated by repeated
Israeli raids. One result has been the growth of "solidarity
between the Palestinian resistance and the Lebanese Arab-
Muslim nationalist groups . . . and it appears that the Palestinians . . . served as a catalyst for Muslim nationalist
discontent and a model for organizing it. A grimmer consequence was further erosion in the legitimacy of Lebanon's
political institutions."[36]
     Christian militants, like the Kataib, have charged
repeatedly that the Palestinian presence in Lebanon provoked
the country's political turmoil and civil war. In their
eyes the guerrillas are seeking to take over Lebanon as
they sought to take over Jordan in 1970 and that they constitute a state within a state whose irresponsible and
reckless military adventures against Israel are principally
responsible for the counter raids by the Israelis. In

addition Christians blame the Palestinian presence as
being largely responsible for the increased polarization
of Lebanese society. In so delicately structured a confessional "balance of power" system so radical a force as
an aggrieved Palestinian community could but disturb and,
inevitably, severely disrupt Lebanon's consociational
stability. This is exactly what Lebanon's Christian
community saw developing in the late 1960s and early 1970s.
Rightly or wrongly Christian militants have become apprehensive that if the confessional system is changed they will
become a defenseless and persecuted minority. The 1975-76
civil war simply confirmed what Lebanese nationalists had
always feared: the formal abolition of confessionalism,
without supplanting it by a higher social order, would lay
the state open to abuses by communities bound to be strengthened from outside in undermining the foundations of the state.
    The Christian response to Palestinian revolutionism
has been drastic, indeed fanatical. Born of fear, disarray,
and desperation radical Christian nationalism, tinged with
unmistakable isolationist, atavistic, and neo-fascist tendencies, has reemerged among Lebanon's formerly most
"moderate" and "progressive" Christian-dominated political
organization. Spurred by the possibility of being "drowned"
in a Muslim sea the Kataib, long representing conciliatory
Christian interests and the most vocal advocate of confessional democracy, abandoned, in the early 1970s, its
previous efforts at promoting reformist principles and,
instead, reverted to its fundamentalist origins remembering,
in the process, its "deep anti-Muslim prejudices." Thus,
in the name of preserving the essential physiognomy of the
system, "it engaged in provocative attacks. It escalated
the conflict to such a degree that it was no longer protecting the pluralist system but feeding the flames of
partition--promoting the idea of an all-pure Maronite
enclave."[37]
    Partition, most Lebanese Christians now agree, including
the Kataib's president, Pierre Gemayel, based on his recent
public declarations including a December 9, 1977, Paris
press conference,[38] is undesirable because it is tantamount
to Christian isolation and inexpedient because no major power
seems ready to encourage it. Yet there remains the Maronite
Christians' adamant conviction that they must never again
be vulnerable to Muslim influence. This view, in its most
acceptable guise, calls for a major decentralization of
government (a la Swiss cantons) and a larger degree of
local autonomy. From the Maronite point of view confessional
democracy cannot be revived so long as Lebanese Muslims
reject the validity of a pluralist social arrangement which
respects and gives political expression to primordial,
ethnic, and communal sentiments. The relative ease with
which Lebanese Muslims and other pan-Arabists disengaged
from their national and "natural" ties with their Christian
compatriots to make common cause with Palestinian nationalist

aspirations however injurious such aspirations may have been to Lebanon's own national interests brought home an important lesson of political survival to militant Christians. If minority rights cannot be guaranteed "democratically" and communal loyalties accorded system-wide legitimacy then survival depends on the radicalization and mobilization of ethnic sentiments with the creation of appropriate instrumentalities for defense and development. Such is the current perspective of Lebanon's Maronite community particularly as represented by the Kataib although such sentiment also has wide appeal among non-Catholic Christians.

Returning to the four alternate modes of politically integrating fragmented multiethnic societies, one of the more serious consequences of the 1975-76 sectarian war has been virtually to eliminate the pluralist, assimilationist, and even secessionist-separatist options thereby leaving Lebanese society subdivided into highly segregated pockets by relatively ethnically homogeneous geographical cantons. Such a political arrangement can only sustain and encourage sectarian division and impede the development of an institutionally heterogeneous nation-state. Until such time as a new pluralist formula can be arrived at, however, it seems certain that radical Christian nationalism will continue to attract the support of those groups whose political definition of self remains strongly rooted in the "gross actualities" of blood, religion, and tradition. For those concerned with policy and the formulation of a more viable interconfessional arrangement for Lebanon there must be a renewed appreciation of the ethnic dimension in national political life. The country's political collapse and social disintegration revealed, as never before, that, while there are class realities, there are also ethnic realities and in Lebanon, as increasingly elsewhere in the Third World, they are the dominant realities. Analysts and ideologues are still insensitive to these "new" old realities. Indeed, a sense of political identity formulated without explicitly incorporating the ethnic dimension appears to be doomed to failure which, in the always volatile Middle East, carries with it ominous and foreboding implications for both regional and international politics.

NOTES

1. A plethora of journalistic and analytical accounts describing the causes and consequences of Lebanon's latest civil conflict have recently appeared. Among the more noteworthy include: Kamal S. Salibi, *Crossroads to Civil War: Lebanon 1958-1976* (Delmar, New York: Caravan Books, 1976); Michael C. Hudson, "The Lebanese Crisis: The Limits of Consociational Democracy," *Journal of Palestine Studies*, vol. V, nos. 3-4 (Spring-Summer 1976), pp. 109-122; Michael C. Hudson, "The Palestinian Factor in the Lebanese Civil War," *The Middle East Journal*, Vol. 32, No. 3 (Summer 1978), pp. 261-278. Marius Deeb, *The Lebanese Civil War* (New York: Praeger Special Studies, 1978). Joseph Chamie, "The Lebanese

Civil War: An Investigation into the Causes," *World Affairs*, vol. 139, no. 3 (Winter 1976-77), pp. 171-188; Enver M. Koury, *The Crisis in the Lebanese System: Confessionalism and Chaos* (Washington, D.C.: American Enterprise Institute for Public Policy Research, 1976); Thierry Desjardins, *Le Martyre du Liban* (Paris: Plon, 1976); and Pierre Vallaud, *Le Liban au Bout du Fusil* (Paris: Hachette, 1976). "Liban," *Revolution Africaine* (Algiers), No. 740 (April 26-May 2, 1978), pp. 1-32 (supplement).

2. Probably the most persuasive articulation of this phenomenon remains that of Karl W. Deutsch, *Nationalism and Social Communication: Inquiry into the Foundation of Nationality*, 2nd edition (Cambridge, Mass.: The M.I.T. Press, 1966). See also his *The Nerves of Government Models of Political Communication and Control* (New York: The Free Press, 1966).

3. Hudson, "The Lebanese Crisis," p. 115. Much of the arguments presented in this and the preceding paragraph are derived from Hudson's informative article.

4. Lebanese confessionalism has been the object of extensive study and analysis by numerous scholars. Good general accounts may be found in Kamal S. Salibi, *The Modern History of Lebanon* (New York: Frederick A. Praeger, 1965); Albert Hourani, "Lebanon: The Development of a Political Society," in *Politics in Lebanon*. Edited by Leonard Binder (New York: John Wiley and Sons, Inc., 1966), pp. 13-29; Leila M.T. Meo, *Lebanon: Improbable Nation* (Bloomington, Indiana: Indiana University Press, 1965); Clyde G. Hess and Herbert L. Bodman, "Confessionalism and Feudality in Lebanese Politics," *Middle East Journal*, vol. 8 (Winter 1954), pp. 10-26; and Ralph E. Crow, "Religious Sectarianism in the Lebanese Political System," *Journal of Politics*, vol. 24 (August, 1962), pp. 489-520. See also Michael C. Hudson, *The Precarious Republic: Political Modernization in Lebanon* (New York: Random House, 1968), David and Audrey Smock, *The Politics of Pluralism: A Comparative Study of Lebanon and Ghana* (New York: Elsevier, 1975), and Michael W. Suleiman, *Political Parties in Lebanon* (Ithaca, N.Y.: Cornell University Press).

5. For the text of the *mithaq* see George Dib, "Selections from Riadh Solh's Speech in the Lebanese Assembly (October 7, 1943) Embodying the Main Principles of the Lebanese 'National Pact,'" *Middle East Forum*, vol. 34 (January, 1959), pp. 6-7. For an interpretation of the National Pact by the Maronite president, Bishara al-Khuri, see *Haqaiq Lubnaiyyat* (Lebanese Truths) (Harisa: Matba'at Basil Ikhwan, 1960-61).

6. Good general studies on aspects of Lebanese feudalism may be found in Iliya F. Harik, *Politics and Change in a Traditional Society: Lebanon, 1711-1845* (Princeton, N.J.: Princeton University Press, 1968) and William R. Polk, *The Opening of South Lebanon, 1788-1840: A Study of the Impact of the West on the Middle East* (Cambridge, Mass.: Harvard University Press, 1963). See also Albert H. Hourani, *Syria and Lebanon: A Political Essay* (London: Oxford University Press, 1954) and Kamal S. Salibi, *The Modern History of Lebanon*.

7. Hudson, "The Lebanese Crisis," p. 117.

8. For a brief but balanced critique of this position see Marc Ferro, "Le Defi des Ethnies: Critique du Marxisme ou Critique du Capitalisme?" *Le Monde Diplomatique* (Paris) (December, 1976), p. 34.

9. Cynthia H. Enloe, *Ethnic Conflict and Political Development* (Boston: Little, Brown and Company, 1973), p. 40.

10.   The theoretical applicability of this phenomenon to other
Third World societies is well treated in the following: Donald
Rothchild, "Ethnicity and Conflict Resolution," *World Politics*,
vol. XXII, No. 4 (July 1970), pp. 597-616; Donald L. Horowitz,
"Three Dimensions of Ethnic Politics," *World Politics*, vol. XXIII,
no. 2 (January 1971), pp. 232-244; Walker Conner, "Nation-Building
or Nation-Destroying?" *World Politics*, vol. XXIV, no. 3 (April
1972), pp. 319-355; and Robert Melson and Howard Wolfe, "Modernization and the Politics of Communalism: A Theoretical Perspective,"
American Political Science Review, vol. LXLV, no. 4 (December
1970), pp. 1112-1130.

11.   Clifford Geertz, "The Integrative Revolution: Primordial
Sentiments and Civil Politics in the New States," in *Old Societies
and New States: The Quest for Modernity in Asia and Africa*.
Edited by Clifford Geertz (New York: The Free Press, 1963), p. 108.

12.   Enloe, *Ethnic Conflict and Political Development*, p. 15.

13.   Samir Khalaf, "Primordial Ties and Politics in Lebanon,"
Middle Eastern Studies, vol. 4 (April, 1968), p. 267.

14.   *Ibid.*

15.   This theme is elaborated upon in a broader comparative
framework in John P. Entelis, "Ethnic Conflict and the Problem
of Political Identity in the Middle East," *Polity* (1978).   See
also Itamar Rabinovich, "Religion and Nationalism in the Middle
East: The Case of Lebanon," The Shiloah Center for Middle Eastern
and African Studies (Tel Aviv University), Occasional Paper No. 51,
February 1977, and Suad Joseph and Barbara L. K. Pillsbury, eds.,
Muslim-Christian Conflict (Boulder, Colorado: Westview Press, 1978).

16.   Iliya F. Harik, "The Ethnic Revolution and Political Integration in the Middle East," *International Journal of Middle East
Studies*, vol. 3, no. 3 (July 1972), p. 310.

17.   Labib Zuwiyya Yamak, *The Syrian Social Nationalist Party:
An Ideological Analysis* (Cambridge, Mass.:   Harvard University
Press, 1966), p. 36.

18.   This point of view is forcefully put forth in Clovis
Maksoud, "Lebanon and Arab Nationalism," in Binder (ed.), *Politics
in Lebanon*, pp. 239-254.

19.   Hisham B. Sharabi, *Nationalism and Revolution in the Arab
World* (Princeton, N.J.:   D. Van Nostrand Company, Inc., 1966), p. 96.

20.   *Ibid.*

21.   A recent, 1976 study on the economic status of Lebanese
social groups according to sectarian affiliation sustains what has
been a socio-economic fact since the 1920s: Christians are
wealthier, more educated, better clothed and housed, and in more
prestigious occupations than the Muslims.   J. Chamie writes: "With
whatever reasonable criteria one chooses to utilize, the social and
economic differentials between the religious groups are unmistakably
clear: non-Catholic Christians and Catholic at the top, Druze
around the middle, Sunnis near the bottom, and Shi'as at the very
bottom."   Chamie, "The Lebanese Civil War," p. 180.

22.   Harik, *Politics and Change in a Traditional Society:
Lebanon*, 1711-1845, p. 128.

23. Zuwiyya Yamak, *The Syrian Social Nationalist Party: An Ideological Analysis*, p. 36.

24. An anonymously-authored pamphlet published around 1945 somewhere in the United States.

25. Charles Corm was probably the leading contemporary exponent of this doctrine. See Charles Corm, *La Montagne Inspirée* (Beirut, 1934).

26. On the dynamics of Lebanese nationalism see Maurice Harari, "The Dynamics of Lebanese Nationalism," *Current History*, vol. 36 (February 1959), pp. 97-101 and Pierre Rondot, "Lebanese Institutions and Arab Nationalism," *Journal of Contemporary History*, vol. 3 (July 1968), pp. 37-51. The Kataib's development of Lebanonism is treated in John P. Entelis, *Pluralism and Party Transformation in Lebanon: Al-Kata'ib, 1936-1970* (Leiden: E. J. Brill, 1974), pp. 68-83; John P. Entelis, "Belief-System and Ideology Formation in the Lebanese Kata'ib Party," *International Journal of Middle East Studies*, vol. 4, no. 2 (April 1973), pp. 148-162; and John P. Entelis, "Reformist Ideology in the Arab World: The Cases of Tunisia and Lebanon," *The Review of Politics*, vol. 37, no. 4 (October 1975), pp. 513-546.

27. See, for example, Michel Chiha, *Liban d'Aujourd'hui* (Beirut: Editions du Trident, 1949); "Lebanon at Home and Abroad," *Les Conferences du Cenacle*, XX (1966), pp. 15-170; "Le Liban dans le monde: perspectives d'avenir," *Les Conferences du Cenacle*, V (December 1951), pp. 256-282.

28. See "Le Libanisme, une doctrine," *Action* (Beirut) (December 1956), pp. 1134-1139 and Jacques Nantet, "Le Patrimoine libanais: aspect historique," *Action*, vol. XXVI (January 1967), pp. 60-65.

29. For a historical analysis of the party's founding and developments see John P. Entelis, "Party Transformation in Lebanon: Al-Kata'ib as a Case Study," *Middle Eastern Studies*, vol. 9, no. 3 (October 1973), pp. 325-340 and John P. Entelis, "Structural Change and Organizational Development in the Lebanese Party," *Middle East Journal*, vol. 27, no. 1 (Winter 1973), pp. 21-35. See also Frank Stoakes, "The Supervigilantes: The Lebanese Kataeb Party as a Builder, Surrogate and Defender of the State," *Middle Eastern Studies*, vol. II, no. 3 (October 1975), pp. 215-236.

30. For full details, see Entelis, *Pluralism and Party Transformation in Lebanon: Al Kata'ib, 1936-1970*, pp. 84-152.

31. See Fahim I. Qubain, *Crisis in Lebanon* (Washington, D.C.: The Middle East Institute, 1961) for an adequate treatment of the 1958 civil war.

32. On the Nasserite phenomenon see Hrair Dekmejian, "Marx, Weber and the Egyptian Revolution," *The Middle East Journal*, vol. 30, no. 2 (Spring 1976), pp. 158-172. On the failure of charismatic leadership in Nasser's Egypt see John P. Entelis, "Nasser's Egypt and the Failure of Charismatic Leadership," *Orbis*, vol. XVIII (Summer 1974), pp. 451-464.

33. Kamal S. Salibi, "The Lebanese Identity," *Middle East Review*, vol. IX, no. 1 (Fall 1976), p. 12. Reprinted in this

volume. See Chapter 16.

34. Even within Lebanon itself 1977 estimated figures of sectarian affiliation reveals the following distribution: Muslims, 60%, (Shiites, 27%; Sunnites, 26%; and Druzes, 7%); Christians, 40% (Maronites, 23%; Greek Orthodox, 7%; Greek Catholic, 5%; and other Christians, 5%). See Rafic Boustani, "Les deplacements de population risquent d'avoir des effets durables pour l'economie," *Le Monde*, November 20-21, 1977, p. 18.

35. A detailed analysis of the events preceding the Cairo agreement can be found in John P. Entelis, "Palestinian Revolutionism in Lebanese Politics: The Christian Response," *The Muslim World*, vol. LXII, no. 4 (October 1972), pp. 335-351.

36. Hudson, "The Lebanese Crisis," p. 116.

37. *Ibid.*, p. 117.

38. See *Le Monde*, December 11-12, 1977, p. 3.

18
Mu'amar Qadhafi's New Islamic Scientific Socialist Society

Raymond N. Habiby

Al Fateh is an Islamic Revolution. [1]

The Glorious Qur'an is the Shari'a [law] *of Our New Socialist Society.*

These are but two of the many billboards displayed on walls in Libya. The billboards carry either direct quotations from the two *Green Books* [2] authored by Col. Mu'amar Qadhafi, the leader of Libya, or statements offering explanations or expressing support for the two books. No wall in Libya is spared the brush, or the glue, or the paper. Some of these billboards are even floodlit, permanent fixtures. [3]
In green lettering on a white background, the two billboards quoted above best represent the Libyan leader's attempt to convince the Libyans and the outside world that what he is after is the redevelopment of Libya on the basis of the teachings and dogma of Islam or, better still, how he has interpreted the Islamic teachings and dogma. Since his second *Green Book*, entitled, *The Solution of the Problem of the Economy, Socialism,* [4] hit the stands in late 1977, Col. Qadhafi has lost no time in initiating the implementation of its provisions. Because of its radical approach, it has generated a good deal of criticism among a segment of Libyans, and Col. Qadhafi, in his address in Green Square, Tripoli, on November 19, 1978, on the occasion of the Muslim *Curban Bairam,* took this time to respond to his critics. His

Mu'amar Qadhafi's New Islamic Scientific Socialist Society is reprinted from *Middle East Review*, Vol. XI, No. 4, Summer, 1979.

socialism, he said, was an Islamic scientific socialism.
In this most revealing speech,Qadhafi fully developed
his ideas about Islam and his interpretation of Islamic
teachings and dogma. He ridiculed those who entertain
a feeling of guilt whenever they stage a revolution just
because they are Muslims: "The truth is that Islam is
a great revolution, nay, it is a world revolution," he
declared[5] (p. 13). "The voice of truth and the Islamic
revolution must echo in every part of the world" (p. 18).
As to the part he and Libya would play, "We, here in
Libya, are not ashamed to see a progressive revolution
start from the extreme left, yet we will never give up
Islam, and we will prove to the world that what has become of the Muslims has nothing to do with Islam...
Precisely on the contrary, Islam calls for progress"
(pp. 17-18).

He recognized the "backwardness of the Islamic
nation from Indonesia to Mauritania," but "this has
nothing to do with Islam" (p. 21). It is the result
of a number of factors, not least of them, the wrath of
God. "God is angry with those who forsake Islam. His
wrath manifests itself in backwardness, hunger, disease,
imperialism, reactionary style of life, and a dictatorship
installed over them from within" (p. 20). "God subjects
them to any of these evils from within or from without"
(p. 21).

He was quick, however, to give glad tidings to the
Muslims of the world. "The Muslims of North Africa, and
of Libya in particular, have awakened, and have raised
the banner of the Islamic revolution. Socialism is being
realized in Libya. The chains of exploitation are now
broken...the chains of slavery...the chains of humiliation
...equality is being achieved and we hear again the name
of God. True Islam is being revealed, Islam, the religion
of freedom, the religion of progress, the religion of
equality, the religion of justice..." (pp. 21-22).

In this Islamic revolution, which will, in the end,
reach the whold world, because Islam is a universal
religion, "You Libyans are to play a big role in leading
the new revolution," he declared, "the revolution of
the emancipation of Islam, the emancipation of the subjugated masses... You are to play a leading role in
preaching the Islamic revolt, the new socialism. This
is the *jihad* (Holy War). Now there is hope. Now the
Islamic revolt has begun. There is hope that Islam will
again emerge in its true form" (pp. 22-3).

ISLAMIC SOCIALISM

In his two *Green Books* and in his speeches, Col.
Qadhafi preaches what he calls Islamic socialism. He

is a devout practicing Muslim who believes in the
universality of Islam--Islam which is both religion and
state. He is a "thinker"[6] who feels he has succeeded in
unlocking the truth of God's word as it was revealed in
the Qur'an for the benefit of mankind as a whole and the
world at large. In his view, he is doing the world a
service. Having already solved the problem of democracy
in his first *Green Book*, he has now, in his second, solved
the problem of the economy--two problems which have defied
man's ingenuity over the centuries. To Qadhafi, political
democracy and social and economic justice lie in the
teachings of true Islam--that is why the early Muslims
were progressive: because they understood Islam (p. 23).
"Islam had opened the minds of Muslims in order to enable
them to harness the powers of the universe, air, space,
the sun, the moon, the stars, oceans, seas, the sky and
the earth, and place them in the service of man, for God
has said that they are placed in the service of man"
(p. 23). "It is our duty to show the world that algebra,
arithmetic, geometry, astronomy, medicine, watch-making,
are all the products of Islamic thought. Without them,
the world would never have arrived at those thresholds of
knowledge" (p. 23). Answering his own question as to why
the early Muslims had attained all this knowledge, he
declared, "The Qur'an directed their thinking... The
Qur'an told them: "Think...think" (p. 23). "There are
secrets in the Qur'an and verses you do not understand
so far. There are truths you have not fathomed, truths
which made the Muslims who knew the Qur'an attain all the
knowledge I have told you about. Now we do not understand the Qur'an, so we do not understand anything...
This is why we say that artificial rain is wrong and going
to the moon is wrong. Muslims should have been the first
to do all this" (p. 24). "The fact that we do not possess the know-how in atomic energy or technology has nothing
to do with Islam" (p. 10).
     Return to Islam, and all the problems of the world
will be resolved. This, in essence, is what Qadhafi
teaches in his two *Green Books*. As he told his audience
in November 1978, "Why did we say that the Qur'an is the
shari'a of society? Read the Qur'an and you will find
in it all knowledge. It explains everything" (p. 24).
He ridiculed those Muslims who know so much about so many
books yet do not know the Qur'an. "When you leave here,"
he exhorted his listeners, "read the Qur'an. You will
feel as if you are reading a new book, as if you had never
heard of it before...as if you are reading it for the
first time" (p. 22).
     He was also critical of those who claim that socialism
leads to underdevelopment. These people are not true
Muslims, as were the "early enlightened Muslims who under-

stood Islam" (p. 23).   He was also critical of those
Libyans who, when they have the benefit of the *Green
Book*, still yearn for French, Roman, Italian or other
law, "yet claim to be Muslims" (p. 23).   "Now that the
Islamic revolt has begun... There is hope that Islam
will emerge in its real form" (p. 23).   "This is great
news to the Muslims...the rise of the new Islamic
scientific socialist revolution in Libya" (p. 24).
Iran, he claimed, would be next in line to embark on
this world-wide revolution.   "The Muslim masses in Iran
are on the move... Perhaps the Muslims of Iran will
emerge victorious and a new peoples' revolt will emerge
and another Muslim people will be liberated... Thus the
revolt will spread, the new revolt, the revolt of Islam
will spread" (p. 24).

For his Muslim audience, and Muslim skeptics, he
had this note of warning: if the "revolt of Islam, the
revolt of truth, socialism and knowledge fails, the world
will say that Islam is a synonym for backwardness, and
is a class system.   The people will leave Islam--your
sons, grandsons--in the future...in one hundred years,
five hundred years, or a thousand years, none of them
will be Muslims" (p. 24).   To those who still insisted
that not what the *Green Book* contains but what they
preach is Islam, he said, "Whenever you say this (i.e.,
their own preaching) is Islam, you are actually driving
your children to give up Islam.   They will embrace any
doctrine which advocates equality" (p. 19).

Qadhafi was stressing Islam in Libya, a devout
Muslim country.   And not surprisingly, at the last meeting of the Fourth General Peoples' Congress, Libya's
supreme legislative council, in Tripoli in December 1978,
a resolution was passed stating that one of the grounds
for the abrogation of Libyan citizenship is a person's
abandonment of Islam for another religion.[7]   Qadhafi's
efforts to combine Islam with modernization are not new
in the Islamic world.   They began when leaders like Jamal
al Din al-Afghani and Imam Muhammad Abdu, in the days of
the ailing Ottoman state, sought for reasons for the
stagnation of the Islamic empire.   Those who followed
them, to modern times, either advocated a complete separation of state and religion in order to produce a modern
state, or the reinterpretation of the Qur'an and the
Hadith (sayings) to produce a modern Islamic state, which
would match or surpass the viability and development of
the states of the West and ward off the inroads of imported doctrines like communism, fascism, etc.   Col.
Qadhafi, who belongs to the latter school of Islamic
thought, believes that he has the answer.   The Qur'an
and Islam, which are universal, are valid for all time
and can serve the modern state and society.   These are

his "glad tidings to Muslims."

GOD AND ECONOMICS

Col. Qadhafi sees his *Green Books* as the guides to
a total Muslim universal emancipatory system. Any similarities with other systems are only incidental. Thus,
as billboards in Libya proclaim:

> *The Green Book Provides for the Final Emanci-*
> *pation of Man.*
>
> *The Green Book is the Guide for the Whole*
> *of Humanity on its Ultimate Journey toward*
> *Emancipation.*
>
> *The Green Book is the Hope of the Toiling*
> *Masses.*

And, stressing the role of Libya, a billboard reads:

> *Our Nation Heralds to Other Nations the*
> *Beginning of the Age of the Masses.*

In his November 1978 speech, Qadhafi made full use
of the Qur'an and the *Hadith* to answer his critics and
to warn them of God's wrath. The Qur'an, he attempted
to demonstrate, supports his economic theories and the
role of the Muslims. According to *Sura Imran*, III:110,
"You are the best people given to other peoples." As
in *The Heifer*, V:143, "You are selected for the mission
... Muslims have a knowledge of religion and are given
a message to the world."[8] Quoting from *The Bee*, XVI:89,
"For we have sent down to thee a book explaining clearly
everything, and a guidance, and a mercy, and glad tidings
to the believers," he added, for emphasis, "This book is
the Qur'an. This is Islam... It is not misery. It is
not evil. It heralds prosperity and happiness. To whom?
To the Muslims who embraced it" (p. 8).
He was also critical of those who interpret Islam
to mean "palaces, money, gold, silver, concubines, wives
and children," yet who claim it is wrong to reach the
moon, that heart surgery is wrong and that progress is
wrong, and he reminded them of the words of the Qur'an
(quoting from *The Covered*, LXXIV:11-17) "Leave me alone
with him I have created, and for whom I have made extensive
wealth, and sons that he may look upon, and for whom I
have smoothed things down. Then he desires that I should
increase! nay, verily, he is hostile to our signs! I
will drive him up a hill" (p. 11).

Then he reminded his audience of what the Prophet Muhammad had said about a society of masters and slaves, of hungry and overfed, and quoted the *Hadith*, "He who goes to bed with a full stomach and his neighbor is hungry is not one of us" (pp. 23-4).

To those who see Islam as capitalism, he said that capitalism stood for hoarding gold and silver and quoted from the Qur'an (*Night Journey*, XVII:16), "And when we desired to destroy a city we bade the opulent ones thereof (i.e., the capitalists) and they wrought abomination therein (the consequence of corrupt capitalism) and its due sentence was pronounced, and we destroyed it with utter destruction" (p. 11).[9] What they had just heard, he reminded his listeners, was the word of God and not that of Mu'amar Qadhafi (p. 12). Then he asked, "But what does the Qur'an say of the rich, of the capitalists, and those who oppose socialism? Socialism is equality, joint participation of the citizens in the wealth of the country. This is socialism. What does the Qur'an say? 'And leave me and those who say it is a lie, who are possessed of comfort, and let them abide for a while. Verily, with us are heavy fetters and hell-fire, and food that chokes, and mighty woe!' (*The Enwrapped*, LXXIII: 11-13). This is for those capitalists who deny Islam, and who reject Muhammad... This is what God has prepared for them on the day of resurrection... They are the capitalists who reject equality with their slaves, with their women, with the poor, and reject equality among the sons of the Islamic nation" (p. 12).

The capitalists "desire to be God on earth, with slaves prostrating themselves before them... If you rise against a capitalist and seek equality he replies 'God in Islam forbids this.' He denies you your money and the product of your sweat. The capitalist acquires the money of the poor. He is rich with their money. Isn't this what God meant when he said in the Qur'an: 'Do not devour your wealth among yourselves in vain'? They reverse this verse and then claim that socialism is against religion" (pp. 13-14). At this point, Col. Qadhafi draws a parable: "What," he asks, "was the relationship between the Prophet Muhammad and his uncle, Abu Lahab, or Abu Jahl? It was one of armed struggle. What did God say about Abu Lahab? 'Abu Lahab's two hands shall perish, and he shall perish' (*Abu Lahab*, CXI:1-4). Why? Because 'His wealth will not avail him, nor what he has earned! He shall broil in a fire that flames.' Why did God curse him? Because he was a non-believer. He refused to accept the call of justice. Why? Because he was rich. Who said that? God! It is clear that Abu Lahab was rich and because he was rich his eyes, ears and mind were shut. He could not hear the word of truth" (p. 18).

The rich are doomed. Even in Libya, "They enslave the workers, the farmers and everyone of you. Their religion is the dollar. They smuggle out money, gold and foreign exchange. They do not worship God or serve their country or make good the agricultural land they had laid to waste. One owns a building with one hundred apartments, yet another lives in a shack. One has concubines, yet another is unable to secure a loan from a bank to marry one wife. One owns a luxury car which he replaces every month (as in the other rich Arab countries), yet another has to go barefoot. Is the Islam that they want palaces, gold and silver? Didn't God say, 'But those who store up gold and silver and expend it not in God's way--give them glad tidings of grievous woe!' (*Repentence*, IX:34). And what did the Prophet say in the *Hadith*? 'People are equal like the teeth of a comb.' If one lives in a shack, and another in a palace, are they equal? One has so much money, he does not know what to do with it and smuggles it out to Europe, and another does not have the money to feed his children, so he works twenty-four hours a day. Are they like the teeth of the comb? Isn't this a clear departure from the *Hadith*"? (p. 22).

Qadhafi's second *Green Book*[10] presents, again, as his "solution" to the world's ills, his Third Universal Doctrine, which, he claims, is based on natural law and which will replace and supercede all other doctrines and resolve all the global economic problems once and for all, on the basis of "a new socialist society, which is a happy society, because it is free. Happiness will be achieved by satisfying the spiritual and material needs of man" (p. 19). He specifically points out that "The *Green Book* not only solves the problem of material production but also provides a comprehensive solution to the problem of human society, so that the individual may be both materially and spiritually liberated... This is the final solution, that will produce happiness" (pp. 26-7). It is to be achieved by "satisfying (man's) needs, eliminating exploitation by others, ending tyranny and finding the way toward a just distribution of society's wealth" (p. 31). "It is the theory of liberating man's needs to emancipate him" (p. 32). "It is the new socialist society, the culmination of man's struggle to attain his freedom and achieve happiness by satisfying his needs" (p. 31). And this "should be done without exploiting or enslaving others" (p. 32).

All previous attempts to resolve this problem have been either cosmetic in nature or merely acts of charity (p. 4). "Even in those cases where ownership is now public ownership, this is not a solution. Here, assuming

that the authority which monopolizes ownership is the
authority of the people, public ownership is acquired
in the interest of society at large and not that of the
workers... In both public and privately owned establish-
ments, the workers are wage earners" (pp. 5-6). "The
solution lies in the abolition of the wage system...
and a return to the law of nature...which provides for
equality among the factors of production...namely:
raw materials, the instrument of production, and the
producers... Each factor must receive an equal share
in production" (pp. 7-8). "The failure of all attempts
so far, in so far as they disregarded the law of nature,
makes it imperative to return to it" (p. 11).

All previous attempts failed to resolve the problem
because of their concentration on the problem of ownership, while the real problem is that of the producers,
who have remained wage earners. The lot of the wage
earners has improved over the years as a result of the
benefits they have secured, but this has not solved the
basic problem (pp. 2, 3).

Qadhafi appears to differentiate between three types
of economic activity: domestic help, industrial production
involving raw materials, machinery and workers and agricultural production involving the utilization of land by
man--and now with the help of machinery.

Regarding industrial production, or manufacturing,
Qadhafi sees that, in the days of manual production, the
process involved two factors: raw materials and man the
producer (p. 9). Animals were soon added, to be replaced
later by the machine. "Although the factors of production
have, over the years, changed quantitatively and qualitatively, the essential role of each factor has not changed
(p. 10). This is why it is still necessary for production
to be divided into three equal shares: a share for each
factor of production. This is so basic to the solution
of the problem of the economy because the producers
become partners instead of wage earners.

An exception, however, is agriculture as an economic
activity. It involves land and man--unless a machine is
used. In this case, three factors exist, and production
is then split into three equal shares (pp. 13-14).

The same rule does not apply to domestic help, and
therefore Qadhafi proposes that domestics be granted the
status of public employees (pp. 37-9).

FORMS OF OWNERSHIP

In his new, socialist society, Qadhafi delineates two
forms of ownership as being a natural solution. One is a
system of private ownership, to satisfy an individual's

needs without an exploitation by others. The other
is socialist ownership, with the producers becoming
partners in production. This socialist ownership
replaces the type of private ownership which produced
a class of wage earners who had no rights to what they
produced (p. 32). What they produced belonged to private
ownership. He holds that "the attainment of freedom depends on the extent of man's ownership of what he needs
...ownership which is personal and is sacredly guaranteed"
(p. 33). "Otherwise you will live in a state of anxiety
which will do away with your happiness and freedom"
(p. 35).

While the *Green Book* does not explicitly say so,
it nevertheless appears that all productive or manufacturing industries will come under the socialist
type ownership, with the workers (who are to be called
producers) as partners and receiving a share of the
production. Agricultural land will be "used," that is,
possessed by the farmers, but not owned by them. There
will be two types of homes, private and socialist-owned.
Private ownership will include an individual's house,
means of transportation, clothing, food, a livelihood
and the like.

Qadhafi desires a happy society; happy because it
is free. Freedom lies in liberating man's basic needs.
If these needs are controlled, man can be exploited and
enslaved. He lists four basic human needs: (1) Food;
(2) A dwelling place, (3) Clothing; (4) Transportation
(p. 33), but discusses them under three headings, namely,
(1) A dwelling place, (2) A livelihood; (3) Means of
transportation (pp. 16-18).

An individual should own his own dwelling, but the
house he owns should be for his own use and not to rent
out. To build and own a house to rent out would be an
attempt to control a need for another person (p. 16).
Some means of transportation is also a necessity for a
man and his family. "You own it, for in a socialist
society, no man or authority can possess means of
transportation for hire, as this would lead to controlling the needs of others" (p. 18). As to income, or
a livelihood, in a socialist society, Qadhafi points out
that this should never be a wage or an act of charity,
but that it can be owned as private property. "There
are no wage earners in a socialist society. There are
partners" (p. 17). Your livelihood comes from a partnership in a production unit, or the use of agricultural
land, or the performance of a public service."

In this new society, man will have three alternatives.
(1) He can be self-employed in order to guarantee his
material needs; (2) He can work for a socialist corporation and be a partner in production; (3) He can perform a

public service to society, which would then provide
him with his material needs (pp. 19-20). In all this,
however, "man's legitimate economic activity is solely
the satisfaction of his needs. No person has the right
to economic activity that provides him with more than
is necessary to satisfy his needs, as any amount he
acquires in excess of his needs is actually taken from
the needs of others" (pp. 20-21).

A society's wealth must be equally distributed,
each citizen receiving one unit. "The disabled and the
insane have the same share as the healthy" (p. 30).
If this system is not followed, there will be rich and
poor, and exploitation will prevail (p. 29). Individuals
can save as much as they want for their own needs (p. 30)
but "what is left beyond the satisfaction of individual
needs shall remain the property of the members of society"
(p. 29). "There is still room for the skillful and the
industrious. While they do not have the right to acquire
the share of others, they can utilize their skill in
managing what they receive to satisfy their needs and
benefit from that (pp. 20-30). Individual differences
in wealth, in the new socialist society, are "only per-
missable for those who perform a public service. Society
will allocate for them a share of wealth commensurate with
that service" (p. 31). He does not clarify, however,
whether this distribution of society's wealth will take
into consideration and include what a person will acquire
as income from permissible economic pursuits.

Qadhafi also answers two anticipated criticisms
of his system. One might say, he writes: The present
system is producing, so why change it? And one might
ask, also, whether his system provides an incentive to
produce. A level of production is attainable even under
a bad system, he responds, because it is a matter of
survival. A person has to work in order to obtain some
income to live on. "The best proof is that in capitalist
societies production accumulates and expands in the hands
of a few owners who do not work but exploit the efforts
of others who are obliged to produce in order to survive"
(p. 26). Nevertheless, he claims, a system of no wages,
in which the producer is a partner in production and,
as such, receives an equal share with the other two
factors of production provides a system of better incen-
tives. In the present system, he points out, working for
wages has failed to solve the problem of increasing and
developing production (p. 26).

In a special section on agricultural land, Qadhafi
claims that this land "is no one's property. Everyone
can use it by working, farming or using it as pasture
for their flocks. A man can use this land so long as he
does not employ others, and to the extent that he satisfies

his needs. His heirs can inherit the use of the land, and can use it in the same manner to satisfy their needs. In all this, man has possession, but not ownership, of the land (pp. 18-19).

Another section deals with domestic workers, or help, paid or unpaid. He calls them the slaves of our modern age. In a socialist society of partnership in production, the natural, socialist law does not apply to them. The solution is, therefore, that "the house shall be serviced by its occupants." Necessary services are to be provided "not by servants, but by employees, who can receive promotion as house workers and can enjoy social and material safeguards like any public service employee" (p. 39).

With all these changes, workers will cease to be called "workers" and will be referred to instead as "producers." In Qadhafi's modern society, the masses of ignorant, illiterate workers will be replaced by a limited number of technicians, engineers and scientists. This will mean the gradual disappearance of trade unions, which will be replaced by professional and technical syndicates (p. 15).

Qadhafi sees, in the growing power of the trade unions in capitalist societies, the means of transforming these capitalist societies of wage earners into societies of partners (p. 35). And, "sooner or later, under the guidance of the *Green Book*, a revolution to achieve socialism will begin, with the producers (the former workers) seeking to acquire a share in what they produce. They will "change their demands, and instead of asking for increased wages, will demand a share in production" (p. 36).

The final step will arrive in a socialist society when profit and money disappear. With full production, the material needs of society will be satisfied. In the final stage, profit will disappear automatically, and there will be no need for money (p. 36). Qadhafi does not explain, however, how his society will function without the institution of money as a means of exchange. And as to profit, he cautions that this is still the driving economic force in pre-socialist societies, so its abolition should not be a step lightly taken. "It must be the result of the development of socialist production. The endeavor to increase profit will ultimately lead to its disappearance" (p. 37).

TURNING THEORY INTO PRACTICE

At best, the *Green Book* is a theoretical discussion of selected aspects of the problem of the economy. It

lacks precise detail as to how these theories will be
applied; how necessity is to be measured; how the
redisposition of land, houses and work will take place
in a real situation, both today and in the future, in
an ever-changing society. Yet, in Libya, steps have
already been taken to implement Qadhafi's second *Green
Book*. All persons living in rented homes have become
the owners of these homes. Persons owning more than
one house or apartment have had to choose which one
they wished to retain for themselves and their children.
In a major speech on September 1, 1978[11] Qadhafi called
on the workers of Libya to begin the implementation of
the *Green Book's* guidelines by taking over their factories,
and thus becoming partners in them. The Libyan newspapers
have, since then, and on a daily basis, devoted special
sections to reports of these take overs. Plans are in
progress for the reassignment of agricultural land and
the implementation of the *Green Book's* guidelines dealing
with the communications system.

All this explains the flood of billboards one sees
in Libya, proclaiming:

> *Partners, Not Wage Earners.*
>
> *The House Belongs to its Occupant.*
>
> *Equality, Equality.*
>
> *Victory for the Workers Over the Capitalists.*
>
> *Freedom for the Toilers -- Freedom for the Masses.*
>
> *Authority in the Lands of Al Fateh Resides in
> the People, and No One Else.*

On December 23, 1978, *Al Fajr Al Jadid*, Libya's
leading newspaper, carried this front page, four
column headline:

> *Textile Workers in France's Department of
> the Loire Occupy Factory in Response to the
> Workers' Revolution in Al Jamahiriya* (Libya).

The story began: "The revolution of the workers
in the land of the great *Al Fateh* has had a response
in France, where the textile workers in France's
Department of the Loire occupied the factory." Following a lengthy report of the incident, *Al Fajr Al Jadid*
concluded:

The action of the French workers was a decisive

rejection of the oppressive relationship between workers and capitalists in exploitative capitalist society. These are the relationships that the workers in *Al Jamahiriya* have trampled underfoot and destroyed forever, and that are now replaced by the relationship of partners, not wage earners!

NOTES

1. Literally, *Al Fateh* means "the beginning," in Arabic. *Al Fateh* of any given month is the first of the month. The Libyan Revolution was started on September 1, 1969, so it is regularly referred to as *Al Fateh*.

2. For a discussion of the first *Green Book*, see R. Habiby, "Qadhafi's Thoughts on True Democracy," *Middle East Review*, Vol. X, No. 4, Summer, 1978, pp. 29–35.

3. I saw so many billboards in Libya during my short visit there, December 17–23, 1978. They were in Tripoli International Airport, in my hotel, added to the names of stores, and everywhere.

4. The first edition in Arabic is dated November 1977 and is published by The General Printing, Distribution and Advertising Co., *Jamahiriya* (Libya).

5. This and other quotations from the speech are from the Arabic text of Col. Qadhafi's November 10, 1978 speech in Green Square, Tripoli, as published and distributed by the Libyan Government.

6. The back cover of the Arabic text of the Second *Green Book* says, "The Thinker, Mu'amar Qadhafi, having given us the final solution to the problem of democracy in the first chapter of the *Green Book*, will, in the second chapter..." etc.

7. *Al Fajr Al Jadid* (Libya's main Arabic Daily), December 21, 1972, p. 2.

8. All the translations of the Qur'an are from *The Koran*, translated by E. H. Palmer, Oxford University Press, London, 1960. (First published in 1900).

9. Words added to the Qur'anic verse in parenthesis are Qadhafi's.

10. I have compared the Arabic and the English texts published by the Libyan Government. The many mistakes in the English text made me turn to the Arabic. All references in this article from this point on are to the Arabic edition, dated November, 1977 and published by the General Printing, Distribution and Advertising Co., *Jamahiriya* (Libya).

11. *Al Fajr Al Jadid*, September 2, 1978. "The revolution is workers taking over all the production positions in the country. They should advance as of today to free themselves from wages, the chains of bondage and the domination of others."

19
Qadhafi's Thoughts on True Democracy

Raymond N. Habiby

Libya, in the fifties, was considered so poor
that it could hardly merit attention. Oil was struck
in 1959 and the situation changed dramatically. By 1977,
Libya had become the world's seventh largest oil producer,
with oil revenues in excess of $8 billion a year and gold
and foreign currency reserves in excess of $3 billion.
This definitely projects a bright economic picture for
a country which, while larger in size than the state of
Alaska, is 90% desert and is inhabited by only 2.6
million people.

On September 1, 1969, a coup brought about the end
of the monarchy which had ruled Libya since Independence
Day in 1951, and the Libyan Arab Republic was proclaimed.
The coup was led by a young Army lieutenant, Mua'mmar
Qadhafi. On December 11 of that year, the new Revolution
Command Council (RCC) issued a Constitutional Declaration
which has, for all practical purposes, served as the
"constitution" of the new Republic.

Qadhafi, now thirty six, is a deeply religious man
who considers himself the champion of all the Arab and
Islamic causes. He is openly against what he sees as
Western imperialism, and Communism does not appeal to
him either.[1] He is convinced that Israel has no place
in the Arab world and that, in order to destroy Israel,
Arab unity must first become a reality and this is only
possible once all the Arab regimes follow his system of
planned radicalism. He sees his role as that of a new
Arab Saladin, destined to destroy the foes of Islam and
all the "corrupt" dynasties and regimes. He is the sword

Qadhafi's Thoughts on True Democracy is reprinted
from *Middle East Review*, Vol. X, No. 4, Summer, 1978.

of Allah turned on the enemies of Arabism and Islam.

Qadhafi has rejected both capitalism and communism
as viable systems and asserts that his own doctrine,
the Third Universal Doctrine, which bases itself on the
foundations of the morality of religion and the humani-
tarianism of socialism, is the inevitable successor, his
Doctrine is, thus, the "final solution to the problem
of the liberation of man."

Starting in 1974, and with the help of Moscow,
Qadhafi has built up an arsenal of weapons now estimated
to include at least 1200 battle tanks, 1000 scout and
armored personnel cars, Soviet surface-to-air missile
systems, large numbers of Russian SCUD and FROG-7
artillery missiles, 110 French Mirage jet fighters, 2
squadrons of Russian MiG-23's, a dozen TU-22 bombers,
a number of helicopters, and possibly a number of MiG-25
Foxbats.[2] Qadhafi calls this stock of weapons "the
arsenal of Islam."

THE THIRD UNIVERSAL DOCTRINE

Qadhafi's thoughts on a Third Universal Doctrine
seem to have taken shape in 1974. The Doctrine is not
one we normally associate with the stand of Third World
nations in a world dominated by the two superpowers.
To Qadhafi, the Doctrine is the final answer "to man's
fight through the ages to attain political, economic
and social freedom." It will triumph, and will replace
both capitalism and communism. And he is certain this
will happen, because the Doctrine is "based on the laws
of nature and the divine nature of religion."

Qadhafi published the first of a series of *Green
Books*, in which he presents and analyzes his thoughts
and arguments in support of the political facet of his
Doctrine, namely his "solution for the problem of
democracy," in 1975. The first *Green Book* is 48 pages
long and 3" by 5" in size. It is required reading for
all Libyan citizens and is taught to all levels of students.
Sold for one Libyan Dinar ($3.35), it has already been
through a number of printings.

The second *Green Book* was published in the fall of
1977. It deals with the economic facets of the Third Universal Doctrine. (A third *Green Book* deals with the social
aspects of the Doctrine.)

The first *Green Book* is important, not simply because
it helps us analyze Col. Qadhafi's thoughts, but also because the Libyan political structure is being remodeled
along the lines of the Third Universal Doctrine. Anyone
visiting Libya nowadays[3] is bound to notice the huge
posters flashing direct quotations from the *Green Book*,

and all political meetings and rallies are punctuated
with direct quotations from the Book. Here are some
of them:

> *There can be no democracy without People's*
> *Congresses.*

> *Parties are tools used in destroying democracy.*

> *A partisan is a traitor.*

> *Representative Assemblies make a mockery of*
> *democracy.*

> *There is no substitute for the people, and*
> *representation is a farce.*

> *A Representative Assembly amounts to rule*
> *in absentia.*[4]

   To discover what Qadhafi means by all this, and to
be in a better position to follow political developments
in Libya (and, hopefully, to obtain a proper perspective),
one has to be acquainted with the *Green Book* (*Al Kitab*
Al Akhdar, in Arabic).
   In February, 1977, Col. Qadhafi took the first
step when he abolished the RCC and turned over its powers
and duties to the General People's Congress, an institution
described in the *Green Book*. The name *Libya* was also
changed from the Libyan Arab Republic to the Socialist
People's Libyan Arab Jamahiriya.[5] The Libyan Government
chose not to translate the word "Jamahiriya," which is the
Arabic word for "multitudes" or "the masses," and the
Libyan Government, radio, T.V. and newspapers now either
use the long new name or simply call the country *Al*
Jamahiriya, probably with the intention of stressing the
role which the masses are to play in Qadhafi's concept
of Democracy.[6] For, after all, the title of the first
Green Book is "The Solution for the Problem of Democracy:
The Sovereignty of the People."
   Given the role which Col. Qadhafi has set for himself
and for Al Jamahiriya (Libya) to play, one cannot dismiss
his thoughts as immaterial. Is it possible that, one day,
Qadhafi's thoughts, political, economic and social, might
find acceptance in those countries now seeking Libya's
petrodollars? Or would Qadhafi's arsenal eventually be
used to implement his thoughts? At different times in
history, and in the twentieth century in particular, the
world has belittled other works only to discover their
impact on certain regions of the world.
   It is not the purpose of this paper to analyze

Qadhafi's political doctrine in terms of its political
soundness or practicality. This paper is by choice
limited to an analytical exposé of Qadhafi's thoughts
on "Pure Democracy." It supplies his own explanations
and justifications.

On Political Systems

The Libyan leader devotes a good part of his book
to a criticism of the so-called "accepted foundations of
traditional democracy," namely elections, representative
assemblies, political parties, the class system and
referendums. He believes that every one of them has
failed to produce a democracy; they have all produced
dictatorships. Qadhafi then presents his own concept
of democracy, or what he calls the Third Universal
Doctrine, in which democracy is "The people supervising
itself." This system does not call for a constitution,
since constitutions are "man-made laws which embody the
viewpoints of the dictatorial regimes of the world."
Lastly, he addresses himself to the question of how a
free press should function in a democratic society.

In justification of his doctrine, Qadhafi presents
the thesis that all existing political systems are the
result of either an armed or peaceful struggle to attain
power, and be it a group, a clan, a faction, a tribe, a
political party, or an individual, when any of these wins,
the people are the losers. This only means the defeat
of true democracy.[7]

Qadhafi maintains that the regime of a candidate
who wins an election by 51% of the vote is a dictatorial
government, since 49% of the voters will be ruled by someone they have not elected. In those instances of a more
than two-way fight, it is possible for the losers to
command more votes than the elected representative, yet
he is declared "legally and democratically elected"
(p. 4). "These are dictatorial systems and make a mockery
of democracy," he writes.

To Qadhafi, the "accepted foundations of democracy"
are "representative assemblies," "political parties,"
"the class system," and "referendums." None of these
systems, he finds, can produce a "true democracy." This
is the "Number One political problem of all human societies
today" (p. 3), and once this is resolved, men will put an
end to the age of oppression and dictatorial rule and
replace them with the authority of the people. He assures
us that the *Green Book* contains the "final solution to
the problem of the system of government" (pp. 25-26).

National assemblies are also summarily dismissed
as fake representation of the people and a makeshift
system for resolving the problem of democracy. This is

so even though national assemblies have been and are still the "backbone of traditional democracy" as practiced in the world today (p. 6). Democracy is then the people, not their representatives; representative assemblies stand as a legal barrier between the people and the exercise of authority. Qadhafi contends that by their monopoly of authority, representative assemblies have isolated the masses from politics. "The masses were left with the outer form of democracy, namely with agreeing to cast their votes in the ballot boxes" (pp. 6-7).

Qadhafi also rejects the system of electing deputies either from districts or through party lists or coalitions of parties because, once the elections are over, "the deputy monopolizes the new authority given to him and begins to act as the deputy of the people. He is given immunities and a measure of sanctity, yet the citizens are denied them" (p. 8). It is not democratic for a deputy, once elected, to deputize for thousands, hundreds of thousands, or millions of citizens so long as he is not linked to the voters by a popular organization system (p. 8). It is the duty of the people then to say, loud and clear: "No one can represent the people" (p. 9).

The Libyan leader also dismisses as undemocratic a government resulting from a party victory in an election, because the deputies are representatives of the party, not the people. The same can be said of party coalitions. He bemoans the lot of the people, who are the prey of political groups competing to snatch authority from them; the people are then left "to stand silently in line to cast their votes the way they cast a piece of paper into a garbage can" (p. 9). And, what is more, elections are demagogic systems in which the voters are bought and tossed around. The poor stand no chance; only the rich win elections (p. 9).

Delving into history in support of his point of view, Qadhafi finds that the concept of representative assemblies was one advocated by philosophers, thinkers and writers at a time when the people were herded like cattle by kings, sultans and conquerors. It was only natural that the most these people could hope for then was to have someone represent them before the rulers, something which the rulers had persistently refused to accept (p. 10). Qadhafi cannot, therefore, he writes, see how now, in the days of the "victory of the republics, and the beginning of the age of the people, democracy would be nothing more than a system in which a few deputies represent the multitudes of people." He then immediately points out that the "worst dictatorships the world has so far experienced have co-existed with representative assemblies" (p. 11).

The political party is, to Qadhafi, "the latest

instrument of dictatorial rule" (p. 12). Parties clothe
themselves with the garments of democracy so that they
have councils, committees and propaganda, yet the truth
is that parties are "a system in which the part rules
the whole" (p. 12).

Explaining what a political party is to him, Qadhafi
defines it as "a collection of persons of the same
interests, the same viewpoints and the same doctrines,
or persons who live in the same geographical locale.
They form a party to attain their ends and impose their
doctrines on the whole of society. They seek authority
in the name of implementing their programs" (p. 13).
Ridiculing parties, Qadhafi asks: "How could a party
rule a people, who are composed of a variety of interests,
moods and doctrines?" (p. 13). To Qadhafi, parties are
established to rule those persons who are outside the
confines of the party and, "to attain this, the party
has to seize power" (p. 13).

Political parties, Qadhafi insists, are forces of
disruption in any nation, since, in their struggle to
attain power, they destroy the accomplishments of those
who preceded them, even if these accomplishments were
for the good of society. This is why the intra-party
struggle proceeds at the expense of the vital and supreme
interests of society, and why, while one party wins and
the other or others lose, it is always the people and
democracy that are really the losers (p. 15). Pointing
to what he calls a major weakness of political parties,
he says that they take bribes and can be bought, "from
within and from without" (p. 15).

The Libyan leader does not seem to have much faith
in the opposition. He does not see the opposition as
playing the role of watchdog over the interests of the
people. In his view, the opposition simply "keeps watch
over the ruling party, waiting for the time and place
to replace it in power" (p. 16).

In his final criticism, Qadhafi asserts that a
political party can only represent a segment of the
people, yet the "sovereignty of the people is indivisible."
The party claims that it rules on behalf of the people, yet
the people cannot have representatives. "For all these
reasons, the party is not different from the tribe or
factions. All of them are bad, and they function to
destroy society" (pp. 17-18).

On Classes

Qadhafi also disapproves of the class system, which
to him is no different from the political party, the tribe,
or factions. A class, he writes, seeks to further its own
interests and not those of the people and must, by analogy,

be considered dictatorial even if, as he believes,
class and tribal coalitions are superior to political
parties. Why? Because peoples originally began as
tribes and are now structured into classes. Political
parties, on the other hand, can never encompass all
the people and will always be a minority vis-a-vis the
people, i.e., the majority. In the process of destroying
one another, Qadhafi holds, parties, tribes and classes
resort to the logic of force, which is alien to true
democracy and is therefore dictatorial (p. 21).

Whenever a class destroys all the other classes in
a society, it inherits all the characteristics of the
society which the destroyed classes represented. The
victorious class then becomes the material and social
base of that society. As an example, Qadhafi writes, if
the working class succeeds in destroying all the other
classes, it will surely inherit all the characteristics
of the old society and, in time, all the old characteristics will re-emerge through the working class and the
old society will be reproduced. Factions will develop,
which will be followed by a new class structure and the
renewal of the struggle to rule the society (p. 23).
Every society undergoing a class struggle was at one
time a one-class society and, in time, as a result of
the law of inevitable development, other classes
developed.[8] It is, therefore, a waste of time to try
to solve the problem of who rules by unifying the base
of a society (pp. 23-24).

Dealing with the last so-called accepted foundation
of traditional democracy, namely the referendum system,
Qadhafi also dismisses it as a "mockery of democracy"
because "those who say 'yes' and those who say 'no' do
not really express their will... They are only allowed
to say 'yes' or 'no'." Such a system is "the worst
and most oppressive dictatorial system," for those who
say "yes" and those who say "no" must be allowed to
explain why. "Referendums, like elections, are resorted
to as a coverup. They seek to cover up the failure to
resolve the problem of the system of government, a system
based on the rule of the people, because the people can
have no representatives" (p. 25).

The Doctrine of Democracy

True democracy is direct democracy, yet it is
impossible for all the citizens to discuss and formulate
policy. The great and practical system to attain direct
democracy is to be found in the Third Universal Doctrine,
which will resolve the problem of democracy in the world
once and for all. The masses will be left with nothing
to do but to "fight to destroy all existing dictatorial

systems in the World" (p. 30).

What then, is Qadhafi's "system," or Third Universal Doctrine? In order to produce "true democracy," Qadhafi divides the people or citizens into basic people's congresses. Each basic people's congress would then select a leadership committee and the leadership committees combined would form the people's congress of the region, as distinct from the basic people's congresses. The basic people's congresses would also select people's committees for administration, whose function is to take over all government administration, so that all societal services are, from then on, operated by people's committees. These people's committees are held accountable to the basic people's congresses, the bodies which formulate policy and supervise its implementation.

Qadhafi explains that his system would transform government administration into people's administration. Traditional government supervision would become supervision by the people. This, for him, is very important, because the end product is a complete change in the traditional definition of democracy. This change is from "democracy is the people supervising government" to the more correct definition, of "democracy is the people supervising itself" (pp. 30-31).

Qadhafi appears to believe, however, that certain groups of citizens merit membership in more than one basic people's congress. Workers, farmers, students, merchants, tradesmen, professionals and employers, while belonging to their basic people's congresses, are also required to form syndicates and trade unions which, in turn, like the basic people's congresses, have people's committees and leadership committees (p. 32).

Once the basic people's congresses, people's committees and trade unions and syndicates begin to function, the results of their deliberations are sent to the General People's Congress to be put into final form. The General People's Congress is a meeting of the leadership committees of the basic people's congresses, the people's committees and the trade unions and syndicates. The General People's Congress meets once a year and its resolutions--which appear to be regarded as "laws"--once passed, are then transmitted to the basic people's congresses, the people's committees and all the trade unions and syndicates, which then begin the process of implementation (p. 32).[9]

What, then, is the difference, in Qadhafi's plan, between the General People's Congress and traditional representative assemblies? To Qadhafi the General People's Congress is not a meeting of individuals but a convocation of the basic people's congresses, the people's committees, the trade unions, the syndicates

and all the professional associations, while traditional
representative assemblies are meetings of individuals
(p. 33). "In such a system, the people become the system
of government, and finally the problem of democracy in
the world will have been resolved" (p. 33).

Is there a need for a constitution in this system
of direct democracy? Will the people in the long run
assume positions incompatible with the demands of a
healthy system? The Libyan leader's response to the
first question is an emphatic "No!" because present-day
constitutions are not "the law of society," but are "man
made laws and contain the views of the dictatorial regimes
of the world." Persons first decide how to control groups
of people, then write a constitution for them which they
are forced to obey (p. 36). This is unacceptable to
Qadhafi, since it would only mean that the will of the
dictatorial regimes has replaced the law of nature,
which is the logical law of men wherever they might be,
because all men are the same (p. 37). Constitutions are
not permanent, can be changed and are in fact changed,
but the "law of Society" is not subject to change and
serves as the final arbiter as to what is right and wrong.
It defines the rights and obligations of individuals.
In fact, freedom is threatened if the law of Society is
changed by political regimes (pp. 38-39).

In arguing against constitutions, the Libyan leader
writes that state laws promulgated under a constitution
are replete with corporal punishment, yet the laws of
society and custom hardly ever provide for such and are,
on the whole, moral in character. Punishment, in religion,
is in the hereafter, and if religion ever provides for a
worldly punishment it does so in extreme cases if necessary
for the good of society. He stresses that religion is the
reaffirmation of the law of nature, therefore any law
not based on religion is the work of one man against
another, and such laws are void because they lack their
natural source, namely, custom and religion (p. 40).

Finally, Qadhafi addresses himself to the question
of who, in a direct democracy, watches over society to
insure that there is no deviation from the law. The
Libyan leader maintains that society must be its own
guardian, because if any other authority assumes this
function then the whole system becomes dictatorial.
Society will provide its own system of supervision through
the basic people's congresses and committees which form
the General People's Congress (pp. 40-41). In the "so-
called democracies," which Qadhafi calls the "dictatorial
systems of the world," society's only means of correcting
a deviation is force, namely, revolt against the system
of government. The use of force is not a democratic
method, and only a percentage of society has either the

means or the will to take part in acts of violence.   In
Qadhafi's system, if there is a deviation from the laws of
society, such deviation would be the deviation of the whole
and is then corrected by the involvement of the whole,
which is the democratic procedure and, since no group
exists outside the system, the deviations are corrected
from within and not from without (p. 43).   Qadhafi seems
to consider this the greatest asset of his Doctrine.

What is the role of the press in Qadhafi's system of
direct democracy?   The Libyan leader considers the press
the means of expression of society and not of a person or
a corporate group.   The logic of democracy, then, dictates
against individual or corporate ownership.   "If a person
owns a newspaper, it is his own and will naturally express
his own point of view.   No one can claim it represents
public opinion."   Democracy cannot permit a person to own
a public information system, but it gives him the right to
express himself by all possible means, "even in a crazy way,
to prove his lunacy" (p. 45).   A paper owned by the Chamber
of Commerce can only represent the views of the Chamber of
Commerce.   "A democratic paper is one published by a people's
committee representing the different segments of society.
This is the only way the press or any means of communication
can express the views of society as a whole, whereas a paper
owned by the medical profession or the Bar Association can
only express the views of the owners" (p. 46).

For Qadhafi, this would also solve the "problem of
the free press" which is also a product of the general
problem of democracy.   The Third Universal Doctrine is, in
his view, the only solution, and he warns that "unless the
age of democracy dawns, the age of anarchy and demagogery
will set in" (p. 47).

What next?   Qadhafi concludes with the following
statement:

> This is the conceptual framework of true democracy,
> yet in real life it is always the strong who rule.   In
> other words, the strongest segment of any society rules
> (p. 48).

One is bound to ask what the point is of this utopian
concept if the strong are bound to rule?   The *Green Book*
presents a variety of utopian thoughts, but does not seem
to involve itself with the practical, day-to-day application
of the concepts presented, in a real government situation.

NOTES

1.   The Communist Party is illegal in Libya and its members have
been prosecuted.

2.   These figures appeared in *U.S. News and World Report*,
April 10, 1978, p. 39.

3. The author spent the 1975-76 academic year in Libya as a visiting professor at the University of Benghazi. While he was there, the university was renamed Qar Yunis University.

4. These translations and all other quotations from the *Green Book* in this article are from the Arabic as translated by the author.

5. This is the exact Libyan Government translation as it appeared in a full-page Government-paid advertisement in *The Christian Science Monitor* of April 7, 1977, p. 7.

6. For example, see *Al Jihad* of Libya of March 25, 1977, p. 1. The banner headline (in Arabic) reads, "Al Jamahiriya Attains a World-wide Development Record."

7. The *Green Book* , p. 4. Here, pages refer to the Arabic text and have been translated or paraphrased by the author.

8. Qadhafi appears to be arguing against the class logic of communism.

9. This is not very clear since the cabinet, in Libya, still "legislates" by decree under the "Constitutional Declaration of 1969" and laws come into effect upon their publication in the *Official Gazette*.

20
The Creation of Saudi Arabia and the Erosion of Wahhabi Conservatism

George Linabury

It is customary to attribute the establishment of the Saudi state to the singlehanded efforts of Ibn Saud. This paper does not seek to denigrate the accomplishments of that great desert chieftain, but rather to demonstate Great Britain's singular--one might even call it unique--role in the emergence of the Saudi state. Similarly, the United States is generally considered to have replaced His Majesty's Government in Arabia in the post World War II period, when the former was transformed from an empire into a nation. The implication is that the American role was similar, if not identical, with the British one. This paper seeks to examine the different effects of the two Powers on the desert kingdom, and to bring more sharply into focus the emergence of Saudi Arabia, the erosion that has taken place in its conservatism and the imponderables this situation poses.

THE BRITISH CONNECTION

Britain's special treaty relationships with the small principalities or sheikdoms of the Persian Gulf date from the early nineteenth century and had as its objective the suppression of piracy and the curbing of the slave trade. In abandoning these lucrative occupations, the sheikdoms generally agreed to British control over their foreign relations and to the nonalienation of their territories without prior British approval.

The Creation of Saudi Arabia and the Erosion of Wahhabi Conservatism is reprinted from *Middle East Review*, Vol. XI, No. 1, Fall, 1978.

The Ottoman Sultan also exerted some influence along the east and west coastlines of the Arabian Peninsula, but left the barely accessible central desert regions to the Bedouin tribes, the most powerful of which was led by the pro-Ottoman Ibn Rashid. The "Sick Man of Europe," as the weakened Ottoman Empire was called in the West, was consistently buttressed by the British Government in order to avoid a European scramble to dismember it, for that would inevitably have triggered a Great Power war. However, when London concluded that British imperial interests were at stake, carefully calculated "responses," adequately supported by Britain's then preeminent position in the world, were not uncommon.

At the turn of the century, such a situation presented itself with the scheme to build a railroad from Berlin to Baghdad and, later, to extend its terminus to Kuwait, on the Persian Gulf. The possibility of linking other European Powers to the Gulf via the railway over territories that Britain had come to look upon as part of its imperial route to India, was contrary to the perceived British interests. Accordingly, the British offered the willing ruler of Kuwait, Sheik Mubarak ibn Sabah, the opportunity of joining the elaborate treaty structure which London had erected with such care. Sheik Mubarak knew from experience that the British were interested only in his external relations, and so their presence would prevent those meddling Ottoman Turks from interfering in his internal affairs. Mubarak gladly, therefore, surrendered control of his external affairs to His Majesty's Government. In addition, he agreed never to cede, sell, mortgage or lease any of his territory without prior British approval, which quite effectively allowed London to prevent the railroad from approaching any feasible area in the northern reaches of the Persian Gulf. Soon thereafter, British sensitivities regarding Gulf affairs brought a halt to tribal skirmishing between the Rashidis and the Kuwaitis; the British convinced the Sublime Porte, (i.e., the Ottoman Government) to restrain its protegé, Ibn Rashid, while they would likewise restrain Mubarak. Understandably, Britain's anxieties were raised when the Porte attempted to land troops in Kuwait, and Britain moved quickly to prevent this action. The result of these events was to restrict Ottoman expansion in Arabia, but an important side effect worked to the advantage of Ibn Saud, a desert sheik who was seldom on good terms with the Ottoman Turks and their client, Ibn Rashid.

'Abd al-'Aziz ibn 'Abd al-Rahman al Faysal al Saud, popularly known in the West as Ibn Saud,* had been testing his arch foe, Ibn Rashid, but had fared none too well in

---

*He is generally known as 'Abd al-'Aziz in Arabia.

this effort.   Fortunately for him, Sheik Mubarak came
to his rescue by giving him sanctuary.   In Kuwait, the
Saudis licked their wounds and planned a daring assault
on Riyadh, then the Rashidi fortress in central Arabia
and today the capital of the Saudi Kingdom.   The assault
(in 1902) was successful, and the foundation of the
modern Saudi state was laid.   British policy, by curbing Ottoman power in the Gulf region and hindering the
designs of the Rashidis, had been of signal service to
the desert warrior who was to give his name to a new
Arab kingdom.
      Additional attempts by the Sublime Porte, which
dispatched troops to the area to further Ottoman influence in Arabia, were turned aside by British diplomacy.
Not unnaturally, Ibn Saud began to put out feelers to the
British for direct assistance, but his overtures went
unanswered by a British Government which did not wish,
unnecessarily to embarrass its relations with the Porte.
Nevertheless, and to the chagrin of the Turks, the British
Government did post Captain S. G. Knox to Kuwait to act
as Political Agent--to observe Ottoman military movements
and to cultivate good relations with Mubarak--and only
incidentally to keep an eye on the struggle still taking
place in the interior between the Saudis and the Rashidis.
      By 1906, the Rashidis had suffered a serious defeat
at the hands of the Saudis.   The few Ottoman troops
stationed in the province of Najd, in northern Arabia,
began deserting their posts due to the extreme heat and
an outbreak of cholera.   The token Ottoman occupation of
northern Arabia collapsed, leaving the Saudis free to
continue to cultivate their position.   Still another Saudi
feeler to the British went unanswered, although innocuous
conversations were held with Captain William Shakespear,
who had replaced Knox.   The Saudi offer of trading privileges
in return for the protection of British sea power did not
entice London, which was far more interested in concluding
a comprehensive settlement of international problems with
the Ottoman Turks than in being diverted by tribal machina-
tions in the interior of Arabia.
      The situation changed, however, in 1913, when Ibn
Saud captured the east coast province of al-Hasa from the
Ottomans and was thereby brought into the sphere of British-
Gulf politics.   Still, the British moved cautiously, now
more than ever concerned about the direction of Ottoman-
German relations.   Ibn Saud was informed that as long as
he did not disturb the peace in the Gulf area, His Majesty's
Government would continue to maintain friendly relations
with him.   These British-Saudi contacts did not go un-
noticed in Constantinople, where the Porte's suspicions
about British motives grew apace.   Uneasy about the way
events were developing, the British informed Ibn Saud in

writing not to take any further independent action.
But the British balancing act swung in the Saudis' favor
again in the early spring of 1914, when the Porte recom-
menced military preparations for a campaign against the
Saudis. It was this extension of Ottoman power in an
area of significant British interests, not Saudi well-
being, that impelled Britain to warn the Porte that His
Majesty's fleet would prevent the landing of Ottoman
troops in eastern Arabia. To Ibn Saud the results of
this warning were of more pressing interest than the
British rationale behind them.

The outbreak of the Great War found the Turks
firmly ensconced on the German side and the British
shifting gears. London conceded that because of Ibn
Saud's foothold on the Gulf and his control of the interior
"we cannot touch him. It is essential...to carry him with
us in any settlement of Arabian affairs that may be proposed."[1] This revelation was formally expressed in the
1915 treaty between the two parties which, in effect,
created a semi-protectorate status over Saudi domains
through the now traditional nonalienation bond, Saudi
noninterference in the affairs of the Gulf sheikdoms in
special treaty relations with Britain and relinquishment
of control over Saudi foreign relations. Unlike similar
treaties with Gulf rulers, however, Ibn Saud agreed to be
guided by British advice only if this was not damaging
to his own interests, thus attesting to his preferential
treatment. An annual subsidy of £60,000, and British
military assistance, rounded out the agreement.

The Saudi-Hashimi Struggle

In order to relieve the pressure on their Indian
troops, which had landed in Basrah, in southern Iraq,
the British sought to employ Saudi Bedouin in an attack
on Ibn Rashid. But Ibn Saud saw his position as precariously poised between the Rashidis in northern Arabia
and the Ottoman Arab governor of the Hijaz, Sharif Hussein
ibn 'Ali, scion of the Hashimi House, in western Arabia.
To exhaust his troops in a showdown battle with the
Rashidis might leave him in a weakened position to deal
with Hussein, whose enmity to the Saudis was great, and
was returned. Further complicating these tribal maneuver-
ings was the fact that Hussein, with British assistance,
had seceded from the Ottoman Empire in 1916, declared the
Arab Revolt and provided his own Bedouin troops in western
Arabia to protect the British right flank in its drive
from Egypt to Damascus. The Saudi-Hashimi rivalry drove
the British from one frustration to another, but they
strove assiduously to keep their two Arabian allies from
coming to sword's point. Then the tide of war moved

northward and westward, placing Hussein in a more
strategic position in British war strategy. Left in
the backwater of military events, Ibn Saud became more
of local than imperial value.

British admonitions to avoid a breach in the midst
of the war notwithstanding, relations between the two
Arabian leaders reached a critical juncture over the
ownership of the oasis town of Khurmah in the eastern
Hijaz near the frontier with Najd. Hussein had
appointed Khalid ibn Lu'ay as amir (governor) of Khurmah,
but Ibn Lu'ay switched his allegiance to the Saudi camp
when he was converted to Wahhabism* by its zealous
missionaries. The population of Khurmah followed their
amir, and so, without raising a finger, Ibn Saud acquired
an ally and an important oasis settlement.

Saudi religious conservation may be dated from this
time: Ibn Saud was now the Wahhabi leader.**

Meanwhile, Hussein's troops were busy besieging the
Turks at Medinah--but they could easily be transferred
to Khurmah. This eventuality the British were bent on
avoiding at all costs; it would leave Ottoman troops
free to maneuver in their rear. To Hussein the British
therefore anxiously played down the importance of the oasis
town as compared with the siege of Medinah, which was
directly connected with the war effort. Identical notes

---

*The Wahhabis (*Wahhabiyya*) are an ultraconservative
puritan Sunni Muslim sect which arose in the Arabian
peninsula in the latter half of the eighteenth century,
founded by Muhammad Ibn Abd al'Wahhab, who came from
Najd. His teachings were adopted by Muhammad Ibn Saud,
sheik of the Dar'iya region, and the house of Saud became the leader of the Wahhabis.

The Wahhabis have felt that Muslims have abandoned
their faith in one God and distorted the Muslim religion
through innovations which run counter to pure Islamic
faith. They accept only the Qur'an and the early *Sunna*
(Tradition) and reject all later developments and interpretations in Islamic theology and mysticism. They
reject veneration of saints and tombs, prohibit the
decoration of mosques, and ban luxury. All Muslims
who do not accept their interdicts are regarded as
heretics. (Eds.)

**Perhaps because of his sojourn in Kuwait and his
attendance at the counsels of Mubarak, however, he
was one of the less fanatical adherents of the sect,
for practical politics, and British power, had made
their impression upon him.

were hurried off to both Arab leaders, informing them
that His Majesty's Government "must insist, under pain
of severe displeasure, that neither party take any
action which is likely to lead to an open breach."[2]
Hussein's forced inaction at Khurmah, however, was
interpreted by the tribes, fickle in their loyalties
and determined to be on the winning side, as a sign of
Hashimi weakness.   The British-enforced *status quo*
left Khurmah in Saudi control and eventually (1925)
provided a strategic point of departure for the Wahhabi
invasion of the Hijaz.

When the war ended, Britain's interest in the Hijaz
centered upon its holy cities of Mecca and Medina and on
the necessity of safeguarding the pilgrimage traffic
from British India, with its large Muslim population.
Britain was unwilling, perhaps unable, to translate this
interest into military involvement in the Saudi-Hashimi
confrontation so as to avoid a disruption of the peace
and tranquility of the region.   It was willing, however,
to use diplomacy to bring the two sides together, but
would go no further.   Accordingly, Hussein's request for
British aircraft for use against the Wahhabis was refused.
When Hussein took the initiative, by purchasing six Italian
planes, London intervened with the Italian Government and
persuaded it to refrain from further provocative activity.
Understandably, Britain thereafter found Hussein increasingly difficult to deal with, especially when he
refused to ratify the Treaty of Versailles.   To Hussein,
this would have meant his acceptance of the mandate system
and British and French control over the Arab lands, a state
of affairs that ran contrary to the Sharif's dream of
leadership over a great Arab nation.   Such was his chagrin
that when the short-lived Arab state in Syria fell to
French military intervention, even members of Hussein's
own family found him irascible, and actually concluded
that he had lost his mind![3]

The British Treasury, feeling the pinch of postwar
economies, had already cut Hussein's £200,000 war-time
subsidy by half--while maintaining Ibn Saud's subsidy at
the original amount of £5,000.   And Britain continued to
pressure the obstreperous Hussein.   His reduced subsidy
was withheld until such time as he changed his attitude
about signing the Versailles Treaty.   He never did.

Ibn Saud, who continued to receive his regular
subsidy, had conquered the Rashidi stronghold in northern
Arabia, thus ending the rule of one of his two Arabian
rivals.   An agreement with the British in 1922 formally
recognized his northern border with Transjordan and Iraq.
As Anglo-Saudi relations grew more amicable, the Wahhabi
leader felt he could move against the Hijaz with impunity.
When Hussein unilaterally assumed the title of Caliph

without the prior concurrence of a large representative Muslim body, this step not only released a storm of indignation among the Arabs but did nothing to prevent the Wahhabis from forcibly taking the important city of Tayif, near Mecca. Again, Hussein's effusive appeals to the British for material assistance fell on deaf ears. In the early fall of 1924, the British Foreign Office informed the "caliph" that it would adhere to its traditional policy of noninterference in what it chose to call Saudi-Hashimi "religious" affairs.

Hussein's own people finally convinced him to abdicate in favor of his son, 'Ali. The distraught monarch was hustled off into exile in Transjordan, where he promptly continued his intrigues against the Wahhabis. Fearful that this might provoke a Saudi incursion into Transjordan, the British packed Hussein off to Cyprus. Hashimi fortunes continued to decline, and in 1925 'Ali capitulated and the Hijaz was occupied by Ibn Saud and the Wahhabis.

The Saudi domains now spanned the Arabian Peninsula from the Red Sea to the Persian Gulf and, in May, 1927, the British lost little time in officially recognizing the fact by concluding the Treaty of Jiddah. His Majesty's Government recognized the complete and absolute independence of Ibn Saud's kingdom. The quasi-protectorate status of the 1915 treaty was buried. The new treaty indicated an agreement concluded among equals, if not in power, at least in mutual respect. At a time when most of the Arab world was controlled by the imperialist powers, the Saudi position was indeed unique, due to a great extent to British policy.

THE AMERICAN CONNECTION

The Americans came to Saudi Arabia in 1933 and found oil. The culture shock provided by the first event and the immense revenues provided by the second began to erode the ultra-conservatism of the puritanical Wahhabis, albeit slowly. Standard Oil Company of California had estimated that its discovery of petroleum on the island of Bahrain, a scant 12 miles off the east coast of Arabia, made it reasonable to expect to find more within the similar geological structure on the mainland, and they were right. The first well went on stream in March 1938 and the first tanker was loaded in the spring of the following year. This bonanza was interrupted by World War II, during which production was shut down.

The war also affected the pilgrimage traffic to Mecca, the main source of income for Ibn Saud. The cost of running his kingdom was temporarily alleviated by

Britain and by the oil company, but the Wahhabi leader
demanded a great deal more--he wanted $6 million.
Standard of California decided to interest the U.S.
Government in providing the money by way of lend-lease
legislation, with future oil royalties as collateral.
President Roosevelt was not enthusiastic. He suggested
that since the Reconstruction Finance Corporation was
lending Great Britain $425 million, the British use
some of that money to bail Ibn Saud out. The American
oil company was pleased to be relieved of the financial
burden, but irked by the fact that the British would
be getting the credit for providing money which actually
came from the United States. The company was, in
addition, suspicious of British intentions; Britain
might, eventually, try to take over the American oil
concession. At the end of 1942, Standard Oil of California, along with the Texas Oil Company, which had become a partner in the oil venture, prevailed upon Harold
Ickes, Petroleum Administrator for War, to intercede
with Roosevelt once again. This time they were successful. The President wrote a note to the Lend-Lease
Administrator in which he said that "...in order to
enable you to arrange lend-lease aid to the Government
of Saudi Arabia, I hereby find that the defense of Saudi
Arabia is vital to the defense of the United States."[4]
Not only had the two oil companies been relieved of the
burden of financing Ibn Saud, but their prestige in
Arabia rose, for they had facilitated the "arrangements."
The U.S. was committed to the protection of the American
concession and the possibility of British penetration
was removed.

Ickes was elated too. He drew up a plan which
allowed the U.S. Government to acquire control of the
Saudi concession from the oil companies. When this hit
a stone wall of opposition from the oil companies, Ickes
came up with an alternate proposal. The U.S. would
build a pipeline across northern Arabia to the Mediterranean.
The companies resisted this idea as well. They decided to
build the pipeline themselves and acquired two additional
partners to help finance the project. Exxon and Mobil
(then Standard of New Jersey and Socony-Vacuum) joined
them to form the Arabian American Oil Company (ARAMCO).
This merger solved several problems for the oil companies.
The original owners needed outlets for additional production in order to provide increased royalties to a
demanding ruler; the new partners were seeking additional
crude supplies from the Middle East in order to meet increased market demands. In September 1950, the Trans-
Arabian Pipe Line Company (TAPLINE), owned by the companies
of ARAMCO, for the first time conveyed Saudi Arabian crude
from the producing fields on the east coast 1,068 miles

across Arabia, Jordan and Syria to the Lebanese terminal
at Sidon on the Mediterranean.

THE PROCESS OF EROSION

It was becoming increasingly difficult for American
oilmen to live as the first American oilmen did who came
ashore in eastern Arabia, wearing Arab clothes and growing beards in order to make themselves less conspicuous
in the local conservative Wahhabi population. In the
early days, a Saudi Arab who passed an American in the
streets of Riyadh would hastily turn his head away in
order not to be polluted by the gaze of the Christian
infidel, but that type of behavior had become increasingly
rare.
      The Saudis had also begun to change. For the TAPLINE
venture, Ibn Saud did not demand royalties but services.
He wanted to build up his country's northern frontier,
which bordered on not always friendly Jordan and Iraq.
Where there had been nothing but sand and sky and the
infrequent movement of Bedouin tribes there now appeared
four pumping stations, complete with American civilization
in miniature: American wives in Western dresses, American
movies, safety rules, cafeterias, swimming pools, clinics,
pay scales, golf courses and American ideas of punctuality,
etc. The Saudis quickly learned that they would have to
learn English in order to advance, and learn they did, even
to the point where some became literate in English while
remaining illiterate in Arabic. Gradually, they became
part of two cultures, with not always a clear idea as to
when to employ one and not the other. The company built
concrete office buildings for local officials, air
conditioned and equipped them, provided a fleet of cars
for designated local government officials with free gasoline
and repairs, and built four airstrips for TAPLINE and other
aircraft. Equally significant, if not even more so, was
the construction of the only road across northern Arabia
linking Jordan, Syria and Lebanon with the eastern part
of Ibn Saud's realm. Over this road came the products
and culture of the Middle East and Europe. TAPLINE built
four hospitals, containing the latest equipment and the
finest doctors. (The nurses were all Arab men. The
government eventually insisted that female nurses be
provided--until it discovered that most of these nurses
would be Lebanese of Armenian extraction. Armenian
meant Russian, and Russian meant godless communism.
Years went by until this conservative attitude changed.)
TAPLINE also built and maintained four schools for Saudi
boys and then also girls' schools, at government urging.
The company drilled water wells, which supplied not only

its own facilities but also the local government buildings,
town cisterns and camel troughs for the use of the Bedouin.
It sponsored community development projects, often providing
free services and engineering advice, such as on the establishment of private electric companies, garbage disposal
facilities, etc. It partially subsidized concrete housing
developments and made its purchases from the area's business-
men. Towns sprang up around each of the four pumping stations,
and their populations grew steadily. The shape of northern
Arabia was changing and so was its lifestyle. A similar
situation on a larger scale took place in the ARAMCO area
in eastern Arabia.

"Arabian Peninsula" *Jazirat al-'Arab* in Arabic means,
literally, "Island of the Arabs." If an island connotes
insularity, then the Arabian Peninsula is an island, sur-
rounded on three sides by water and to the north by the
Great Syrian Desert, as formidable a barrier as is any body
of water. This "island"--and the conservatism that it helped
to perpetuate--was now breached, and the process of Westernization (the Saudis prefer to use the word "modernization")
has not been reversed. To see this process at work one may
visualize sitting in a Bedouin tent while one's host listens
intently to Radio Cairo relayed on his transistor radio as
he pours a cup of tea out of a pot made in Czechoslovakia
while his children pour water from a 55-gallon drum recently
filled with oil and haul the water into the desert in his
new Ford pick-up. It is evident during a religious holiday
when, at the governor's palace, the Qadi (religious judge)
pointedly asks the local bank director why he charges
interest (a procedure forbidden by Islamic law) and the
banker replies that this is not interest but merely a service
charge. And, all the while, the governor sits between his
two guests, saying not a word in admonition. In Jiddah,
a complex of 32 government-sponsored apartment buildings
is being erected for middle-income Saudis whose parents
lived in tents or mud houses. An incredible building effort
foresees the construction of two industrial cities, Yanbu'
on the Red Sea and Jubayl on the Persian Gulf, at a cost
of $30 billion.

Not only the accumulation of material goods, purchased
with petro-dollars, fuels the revolution of rising expectations, but also the very presence of the Americans and other
foreigners and the life-style they bring with them. Approximately 30,000 Americans now live in Saudi Arabia. By the
early 1970s there were about 300,000 foreigners in the
country and 500,000 were planned for. It is estimated that
by 1980, one out of every five or six persons, and one out
of every three workers in Saudi Arabia will be foreigners.
Many of the technical personnel from the Western countries
bring their families with them. To keep them in the
country, the Saudi Government is promoting an international
school system, with an American curriculum where the language
of instruction is English. (Muslim children may not attend.)

True, many of these foreigners are in the country only for the duration of their contracted jobs and are often isolated from the mainstream of Saudi life. They are not always happy with their standard of living or their working conditions, and are therefore a source of potential discontent. The construction work in which they are generally employed is going on at a frenzied pace, but problems abound. Jiddah port, on the Red Sea, into which came much of the $3.6 billion of American merchandise pouring into Saudi Arabia in 1977, experiences unloading delays of 125 to 150 days, with some ships standing by for 200 days. The problem is not exclusively lack of physical port facilities but also lack of organization, customs delays, papers missing, etc. ARAMCO has noted that a major company concern is the increasing frequency of automobile accidents on the overcrowded highways of the Eastern Province. It has urged its employees to leave their cars at home and has put 50 new air-conditioned buses into service, bringing its total fleet to 300.[5]

A significant sign of conservation is the traditional attitude toward women. In Saudi Arabia they are heavily veiled, forbidden to drive cars or to travel alone and have little opportunity for public employment. Nevertheless, about 250,000 Saudi girls attend public schools and 11,000 are university students, with half of the latter studying abroad. If the sociologists are right--that to teach a man is to teach an individual, but to teach a woman is to teach a nation--then the Saudi social fabric is already being jarred. Women's liberation, however, is not in Saudi Arabia a matter of revolution but rather of evolution. Here and there women radio and TV announcers, physicians, psychologists, newspaper columnists and teachers are to be seen. Of paramount importance is the attitude of the men toward the emancipation of women. That too is changing, especially among the younger, educated Saudis. More than one young Saudi has informed this writer of his recent marriage to a Syrian, Jordanian or Iraqi girl, because he could not find an educated Saudi spouse. In time, this could undermine the preference for cousin marriages which made tribal and village societies such closely knit units. Some high ranking government officials have cautiously proposed that women be allowed to work--for the very practical purpose of alleviating the Saudi labor shortage. The process is underway, but rapid progress is problematical: the Saudis have certainly followed with concern the [1978] riots in Iran due, in part, to the Shah's policy of taking some steps to emancipate Iranian women. The religious elite in Saudi Arabia still plays a powerful role in the education establishment. Helping to undermine this role, however, this writer believes, are the 8,000 students between the ages of 20 and 30 studying at United States colleges.

The emergence of a middle class is also eroding the traditional structure.[6] This group is made up of managers,

administrators, technicians, clerks, teachers of modern
subjects, lawyers, scientists, army officers and others
in government and business. They have prestige and socio-
economic power, and occupy their positions because of
personal qualifications, not their royal family ties.
Their numbers are small and, to date, they have avoided
immersing themselves in political matters. As development
plans move forward, however, it is safe to assume that this
option will reverse itself. The Arabic word for "old man,"
sheik, is also a title of respect. Yet the middle class
may, in time, challenge the hallowed position of age and
experience with a more lethal weapon: a modern, secular
education.

CONCLUSION

     In a part of the world where the imperial powers,
especially the British and the French, staked out claims
and interfered in the internal affairs of the indigenous
inhabitants, where spheres of influence were common and
the League of Nations mandate system flourished, British
and Saudi interests curiously complemented each other.
The by-product of Britain's policies helped to bring into
being the Wahhabi state. Britain's primary area of interest
was the periphery of the Arabian Peninsula. Consequently,
the British played a dual role: they assisted in the establishment of Saudi Arabia but simultaneously allowed the
ultra-conservative Wahhabi doctrine to flourish in the
interior at a time when most other Arab countries were being
acculturated by the presence of the Europeans. By contrast,
the Americans, in their search for oil, penetrated into the
desert with their families and their civilization. The
British subsidized Ibn Saud but just enough to keep his
government afloat. The petroleum that the Americans
discovered provided, eventually, more money than the
Saudis could spend. The petro-income speeded up the
erosion of conservatism, slowly at first, but with increasing
momentum in more recent years. This conservatism, which emphasized faith, community and tradition and was so long
preserved by British policy, Wahhabism and geography, now
began to be buffeted by reason, individualism and change.
     The imponderables which this condition portends are
impossible to forecast, but most observers see little possibility of radical, abrupt change. Overall this may be true,
but spotty aberrations could appear. The 1973 oil embargo
comes to mind. The proliferation of the Saudi family
throughout government may become an irritant to the rising
middle class. The next succession in government may not be
as well orchestrated as it has been in the past. With
potential enemies near her borders, the Saudis "are building
an army whose officer corps...may contain a Colonel Quadafi
[sic]."[7] Indeed, the financial rewards of a military

upheaval are enticing, and this form of discontent has its history in the Middle East. Also, as the "banker" for Egypt, Syria and Jordan, the Saudis have been drawn deeper into these countries' affairs, and this might produce unsettling effects at home.

Will Saudi Arabia continue to expand oil production to accommodate the United States, even though she cannot use the additional revenues? Would she impose another oil embargo or production cutbacks if movement toward an Arab-Israeli peace bogs down? What might be the consequences for Israel of a Saudi Arabia which decides to become more adventurous in international politics? Will the Saudis be flexible on the subject of East Jerusalem? Only time will provide the undisputed answers, but it will be instructive to analyze each of these questions as Wahhabi conservatism recedes slowly into the past.

NOTES

1. St. Anthony's College, Oxford, Middle East Centre, DS 42.1, Note by India Office on Arabia, 26 April 1915.

2. Foreign Office File 686/15, Political Department, Baghdad, to Arab Bureau, 28 August 1918.

3. Colonial Office File 727/2, T. E. Lawrence to Foreign Office, 16 September 1921.

4. Benjamin Shwadran, *The Middle East, Oil and the Great Powers* (3rd ed.; Jerusalem: Israel Universities Press, 1973), p. 319.

5. ARAMCO's annual report to the Saudi Government, *ARAMCO 1977*, p. 12.

6. For a detailed examination of this subject see William Rugh, "Emergence of a New Middle Class in Saudi Arabia," *Middle East Journal* (Winter 1973), 7-20.

7. John C. Campbell, "Oil Power in the Middle East," *Foreign Affairs* (October 1977), 104.

21
Islam and Political Values in Saudi Arabia, Egypt, and Syria

R. Stephen Humphreys

Most observers of the Arab world would agree that Islam is currently playing a strikingly active role in the political life of that region--more so, perhaps, than at any time since Nasir's seizure of power in Egypt in 1954. It thus seems an appropriate moment to reconsider an old (but recently rather neglected) problem in Middle Eastern studies, that of the ways in which Islam may affect the political values and policy choices of the ruling elites in preponderantly Muslim countries.

Insofar as Islam can be demonstrated to have a substantial and predictable impact on political behavior, it is clearly of high importance for American and European policy planners to develop a valid understanding of this impact. Such an understanding must work at several levels. In everyday, pragmatic terms, it must involve a sense for the religious implications of specific policies and issues--for example, those aspects of the Arab-Israeli dispute, such as the ultimate disposition of the holy places in Jerusalem and Hebron, which might engage the religious values of the Saudi political elite; or the degree to which popular resistance to family planning in Egypt may be felt and expressed in terms of Islamic values. These two issues and perhaps a few others are obvious, overt cases of the intertwining of religion and politics, and they are so understood by almost everybody who has occasion to deal with the Arab states. But such an *ad hoc* issue-oriented understanding is very likely to degenerate into an empty repetition of slogans and rules of thumb, and is in any case inadequate to deal with the subtler and deeper ties between these two aspects of social life. What is needed is a more systematic sense of how political issues are felt to be religious issues

Islam and Political Values in Saudi Arabia, Egypt and Syria is reprinted by permission of *The Middle East Journal*, Vol. 33, No. 1, Winter, 1979.

as well among many groups in Arab Muslim societies. In
more formal terms, we wish to define a model of cultural
behavior in which a set of conceptions identified as religious in nature can act to create effective political
norms.

Among many possible approaches to this problem, I have
chosen one which consists in trying to define the elementary
religio-political orientations available to contemporary
Muslim statesmen, then in exploring how these orientations
are reflected in the political structures and policies of
three quite disparate states (though all three are united
in being both Arab and predominantly Sunni Muslim). The
orientations which I shall define represent simply the
polar extremes implicit in contemporary Muslim thought;
*they are ideal types, not a descriptive classification of
empirical reality.* But by beginning with ideal-typical
orientations, each of them distinguished by a high degree
of coherence and logical/emotional consistency, we may better
appreciate both some of the key values underlying political
behavior in the Arab world and many of the problems obstructing
the realization of these values.

When we say that Islam affects politics, what do we
mean? "Islam," by itself, is a highly diffuse and equivocal
term. It is used both by outside observers and members of
the Muslim community to refer to personal faith, theological
doctrine, cultural attitudes, patterns of everyday behavior
(both normative and actual), and a multitude of organizational
structures--all without any clear or explicit differentiation.
All of these things, moreover, do enter into the shaping of
political values because all are equally a part of Islam as it
is understood by its adherents. However, I believe that these
various aspects of Islam can be comprehended in a simpler and
analytically more adequate way by saying that Islam may influence political values (and hence political behavior) on
three levels: 1) as a religion strictly speaking--*i.e.* as a
system of theological beliefs and transcendentally fixed
ethical duties; 2) as an ideology; 3) as a symbol of cultural
identity. It is the interaction of these three modes of
religion which produces a distinctive religio-political
orientation.

Islam has of course never been monolithic; it has never
meant the same thing to all Muslims, and this diversity of
understanding has always been a fruitful source of social and
political conflict. But in pre-modern times all at least
shared a specifically religious interpretation of life; for
everyone, all events could be given meaning and value in
terms of some conceptual framework founded on the undoubted
facts of the Unity of God and the Prophethood of Muhammad.
Since the mid-nineteenth century, however, the intellectual
avant garde in Muslim lands, including many members of the
political elite, have increasingly been attracted by secularist
ideologies (liberalism, positivism, racial nationalism,
Marxism, etc.). As the circumstances of material life came

more and more to be dominated by Europe, European modes of
thought seemed to many to be a more adequate instrument
for dealing with reality. The stock of ideas thus introduced
into the Arab world is a very disparate one, to be sure, but
for our purposes the whole body of them may be called
Secularism, since all these ideologies concur in resolving
the main questions of value and meaning according to this
worldly criteria, while relegating revealed religion to (at
best) the role of guardian of the individual conscience.
Among Muslims who have become conversant with secularist
thought and are aware of its powerful and manifold appeal,
but who wish to preserve the essence of their tradition,
one can identify two types of response to this challenge,
responses which I shall call Fundamentalism and Modernism.
These, together with Secularism, can be taken as the three
polar orientations around which tend to cluster the thought
and behavior of Muslims (or at least persons of Muslim
heritage) in the contemporary world. It should be stressed
again that these three orientations are ideal types, abstracted
from a complex reality in which the values and attitudes of
any one person are likely to contain an admixture of all three,
tending towards one or the other according to the issue involved. From another point of view, Fundamentalism, Modernism
and Secularism are not the terms used by Muslims themselves
to describe the current religious situation--at least not
in the way in which I am using them--and they might not be
acceptable to many persons who do in fact adhere to the ideas
which they name.
     We may define Fundamentalism as the reaffirmation, in a
radically changed environment, of traditional modes of understanding and behavior. In contrast to conservatism or
traditionalism, which assumes that things can and should go
on much as they have for generations past, Fundamentalism
recognizes and tries to speak to a changed milieu, an altered
atmosphere of expectations. Fundamentalism is by no means
a blind opponent of all social change, but it insists that
change must be governed by traditional values and modes of
understanding. In an Islamic context, Fundamentalism asserts
not only the literal truth of the Qur'an but also that its
commandments, legal as well as ritual, are fully incumbent
on modern man. Specifically, it affirms the continuing
rightness of the Qur'an's prohibition of intoxicants and
interest on loans, its rules for divorce and inheritance
(which generally favor the male), its permission of plural
marriage, and its penalties for certain criminal acts (*e.g.*
amputation of the hand for theft). In some circumstances
it may be impossible to fulfill the Qur'an's commands and
prohibitions, but they remain valid all the same. For
Fundamentalism, the Qur'an is not the only source of value;
the conduct of the Prophet and the first generation of believers is also normative. Given changing circumstances,
one cannot always imitate them exactly, but one can at least
study their example and try to act as they would have done

in the same situation. Finally, Fundamentalism reveres the
lawyers and theologians of medieval Islam, and especially
the vast structure of ritual, moral norms and positive law
(collectively called the *shari'a*) which they created. The
shari'a is a comprehensive description of the behavior expected
from every Muslim. If it cannot be instituted in its totality
in a modern state (and in fact never has been) it nevertheless
remains the sole valid basis for personal conduct and social
life. On the question of whether the *shari'a* can be modified
so as to fit modern circumstances, Fundamentalism displays
two somewhat contradictory tendencies. On the one hand, some
Fundamentalists regard the *shari'a* as a fixed corpus of
commands and prohibitions; its established injunctions cannot
be altered and may be added to only when situations arise for
which it contains no clear directives. Other Fundamentalists,
however, would prefer to emphasize the *sources* of the *shari'a*
(Qur'an, prophetic teaching and example, the attitudes of the
early community) and the juristic processes (*fiqh*) by which
these sources or raw materials can be elaborated into a
comprehensive code of conduct. But it should be noted that
in specific cases, even the adherents of this latter approach
will tend to accept the traditional formulae defined by the
medieval jurists.

     To repeat a point made above, Fundamentalism is more a
tendency than a current social reality. It is a set of
attitudes approximated among many groups and individuals, but
totally and exclusively subscribed to by very few. Because
of its focus on history and scripture, Fundamentalism is an
orientation which can only appeal to persons of some education,
those who are aware of and feel an affinity for the high
culture of traditional Islam. Fundamentalism is decisively
not a folk religion of the illiterate or semi-literate peasantry
and proletariat, though in some circumstances its themes may
be very effective in mobilizing the Islamic sentiments and
sense of identity among such groups. (The anti-imperialist
struggle in the Arab world, for example, has drawn heavily
on Islamic symbols, as have the campaigns to create a broadly
based national consciousness). At the same time, Fundamentalism
is an orientation perhaps most common among groups which find
themselves being pushed aside or threatened by the evolution
of society. Almost everywhere, these include the artisans and
shopkeepers of the great cities, the merchants and middling
landowners of the provincial towns, and of course the guardians
of the old Islamic tradition, the *'ulama'*. But Saudi Arabia
demonstrates that a very broad commitment to Fundamentalist
ideals can be maintained even among a modernizing, techno-
cratic elite. And the anti-constitutional riots in Syria
during the winter and spring of 1973 show that Fundamentalist
ideas remain powerful symbols for mobilizing mass action.
In any case, one cannot deny that Fundamentalism has a strong
intellectual and emotional appeal even to those Muslims who
do not fully accept its premises--partly, no doubt, because
of its internal consistency and forthrightness, but also

because it stands as a reproach to many partly secularized
Muslims, men and women who have become uneasy about their
accommodation to the modern world and who despair of their
future in it.

Modernism, the alternative response to the Secularist
challenge, yields nothing to Fundamentalism in its reverence
for the traditional foci of Islamic thought: the Qur'an, the
life of the Prophet, the example of the first Muslims, the
shari'a. But Modernism not merely reaffirms but also re-
evaluates, from top to bottom, the significance of these
things for modern life. If the Qur'an remains undoubtedly
the Word of God, its commands are to be understood as a call
for human progress. Modernism points to the Qur'an restriction
of slavery, its enhancement of the status of women, its limitations on the right of private vengeance, its consistent
appeal for charity and social solidarity. These things were
a great step forward in the social milieu of seventh century
Arabia, and they are processes not yet completed in the
twentieth century. To bind oneself by the literal sense of
the Qur'an's commands and prohibitions would be in many cases
to defy the true meaning of God's word. For Modernism as
for Fundamentalism, the Prophet and the early Muslims are
models to be emulated, but with an altered emphasis. It goes
without saying that one can no longer imitate their actions;
therefore one must seek the underlying moral purpose of their
acts and model his conduct on that. The *shari'a*, finally,
may well be the highest achievement of traditional Islam,
but Modernists recall that it was shaped by scholars who were
concerned to deduce an Islamic way of life which would fit
the conditions of their time. The *shari'a* thus cannot be
understood as a fixed repository of commands and prohibitions
but should be viewed as the end result of a long process of
jurisprudence. Modernism in fact prefers to stress the
underlying concepts of Islamic jurisprudence, especially
maslaha ("the public good") and *ijtihad* ("independent juristic
investigation"), and hopes to use such concepts to produce
modern legislation which will both embody the highest ideals
of Islam and be eminently suited to modern life. The *shari'a*'s
positive precepts are not to be abandoned lightly--many are
still valid, many others are suitable for contemporary society
with some modification--but they are not sacrosanct.

Modernism has always seemed attractive to outside
observers of the Muslim world, but its fortunes within that
world have been uneven. For this many reasons might be
offered, but I will propose only two. First, Modernism has
not been able to achieve a synthesis as comprehensive and
internally consistent as that to which Fundamentalism can
appeal; it remains a series of sketches and essays, though
some of these are brilliant and suggestive. Second (and I
suspect more important) Modernism finds it difficult to defend
itself from the Fundamentalist charge that it is merely a
cover for moral laxity and secularism. From a Fundamentalist
perspective Modernism is simply an excuse for setting aside

the traditional doctrines whenever they seem inconvenient
or embarrassing. And it must be admitted that this charge
has some merit, for Modernism has had a particular appeal
as a slogan to certain political leaders who have on many
occasions displayed strongly secularist tendencies--Nasir
of Egypt, Bourguiba of Tunisia, or Hafiz al-Asad of Syria.
A Modernist orientation is perhaps most likely to be found
among the Westernized intelligentsia and professionals--but
these are precisely the groups whose attitudes are generally
most alien to the great mass of the population, and among
whom secularism and overt hostility to religion have struck
the deepest roots.

In spite of its problems, however, one should not
entirely discount Modernism's impact on the contemporary
Muslim consciousness. For one thing, its two great Arabic
classics (Muhammad 'Abduh's *Risalat al-Tawhid* and Muhammad
Husayn Haykal's *Hayat Muhammad*) have sold very widely indeed.
Likewise, the interpretations of Islam taught in the government schools of Egypt, Syria and elsewhere are almost certainly Modernist in inspiration. Finally, and rather surprisingly, the works of the leading publicists of the Muslim
Brethren, written in the late 1940s and early 1950s, are
militantly Fundamentalist in tone but distinctly Modernist
in content. In spite of the Nasir regime's bitter conflict
with the Muslim Brethren, works by at least two of its members
(Sayyid Qutb and Mustafa al-Siba'i) were widely disseminated
in revolutionary Egypt and plainly contributed much to the
official ideology of Arab Socialism.

We have so far described Fundamentalism and Modernism
as religious systems, and we have seen that even on that
level these orientations have important political implications.
But because Islam claims to regulate in quite specific ways
the personal conduct of believers and even the organization of
the community, Islam has always been not only a system of
belief but an ideology. As an ideology, it provides a conceptual framework in terms of which public issues are perceived
and articulated; moreover, it defines the bases of solidarity
and cohesion within society as well as the politically relevant
groups of society and their appropriate roles. From this, it
follows that there are political consequences to these religious
orientations of a far more systematic kind than we have yet
discussed. Each orientation implies an ideal polity which it
must struggle to achieve to the fullest extent possible.
Without attempting a comprehensive definition of politics within
an Islamic order, we can assert that the critical foci of any
serious political discussion would be the following: 1) the
religious identity of the political elite; 2) appropriate
sources of public law; 3) acceptable forms of government;
4) the role of religious specialists in politics; 5) the
political significance of Muslim solidarity.

Fundamentalism tries to maintain the political outlook
of the great Sunni jurists writing between the eleventh and
fourteenth centuries. In modern terms, this outlook can be

formulated in the following manner:

1) In a Muslim country, the entire political elite should be practicing Muslims. Non-Muslims are certainly to be tolerated as members of society and their liberties are to be protected, but they should not be rulers over Muslims--which is to say that they should not wield independent policy making authority.

2) The *shari'a*, according to some traditionally accepted mode of interpretation, should be the entire law of the state. Indeed, the state properly has no autonomous legislative powers, but only the right to issue such administrative regulations as will enable the *shari'a* to be enforced. Moreover, if circumstances make it impossible to enforce some aspects of the *shari'a* (*e.g.* the dicta concerning slavery or relations with non-Muslim states), it is better to set these portions aside altogether and rule through overtly secular state decrees. For in no case is one entitled to tamper with the *shari'a*, modifying or reinterpreting it to suit current whims and sensibilities.

It is true that many Fundamentalists would not subscribe to this extremely rigorous doctrine. They would concede that much of the *shari'a* is ritual commandment or moral precept rather than law in any proper sense, that even in its truly legal portions it is full of contradictions and ambiguities, that many of the exigencies of contemporary life are inadequately provided for. Traditionally, such problem were assigned to the judiciary, which would deal with them on a case-by-case basis through the exercise of *ijtihad*. But it may be that justice and the public interest (which are the true goals of the *shari'a*) are better served by permitting the state to issue a codified version of the *shari'a*. But such legislation must adhere as closely as possible to the traditional texts; moreover, the letter of the *shari'a* cannot be employed against its evident spirit, nor may weakly attested opinions be preferred to the authoritative interpretations of the great jurists. In short, the legislator's work is one not of creation, but merely of harmonization and clarification.

3) As to the form of government, traditional juristic thought recognized as fully legitimate only the universal caliphate, in which one man made a contract with the entire Muslim community to wield all executive and judicial authority on its behalf. But with the collapse of the caliphate the Sunni jurists were compelled to deal with the reality of military dictatorship, government overtly based on main force. After quite literally some centuries of soul searching, a solution was finally attained in the work of Ibn Taymiyya and Ibn Khaldun: *any* government, however it came to power, was legitimate so long as it ruled in full accord with the *shari'a* and framed policy through close consultation with the *shari'a*'s recognized interpreters, the *'ulama'*. Modern Fundamentalism must likewise contend with reality,

in this case the widespread existence of popularly elected
assemblies which claim the authority to make law. Fundamentalism in general concedes them this authority only in
a very restricted sense, if at all (see Para. 2 above). On
the other hand, some spokesmen welcome popular assemblies
as an effective way of realizing the Qur'an's injunction to
rulers to seek consultation. Moreover, they can be a useful device for checking the acts of secularizing despots.
On the whole, they present no more difficult a problem for
Islamic thought than did the military dictatorships of the
middle ages.

   4) Even in contemporary states, the *'ulama'* must have a
decisive voice in articulating, or at least reviewing and
ratifying, all governmental policy, for no other group has
a sufficient knowledge of and commitment to the *shari'a* to
ensure that policy conforms to its demands. The institutional structures for doing this are a matter of simple
utility, but they should not compromise the independent
judgment of the *'ulama'*.

   5) Finally, Islam should be the main basis of solidarity,
both among the citizens of any one country and in the relations among Muslim states throughout the world. Obviously
there are other sentiments which underlie social cohesion--
ethnic identity, patriotism, common citizenship--and these
are perfectly legitimate so long as they do not outweigh
the duty of Muslims to be brothers to one another.   In
foreign affairs, plainly one cannot avoid dealings with
non-Muslim states, but these should be regulated on the
basis of necessity and utility to the Muslim community.

   Among the major Arab states (and even Muslim states
generally) Saudi Arabia is the only one which closely
approximates the Fundamentalist criteria. With the partial
exceptions of Libya and Morocco, it is alone in relying on
religion as its main basis of legitimacy. It is certainly
true that the House of Sa'ud has acquired many claims to
the loyalty of its subjects. Among these would be the
prestige which Bedouin society traditionally accords to
the wealthiest, most prolific and militarily most effective
families in its midst. Another such claim would be the
dynasty's success in imposing and maintaining a *Pax Saudiana*
over the once turbulent and still proud tribes of the
Peninsula, and in undertaking (even before the advent of
oil wealth) a successful program of sedentarization.
Finally, but only in the last two decades, the Saudis have
been able to distribute lavish and growing material rewards
among their followers. But at bottom, the capacity of the
House of Sa'ud to command assent rests on its maintenance
of the alliance made two centuries ago (in the 1700s) between
the reforming *shaykh* Muhammad ibn 'Abd al-Wahhab and the
Bedouin chief Muhammad ibn Sa'ud. This alliance was based
on Ibn Sa'ud's commitment to use his military prowess to
realize the rigorous religious reform advocated by Ibn

'Abd al-Wahhab throughout the Arabian Peninsula. The same
program inspired 'Abd al-'Aziz's restoration of the Saudi
kingdom in the early decades of this century. Even today
the descendants of Ibn 'Abd al-Wahhab constitute a clan
whose prestige and influence are second only to those of
the ruling family itself. The two families are closely
linked by marriage, and many high government posts are held
by members of the *shaykh's* family. Altogether, then, the
membership of the Saudi political elite as well as its claims
to authority accord unusually well with Fundamentalist
criteria.

Much of the same harmony of ideal and reality is found
in the Saudi legal system, for it is based largely on the
shari'a as traditionally used and understood. An early conflict between ruler and *'ulama'* may help to bring out the
significance of this point. In 1927 King 'Abd al-'Aziz
proposed to codify the legal materials in the *shari'a* on
the basis of the doctrines in it which conformed most rigidly
to the Qur'an and the example of the Prophet. Such a project
might well seem absolutely unobjectionable in a religiously
oriented state, but *'ulama'* resistance compelled the king to
forego it. In their minds, codification meant tampering,
the selection of some of the traditional texts and the
suppression of others, and it required *shari'a* materials to
be arranged according to foreign criteria. The state, in
short, would be arrogating to itself the right to manipulate
God's law to suit its own needs--a process which once begun
could not easily be checked.

Finally, Islamic identity is vital not only to the
internal political structure of Saudi Arabia but also to
its foreign affairs. It is of course well known that during
Nasir's later years, all Arab states were willy-nilly divided
into "progressive" and "reactionary", and that in the hope of
countering Nasir's initiatives King Faysal spent much effort
trying to construct an Islamic Pact. The project ultimately
came to nothing and proved unnecessary after Nasir's demise;
still, it suggests the ideological orientation which seemed
most significant and effective to the late monarch. The
current regime is using its vast cash reserves to support a
change from alliance making to institutionalized development
aid, as embodied in the Saudi Development Fund and the Islamic
Development Bank. The latter, at least, intends to give
development loans, at no interest, to Muslim countries and
Muslim minority communities only. Finally, one might note
the annual pilgrimage, which lends prestige to the Saudis
and gives some occasion for statements on the need for
world wide Islamic solidarity.

Saudi Arabia is clearly a critical test case for
Fundamentalism, for that country's experience will demonstrate
whether it is possible to reconcile sudden and immense wealth,
rapid technological change and strict adherence to the norms
of traditional Islam. So far, one must admit, the Saudis have
done rather well, but they still confront some serious problems.

The most obvious of these is the corruption and demoraliza-
tion among the elite induced by the influx of oil revenues
after World War II--a trend only partially checked by King
Faysal. But doubtless more significant is the simple
incapacity of the *shari'a* to meet all the needs of a modern
state. As long ago as 1931 King 'Abd al-'Aziz set aside the
commercial chapters of the *shari'a* with his Regulation on
Commerce. This Regulation, still generally in force, was
derived from the Ottoman Commercial Code of 1850, which was
itself based on French models. (The Saudi version, however,
does omit all reference to interest.) Likewise, the country's
vital oil concessions were drawn up in terms of Western
contract law, though internally the civil procedures of the
shari'a are still relied upon. Finally, Saudi Arabia has
bowed to Western moral-legal norms in its abolition of the
slave trade (in 1936) and later of slavery *per se* (in 1962).
None of these things fatally weakens the country's religious
foundations; indeed, the bulk of its institutions and the
whole tone of its public discourse are witness to the integrity
of its vision of Islam. But enough compromises have already
been made to suggest that the future is not wholly secure
from Secularist corrosion.

One of the advantages of the Fundamentalist evaluation
of the state is that it is clear cut; it is fairly simple
to discern how closely any given polity conforms to its
criteria. Such is regrettably not the case with the Modernist
analysis, for while the theoretical distinctions between
Modernist and Secularist views of politics are very clear,
the practical consequences of these views overlap freely.
The problem is two-fold. On the one hand, Modernism believes that a critical understanding of contemporary social
reality is essential to any attempt to give Islamic value
and meaning to that reality, to rethink Islam so that it
may fully meet the needs of modern man. On the other,
Secularism is perfectly willing to appeal to Islamic cultural
and religious symbols whenever popular attitudes seem to demand this. It is thus often very difficult to decide whether
a government is sincerely trying to meet the high standards
set by Modernism or is simply making those compromises with
social reality which Secularism readily allows for. Because
of this ambiguity it seems best to consider simultaneously
the political outlook of both orientations.

> 1) Secularist ideologies insist that an individual's
> religious affiliation can have no political consequences;
> any person should be able to hold any office in the state,
> and the legal status of all citizens must be equal. As a
> practical matter, however, one may permit Muslims a monopoly
> of the most sensitive posts until social attitudes have
> evolved sufficiently to make this expedient unnecessary.
> Modernism here is in a dilemma: it appreciates the concept
> of equal citizenship, but it also wishes to create a state
> in which specifically Muslim values underlie citizens'

rights and duties. Perhaps the most common solution
(in cases where there is a significant non-Muslim population) is to require the head of state to be a Muslim while
leaving parliamentary and cabinet office open to non-Muslims.
In this way it is possible to recognize (though not in a
logically fully satisfying manner) two highly valued
principles, civic equality and a Muslim polity.

2) Both Modernism and Secularism concur in some form of
the principle of popular sovereignty, from which it follows
that the right to legislate rests with the people and its
authorized representatives. But Modernism wishes to control
this right by insisting that it be exercised in accordance
with the spirit of the Qur'an and the Prophet's teaching.
How does one preserve this spirit? Here Modernism is
ambivalent, for it has so far evolved no systematic jurisprudence by which specific legislation may consistently be
derived from these basic sources. A common, though perhaps
not very satisfying, device is to utilize *shari'a* materials
wherever possible, but this requires an admission that it is
legitimate to rip these out of their original contexts and
apply them in new ways. However, this approach at least
permits legislation to retain some Islamic coloring while
a new jurisprudence is worked out; at the same time, it
recognizes the Modernist principle that the Muslim community
must be free to legislate in accordance with its current
needs.

Secularism, of course, recognizes no rationale for law
save contemporary utility. Secularist governments may
certainly draw on the *shari'a* for specific enactments where
popular custom and sentiment so demands--family and personal
status law is the classic case in point--but ultimately the
shari'a is no more than a human construct, appropriate perhaps to a certain stage of social evolution but subject to
the law of change and progress.

3) As in the case of Fundamentalism, it is really not
possible to identify the forms of government called for by
Modernism and Secularism. The latter orientation, of course,
informs a vast range of political ideologies and requires
no further comment here. Modernism, because of the circumstances of its birth and development, has an historical
affinity for parliamentary liberalism. Many Modernists
have argued that a Muslim community can act to preserve
its identity and its best traditions only if effective
political authority is vested in the community itself.
Such arguments are commonly buttressed by appeals to the
Quranic injunction calling on the Prophet to consult with
his people and to the primitive caliphate, which is interpreted as an egalitarian and democratic regime. On the
other hand, the sorry record of many parliamentary regimes
in the Muslim world has been profoundly disheartening, and
Modernists who wish to have some impact on policy making
have had to enter marriages of convenience with whatever
regimes lie to hand.

4) Since Secularism regards religion as entirely a
personal matter, it defines no specific role in the political
process for the spokesmen of religion. The support of the
'*ulama*' may of course be sought if that will contribute to
the success of controversial policies, but that is much the
same as seeking an accommodation with any other powerful
group. Modernism, on the other hand, would like to assign
a constitutional role of consultation and revision to the
'*ulama*', or some equally authoritative body of interpreters
of Islam. Unfortunately, the '*ulama*' as presently constituted are out of touch with current needs and realities
and there is no other group adequately trained in the
sacred texts to replace them. What is needed (but does not
yet exist) is a radical reform in the educational system so
as to produce scholars capable of applying traditional
knowledge to contemporary problems.

5) Modernism seems generally to replicate the Fundamentalist analysis of religion as the proper basis of social
cohesion and international cooperation. Given conditions
in the real world, of course, Modernists are sometimes uneasy about the governments with which Islamic solidarity
would link them, but that fact does not alter the ideal.
Secularist attitudes in this matter are apparent and need
not detain us.

We shall not find among the Arab states any which are
fully and unambiguously Modernist or Secularist. In most
countries the majority of the political elite are inspired
by one or the other of these orientations (at least as
evidenced by their public statements), and yet they are
not free to make either of them the basis of a systematic
policy, even if they knew how. If government is to be
legitimate and effective, it must to some degree conform
to the values and sense of self identity of its subjects.
No purely Secularist ideology, however, is acceptable today
to the vast majority of the Arab masses, and even highly
secularizing regimes must be prepared to justify their
programs in terms of Islamic symbols, to show that their
policies do not contradict "Islam" even if they are not
primarily inspired by it. Modernism, hampered by its
vagueness and lack of a clear program, is subject to attack
from both sides, especially at times of social crisis and
ideological confusion. Still, there are clearly states with
tendencies in one direction or the other, and we cannot
ignore their attempts to resolve the political dilemmas
of Secularism and Modernism simply because they have not
entirely succeeded.

Egypt is perhaps the classic case of a Modernist-
oriented state, but it has by no means been a pure or
consistent adherent of this tendency. In no other land,
certainly, are the preconditions for a Modernist stance
towards politics better met. To begin with, Egypt was an
early and committed modernizer, in that it has since the

early nineteenth century increasingly shaped its laws and
institutions in accordance with contemporary European models.
Moreover, by the end of World War I at latest, Egypt had
produced a substantial number of men who were thoroughly
familiar--one might even say imbued--with European modes of
political thought and behavior. At the same time, Egypt
was one of the cradles of Islamic Modernism, which has been
a constant and influential strain of thought there since the
1890s. Modernism in Egypt, moreover, has been represented
not only by thinkers but also by men in a position to shape
public policy. In this regard it suffices to mention
Muhammad 'Abduh, chief *mufti* under Lord Cromer's administration; the three reform-minded rectors of al-Azhar (Mustafa
al-Maraghi, Mustafa 'Abd al-Raziq, and Mahmud Shaltut); and
'Abd al-Razzaq al-Sanhuri, who was largely responsible for
drafting not only the Egyptian Civil Code of 1948 but also
the Iraqi Civil Code of 1953. Even Jamal 'Abd al-Nasir,
who was in so many ways a secularizing figure, rather consistently invoked Islamic symbols within a Modernist framework in order to legitimize both his foreign policy and his
Arab Socialist ideology. Even if his true personal orientation was not of Modernist inspiration, it remains the case
that he found Modernism to be the most appropriate vehicle
for conveying his socio-political goals to the Egyptian
people.
     The continuing influence of Modernism in Egypt is
perhaps best evidenced by the debates on the proper role
of Islam which underlay the Constitution of 1971. From
the outset all parties agreed (overtly, at least) that the
new constitution must name Islam as the state religion, and
there was likewise broad consensus that the *shari'a* should
be in some sense a basis of legislation. But the precise
role of the *shari'a* was hotly disputed, with some circles
saying that legislators should operate simply according
to its spirit, while others demanded that it be rigidly
adhered to as the sole material source of legislation. In
the end, the relevant passage of the constitution (Art. 1:2)
was phrased as follows: "The principles of the Islamic
shari'a are a major source of legislation." On the face
of it, this would appear to be a liberal Modernist position,
and the intent behind it was clearly brought out by the
comments of a member of the drafting committee. By the
shari'a, he asserted, we should understand not the whole
corpus of medieval jurisprudence but only the Qur'an and
the authentic teaching of the Prophet. This approach, he
continued, was fully in accord with the best and most
ancient practice, for if one examined the conduct of the
first generation of Muslims, it was plain that they were
guided not by blind adherence to fixed rules but by their
sense of how best to serve the public welfare.
     Two points in these constitutional debates deserve
attention. First, the formal identification of Egypt as
a Muslim state, which was of vital importance to men of

both Fundamentalist and Modernist tendencies, could not
have displeased Secularist circles in the government. This
is so not only because these circles would recognize that
Islam was an essential element in the cultural identity of
most Egyptians, but also because such an identification would
justify the state in continuing its long established policy
(dating from the 1890s) of an evercloser supervision and
control of the Muslim religious establishment. As to the
shari'a's role in legislation, it is a moot point whether
the constitution makers were sincere or hypocritical in the
definition they proposed, but through the formulation of
Art. 1:2 they clearly did assert that if Egypt was to be
an Islamic state, it would also be a modernist one.

No Arab state has been so frankly and vigorously secularizing as have Turkey and Iran. Still, Secularist tendencies
are not difficult to identify among contemporary Arab governments, and none has been so bold (and at the same time so
frustrated) as Syria since the Ba'thist seizure of power in
1963. The Ba'thist ideology professed by the current regime
and imbedded in the 1973 Constitution is ultimately the
creation of a Syrian Christian, Michel 'Aflaq; the party
itself was founded by 'Aflaq and a Sunni Muslim, Salah
al-Baytar; and since the late 1940s the Ba'th has found a
disproportionate number of adherents among two of Syria's
minority sects, the Nusayris (generally called 'Alawis) and
the Druze. It is true that Islam has an important place
in Ba'thist thought--not, however, because of the truth of
Islam's social and religious teachings, but because it is
a vital constitutive element in Arab nationalist consciousness. In all this, clearly, neither Fundamentalism nor
Modernism has had any significant role to play.

One's impression is that Islamic symbols are much
less a part of official political discourse in Syria than
in Egypt, in spite of the evident conservatism of religious
and social mores even in the largest cities, Damascus and
Aleppo. It might be argued that Syria provides a rather
favorable milieu for political Secularism, for both demo-
graphic and historical reasons. To begin with the former,
three-quarters of her population is Sunni Muslim, but this
still leaves a proportion of other confessional communities
too high to be ignored in the political process, at least
in the context of an integrated modern state. The historical
reasons favoring Secularism are two: 1) since 1966 Syrian
politics has been dominated by military men of Nusayri
background, who have every interest in not calling attention
to their sectarian status; 2) on a deeper level, for many
of the Syrian political elite, the present Syrian Arab
Republic is an artificially truncated entity which ought to
include Lebanon and Palestine as well--but such an eventuality
would only increase the proportion of confessional minorities
in the country, so that the erection of an Islamic state would
be even harder to justify than it now is. In any case, it is
true that Islam has never been recognized as the official

state religion in any of Syria's post-independence constitutions, though both the 1950 and 1973 documents have given
it a special status by identifying the *shari'a* as a principal
source of legislation and by stating that the head of state
must be a Muslim. The 1973 Constitution was indeed a critical
test case for political Secularism in Syria, for its publication in draft form in January 1973 provoked a storm of
protests and riots which ended only in April at a cost of
scores of lives. Whatever the "real" causes of the violence,
it claimed to be directed at the irreligiousness of the
draft constitution, which recognized Islam only by naming
the *shari'a* as a main source of legislation. This clause,
however, was inserted in no very prominent place, and its
curt matter-of-factness was in striking contrast to the
fervent Ba'thist rhetoric of the rest of the text. President
al-Asad quickly agreed to a compromise clause stating that
the President must be a Muslim, but when this failed to quell
the disorder he steadfastly refused to take the final step
demanded by the protesters, that of naming Islam as the
state religion.

Although we can identify the dominant tendency in Egypt
and Syria, we cannot, however, say that either state has fully
realized the vision of politics implicit in this tendency.
Since the 1952 revolution, Egypt has been deeply tempted by
Secularism and Fundamentalism simultaneously. On the one
hand, the Nasir regime showed itself determined to reduce if
not eliminate the autonomy of the country's religious institutions. Hundreds of privately endowed mosques were taken
over by the government. Al-Azhar was subjected to a thorough-
going reorganization which effectively made it just another
state university, though admittedly one with a prestigious
school of religious studies. Finally, the *shari'a* courts
which had heretofore administered the personal status law
were consolidated with the national courts (responsible for
civil and criminal law) in 1956, thus stripping the *'ulama'*
of their last stronghold in the judicial system. But in
spite of these shows of force, neither Nasir nor his successor
has dared to promulgate, or even to submit for open discussion, a long-promised reform of Egypt's family and personal
status codes (enacted in 1921 and 1929, and adhering closely
to *shari'a* rules). It is taken for granted that any such
reform will reduce the current legal role of *shari'a* norms,
thus eroding the capacity of traditional Islamic values to
shape personal behavior. But since Islam has always been
understood to govern everyday activity as well as belief
and ritual, any such change will strike at the very heart
of what it means to be a Muslim. In the minds of many
Egyptians (probably a large majority), legal "reform" in
this area would be tantamount to surrendering Egypt's claim
to be a Muslim state and society.

Likewise, the Syrian regime continues to be bedeviled
by the profound Sunni Muslim loyalties of three-quarters of
the country's people. Some commentators have proposed that

although the Sunni bourgeoisie of Syria have articulated
their discontent with the Ba'thist regime in Islamic terms,
the real basis of their hostility is their exclusion by it
from meaningful political participation. There is merit in
this interpretation, and the regime's partial success in
inducing political acquiescence among this group by giving
its members a change to enrich themselves as importers and
contractors in a liberalized economic climate would seem
to reinforce it. Nevertheless, it remains true that a
secularizing government cannot reform the country's *shari'a*-
based personal status code of 1953, for much the same reasons
restraining the Egyptian authorities. Likewise, President
Hafiz al-Asad, whose Nusayri sect is held by many Syrians
to be not only heretical but even completely non-Islamic,
has had to go to great lengths to demonstrate that he is
a true Muslim and that his sect expounds a legitimate variant
of Islamic revelation. (These steps have included attendance
at public worship in the mosque, where Nusayris are never
found, and gaining a formal opinion from the chief of the
"Twelver" Shiite community of Lebanon that the Nusayris are
a branch of the Shi'i faith.) For Syria, a Secularist
political order remains an aspiration which must be deferred
to the distant future.

Of the three religio-political orientations which we
have examined, therefore, only Fundamentalism is embodied
in a political system in a reasonably unalloyed form. As
we have suggested, this is partly due to its internal consistency and powerful emotional appeal as a symbol of
cultural identity, and partly also to the unique alliance
between religion and politics which created the Saudi kingdom.
But it owes something to current circumstances as well. Saudi
Arabia's vast wealth is owed to the very recent exploitation
of a resource which--so far at least--has required little
ideological change. The oil revenues of Saudi Arabia have
in a sense liberated it from the necessity to choose between
tradition and modernity. Such is not the case in resource-
poor and culturally far more heterogeneous countries like
Egypt and Syria. These states, facing enormous economic
pressures, are compelled to undertake a massive transformation of their social structures if they are to have any
hope of freeing themselves from poverty and economic dependence. But social change of this magnitude almost inevitably
implies ideological transformation as well. On another
level, many segments of Egyptian and Syrian society have
developed cultural ideals and aspirations during the past
century which simply cannot be met within the rigid framework of Fundamentalism. For Egypt and Syria, whatever
obeisance may be paid to Fundamentalist norms from time to
time, the future must lie with Secularism or Modernism.

What does all this mean for Western policy in the Arab
world? Certainly it shows that Islam is not a matter of a
few emotional issues only--an irrational aspect of affairs
which may be quarantined, so to speak. Rather, the

relationship of Islam to politics is fundamental and
systemic. Almost all political activity has important
implications for the role of Islamic values in public life,
and these implications are likely to be of vital significance
to some major group either in the political elite or in
society at large. More than that, the contrasting religio-
political orientations of the region (especially in heterogeneous countries like Egypt and Syria) ensure that there
can be no real consensus even among the political elite as
to what are the true Islamic values or how they ought to be
reflected in public policy. It is thus in the nature of
things that there will be much uncertainty, confusion and
inconsistency in the definition of policy goals and in the
choice of strategies to attain them. It should be apparent
from our argument above that this situation is not a symptom
of fickleness and irrationality, but is the predictable
consequence of a still unresolved clash of value systems--a
clash felt not only between opposing groups but in the minds
of individuals.

The concrete meaning of this analysis for Western policy
can be seen when we move to a consideration of specific
countries and situations. It is no small irony that the king-
pin of American policy in the Arab world is Saudi Arabia,
a state whose most basic political values are profoundly
incommensurate with our own. This fact in no way implies
that the Saudis are unreliable allies, since they and the
United States share many common interests and perceptions--
that a serious program of oil conservation is essential to
the long term interests of both countries, for example, or
that regional stability is best served by active support for
conservative or at least non-revolutionary regimes--and there
is no reason to suppose that this community of interests will
change soon. Nevertheless, the religio-political orientation
underlying Saudi policy may well lead to difficulties on
other, equally vital issues. Thus, it is a common American
notion that socio-economic development requires a rationalization of legal and political institutions along familiar
Secularist lines, whether liberal-democratic or Marxist.
The Saudi government, however, very strongly believes in a
reassertion of traditional Islamic norms and is not reluctant
to encourage recipients of its assistance to take such steps.
Egypt, whose fragile economy has been largely underwritten
by Saudi Arabia (along with other conservative Gulf states)
since 1967, is especially subject to such pressures. Where
traditionalism is expressed chiefly through such gestures
as reestablishing Quranic criminal sanctions, it may present
no real problem to Western or Egyptian development planners.
But other aspects of Saudi Fundamentalism, such as its strong
opposition to birth control or its restrictive attitudes
towards women as professionals and modern-sector workers,
might well have grave consequences if they were to be insisted upon as a *quid pro quo* of Saudi assistance. This
is a kind of issue which seems very likely to become a point

of contention between Western and Saudi development aid
officials, especially as Saudi Arabia plays a growing role
in regional economic development.

The problems (or potential problems) presented to
Western policy by Islam in Egypt and Syria are, as one would
expect, in striking contrast to those we have just described.
For rather different reasons, both countries face a long
term crisis of legitimacy, and in both, the challenge comes
from two directions, a Fundamentalist "right" and an extreme
Secularist "left." In Egypt, the crisis stems from the
failure of two distinct but closely related governments to
deal effectively with the country's massive social problems.
In the eyes of many Egyptians, the failure is not one of
specific persons or policies only, but is an indictment of
the whole political system and the ideology underlying it.
Thus Nasir's attempt at a socialist mobilization of Egyptian
society--a very moderate attempt when measured against the
Soviet Union or China--and Sadat's uncertain liberalism stand
accused, and with them the sort of Islamic Modernism which
they have called upon to legitimize them. In these circumstances it is no surprise that a frankly Marxist solution
should appeal to many intellectuals and army officers. It
is less obvious why other segments of the elite should be
tempted by Fundamentalism, but it is undeniable that this
orientation has recently become powerfully attractive in
circles where it would have been summarily rejected ten
years ago. One explanation of this phenomenon is certainly
the failure of acceptable alternatives over the past 25 years,
which has caused a critical loss of confidence in the value
and power of non-traditional ideologies. But just as important would be the economic success of Saudi Arabia and
Qadhafi's Libya, which has enormously enhanced the
credibility of Fundamentalist socio-political attitudes.

In Syria, we have a government whose legitimacy is
always in question, whatever the success or failure of its
policies. The Sunni majority of the population remains
profoundly resentful of a Ba'thist government which is both
Secularist in orientation and dominated by men of Nusayri
background, and this resentment (as we have seen) is easily
mobilized. At the same time, there are clearly important
factions within the Ba'th itself (not to mention the numerous
other leftist parties of Syria) which are offended by Asad's
concessions to traditional religious sentiment and the
economic interests of the bourgeoisie. These groups are
eager to reinstate a purer and more rigorous radicalism and
will certainly exploit any opportunity to replace the present
regime with one more to their taste.

The crisis of legitimacy in Egypt and Syria presents
American policy with a difficult dilemma. On the one hand,
for the first time in many years the United States has
achieved a *modus vivendi* with both countries which allows
it to exert some influence on their foreign and internal
affairs. On the other, it dare not push very hard,

because neither government has much room to make obvious,
public concessions or compromises. For Egypt, the main
constraint seems to be one of time; Sadat must begin to make
visible progress on Egypt's multifarious problems very soon
if he hopes to remain in power. For Syria, the fundamental
difficulty is that Asad has to satisfy the values and
aspirations of two deeply suspicious and mutually hostile
groups; as a result, his dealings with the United States, or
any other major power, must be determined almost exclusively
by his estimate of the balance of internal political forces.
Both in Egypt and Syria, Western policy makers find themselves
dealing with a profound conflict of values and ideologies which
they have almost no power to influence. In both cases, they
will be forced to content themselves with an uncertain future
which gives little scope for long term planning. In such a
situation, the only effective guide to policy is a precise
understanding of the ideological turmoil which is shaping
the overt struggle for power. And in this clash of ideologies,
attitudes toward and interpretations of Islam are a vital
element.

BIBLIOGRAPHY

     In a paper of this kind there seems little point either
to footnotes or to a formal bibliography; on the other hand,
I do think it appropriate to indicate those readings which
have supplied specific information or which have helped me
in rather direct ways to reach the conclusions which I give
here.
     Islamic and Arabic thought in the twentieth century has
been the subject of many studies, though none of these has
followed the tripartite typology which I use here. The best
known and most challenging analyses of religious thought
are H.A.A. Gibb, *Modern Trends in Islam* (Chicago, 1947) and
W. Cantwell Smith, *Islam in Modern History* (Princeton, 1957),
to be supplemented by the more recent surveys of Kenneth
Cragg, *Counsels in Contemporary Islam* (Edinburgh, 1965),
and Ali Merad, "Islah," *Encyclopaedia of Islam* (new ed.),
IV, 141-163. A useful though not very profound survey of
the writings of the *'ulama'* of al-Azhar during the 1960s
can be found in Hava Lazarus-Yafeh, "Contemporary Religious
Thought among the 'Ulama' of al-Azhar," *Asian and African
Studies* (Annual of the Israel Oriental Society), VII (1971),
211-236. The doctrines of the Muslim Brethren are per-
ceptively and sympathetically presented in the superb study
of Richard Mitchell, *The Society of the Muslim Brothers*
(London, 1969). Among the many statements of Modernism,
the most consistent and convincing is surely to be found
in the work of the Pakistani scholar Fazlur Rahman, most
notably his *Islam* (New York, 1966). The slow emergence of
Secularist modes of thought in the Arab world is luminously
presented in Albert Hourani, *Arabic Thought in the Liberal*

Age, 1798-1939 (London, 1962). Leonard Binder, *The Ideological Revolution in the Middle East* (New York, 1964), though frightfully obscure in places, contains a revealing and ironic analysis of Nasirist and Ba'thist ideology. Finally, one may consult a perceptive though partisan article by an Egyptian leftist commentator: Michel Kamel, "Dialogue entre l'heritage culturel et le modernisme dans la pensee egyptienne contemporaine," *Travaux et Jours*, no. 46 (Jan-March 1973), 53-72.

The problem of law and legislation, so fundamental to our analysis in this paper, is dealt with in a formalistic but very exact manner in the excellent survey of Norman Anderson, *Law Reform in the Muslim World* (London, 1976).

Information on religion and society in Saudi Arabia has been hard to come by since Philby's day; among recent references, Derek Hopwood, ed., *The Arabian Peninsula: Society and Politics* (London, 1972), is brief but scholarly.

Syria likewise has been neglected rather badly. Tabitha Petran, *Syria* (London, 1972), is an intensely partisan work, written from a Syrian leftist (but non-Ba'thist) perspective, but it remains a very intelligent and revealing modern history of the country. The 1973 Constitution is reproduced (in an unofficial English version) in the *Middle East Journal*, XXVIII, no. 1 (Winter 1974), 53-66. By far the best account of the tumult surrounding it is that of John J. Donohue, "La nouvelle constitution syrienne et ses detracteurs," *Travaux et Jours*, no. 47 (Apr-June 1973), 93-111.

On Egypt there is of course an overwhelming mass of material, though little of it bears specifically on the problems here discussed. Morroe Berger, *Islam in Egypt Today* (Cambridge, 1970) gives some useful data on the institutional aspects of religious life, and Daniel Crecilius, "Al-Azhar in the Revolution," *Middle East Journal*, XX, no. 1 (Winter 1966), 31-49, discusses Nasir's reshaping of this center of learning. The different modes of religious life and feeling are portrayed in Michael Gilsenan, *Saint and Sufi in Modern Egypt* (Oxford, 1974). The 1971 Constitution is given in the *Middle East Journal*, XXVI, no. 1 (Winter 1972), 55-77; and in the following issue of the same journal the debates accompanying its drafting are surveyed by Joseph P. O'Kane, "Islam in the New Egyptian Constitution: Some Discussions in *al-Ahram*," *MEJ*, XXVI, no. 2 (Spring 1972), 137-148. Finally, one should mention the most systematic attempt to analyze Nasir's ideology and its relationship to his public policy: R. H. Dekmejian, *Egypt under Nasir: A Study in Political Dynamics* (Albany, N.Y., 1971).

22
Islam in Sudanese Politics

Gabriel R. Warburg

On March 27, 1970, Sudanese President Ja'far Muhammad
al-Numeiri ordered the bombardment of Aba Island, the stronghold of the *Ansar*, the major popular Islamic movement in the
Sudan. Between five and twelve thousand *Ansar* were
killed, including their spiritual leader the Imam al-Hadi
al-Mahdi, both on the island itself and in later skirmishes.
Following this massacre it was widely assumed that the power
of sectarian politics in the Sudan had been crushed. Yet,
six years later, in July 1976, the *Ansar* led a daring, though
abortive, *coup* against President Numeiri with the aid of
Libyan weapons and financial support. Another year passed
and on July 8, 1977, President Numeiri travelled to Port
Sudan to meet al-Sadiq al-Mahdi, the leader of the *Ansar*.
and the instigator of the July 1976 *coup*, and signed with
him an eight-point agreement for "National Reconciliation."
Thus, after more than eight years of military rule, with all
political parties except the Sudan Socialist Union (SSU) outlawed, the power of the *Ansar*, was still strong enough to
warrant an attempt by Numeiri to arrive at a settlement with
the most consistent enemies of his regime.
What was the source of this power? The *Ansar*, in their
'modern' form, first appeared on the Sudanese political scene
during World War I, when their founder and spiritual leader,
Sayyid 'Abd al-Rahman al-Mahdi, was recruited by Sir Reginald
Wingate, Governor-General of the Anglo-Egyptian Sudan, to
combat Muslim propaganda emanating from Istanbul.[1] Having
fulfilled this task successfully, the *Ansar* went on to collaborate
with the British authorities in fighting against Egyptian
nationalism, which reached new heights in the years 1919-1924,

Islam and Politics in the Sudan is reprinted by permission of *Jerusalem Quarterly*, Vol. 13, Fall, 1979. It
has been excerpted and updated by the author.

and one of whose aims was the 'unity of the Nile Valley'.
But in both cases the *Ansar* were far from reluctant in their
support of Britain's aims, since they regarded both Turkey and
Egypt as corruptors of Islam and the usurpers of Sudanese
independence in the nineteenth century. They were thus more
than willing to collaborate with Britain against their northern
neighbours. But what the British authorities did not foresee
at the time, was that the *Ansar* were creating a power base in
the Sudan which was to become a dominant factor in Sudanese
politics, despite British efforts to curtail it. Indeed, on
the eve of the Sudan's independence, in the years 1953-1956, it
became clear that despite the emergence of an educated elite
with political aspirations, the real masters of Sudanese
politics were the leaders of popular Islam, and primarily the
heads of the *Ansar*, (Sayyid 'Abd al-Rahman al-Mahdi), and of
the *Khatmiyya* (Sayyid 'Ali al-Mirghani).

It was under these circumstances that the Sudan had its
first experiment in democratic parliamentary government. Hence,
it is probably no wonder that parliamentarism, dominated by
the two major religious sects: the *Ansar* and the *Khatmiyya*,
had no real chance to survive. Its first lease on life came
to an abrupt end in November 1958, when the army, as elsewhere
in the Middle East and Africa, took over. But even the Sudanese
venture in military rule was unique in that the Army's chief
of staff, Ibrahim 'Abbud, first sought the blessing of the
religious leaders of the *Ansar* and the *Khatmiyya* and only then
made his bid for power.[2]

In a statement to the Commission of Inquiry, formed in
1964 after 'Abbud was deposed in order to investigate the
reasons for the military *coup* and the alleged crimes of the
military regime, General 'Abbud stated the following:

> ...A few days before parliament was due to resume its work I
> was approached by Abdullah Khalil. He informed me that the
> political situation was going from bad to worse; serious
> and dangerous events might result from this situation and
> there is no way out but for the army to take over...Abdullah
> Khalil, three days before the *coup d'etat* came to see me
> again to make sure of the developments of our plans. I assured
> him that everything was being carried out according to plan
> and that we will take over before 17 November. Abdullah
> Khalil said to me 'May God help you and give you success'...

According to some sources, Sayyid 'Abd al-Rahman al-Mahdi
was himself interested in the military takeover, having
been persuaded by 'Abdallah Khalil that following the *coup*
he would be declared President of the Sudan, a position he
had craved for many years.[3]

The force of popular Islam expressed itself throughout
the whole period of 'Abbud's regime. The law for the dis-
persal of the parties and the confiscation of their property
did in fact hit the *Umma* and the People's Democratic Party,
the political arms of the two sects. However, the *Ansar*

and the *Khatmiyya* themselves were not only unhurt by these
measures, but in fact began to fulfill some of the functions
that had previously belonged to their respective parties.
The *Ansar*, under their new leader Siddiq al-Mahdi,[4] reorganized and created a hierarchy of party-like institutions,
both at the centre and in the provinces. Siddiq's power and
self-confidence rose to such an extent that in October 1959
he demanded of 'Abbud that he end military government and
revive democratic parliamentary institutions. The leaders
of the *Ansar* did not even hesitate to attack 'Abbud for, in
their opinion, selling the rights of the Sudan by signing
the Agreement for the Division of Nile Waters with Egypt on
November 8, 1959. Siddiq's declaration of the *Ansar*'s loyalty
to 'Abbud in May 1960, stressing that his activities and the
activities of the *Ansar* were solely religious, was lip service
only.[5] In November of the same year, Siddiq's name appeared
at the top of a list of twenty religious and political leaders
on a petition to the military authorities, demanding that they
return to their barracks.[6] In March 1961 Siddiq reiterated
his demand, declaring that the military regime had extracted
the state from a crisis, but that its continuation in power
was now doing more harm than good.[7] Despite his repeated
demands for the cessation of military government, the authorities
refrained from attacking Siddiq or the *Ansar* and, apart from
attempts to restrict their economic power, left them to operate
freely. Even in June 1961, following a railwaymen's strike,
when a letter of protest from all the veteran political leadership, including Siddiq, was sent to 'Abbud, the authorities
still did not dare to harm the head of the *Ansar*. All the
other leaders were arrested and exiled to Juba, capital of
Equatoria, while Siddiq continued his activities unhindered.[8]
Only in August of the same year, after a bloody clash at the
Mahdi's tomb between young demonstrators of the *Ansar* and the
army, was Siddiq placed under house arrest for a short period,
and a number of leading *Ansar* were imprisoned.[9]

  Siddiq died in October 1961 and the leadership of the
Ansar passed to his brother al-Imam al-Hadi al-Mahdi. Siddiq's
son, al-Sadiq, was designated to lead the *Umma* party and was
ordered by his father, before his death, to continue the
struggle for the return of political freedom and democratic
rule to the Sudan. But the struggle for a return to civilian
rule was undertaken predominantly by the educated and professional classes, led by the Communist Party, rather than
by the religious sects. In October 1964 a civilian revolution,
which spread from the University of Khartoum and developed
into a nationwide political strike, toppled the military
regime. 'Abbud and his colonels were replaced by the first non-
sectarian government in the history of the independent Sudan.
However, the transitional government of October 1964 - with
its strong leftist leanings - could not survive for long
against the predominant sectarian forces. In February 1965,
the prime minister was forced to resign and a new government
in which the traditional forces predominated once again came

to power and led the country to the general elections of
May 1965. The brief, non-sectarian interlude thus came
to an abrupt end and the sectarian divisions which had
harrassed Sudanese politics in the turbulent years between
1956 and 1958 were back in force. The only real difference
between the two periods is that the two major sects, the
Ansar and the *Khatmiyya*, had lost their old and venerated
leaders and hence were divided and lacked cohesion. The
split was particularly harmful to the *Umma* party, in which
al-Sadiq al-Mahdi challenged the more experienced politician
Muhammad Ahmad Mahjub, thus splitting both the party and the
Ansar. Indeed, in the April 1968 elections, the last democratic elections before the army resumed power, the split within the *Umma* first led to bloody clashes on Aba Island and
later resulted in a humiliating defeat for both factions of
the *Ansar*. It was this defeat, and the resulting ascendancy
of the *Khatmiyya*-dominated Democratic Unionist Party, which
persuaded al-Sadiq and al-Hadi al-Mahdi to agree that the
first would become prime minister and the second president
in the next elections. Mahjub commented bitterly:

> ...They thus seemed to consider the rule of the state a booty
> to be inherited and divided between them, to the exclusion
> of the other members of the party who did not belong to the
> Mahdi family...

Thus it seemed that the *Ansar* would reunite, and with *Khatmi*
support it was agreed on May 23, 1969 that the Sudan should
be a presidential republic with an Islamic constitution.[10]
     Two days later, on May 25, 1969, the Free Officers under
Numeiri seized power and declared that they would at last do
away with sectarianism and realize the socialist programme of
the October 1964 revolution. The Democratic Republic of the
Sudan was born. Indeed, the defeat of sectarianism was first
on the agenda of the Communist-backed Free Officers. After the
coup some forty thousand *Ansar* gathered on Aba Island where
their spiritual leader, al-Imam al-Hadi, had returned to.
Numeiri decided to challenge the Imam on his own ground and
declared his intention of touring the White Nile, including
Aba Island. The Imam warned him that the atmosphere was tense
and that he could not guarantee his safety. But Numeiri was
adamant and when he was stopped from landing on the island he
ordered its bombardment by MIGs and rockets, on March 27, 1970.
After two days of bombing and three additional days of fighting,
the remaining *Ansar* capitulated on March 31. Between five
and twelve thousand were killed. Others were killed in the
Ansar quarter of Omdurman, while the Imam al-Hadi was shot
dead while trying to escape to Ethiopia on April 1, 1970.
Muhammad Ahmad Mahjub, though not of the *Ansar* himself,
described the events as:

> ...a brutal massacre; ruthless, senseless and without precedent
> in our history. With little protection and no defence against

air attack, the people were slaughtered in the streets and fields...[11]

Since the Aba Island massacre, in March 1970, the two most prominent surviving sectarian leaders had been in exile. Sadiq al-Mahdi, the Oxford-educated grandson of Sayyid 'Abd al-Rahman, was put on a plane and flown to Cairo where his movements were initially restricted. Later he was allowed to leave Egypt. He has since been involved in building up an anti-Numeiri opposition, especially in the outlying regions of Dar Fur, in the Western Sudan, with the active support of President Qadhafi of Libya. The second leader was Husayn Sharif Yusuf al-Hindi, descendent of the founder of the *Hindiyya* Sufi order,[12] which during the parliamentary 'episode' had joined forces with the *Khatmiyya*, in an attempt to form a religious-political pact against the *Ansar*. On the eve of the Numeiri *coup* he had served as Minister of Finance in the last civilian coalition government under Muhammad Ahmad Mahjub, and had escaped to Aba Island, the *Ansar*'s stronghold, when Numeiri assumed power. Once in exile, Sharif al-Hindi had joined forces with Sadiq al-Mahdi and the *Ansar*, as well as with the outlawed Muslim Brotherhood (the Islamic Charter Front), and had formed the anti-Numeiri National Front. This Front, with the aid of several of the Sudan's neighbours, headed by Qadhafi's Libya, but including at times such strange bedfellows as Saudi Arabia and 'Marxist' Ethiopia, have tried unsuccessfully to topple Numeiri's regime on at least two occasions: in November 1975 and July 1976.

President Numeiri, however, had his own order of priorities. Having crushed the *Ansar's* initial opposition, he dealt a deathblow to his original allies in the Communist Party, in July 1971, following an abortive Communist backed *coup*.[13] The next priority was a settlement with the Southern Sudan, in which Numeiri succeeded in ending the civil war, after seventeen years of strife and bloodshed. The Addis Ababa Agreement of February 1972 was probably Numeiri's major achievement. It provided him with an important ally, with a vested interest in his victory, in the battle against Muslim sectarianism. Numeiri failed, however, in creating institutionalized popular support for his regime. Following in Naser's footsteps, he set up the Sudanese Socialist Union (SSU), as the only legitimate political organization in the country. But like the Arab Socialist Union in Egypt, the SSU was expected to demonstrate its loyalty to the regime without gaining any real stake in the political system.

...A large part of the activity of SSU branches revolved around demonstrations of support for government policy...[14]

Genuine and open debate on government policy leading to real change was negligible. The SSU became a mass organization, lacking grassroot support or independent leadership with a

top-heavy bureaucracy made up largely of presidential
appointments.

In recent years Numeiri has declared his intention to
liberalize the political system, again following the
Egyptian example, this time that of President Sadat. However, as long as the leaders of the National Front remained
in exile and were doing their utmost to overthrow Numeiri,
there could be no real liberalization of the political
system. Following the dismal failure of the *Ansar*-led *coup*
in July 1976, both the leaders of the opposition National
Front and President Numeiri decided to reconsider their
previous strategy. The July 1976 *coup* had been the most
dangerous challenge to Numeiri's regime since the abortive
Communist-inspired *coup* of July 1971. The *coup* was led and
executed by well-trained and equipped *Ansar*, and by the time
the fighting had ended some 700 lives had been lost and 98
additional *Ansar* were later executed. The failure of this
coup, despite the fervour of the *Ansar* who fought to the
bitter end, was due primarily to the loyalty of the Sudanese
army and to the immediate support of the Egyptian units in
the Sudan. The *coup*'s failure convinced the leaders of the
National Front that Numeiri was too strong to be easily
toppled. It convinced Numeiri, who at first claimed that the
coup had been executed by foreign mercenaries emanating from
Libya and Ethiopia,[15] that the National Front and especially
the *Ansar* were too strong to be ignored. Hence he sought
'national reconciliation'.

For Numeiri's regime the return of the leaders of the
National Front to the Sudan, as partners within the SSU,
augured both benefits and dangers. It was clear that neither
Sadiq al-Mahdi nor Sharif al-Hindi would become docile
collaborators with the regime and that their presence could
create an active opposition within the SSU. However, Numeiri
probably believed that as long as they were willing to denounce sectarianism, join the SSU and work within the regime,
their presence in the Sudan would outweigh the dangers of
their continued exile.

On July 8, 1977, Sadiq al-Mahdi was therefore invited
to Port Sudan to discuss the details of reconciliation with
President Numeiri. The eight-point agreement reached between
the two leaders was revealed by Sadiq al-Mahdi in a number of
interviews.[16] According to Sadiq, Numeiri agreed to important
changes in the political system; the release of political
prisoners; a revision of the constitution and neutralism in
the Sudan's international relations. In return the National
Front would end its armed opposition, dismantle its training
camps and return to the Sudan to take part in the national
reconciliation. Indeed, al-Sadiq openly declared his belief
both in the role of the army in the politics of developing
countries and in socialism as an essential model for economic
development. The one-party system, exemplified by the SSU,
was essential for the present stage of Sudanese politics and
all al-Sadiq sought was the restoration of political and

civil liberties and a general amnesty for himself and his colleagues.

The agreement was ratified by the executive of the National Front on July 14, 1977 and at the end of that month some 900 political prisoners belonging to the National Front were released on Numeiri's orders. A law granting general amnesty for 'illegal acts' committed against the regime was passed on August 7.[17] This enabled al-Sadiq, accompanied by twelve leading *Ansar*, to return to the Sudan on September 27, 1977, after more than seven years in exile.[18]

Reconciliation was facilitated in the Sudan not only through amnesty but through major changes in the electoral law to the People's Assembly, which were announced on September 26, 1977.[19] Furthermore, a special committee was appointed by Numeiri in the same month, whose task it was to begin the integration of political exiles into the political, economic and social fabric of the Sudan.[20]

The elections held in February 1978 may be regarded as one of the major fruits of reconciliation. Out of the 304 seats in the People's Assembly, candidates supported by the two main groups within the National Front--the *Ansar* and the Democratic Unionist Party--won thirty seats each, while the erstwhile Islamic Charter Front (Muslim Brotherhood) won twenty seats. If one takes into account that about sixty additional seats were won by so-called independent candidates, especially in rural areas,[21] the fruits of reconciliation seemed impressive. On March 21, 1978, Numeiri appointed six new members to the SSU political bureau, a substantial figure in this prestigious twenty-nine-member body. The new members included al-Sadiq al-Mahdi, Ahmad 'Ali al-Mirghani and Dr. Hasan al-Turabi, the respective leaders of the *Ansar*, the *Khatmiyya* and the Islamic Charter Front.[22] Even more far reaching were the appointments of fifty-one new members of the Central Committee of the SSU, including the above three leaders and many other former anti-Numeiri activists. At the time, Ahmad 'Ali al-Mirghani, in line with *Khatmiyya* tradition, refused to be drawn into active politics and declined the honour conferred upon him by Numeiri.[23] Al-Sadiq declared that he regarded his appointment as premature. Yet, a few months later, on August 3, 1978, he reached an agreement with Numeiri which enabled him to join the central bodies of the SSU.

However, even at this stage, when reconciliation seemed to be progressing smoothly, two questions remained unanswered: first, al-Sadiq's political-executive role in the Sudan and second, his ability to stand by the agreement, namely to bring the anti-Numeiri opposition from Libya and Ethiopia back to the Sudan. Right from the first agreement of July 1977, there were consistent rumours that al-Sadiq would be offered the premiership of the Sudan. Indeed, when in one of his periodic government reshuffles Numeiri assumed the office of prime minister, it was generally assumed that he was doing

so in order to hold the post for al-Sadiq.[24] These rumours
persisted despite constant denials both by al-Sadiq himself
and by Numeiri, who declared that al-Sadiq was not yet ready
to assume executive responsibilities.[25]
    But the second challenge was even more crucial, as it
involved al-Sadiq's credibility as the leader of the National
Front. When it was realized that the armed fighters of the
National Front, whose number was estimated as some 6,000,
were not returning to the Sudan despite the general amnesty
and the appeals of al-Sadiq, the latter was sent on a special
mission to Libya in December 1977 in order to close the camps
and bring his supporters home. Both Numeiri and al-Sadiq
declared their satisfaction with this mission, stating that
all expectations had been fulfilled, the camps in Libya had
been closed and the returning exiles were being resettled in
Dar Fur, Kordofan, as well as in the Blue and White Nile
provinces.[26] However, despite these declarations the return
of the exiles was much slower than expected. Two causes were
named for this setback. The first explained the slow return
as the result of the preparations which had to be undertaken
for their absorption in the Sudan. The second claimed that
the camps would not be closed and the exiles would not return
as long as Sharif al-Hindi remained abroad, as his position
in the camps was superior to that of al-Sadiq.[27]
    In August 1978, al-Sadiq again travelled to Libya in order
to make the necessary arrangements for the return of the Sudanese
emigrants. In a detailed interview with the associate editor
of the official Sudanese monthly *Sudanow*, al-Sadiq expressed
his confidence in the return of the Sudanese emigrants, from
both Libya and Ethiopia, stating that '...in both cases,
they are all Ansar...' thus trying to refute the rumours that
he had lost his credibility in the camps. The slow process,
he explained, was due to the preparations undertaken in the
Sudan, on the one hand, and the strained relations with Ethiopia
on the other. According to al-Sadiq there had always been more
Sudanese emigrants in Ethiopia and despite the strained relations between the two governments, over fifty percent of these
had infiltrated across the borders and returned to the Sudan.
The difference between the camps in Ethiopia and those in
Libya was, as stated by al-Sadiq, that the latter constituted
the elite of the *Ansar*.[28] But whatever the reasons for the
slow progress made in dismantling the camps, the fact remains
that as late as January 1979, the camps in Libya were still
full of Sudanese emigrants.[29]
    No sooner had al-Sadiq announced details of the recon-
ciliation agreement between him and Numeiri than opposition
was voiced from various quarters. Inside the Sudan, it came
primarily from two sectors. The hard-core supporters of the
May 1969 revolution, including members of the original
Revolutionary Command Council (RCC) feared that reconciliation
would undermine their power. Moreover, with the support of
the so-called secular intelligentsia, this group feared a return
to sectarian politics and did not believe in the sincerity of

the al-Sadiq announcements.[30]

But far graver, and probably of greater significance both to Numeiri and to the future of the Sudan, were the doubts and criticisms raised by non-Muslim Southern leaders, who feared that al-Sadiq's return to the Sudan was the first step towards Islamization.

In the Addis Ababa Agreement of February 1972, which brought to an end the civil war between the Arabicized Muslim North and the Negroid Nilotic South, after nearly seventeen years of strife and bloodshed, one of the major bones of contention was religion. The Southerners insisted that there be no attempts to declare Islam the religion of the state, or to create a so-called Muslim republic in that country. Mr. Abel Alier, President of the Southern regional government until the February 1978 elections, tried to minimize these fears:

> ...Sadiq el Mahdi has been granted amnesty after being sentenced to death...A great deal had changed in the time between his departure from the Sudan and his return to Khartoum...We in the South expect him to accept the new situation gracefully...[31]

Others were less optimistic. The government's decision to appoint a commission, chaired by Dr. Hasan al-Turabi, to determine whether Sudanese Law should be revised and brought into line with Muslim *Shari'a*, was regarded by at least one Southern leader, Bona Malwal, as a breach of promise and a threat to Sudanese unity.[32] It led to his resignation as Minister of Information.[33] Religion, stated Malwal, should be left to the individual and should not be forced on the populace through religious laws of the *Shari'a* brand. A year later, while he was already on study leave in London, Malwal reiterated these fears, based on a year's experience with reconciliation. He accused al-Sadiq of attempting to create an *Ansar*-controlled power base in the Western Sudan, thus undermining the country's unity. While Malwal declared his strong support for reconciliation, he opposed al-Mahdi's plans, which would turn the Sudan into an Islamic state in which non-Muslims like himself would be at a clear disadvantage.[34]

Whether Malwal's fears were exaggerated or not is irrelevant. These fears existed in the South on the eve of the February 1978 elections, and the defeat of the pro-government candidates, including Abel Alier himself, was definitely a reflection of this fear and helped Joseph Lagu to assume power in the South.[35]

Differences of opinion regarding reconciliation were not limited to those who feared that Numeiri had compromised the future of the Sudan. Others, both within the *Ansar* and from the ranks of the rival Democratic Unionists in the National Front, claimed that al-Sadiq al-Mahdi had gone too far. The criticism within the *Ansar-Umma* leadership centered

on al-Sadiq, who had decided to disband the independent political body of the opposition, without consulting with his
colleagues who had remained in opposition within the Sudan.
Moreover, rumours were circulating that al-Sadiq had accepted
£200,000 from the Sudanese government as 'compensation' for
the use of his property while he was in exile.[36]   There are
indications that these disagreements involved the Mahdist
family itself, including the late al-Hadi al-Mahdi's two sons:
Wali al-Din and Nasr al-Din, who were especially asked by
Numeiri--not by their first cousin al-Sadiq--'...to involve
themselves and the disciples of the late Imam al-Hadi al-Mahdi,
in national work for the paramount interests of the country...'[3]
     But of much greater impact was the rift within the National
Front between al-Sadiq and his erstwhile ally, Sharif al-Hindi.
The first indication of this rift was Sharif's condemnation of
Sadat's peace initiative and of Numeiri's declaration of support
made in the wake of Sadat's visit to Jerusalem in November 1977.
Thus, somewhat paradoxically, the Democratic Unionists, who
followed in the footsteps of al-Azhari's NUP, and thus were
traditionally in favour of close cooperation with Egypt, had
now taken a step in the opposite direction.
     The Sudanese authorities, prompted by the desire to
speed up reconciliation and probably fearing that al-Hindi
might undermine al-Sadiq's more daring progress, dispatched
a special delegation to London in order to try and reach a
conclusive agreement. On April 12, 1978, an agreement was
signed between vice-president Abu al-Qasim Muhammad Ibrahim and
Sharif al-Hindi, in which the latter agreed to disband the
National Front, dismantle its training camps in Libya and
Ethiopia and hand over its arms to the Sudanese authorities.
In return al-Hindi elicited a promise to gradually lift the
special security measures which had been imposed on the
Sudan since the July 1976 *coup*. To satisfy al-Hindi's
criticism of Sadat, an anti-Zionist resolution was added to
the agreement in which the two sides recognized the legitimate
rights of the Palestinians. Moreover, the Sudanese-Egyptian
agreement regarding gradual integration of the two states was
defined, in this agreement, as the first step towards comprehensive Arab integration. This 'historic agreement', according to al-Hindi, heralded a 'new dawn'.[39]   But despite these
rather bombastic proclamations, al-Hindi did not return to
the Sudan. In an interview published in the London-based
The Middle East, in August 1978, he stated that while he
trusted Numeiri's honesty, he would stay abroad until the
many differences of opinion which still existed between them
had been ironed out.
     How does President Numeiri view these problems? In an
interview with the Lebanese journalist Fu'ad Matar, Numeiri
dismissed both the alleged danger of Communism and the
political power of Sharif al-Hindi's Democratic Unionists
rather lightheartedly. Stating that all Communists had in
fact been released from prison, Numeiri insisted that they
were politically 'invisible' and thus harmless as far as

his regime was concerned. Numeiri continued by dismissing
the importance of Sharif al-Hindi:

> ...As regards brother Sharif al-Hindi I don't think there is
> any problem. We arrived at the solution that should induce
> him to get on a plane and return to the Sudan, but he does
> not come...He has worked in politics and he knows its results,
> and maybe that is why he prefers to play the role of a
> businessman...[40]

Numeiri's attitude was, however, less frivolous when it came
to al-Sadiq al-Mahdi's role in Sudanese politics. He insisted
that:

> ...Sadiq's role will come next year [1979?], which will be
> the year of conferences...so that reconciliation can be
> absorbed and can give the desired effectiveness...

But when asked about Sadiq's present position, Numeiri
retorted with vague generalities such as: '...Sadiq is
still working on consolidating the bases of national
reconciliation...'; or: '...Sadiq is still working on re-
moving the effects of estrangement...' More revealing perhaps was Numeiri's claim that:

> ...Sadiq has asked me several times to excuse him from
> political or executive tasks because he would like to
> have more time to study the situation...

Numeiri also refused to be engaged on the question of
whether his pro-Sadat policy and his open support of the
Camp David accords were in any way a cause for estrangement
between Sadiq and himself. '...I don't think a difference
in opinion should be a reason for destroying our achievements...'
 But while Numeiri still sounded optimistic regarding
the prospects of reconciliation there were already clear
indications that reconciliation had foundered and that
Numeiri's efforts to bring about national unity were back
to square one. The first sign of the crisis was al-Sadiq's
resignation from the political bureau of the SSU on October
21, 1978.[41] In a six-page letter to Numeiri, al-Sadiq
enumerated his reasons for resigning, blaming first and
foremost Numeiri's subservience to Sadat's foreign policy.
However, he later added that internal opposition to reconciliation had halted Numeiri's more forthcoming policy with
regard to amendments to the constitution and the revision
of certain laws.[42] When al-Sadiq left for the United
States, it was claimed that reconciliation had failed.
Indeed the BBC reported, on February 10, 1979, that in a
meeting in Tripoli between Qadhafi, al-Sadiq and al-Hindi
it was announced that reconciliation had come to an end as
a result of the Sudanese government's failure to abide by

the terms of the agreement. In an interview with al-Hindi,
the latter was quoted as defining his agreement with the
Sudan government as a worthless piece of paper. He claimed
that the government had not abided by any of the terms it
had agreed upon and therefore al-Sadiq al-Mahdi had left the
country, and the National Front had resumed its armed struggle
and its popular protest movement in the Sudan, aided by the
opposition to Numeiri, even within the army.[43] Al-Sadiq
al-Mahdi himself was quoted as saying that Numeiri's support
for Sadat's Camp David 'treason', had brought reconciliation
to an end.[44]

The counter-announcements made by Sudanese authorities
claiming that al-Sadiq had only gone to the United States to
accompany his wife who needed medical attention, seemed rather
unconvincing. Numeiri claimed that reconciliation was continuing at full speed and that minor differences of opinion,
regarding primarily the Camp David accords, would not bring
the implementation of the most important policy of the Sudan
government to a halt.[45] However, as long as there is no
indication from either of the two leaders of the National
Front that they are willing to continue with the process of
reconciliation, Numeiri's denials seem to be of little avail.

On October 25, 1979, Numeiri held a meeting with army
and police personnel, aimed at "...the mobilization of national
action...to secure it from sabotage by the enemy of the revolution..." On the same occasion Numeiri emphasized the Sudan's
Arab identity and reiterated its loyalty to the Arab cause.[46]
Even more telling was Numeiri's attendance at the Tunis
Summit Conference organized by the Arab League in November
1979. Having refrained from participating in the Baghdad
Summit in November 1978, this indicated a definite change in
policy. The change became clear when on November 25, 'Abd
al-Hamid Salih, chairman of the Sudan's Peoples Assembly,
made a statement on the Middle East peace process. In it he
asserted that the Sudan had never fully supported the Camp
David accords and now that Sadat's peace efforts had failed,
due to Israeli's intransigence, the Sudan fully supported Arab
solidarity regarding the Arabism of Jerusalem and the creation
of a Palestinian state ruled by the PLO. This point of view
was reiterated a few days later by the foreign relations
committee of the S.S.U.[47]

So it seemed that the combined economic and political
pressures were at last bearing fruit. Numeiri was constantly
accusing Iraq of plotting in the Sudan. But it became quite
clear that the "power blocs" which were accused of being
involved in these intrigues within the Sudan were not limited
to the communists who had been the most convenient scapegoat
ever since their July 1971 coup.[48] In a recent purge of the
S.S.U. political bureau and the reorganization of its secra-
tariat, under Numeiri himself, those who were ousted included
the two sectarian Muslim leaders al-Sadiq al-Mahdi and
Ahmad 'Ali al-Mirghani. It would therefore seem that national
reconciliation which had been declared as the most important

aspect of Numeiri's policy since July 1977, has, at least temporarily, been shelved. Of the three sectarian leaders of the National Front, only Dr. Hasan al-Turabi is still active in Sudanese politics. Sharif al-Hindi, who never returned from his self-imposed exile in London, continued to attack and denounce Numieri, whenever he had an opportunity, promising his audiences that Numeiri's days were numbered and that a popular revolution was not far away. Al-Sadiq al-Mahdi seems to have opted for a rather more ambivalent attitude. In the wake of the Tunisian Arab Summit, al-Mahdi has once again returned to the Sudan and has apparently acted on Numeiri's behalf in helping to reach the resumption of diplomatic relations with Iraq as well as more cordial relations with Libya.[49] In an interview with the Kuwaiti *al-Watan*, conducted in Khartoum on March 23, 1980, al-Mahdi explained his views regarding the Soviet invasion of Afghanistan. He rejected all Soviet explanations regarding this invasion as unacceptable and stated that he had accepted a Soviet invitation to hold more discussions on this topic.[50] So it would seem that al-Mahdi, having resigned from the central bureau of the S.S.U., is nonetheless maintaining a rather low-profile role in Sudanese politics.

Numeiri has in the meantime proceeded with his plans to decentralize his government and to divide the Sudan into six regions which would be governed by their own regional assemblies and governments, similar to that of the southern regions.[51] Should this plan be realized it could change the fortunes of the Sudan and satisfy the diverse ethnic groups which make up the checkered map of the Sudanese population. However, decentralization might also be exploited by the sectarian leaders. Populist Islam of the *Ansari* brand could, for instance, attempt to exploit its power among the Baqqara tribes in Kordofan and Dar-Fur, or among the Fallata in the Jazira and the Blue Nile region. Thus regionalism could be a mixed blessing which, as happened before, will be shelved before it is fully implemented. However, the historical heritage of the *Ansar*, their grass-root support and their concentration in certain regions of this vast country, tend to suggest that their challenge to central government is still accute. If we take into account that the Sudan is torn by immense problems in practically every sphere and that Numeiri, after more than ten years in power, has not succeeded to bring about any real solutions, with the possible exception of the southern problem, the dangers of a populist Islamic uprising in the Sudan seem considerable.

NOTES

1. For details on the history of the *Ansar* until World War II see: G. Warburg, 'From Ansar to Umma: Sectarian Politics in the Sudan, 1914-1945', *Asian and African Studies*, Vol. 9, no. 2 (1973),

pp. 101-153; the *Ansar* were a revival of the Mahdist movement of the 1880s and Sayyid 'Abd al-Rahman was the posthumous son of the Sudanese Mahdi Muhammad Ahmad b. 'Abdallah.

2. K.D.D. Henderson, *Sudan Republic*, London 1965, pp. 129-130; cf. Mohamed Ahmed Mahgoub, *Democracy on Trial*, London 1974, pp. 180-188.

3. Quoted from M. O. Beshir, *Revolution and Nationalism in the Sudan*, London 1974, p. 207; 'Abdallah Khalil was at that time Prime Minister and leader of the *Umma* party, the political arm of the *Ansar*.

4. Siddiq's father, Sayyid 'Abd al-Rahman, died on March 24, 1959.

5. *Middle East Record* (hereafter MER), Tel Aviv 1960, p. 415, quoting from *al-Ayyam*, May 18, 1960.

6. *MER*, 1960, p. 417.

7. *Ibid.*, 1961, p. 469.

8. *Ibid.*, p. 473, quoting from *al-Hayat*, July 12, 1961.

9. *MER*, 1961, quoting from *al-Hayat*, August 25, 1961.

10. Mahgoub, pp. 224-25; cf. Beshir, pp. 215-26.

11. Mahgoub, p. 237.

12. The *Hindiyya* is an offshoot of the *Sammaniyya* Sufi order of which the Mahdi was a leader, before he declared his mission.

13. H. Shaked, et al. "The Communist Party in Sudan, 1946-1971," in M. Confino and S. Shamir, (eds.) *The USSR and the Middle East*, Jerusalem 1973, pp. 335-374.

14. T. Niblock, 'Political System Begins to Relax', *Financial Times Survey*, July 13, 1978.

15. *Arab Report and Record* (hereafter ARR), 1 (1977), p. 19.

16. *The Middle East*, London, November 1978, pp. 12-13; ARR, 14 (1977), p. 608; *Le Monde*, September 13, 1977.

17. Colin Legum and H. Shaked (eds.), *Middle East Contemporary Survey* (hereafter MECS), Vol. I, 1976-1977, New York & London 1978, p. 591.

18. *ARR*, 18 (1977), pp. 796-7.

19. *ARR*, 18 (1977), pp. 797.

20. *MECS*, Vol. II, 1977-1978.

21. *Washington Post*, April 11, 1978; it should be remembered that the leader of the Democratic Unionists had not returned to the Sudan.

22. *ARR*, 6 (1978), p. 211.

23. *Al-Dustur*, April 10-16, 1978.

24. *MECS*, 1976-1977, p. 594.

25. See *e.g.*, *al-Sahafa*, September 10, 1978; cf. interview with Numeiri, *The Middle East*, London, December 1978.

26. *SUNA* (Sudan News Agency), November 25, 1978; *ARR*, 2 (1978), p. 65; *ARR*, 4 (1978), p. 140.

27. *Al-Nahar al-'Arabi wa-l-Duwali*, Paris, January 21, 1978.

28. *Sudanow*, Khartoum, October 1978, pp. 17-18.

29. *ARR*, 1 (January 1979), pp. 6-7.

30. *MECS*, 1976-1977, p. 594.

31. Quoted from an interview with Abel Alier, *Africa*, No. 78 (February 1978), pp. 35-6.

32. *Sudanow*, Khartoum, October 1977.

33. *The Economist*, March 18, 1979, 'A Review of the Sudan'; officially it was stated that Malwal was on 'leave of study' in London.

34. Bona Malwal, 'Reconciliation and the Mahdi', *Sudanow*, Khartoum, December 1978.

35. See interview with Major General Joseph Lagu, *The Middle East*, London, December 1977.

36. *Arabia and the Gulf*, London, January 30, 1978; *al-Dustur*, London, January 9-15, 1978.

37. R. Omdurman, May 30, 1978, quoted by the BBC, June 1, 1978; Numeiri's speech at the opening of the new Mahdist Mosque in Omdurman in February 1979, when he stressed the Mahdist role in the victory of Islam in the Sudan is also indicative: *al-Sahafa*, February 24, 1979.

38. *ARR*, January 1, 1978, p. 21.

39. *ARR*, April 7, 1978, p. 256; Reuter, April 12, 1978; *al-Sahafa*, April 13, 1978.

40. *The Middle East*, December 197-, pp. 55-58; the following, unless otherwise stated, are based on Matar's interview; Sharif was at the time based in London.

41. This was first reported by the Iraq News Agency on October 26, 1978. See *ARR*, 20 (1978), p. 783; *al-Fajr al-Jadid*, October 28, 1978.

42. *Al-Hawadith*, December 29, 1978.

43. *Al-Watan al-'Arabi*, Paris, January 11, 1979; *Events*, London, December 29, 1978.

44. Report from Cairo, quoted by the *The Jerusalem Post*, March 18, 1979.

45. *Al-Hawadith*, January 26, 1979.

46. Quoted by *FBIS-MEA*, V. 209 (26 October 1979), from SUNA, 25 October 1979.

47. *FBIS-MEA*, V. 231 (29 November 1979), quoting SUNA, 29 November 1979, *FBIS-MEA*, V. 229 (27 November 1979), quoting SUNA, 25 November 1979.

48. In an interview with the Saudi Arabian *al-Riyad*, 20 November 1979, Sudan's Vice President and Minister of Foreign Affairs, Rashid al-Tahir, claimed that "the communists have been reduced to small groups and isolated individuals," quoted in *FBIS-MEA*, V. 232 (30 November 1979).

49. *FBIS-MEA*, V. 13 (18 January 1980) quoting Radio Omdurman, 17 January 1980.

50. *FBIS-MEA*, V. 62 (28 March 1980).

51. *FBIS-MEA*, V. 26 (6 February 1980) quoting SUNA, 4 February 1980.

23
Politics, Religion, and Ethnic Identity in Turkey

Jeffrey A. Ross

All ethnic groups seek to define and maintain boundaries for the dual, though highly related, purposes of internal pattern maintenance and external differentiation. Fredrik Barth contends that ethnic boundaries are set through the selection and development of distinguishing cultural traits.[1] The relative efficiency of this process of collective marking is a partial function of the encompassing qualities of the traits that are selected and institutionalized.[2]

Religion is the most all-encompassing, affective, and profound cultural delimiter in most traditional and post-traditional societies.[3] As such, it is admirably suited to serve as a marker of ethnic distinctiveness. Donald Smith effectively conveys the great power of religion--a power that is often not appreciated by social scientists who share a cosmopolitan, secular value mix:

> Religion integrates a traditional society by providing it
> with a common framework of meaning and experience. Through
> the ordinary processes of socialization, the young acquire
> a common set of beliefs and values associated with symbols
> of the sacred. Participation in the same rituals, celebrating
> the same festivals, bearing the names of the same gods or
> saints, shunning the same tabus, members of the society
> are integrated at a profound level. Much of the material
> and artistic culture of the traditional society--art,
> architecture, literature, music, dance--is expressive of
> religious ideas and values. . . The sacred permeates the
> principal social institutions. . . Above all, government
> is sacral.[4]

Many scholars and observers of Turkish affairs have pointed out that religion is the most important basis of interethnic differentiation in the contemporary Turkish Republic, as it was in its predecessor, the Ottoman Empire.[5]

Islam, the religious affiliation of almost 99 percent of
the whole population, is a defining characteristic of membership in the Turkish people.[6]   Indeed, most people in Turkey,
both of the Islamic faith and not of the Islamic faith, view
the label Turk as being synonymous with the label Muslim.
Many would find the suggestion that a non-Muslim could be
a Turk extremely naive if not ludicrous.   The very word that
now is used to signify nationality, *Millet*, has an older
though still valid meaning of religious denomination.   While
a non-Muslim may belong as a citizen to the Turkish state,
Tabiiyet, he can never be a part of the Turkish *Millet*.   In
a very real sense, one's religion is one's nation in Turkey.[7]
Ward and Rustow point this out quite succinctly:

> To this day, an Anatolian villager is as likely to say that
> his nation is "Islam" as that it is "Turkish"; and a member
> of the Istanbul Christian or Jewish minority groups, while
> readily conceding that he is a Turkish citizen, will hotly
> deny being a "Turk."   Integration has thus come slowly in
> Turkey.[8]

    This situation is somewhat ironic in light of the fact
that the Turkish state has maintained an official policy of
secularization since the early years of the Kemalist regime
in the 1920's.   Although committment to secularization has
been modified since the end of the Second World War, all
republican governments have emphasized citizenship and an
image of Turkishness separate from though not antithetical
to Islam.   Evidently, the impact of the state's attempt to
induce an identity modification has been very modest among
the masses, although there has been some success among the
new urban elites.
    While religion may serve as a basis of social differen-
tiation, it may also serve as a powerful basis of social
integration.   The non-Muslim minorities are economically
important but relatively few in numbers, being largely
concentrated in Istanbul and a few other important cities.[9]
Their political impact is, on the whole, not extensive.[10]
The largest and most politically important ethnic minority
in Turkey is the Kurdish population, which numbers some
2,181,000, and is concentrated in Eastern and Southeastern
Anatolia.   Like the smaller Arab population of the Southwest,
the Kurds share Sunni Islam with the dominant Turks.[11]
    There has never been a serious attempt to assimilate
the non-Muslim minorities, but there has been a longstanding
drive to Turkify the Muslim minority groups.   The educational
apparatus has been used to spread the Turkish language among
the Kurds, and state policy has encouraged the decline in
the authority of tribal leaders (*Agas*) and the breakdown
in the cohesion of Kurdish tribal formations.   The state
has even gone as far as to officially deny that a Kurdish
problem exists, classifying the Kurds as "Mountain Turks"
and claiming that their Indo-European language is a Turkish

dialect.[12]

In this paper I shall attempt to empirically investigate the relationship between religion and ethnicity among both Muslim and non-Muslim minorities in Turkey. My data come from a survey that I sponsored and had conducted in January 1975 in Turkey, involving interviews with Turkish citizens who belong to the Armenian, Greek, Jewish, and Kurdish populations. I will use these data to see if Muslim and non-Muslim ethnic groups are characterized by different levels of integration into and perceptions of Turkish society and politics; and to see if religiously observant members of these ethnic groups differ from their non-religiously observant compatriots along these same dimensions. In order to provide tentative answers to these questions, I shall test the following two hypotheses:

> H1 *Muslim minority group members have more positive perceptions of Turkish society and politics than do members of non-Muslim minorities.*

> H2 *Religiously observant non-Muslims in Turkey are more likely to have negative perceptions of the social and political systems than do members of their ethnic groups who are not religiously observant.*[13]

In proposing the first hypothesis, I am suggesting that Kurds, as Muslims, perceive themselves as having more of a legitimate place in Turkish society than do the non-Muslim Armenians, Greeks, and Jews. While a Muslim can, if he wants, become a Turk, this option is closed to non-Muslims. In proposing the second hypothesis, I am also suggesting that ethnic distinctiveness and perceived marginality are stronger for those who are religious than for those who are not. This should be so because ethnic membership in Turkey, as I have described it, revolves around religious delimiters.[14] Those who are not religiously engaged may be attempting to opt out of the system of ethnic stratification that follows denominational lines.

Before presenting the data and findings, I shall very briefly survey the historical record concerning religion and interethnic relations in Turkey. Such a review will show how religion came to serve as an intergroup delimiter, and how it has continued to serve in that capacity. This analysis will put the empirical data into fuller contextual perspective.

HISTORICAL FACTORS

The nomadic Turkish tribesmen who created first the Seljuk and then the Ottoman states were converted to the militant, crusading Islam of the frontier rather than to

the more sophisticated, philosophic Islam of the late
Abbasid court. They identified themselves with Islam to
such a degree that their identity as Turks receded into
the background of their collective consciousness. While
the Arabs and Persians had retained a memory of and a
strong attachment to the glories of their respective pre-
Islamic pasts, the Turks virtually lost theirs.[15] It was
as an Islamic state rather than as a Turkish state that
the Ottoman Empire received its legitimacy. Loyalty to
the Empire rested upon committment to Islam and allegiance
to the Osmanli house's dynastic claim. Over time, the word
Turk was used as a term of derision by the Ottoman elite,
signifying the crude and unlettered peasants and nomads of
Anatolia. Only the Europeans continued to use Turk as a
generic label and refer to the land of the Turks as Turkey.[16]

The Ottoman Empire was a polyglot, multiethnic state
governed by a remarkably cosmopolitan though profoundly
Islamic ruling elite. Indeed, until the eighteenth century,
a majority of the Sultan's subjects were non-Muslims. The
Turks were never a majority in the Empire until the defeat
in the Balkan Wars. Political recruitment did not favor the
Turks over the other peoples of the Empire. Until the reforms
of the early nineteenth century, the sultans practiced
Devsirme, a legalized kidnapping of male Christian children
who were then trained for bureaucratic and/or military service
to the state. Although those so chosen were forcibly converted to Islam and held the status of slaves of the Sultan,
the system, in effect, froze free-born Turkish Muslims out
of positions of political power. The ranks of the *Ulema*,
those who interpreted Islamic law and had quasi-clerical
duties, were one of the few higher career opportunities open
to them.

The rulers of the Empire stressed vertical but never
horizontal integration among their subjects. The organization and administration of the state centered around the
classic *Millet* system in which each religious community was
legally recognized through its own charter, governed by its
own religious law, and led by its own religious leaders.
The religious leaders of each *Millet* acted as judges for
their own people and intermediaries between them and the
state. Turks, Kurds, Arabs, and other Muslims belonged to
the Muslim *Millet*, while Jews belonged to the Jewish *Millet*,
and Greeks, Armenians, Maronites, and others belonged to
their respective Christian *Millets*. Taxation varied for
each *Millet*--non-Muslims were always taxed at a higher
rate than Muslims--and the religious leaders generally
performed the function of tax collector.[17] Mardin notes
that this segmented Ottoman society served to retard the
growth of secondary structures, thereby reinforcing the
dominant role of religion in society.[18]

The non-Muslim *Millets* were tolerated, following
traditional Islamic custom, and forced conversion outside
of the *Devsirme* system was very rare. An ethnic division

of labor based upon religious distinctions developed and
allowed many of the non-Muslim grups to prosper economically.
Indeed, by the nineteenth century, Christians and Jews enjoyed a virtual monopoly on entrepreneurial positions.
Despite this toleration and prosperity, however, non-Muslims
could never rise above a second-class status in which they
were the perpetual inferiors of the Muslims. Unlike the
situation in the early Arab empires, Muslims and non-Muslims
were rigidly segregated and rarely interacted on a social
level.

Prevented from playing a full role in Ottoman society,
the non-Muslims turned inward to their own religious communities and, in the case of the Christians, outward to European
protectors. As the European military ascendancy over the
Empire grew, the Christian minorities became the wedges with
which the Western powers penetrated the Ottoman domain.
Almost every major European power "adopted" a *Millet* as its
own special responsibility and endeavored to preserve its
rights against the "terrible Turks." Such interventions,
often involving force or the threat of force, usually turned
out to the advantage of the intervener. The leading Western
states acquired Capitulations from the sultans that gave them
commercial rights in the Empire and afforded extraterritorial
status to their nationals when they worked or travelled
there.[19] The Capitulations were extended to many Ottoman
non-Muslims when they were able to get *Berats* from European
ambassadors. *Berats*, in effect, conferred quasi-European
citizenship rights upon their holders, making them eligible
for the protections granted foreigners under the Capitulation
treaties.

In the early and mid-nineteenth century a rising Muslim
intelligentsia attempted to respond to the European threat
to the Ottoman Empire through internal, Westernizing reform.
The reformers of the *Tanzimat* sought to appeal to the loyalties
of non-Muslims by advocating a doctrine of Ottomanism--a
design in which a shared sense of Ottoman nationality would
link members of all the *Millets*. Ottomanism was predicated
upon the juridical equality and shared citizen rights of all
the peoples of the Osmanli domain. Unfortunately, Ottomanism
never had much impact beyond a narrow circle in Istanbul--
most Christians, especially those in the Balkans, rejected
it for their own nationalism and most Muslims saw it as a
threat to their divinely-ordained way of life. With the
accession to the throne of Abdulhamid II in 1876, the
Tanzimat came to an end and Ottomanism was replaced with a
somewhat manipulative though emotionally potent Pan-Islamism.

By the late nineteenth and early twentieth centuries,
nearly all of the Muslim and non-Muslim subject peoples of
the Ottoman Empire had turned to nationalism.[20] The Turks,
however, retained a vision of themselves as Muslims first
and foremost. Nationalism came to them in a way that was
very late, somewhat artificial, and extremely problematic.
After the Young Turk Revolution of 1908 deposed

Abdulhamid II, voices of a purely Turkish nationalism came
to be increasingly heard. At the same time, a highly
romanticized variant called Pan-Turanism began to be
expressed by a diverse group of intellectuals and publicists,
many of whom were Turkic emigres from Russia. Ziya Gokalp,
the leading exponent of Pan-Turanism, a doctrine calling for
the unity of all the world's Turks, was himself a Kurd.[21]
With the conclusion of the Balkan Wars, in which most remaining Ottoman Christians and even the largely Muslim Albanians
broke away from the Empire, the leading members of the governing Committee of Union and Progress embraced a Turkish
nationalist and even Pan-Turanist position.[22]

The First World War destroyed the Ottoman Empire and
set in motion the events that ended the Osmanli sultanate
and caliphate. Faced with a real revolt among the Arabs and
a perceived one among the Armenians during the War, the
Young Turk government had responded in a brutal fashion--
the Armenian population of Eastern Anatolia was nearly
exterminated by the Turkish Army in a genocidal campaign
during 1915.[23] Nonetheless, the killing of mostly unarmed
civilians could not compensate for defeat in battle, and
the Turks were forced to surrender in 1918.[24]

The victorious Allies moved in to dismember what was
left of the Ottoman Empire after the military collapse of
1918: an Allied force occupied Istanbul; the British and
French took the Arab provinces as mandates; an Armenian
state was set up in Eastern Anatolia and the Caucasus;
a Greek army moved into the Western Anatolian coastal region;
and the Sultan was compelled to sign the humiliating Treaty
of Sevres in 1920. Many of the non-Muslim minorities quickly
cast their lot with the Allied forces: the Greek communities
on the Anatolian coast supported the Greek army that had
landed at Izmir; the Christians of Istanbul openly fraternized
with the Allied forces, as did the Sultan, and many acquired
Berats; and the remnants of the Armenians fought to preserve
their newly attained statehood.

Reacting to these events, a Turkish nationalist movement
arose in Anatolia around the person of Mustafa Kemal and
did battle with the Greeks, Armenians, French, and the
forces of the Sultan. Even though the collaborationist
Sultan-Caliph and the *Seyh-ul-Islam* had called on the Muslim
faithful to resist the nationalist forces, the latter were
able to appeal successfully to the religious sentiments
of the Turkish masses. The 1919-1922 war against the Greeks,
in particular, was seen by many Turkish Muslims as a *Jihad*
against the invading Christian infidels. When Kemal defeated
the Greeks at the decisive battle on the Sakarya river in
1921, the nationalist Grand National Assembly awarded him
the title of *Gazi* (victor in a holy war). When the nationalists framed their doctrines in the National Pact (1919-1920),
they avoided the controversial and still derisive word Turk,
and spoke instead of Ottoman Muslims.[25]

By 1922 the Kemalists had been fully victorious over

their adversaries. The British, French, and Italians withdrew, the Greeks were routed, and the Armenian state had
been crushed between the Kemalist and Soviet armies. In
1923 the Sultanate was abolished and the capital was moved
from Istanbul, the cosmopolitan imperial capital, to Ankara
in the Anatolian heartland. Between 1923 and 1930 a massive
population exchange with Greece took place in which 1.3
million Greeks were forced to leave Turkey in return for a
much smaller number of Turks. This exchange followed largely
religious lines: ethnic Greeks who were Muslim were not
expelled and ethnic Turks who had become Christians were not
admitted.[26] Resentment and bitterness against the Christians,
combined with some legal restrictions, lasted for many years
and even now, after more than fifty years, emerges in recurring incidents.[27]

Kemal and his colleagues saw the Islamic establishment
as a link to a discredited past and as a barrier to economic
progress and modernization. In 1924 the offices of Caliph
and *Seyh-ul-Islam* were abolished, both positions having been
compromised by the self-serving collaboration of the Ottoman
elite with the Western Allies during the War of Independence.
Soon after, a republic was proclaimed with Kemal as its president, and the republican regime began a concerted attempt to
disestablish Islam and create a secular state along European
lines. One of the most important of the secularization acts
was the dismantling of the legal systems that revolved around
each *Millet*, and their replacement by secular courts administering a unified Western-based legal code. In 1924 the
Seriat courts for Muslims was abolished; in 1925 the leaders
of the Jewish and Armenian communities agreed to submit to
a secular, national code; and the Greek Orthodox followed in
1926, the year of the adoption by the National Assembly of a
modified version of the Swiss civil code.[28] Legally, the
Millet system ceased to exist and was replaced by the concept
of citizenship in the Turkish Republic.

Collective identity based upon Islam and a sacral basis
of state legitimacy could not be easily employed by the
Kemalists since they had directly attacked the traditional
Islamic establishment in their drive to power and firmly
believed that established religion retarded development.
Accordingly, Turkish nationalism, but not its romantic and
unrealistic variant of Pan-Turanism, became the official
doctrine of the Republic. A variety of cultural, linguistic,
and educational policies were pursued that emphasized the
distinctive genius of the Turkish people, and pointed out
their pre-Islamic and possibly their post-Islamic role and
identity.[29] Even though Turkish nationalism soon achieved
the status of an official counter-religion, its hold upon
the masses who still fervently embraced Islam was questionable. Unlike the nationalisms of the Greeks, Armenians,
and other Christian minorities, Turkish nationalism did not
stem from below, from the traditions and aspirations of an
entire people, but from above, from the dictates of a

centralizing state controlled by a narrow modernizing elite. It was a derivative ideology that had to deny much of the past in order to point towards the future.

Among the masses, as is often the case, the new doctrine of Turkish nationalism was absorbed into the dominant Islamic context. The concept of Turk became synonymous with that of Muslim--one could not be one without also being the other. Given the racialist strains in the official doctrine and the Islamic ones in popular nationalism, the non-Muslims were frozen out of full participation in the Republic just as effectively as they had been under the Ottoman Empire.[30]

The Sunni Muslim Kurds had been, by and large, loyal subjects of the Ottoman Empire. Kurdish troops had played an important role in the Armenian massacres, and many Kurds lived on lands and in houses that once had belonged to the departed Armenians of Eastern Anatolia. The Treaty of Sevres had introduced the possibility of an independent Kurdish state--an idea rejected by the Kemalists and quietly dropped by the Western Allies at Lausanne (1923).[31] A large-scale Kurdish revolt erupted in 1925 and further revolts broke out through the mid 1930s, leading to the imposition of martial law in the Kurdish region in 1936 and the forcible removal of many Kurds to Western Anatolia and Thrace, actions that were only softened after World War II. Although these revolts called for the establishment of an independent or at least autonomous Kurdistan, Karpat argues that they were in large part inspired by religious sentiments.[32] In 1925 the Kurdish rebels called for the re-establishment of the Caliphate and a reversal of the official policy of secularism--a policy that brought increased power to the central state apparatus as well as irreligion. Kurdish agitation, followed by official crackdowns and the imposition of martial law, have continued through the 1970s.[33]

Although the Republic had granted full citizenship to non-Muslims, the marginality of the latter was demonstrated during the Second World War. In 1942 the *Varlik Vergisi*, a capital tax designed to increase state revenue and control profiteering, was passed by the National Assembly. The tax was applied in a discriminatory manner so that non-Muslims, who were registered on a separate list, were made to pay at a rate up to ten times that demanded of Muslims.[34] The Western Allies protested this measure and, when the War turned decisively in their favor, the tax was dropped in 1944. The affair produced bitter memories among all concerned: the non-Muslims saw it as a special attack upon themselves and an affirmation of their subordinate status; and the Muslims saw it as another example of the Western powers intervening in Turkish domestic affairs to support the privileges of alien minorities.

This state of affairs has persisted to the present day. If anything, it has been reinforced by the Turkish invasion and partial occupation of Cyprus, followed by the US arms embargo and the retaliatory closure of several US military

and intelligence facilities in Turkey. Kurdish nationalism
has continued to play a political role as Kurdish militancy
in neighboring Iraq and Iran has spilled across the Turkish
border. These inflamations of ethnic conflict have been
paralleled by a modest Islamization of Turkish party politics.
Since the advent of competitive multi-party politics after
World War II, all major parties, including the Kemalist RPP,
have found it necessary to woo voters through covert and
sometimes overt appeals to Islamic sentiments. Necmettin
Erbakan's National Salvation Party has effectively relied
upon Islamic populism and has been a pivotal player in the
making and breaking of a number of government coalitions.[35]
In sum, the non-Muslim minorities are popularly perceived
as resident aliens with ties to foreign powers and the
Muslim minorities continue to be subject to an often counterproductive enforced Turkification.[36]

THE DATA

     The empirical data used in this study come, as indicated
from a January 1975 survey, which includes Kurds, a Muslim
minority, and Armenians, Greeks, and Jews, three non-Muslim
minorities.[37] The sample of 103 was drawn from both metro-
politan Istanbul and Malatya, a small city in Eastern Anatolia.[38]
The sample was evenly spread among the four groups (28.2%
Jewish, 27.2% Greek, 25.2% Armenian, and 19.4% Kurdish), and
all interviews were conducted in an oral, face-to-face format.
These data are suggestive rather than definitive. The sample
size is relatively small, especially when broken down into
each of the four ethnic groups, and the sample could not be
drawn along formal random probability lines because of both
resource limitations and the political sensitivity of the
minority issue within Turkey.
     The survey questionnaire contained a number of items
that sought to measure social and political integration into
Turkish society. In this paper, I will use five separate
measures of social integration and six separate measures
of political integration in order to test the two hypotheses.
The first hypothesis is tested by crosstabulating each of
these measures with the ethnic membership of the respondents.
The second is tested by controlling these crosstabulations
by a measure of the religiosity or lack of religiosity of
the subjects.[39]

FINDINGS: HYPOTHESIS ONE

Social Integration

     The most basic form of integration into a host society
is linguistic. A group cannot hope to play a full role in
the social, cultural, and economic life of a country unless

its members can and do speak the language of that country.[40]
Accordingly, each respondent was asked, through the use of
a four point scale, if he spoke the Turkish language at home.
The data are provided in Table 1.

TABLE 1.   Turkish Language Usage by Ethnic Group

Use of Turkish at home	Greeks (n=28)	Armenians (n=26)	Jews (n=29)	Kurds (n=20)
Always	35.7%	26.9%	37.9%	30.0%
Mostly	17.9	7.7	0.0	25.0
Sometimes	28.6	53.8	55.2	25.0
Never	17.9	11.5	6.9	20.0

$$x^2 = 15.02, \ p = .09 \quad \text{Cramer's V} = .22$$

The data show an important degree of linguistic
acculturation among all four ethnic groups. No fewer than
80% of the members of each group speak at least some Turkish
at home. Differences among the groups, while suggestive,
are not statistically significant. These statistics point
to a real regime success and do not support the hypothesis.
Social integration is highly dependent upon the socialization patterns experienced by a population. Formal education
is a very important part of an individual's socialization in
that it can allow him to broaden his peer contacts or, conversely, to remain within a narrow, ethnically-defined peer
community.[41] I sought to measure this dimension of social
integration by asking each respondent if he had gone to
special minority schools and if he would send his children
to one. The data are presented in Table 2.

TABLE 2.   Attendance at Minority Schools

	Greeks (n=27)	Armenians (n=24)	Jews (n=27)	Kurds (n=18)
Had attended and would send children	88.9%	79.2%	81.5%	16.7%
Had not attended and would not send children	11.1	20.8	18.5	83.3

$$x^2 = 32.11, \ p = .00 \quad \text{Cramer's V} = .58$$

These data strongly and unambiguously indicate a much greater use of special minority schools by non-Muslim than by Muslim ethnic groups. Kurds are, therefore, educationally more integrated into Turkish society than are Greeks, Armenians, and Jews. While these findings support the hypothesis, it must be pointed out that the more urban and affluent non-Muslims have more physical and monetary access to such schools than the poorer, more rural Kurds.

Ethnic particularism is strengthened and social integration is weakened when the members of an ethnic group believe that they are subject to discrimination by members of the majority and agents of the majority-dominated state. Such discrimination gives them little choice other than intensifying their reliance upon communal contacts and institutions.[42] This variable is measured by the following question: "Do you feel any discrimination against your personal rights, your culture, or your community as a whole, due to your ethnic status?" The responses to this question are listed in Table 3.

TABLE 3. Perception of Discrimination

	Greeks (n=19)	Armenians (n=18)	Jews (n=23)	Kurds (n=13)
Perceived discrimination	89.5%	100.0%	60.9%	7.7%
Did not perceive discrimination	10.5	0.0	39.1	92.3
$x^2 = 35.04$, p = .00		Cramer's V = .69		

These statistics show a significant variation among the four groups in their perception of discrimination. The Muslim Kurds, despite martial law and forced Turkification, do not believe themselves to be the object of discrimination. The Christian Armenians, with their memories of genocide, and the Christian Greeks, with their memories of deportation, just as overwhelmingly believe themselves to be the objects of discrimination. The Jews, for whom Turkey once served as a land of refuge, are more divided in their perceptions of discrimination, although a clear-cut majority of the Jews sampled did indeed perceive it. These data provide obvious support for the hypothesis.

Social integration is indicated by an identification with the history of the country in which one lives. If one rejects the affective appeal of that history, one is also likely to reject the society that it symbolizes.[43] Identification with the Turkish past is measured by the following question: "Can you refer to Ottoman history as your history?" The pattern of responses is found in Table 4.

TABLE 4.   Identification with Ottoman History

	Greeks (n=24)	Armenians (n=22)	Jews (n=18)	Kurds (n=20)
Identify with Ottoman history	4.2%	4.5%	66.7%	100.0%
Do not identify with Ottoman history	95.8	95.5	33.3	0.0

$$x^2 = 59.45, \ p = .00 \qquad \text{Cramer's V} = .84$$

The pattern found in Table 4 is much like that found in Table 3: the Muslims strongly identify with Ottoman history, the Christians just as strongly reject it, and the Jews are somewhat divided. This is not surprising in light of the historical record in which the Kurds were strongly attached to the integrative concept of the Muslim *Millet*, the Christians opted for a rejection of Ottomanism in favor of their own ethnonationalism, and the Jews were relatively content with communal autonomy, given the lack of a nationalist alternative under the Empire. These data too support the hypothesis.

The final measure of social integration is the following question: "Do you have faith in the future existence of your community in Turkey?" As Robert Lane points out, confidence in the future and the ability to plan for it are important hallmarks of well integrated individuals and groups.[44] Answers to this question are given in Table 5.

With some modification, the now familiar pattern is found in this table. The Muslim Kurds have the greatest faith in the future of their community in Turkey. Perhaps they define this community in terms of Islam as much as they do in terms of their identity as Kurds. The Greeks have the least faith in the future of their community in Turkey--a perception that may have been reinforced by the Greek-Turkish conflict over Cyprus. Both Jews and, surprisingly, Armenians have relative faith for the future of their communities in Turkey, although not quite as much as the Kurds. The Jews, as we have seen, are consistently more positive about Turkey than the Christians and the Armenians may be trying to make the best of a bad situation considering the fact that they have no alternate homeland outside the USSR.[45] Again, the hypothesis finds support in Table 5.

Political Integration

None of the respondents had been a political activist in Turkey. Many did, however, vote in Turkish elections. Political participation, including voting, indicates a

TABLE 5. Faith in the Future of the Ethnic Community in Turkey

	Greeks (n=14)	Armenians (n=16)	Jews (n=21)	Kurds (n=18)
Yes	35.7%	87.5%	95.2%	100.0%
No	64.3	12.5	4.8	0.0

$$x^2 = 27.82, \; p = .00 \qquad \text{Cramer's } V = .64$$

degree of committment to a society and its political system. Each respondent was asked if he had voted in Turkish elections. The data are found in Table 6.

TABLE 6. Voting Participation

	Greeks (n=19)	Armenians (n=18)	Jews (n=18)	Kurds (n=18)
Voters	63.2%	77.8%	66.7%	94.4%
Non-voters	36.8	33.3	22.2	5.6

$$x^2 = 5.84, \; p = .12 \qquad \text{Cramer's } V = .28$$

Sizable majorities of each ethnic group were voting participants, a striking indicator of political integration considering that appeals to ethnic groups, especially non-Muslims, are relatively rare in Turkish politics. Although the Kurds were the most highly mobilized of the four groups--an impressive fact given their much lower SES--the inter-group differences are not statistically significant. Voting, in this regard, is much like language usage.[46]

While the members of each of the four ethnic groups did not significantly differ in their voting participation, they did significantly differ in their perception of the degree to which the Turkish political system was open to the political recruitment of representatives of the minority groups. Each respondent was asked if he thought that a minority group member could become prime minister, a member of the cabinet, or a member of the National Assembly. Their answers are contained in Table 7.

The pattern of responses is consistent and significant. The Kurds are much more sanguine about a member of their community being recruited for national office than are the non-Muslims. Indeed, the latter seem to harbor

TABLE 7. Perceptions of Minority Political Recruitment

Can a minority group member become prime minister?

	Greeks (n=28)	Armenians (n=26)	Jews (n=29)	Kurds (n=19)
Yes	0.0%	0.0%	0.0%	56.2%
No	100.0	100.0	100.0	47.4

$$x^2 = 48.43, \ p = .00 \qquad \text{Cramer's } V = .69$$

Can a minority group member become a member of the cabinet?

	Greeks (n=27)	Armenians (n=24)	Jews (n=28)	Kurds (n=19)
Yes	0.0%	0.0%	0.0%	84.2%
No	100.0	100.0	100.0	15.8

$$x^2 = 79.51, \ p = .00 \qquad \text{Cramer's } V = .90$$

Can a minority group member become a member of the National Assembly?

	Greeks (n=28)	Armenians (n=23)	Jews (n=25)	Kurds (n=20)
Yes	14.3%	8.7%	4.0%	100.0%
No	85.7	91.3	96.0	0.0

$$x^2 = 65.26, \ p = .00 \qquad \text{Cramer's } V = .82$$

---

no illusions concerning the availability of the prime
ministership or a cabinet post. Kurds, on the other hand,
regularly do get elected to parliament and although the
Kurdish respondents have some doubts about higher office,
a majority of them do not rule it out.

The perception of political freedom is another important indicator of political integration. Those who feel
that they have freedom are more likely to place their
trust in the political process than those who do not.
Each respondent was asked to evaluate the political process
by answering the following highly subjective question:
"Do you feel that you have proper freedom of thought and
speech?" Their replies are summarized in Table 8.

The data once more break down along ethnoreligious
lines. The Muslims are most likely to perceive full freedom, the Christians are least likely to perceive full
freedom, and the Jews are in-between. These data are most
convincing when we recall that the Kurds have had to live
under martial law while the non-Muslims of Istanbul have not.

TABLE 8. Perception of Freedom of Thought and Speech

	Greeks (n=12)	Armenians (n=24)	Jews (n=17)	Kurds (n=14)
Perceives freedom	25.0%	23.5%	58.3%	85.7%
Perceives lack of freedom	75.0	76.5	41.7	14.3

$$x^2 = 15.56, p = .00 \qquad \text{Cramer's V} = .48$$

The final indicator of political integration concerns minority support for the Turkish government's action in an international ethnic conflict, the invasion and partial occupation of Cyprus. Each interviewee was asked if he thought that the government's action in Cyprus was justified. The answers must be evaluated in light of the highly sensitive nature of the question. The answers are in Table 9.

Only the Greeks, for obvious reasons, were lukewarm in their support of the Turkish military action in Cyprus. It is noteworthy that 46.4% of the Greek Respondents declined to answer this question. The Kurds were unanimously in favor of a government action that they may have perceived as a blow for Islam. The Jews and Armenians may be using this issue to demonstrate their loyalty in a low-cost manner. Even if all non-Muslim respondents were less than completely candid in their answers to this question, their reaction pattern is rather revealing. Inter-ethnic solidarity among the non-Muslim minorities, even among the Christians, does not seem to be the case, at least on the Cyprus question.

FINDINGS: HYPOTHESIS TWO

Social Integration

A majority of the interviewees from each of the four ethnic groups reported that they were religiously observant. However, 28.6% of the Greeks, 34.6% of the Armenians, and 34.5% of the Jews claimed that they were not religious. The following data analysis will compare the attitudes and behavior of religious versus non-religious non-Muslims on each of the indicators that were examined in the last section. Only a single Kurdish respondent, as we have seen, reported himself to be non-religious and, therefore, the Kurds are excluded from this analysis.[47]

TABLE 9.   Support for Turkish Action in Cyprus

	Greeks (n=13)	Armenians (n=25)	Jews (n=25)	Kurds (n=20)
Support	53.8%	96.0%	96.0%	100.0%
Opposition	46.2	4.0	4.0	0.0

$$x^2 = 23.86, \ p = .00 \qquad \text{Cramer's V} = .54$$

The data in Table 10 are computed by controlling each of the crosstabulations contained in Tables 1 through 5 by the religiosity or lack of religiosity of the non-Muslim respondents. This will allow us to examine the impact of religious practice upon perceived social integration. The analysis of the data, however, must be tempered by the relatively small sample size in each category that is a by-product of the control technique.

In general, the findings tend to support the second hypothesis and to reinforce one of the observations made in my investigation of the first. Those who are religious tend, on most indicators, to be less integrated into Turkish society than those who are not religious. In addition, religious Jews are generally more integrated than religious Christians, and non-religious Jews are generally more integrated than non-religious Greeks and Armenians. These patterns are most evident in the areas of minority school enrollment--indeed, most minority schools are strongly religious in character--identification with Ottoman history, and faith in the future of one's community. The non-religious are slightly more likely to speak Turkish at home, although Jews do not significantly differ from the others in language use. There are not marked differences, however, between religious and non-religious non-Muslims in their perception of discrimination. Jews, regardless of religious piety, are a bit less likely to perceive discrimination than the others.

Political Integration

Table 11 is generated in the same fashion as Table 10. The crosstabulation between each indicator of political integration and the ethnic identity of the respondent is controlled for religiosity. Again, the analysis is limited by small sample size, and the findings can only be viewed as suggestive.

The attitudinal patterns displayed in Table 11 are rather complex, but provide a degree of confirmation for the second hypothesis. In general, those who are non-religious are more likely to vote than those who are.

TABLE 10. Social Integration Indicators Controlled for Religiosity

Do you speak Turkish at home?

	Religious			Not Religious		
	Greeks (n=20)	Armenians (n=17)	Jews (n=19)	Greeks (n=8)	Armenians (n=9)	Jews (n=10)
Always	35.0%	11.8%	36.8%	37.5%	55.6%	40.0%
Mostly	20.0	64.7	52.6	50.0	33.3	60.0
Sometimes	20.0	11.8	10.5	12.5	11.1	0.0
Never	25.0	11.8	0.0	0.0	0.0	0.0
	$x^2 = 15.29$, $p = .08$		$V = .26$	$x^2 = 3.53$, $p = .74$		$V = .25$

Have you attended a minority school and would you send your child to one?

	Religious			Not Religious		
	Greeks (n=20)	Armenians (n=16)	Jews (n=17)	Greeks (n=7)	Armenians (n=8)	Jews (n=10)
Yes	100.0%	93.8%	100.0%	57.1%	50.0%	50.0%
No	0.0	6.3	0.0	42.9	50.0	50.0
	$x^2 = 4.13$, $p = .25$		$V = .23$	$x^2 = .99$, $p = .80$		$V = .19$

Do you feel any discrimination against your personal rights, your culture, or your community as a whole, due to your ethnic status?

	Religious			Not Religious		
	Greeks (n=12)	Armenians (n=10)	Jews (n=14)	Greeks (n=7)	Armenians (n=8)	Jews (n=9)
Yes	91.7%	100.0%	57.1%	85.7%	100.0%	66.7%
No	8.3	0.0	42.9	14.3	0.0	33.3
	$x^2 = 24.8$, $p = .03$		$V = .58$	$x^2 = 3.74$, $p = .29$		$V = .28$

TABLE 10 (Continued)

Can you refer to Ottoman history as your history?

	Religious			Not Religious		
	Greeks (n=17)	Armenians (n=14)	Jews (n=11)	Greeks (n=7)	Armenians (n=8)	Jews (n=7)
Yes	0.0%	0.0%	45.5%	14.3%	12.5%	100.0%
No	100.0	100.0	54.5	85.7	87.5	0.0

Religious: $x^2 = 49.57$, $p = .00$ $V = .90$

Not Religious: $x^2 = 15.96$, $p = .00$ $V = .83$

Do you have faith in the future existence of your community in Turkey?

	Religious			Not Religious		
	Greeks (n=7)	Armenians (n=9)	Jews (n=14)	Greeks (n=7)	Armenians (n=7)	Jews (n=7)
Yes	14.3%	77.8%	92.9%	57.1%	100.0%	100.0%
No	85.7	22.2	7.1	42.9	0.0	0.0

Religious: $x^2 = 26.07$, $p = .00$ $V = .74$

Not Religious: $x^2 = 7.00$, $p = .03$ $V = .58$

TABLE 11. Political Integration Indicators Controlled for Religiosity

Have you voted in Turkish general elections?

	Religious			Not Religious		
	Greeks (n=16)	Armenians (n=14)	Jews (n=11)	Greeks (n=3)	Armenians (n=4)	Jews (n=7)
Yes	56.3%	71.4%	81.8%	100.0%	100.0%	42.9%
No	43.8	28.6	18.2	0.0	0.0	57.1

Religious: $x^2 = 6.82$, p = .08, V = .29
Not Religious: $x^2 = 6.23$, p = .10, V = .23

Can a minority group member become prime minister?

	Religious			Not Religious		
	Greeks (n=20)	Armenians (n=17)	Jews (n=19)	Greeks (n=8)	Armenians (n=9)	Jews (n=10)
Yes	0.0%	0.0%	0.0%	0.0%	0.0%	0.0%
No	100.0	100.0	100.0	100.0	100.0	100.0

Religious: $x^2 = .30$, p = .98, V = .03
Not Religious: $x^2 = .06$, p = .98, V = .04

Can a minority group member become a member of the cabinet?

	Religious			Not Religious		
	Greeks (n=20)	Armenians (n=16)	Jews (n=18)	Greeks (n=7)	Armenians (n=8)	Jews (n=10)
Yes	0.0%	0.0%	0.0%	0.0%	0.0%	0.0%
No	100.0	100.0	100.0	100.0	100.0	100.0

Religious: $x^2 = .36$, p = .98, V = .03
Not Religious: $x^2 = .06$, p = .98, V = .04

TABLE 11 (Continued)

Can a minority group member become a member of the National Assembly?

	Religious			Not Religious		
	Greeks (n=20)	Armenians (n=15)	Jews (n=15)	Greeks (n=8)	Armenians (n=8)	Jews (n=10)
Yes	14.3%	77.8%	92.9%	57.1%	100.0%	100.0%
No	85.7	22.2	7.1	42.9	0.0	0.0
	x^2 = 26.07, p = .00		V = .74	x^2 = 7.00, p = .03		V = .58

Do you feel that you have proper freedom of thought and speech?

	Religious			Not Religious		
	Greeks (n=5)	Armenians (n=9)	Jews (n=14)	Greeks (n=7)	Armenians (n=8)	Jews (n=10)
Yes	40.0%	44.4%	64.3%	14.3%	0.0%	50.0%
No	60.0	55.6	35.7	85.7	100.0	50.0
	x^2 = 7.38, p = .06		V = .22	x^2 = 7.09, p = .06		V = .28

Do you think that Turkey is justified in its action in Cyprus?

	Religious			Not Religious		
	Greeks (n=5)	Armenians (n=16)	Jews (n=18)	Greeks (n=8)	Armenians (n=9)	Jews (n=7)
Yes	40.0%	93.8%	94.4%	62.5%	100.0%	100.0%
No	60.0	6.3	5.6	37.5	0.0	0.0
	x^2 = 18.88, p = .01		V = .57	x^2 = 7.24, p = .06		V = .23

The Jewish voting rate, however, seems to decline among the non-observant. I cannot easily suggest an explanation other than chance variation--a conclusion supported by the significance tests. The non-religious members of the non-Muslim minority groups are more sanguine about a member of their community becoming a member of the National Assembly than are their religious peers. They are also more likely to support the Turkish government's Cyprus policy--a finding that is most striking when we see that a majority of the secular Greeks approved of the invasion. No one sampled, regardless of piety, believed that a minority group member could achieve cabinet or prime ministerial rank. It seems that both groups are being realistic in this regard, and, therefore, these two questions are not very good tests of the hypothesis. Finally, we see that the non-religious members of the three non-Muslim ethnic groups are less likely to be satisfied with their level of freedom of thought and speech than are their more religious compatriots. This finding, while it contradicts my hypothesis, is in line with Ozbudun's observation that those who are most politically mobilized in Turkey also tend to be the most politically alienated.[48]

CONCLUSIONS

Too many social scientists have implicitly neglected the insights of Weber, Durkheim, and other classical theorists by paying too little attention to the social and political impact of religion. In this study I have attempted to show that religion has long been a powerful organizing force in Turkey and that it still plays a vital role in structuring social and political alternatives for large numbers of people. I have shown that there is significant variation between members of Muslim and non-Muslim minorities in Turkey in their integration or estrangement with the wider social and political systems. Furthermore, there is significant variation among the non-Muslim minorities. The Kurds interviewed in this study, despite years of forced acculturation and military rule, are strongly attached to Turkish social and political institutions. The Greeks and Armenians, however, appear to be generally estranged from the Turkish Muslim world in which they live. The Jews seem to be generally positive about Turkey but they display a number of serious reservations.

Attitudes and behaviors are not only associated with membership in an ethnoreligious community but with an individual's religious committments. Religion plays a role in solidifying feelings of ethnic distinctiveness and apartness. Along most indicators, religious non-Muslims were much more estranged from Turkish society and politics than those non-Muslims who had opted out of

religious practice. It is no paradox that the force that
integrates the Kurds into Turkish life is the opposite of
that which has the same effect on Greeks, Armenians, and
Jews.
     The force of religion in integrating or estranging
a given ethnic population is predominantly social, not
theological. The Muslim Kurds are not only attracted to
their Turkish co-religionists because of a shared body of
doctrines, but because Islam signifies a community to
which they can jointly belong. This same community is
for all practical purposes closed to non-Muslims and even
to Muslims who are not Sunnis. Following the traditions
of *Millet*, it is their own religions that define communal
membership and structure their place in the Islamic-
centered world.
     The secular minorities of the minorities, however,
seem to be moving away from their traditional estrangement into fuller participation in the modern sector of
Turkish social and political life. The secularization
that was imposed by Kemal Ataturk has given them a slight
opening into that world. This opening is very precarious,
as indicated by the responses of many of the non-religious
respondents on several of the questions. The militant
political Islam and racialist Turkism represented by such
figures as Erbakan and Turkes might, however, close this
door and make the already none too secure position of
the minorities, both religious and secular, completely
untenable.

NOTES

     1. Barth maintains that cultural differences result from
inter-group boundary maintenance activities, not vice versa. See
Fredrik Barth, "Introduction," in Fredrik Barth ed., *Ethnic Groups
and Boundaries* (Boston: Little, Brown, 1969), pp. 9-38.
     2. For a discussion, see Harold R. Isaacs, *Idols of the Tribe:
Group Identity and Political Change* (New York: Harper and Row,
1975).
     3. I am referring primarily to the great Western religions,
including Islam, that emerged from the Middle East. Many Asian
religions are more loosely structured and allow for greater social
and ideational pluralism.
     4. Donald E. Smith, *Religion and Political Development* (Boston:
Little, Brown, 1970), pp. 5-6.
     5. See, for instance, Robert E. Ward and Dankwart A. Rustow,
"Conclusion," in Robert E. Ward and Dankwart A. Rustow eds.,
Political Modernization in Japan and Turkey (Princeton: Princeton
University Press, 1964), p. 460; Kemal H. Karpat, *Turkey's Politics:
The Transition to a Multi-Party System* (Princeton: Princeton
University Press, 1959), pp. 251-292; and Bernard Lewis, *The Emergence
of Modern Turkey* (London: Oxford University Press, 1961),
pp. 317-355.

6. This figure includes the four to five million Turkish Shi'ites or *Alevis* (followers of Ali). The *Alevis* were often perceived as a greater threat than non-Muslims by the dominant Sunnis and, as a result, have experienced much greater persecution.

7. These distinctions are discussed by Lewis, p. 338.

8. Ward and Rustow, p. 460.

9. There are approximately 50,000 Greeks, 40,000 Jews, and 32,000 Armenians now living in Turkey. Turkey is among the more ethnically homogenous countries in the world.

10. Dankwart Rustow argues that Christian votes were very important for the Democratic Party's electoral fortunes in Istanbul in the 1950s. The Party represented business interests and advocated a moderate, inclusive nationalism. See Dankwart A. Rustow, "The Development of Parties in Turkey," in Joseph La Palombara and Myron Weiner eds., *Political Parties and Political Development* (Princeton: Princeton University Press, 1966), p. 123.

11. Arabs are estimated by Cohn to make up approximately 1.3% of the population. Due, in part, to the somewhat porous border with Syria, they have effectively resisted assimilation. See Edwin J. Cohn, *Turkish Economic, Social, and Political Change* (New York: Praeger, 1970), pp. 151-154. See also Andrew Mango, *Turkey* (New York: Walker, 1968), pp. 99-100.

12. The left, especially the now-banned Turkish Labor Party, has attempted to appeal to the Kurds' supposed dislike of Turkification. The left has also been able to appeal successfully to the *Alevis*. See Cohn, p. 154.

13. This hypothesis could not be tested among the Kurds as only a single Kurdish respondent reported that he was not religiously observant.

14. Ernest Krausz in "The Religious Factor in Jewish Identification," *International Social Science Journal* 24 (1977), pp. 250-259 reviews data from the United States, Great Britain, and Israel and concludes that Jewish identity is considerably stronger for religious than for non-religious Jews.

15. See Lewis, pp. 8-11. He argues that the word Turk itself, in its use as a descriptor of an entire people, is of Islamic origin.

16. These terms were only officially adopted in 1923 in Turkey.

17. The Ottomans also practiced a feudal form of tax farming.

18. Serif Mardin, "Religion in Modern Turkey," *International Social Science Journal* 24 (1977), pp. 281-286.

19. Capitulation rights were modelled on the *Millet* system. Europeans were, in effect, classified as belonging to a separate self-administering *Millet*.

20. While Greeks, Serbs, Albanians, Bulgarians, Rumanians, Armenians, Arabs, and others turned to ethnonationalism, the Jews did not. Many participated in the Young Turk and Kemalist movements.

21. Although Pan-Turanism defined membership in the Turkic world very broadly, it was never construed to include those of Turkic origin and language who were not Muslim.

22. The leading members of the CUP, such as Enver, Talat, and Cemal, were of diverse ethnic origins. Many, including Kemal, were born in Macedonia. The influence of Pan-Turanism may have been a factor in leading them to enter World War I on the Austro-German

side. Through war, they hoped to acquire territory in Russian
Turkestan and Azerbaijan.

23. Large-scale massacres of Armenians became state policy in
the late nineteenth century. Enver Pasa, Minister of War, appears
to have directly ordered the 1915 massacre in which well over one
million Armenians were brutally murdered. Hitler is reputed to
have referred to the Armenian massacres as proof that a determined
state could get away with genocide.

24. The only major Turkish military victory of the War occured
at Gallipoli. The Turkish commander, Mustafa Kemal, emerged from
the War as the only victorious Turkish general.

25. Ward and Rustow, p. 460.

26. Lewis, pp. 348-349. A smaller population exchange took
place with Bulgaria in this period.

27. There were major anti-Greek riots in Istanbul in 1955.
A good description is found in Karpat, p. 422.

28. For a discussion see Lewis, pp. 266-269.

29. One of the most interesting of these was the Sun Theory,
a doctrine that held that Turkish was the mother of other major
languages and that the prehistoric Turks were the great, though
forgotten, culture bearers and stimulators of antiquity.

30. Lewis, p. 351 notes that "the participation of non-Muslims
in the public life of Turkey actually decreased after the establishment of the Republic." Republican legislation required all citizens
to carry identity cards upon which their religion was stamped.
A similar practice is found in the USSR.

31. For a discussion see Walker Connor, "An Overview of the
Ethnic Composition and Problems of Non-Arab Asia," in Tai S. Kang
ed., *Nationalism and the Crises of Ethnic Minorities in Asia*
(Westport, Connecticut: Greenwood, 1979), pp. 25-26.

32. Karpat, pp. 46-47.

33. Martial law was imposed in a large number of provinces
during the Winter of 1978-79 as a result of both Turkish-Kurdish
and Sunni-*Alevi* violence. Much of the violence was triggered by
the Islamic right.

34. The *Donmes*, the descendents of the followers of the false
Jewish messiah, Sabbatai Tzvi, who converted to Islam along with
him, were taxed at a rate twice that of Muslim Turks. The *Donmes*,
who are prominent in public and business life, have often been
targets of right-wing demagogy.

35. Mardin, pp. 291-294 argues that the NSP utilizes the underground network of the still-banned dervish orders, the *Tarikat*, as
a basis of electoral mobilization.

36. Elements of the Turkish Islamic right have called for
greater Pan-Islamic ties to the Arab states. This has led them
to espouse the Palestinian cause and to view Turkish Jews as a
potential Zionist fifth column.

37. Mr. Cemal Kefadar, then a student at Hamilton College,
conducted the interviews using intermediaries from each of the four
ethnic groups.

38. Most of the Kurds were interviewed in Malatya. All of
the Greeks, Armenians, and Jews lived in Istanbul.

39. The four ethnic groups are socio-economically as well as religiously differentiated. Ethnicity was found to be significantly and strongly related to both income level (Cramer's V = .46) and occupation (Cramer's V = .55). Jews had the highest income levels, while Kurds had the lowest, and the Greeks and Armenians were in an intermediate position. Most Kurds were either peasants or laborers while the non-Muslims were concentrated in entrepreneurial activities.

40. See the cases in Howard Giles and Bernard St-Jacques eds., *Language and Ethnic Relations* (Oxford: Pergamon, 1979).

41. See the analysis in Kenneth P. Langton, *Political Socialization* (New York: Oxford University Press, 1969), pp. 84-119.

42. The effects of discrimination are discussed in Hubert Blalock Jr., *Toward a Theory of Minority Group Relations* (New York: Capricorn, 1967), pp. 186-189.

43. See Jeffrey A. Ross, "The Relationship between the Perception of Historical Symbols and the Alienation of Jewish Emigrants from the Soviet Union," *Western Political Quarterly* 32 (June 1979), pp. 215-224.

44. Robert E. Lane, *Political Thinking and Consciousness* (Chicago: Markham, 1969), pp. 228-311.

45. This is a most sensitive question, and it is not surprising that Greeks and Armenians had a relatively high no response rate.

46. Ozbudun reports that the poorer, more rural and traditional Turks have a generally higher voting turnout than their more affluent, urban compatriots. See Ergun Ozbudun, *Social Change and Political Participation in Turkey* (Princeton: Princeton University Press, 1976), pp. 12-13.

47. Religious observance and belief are not significantly related to the respondents' SES.

48. Ozbudun, pp. 12-13.

24
Religion and Politics
in South Arabia

Robert W. Stookey

The religious element in the long political history of Yemen presents a certain challenge to analysis. Some religious--and irreligious--phenomena that appeared in antiquity have remained operative to our day. At various junctures in the area's turbulent past, on the other hand, it is not easy to assess the respective weight to be ascribed to religious principle, to tribal rivalries, and to personal cupidity or ambition in determining the course of events. The territory, moreover, is not homogeneous, and the diversity in terrain, resources, and outlook has been accentuated by the fact that it has only rarely, and fleetingly, composed a single political unit. Finally, the impact of Western culture, including its secular political norms, differed considerably between the area now comprising the Yemen Arab Republic and the People's Democratic Republic of Yemen, respectively, producing divergent attitudes towards modes of government and the proper role of religious considerations in ordering community affairs. In both, the role of the faith has undoubtedly declined in recent times as a political determinant.

ANTIQUITY AND EARLY ISLAM

The tribal structure of South Arabian society, discernible from the earliest records, has altered appreciably only in recent years. Until well into the Christian era, each of the South Arabian tribes worshiped its own particular deity. The pervasiveness of religion in public affairs varied from tribe to tribe. Ma'in appears to have been ruled in large part by a priestly bureaucracy; the king served as high priest, and public works were constructed in the name, and at the behest, of the God. The cult appears to have held a less preponderant place in Saba, where the monarch or the clan chiefs often

took credit for the building of dams and other community
enterprises. The religious hierarchy played a prominent
role in the transit trade between the Indian Ocean and the
Mediterranean which, with agriculture, formed the basis of
economic life. Temples often served as entrepots where
merchandise was stored for onward shipment after payment
of a tax in support of the cult. Interestingly, the Yemeni
gods were not conceived as rivals or enemies, as was the
case, for example, between Baal and Yahweh in ancient
Palestine. Inscriptions, indeed, might express the respect
of one tribe for the deity of its neighbor. The wars of
conquest among the ancient Yemeni states--Ma'in, Saba,
Hadramawt, Awsan, and Qataban--had as their principal, and
purely secular, objective control over trade and the caravan
routes. During the first centuries of the new era South
Arabia lost its monopoly of the entrepot trade. Seafarers
from Egypt discovered the regime of the Indian Ocean monsoons.
An increasing share of the merchandise was carried in ships
sailing direct from Egypt (and later, Persia) to and from
the Far East, by-passing Yemen and reducing the role of land-
ward transport. Yemen attained political unity under the
Himyarite tribe, but its political capabilities decreased,
along with the central government's control over the restive
tribes.

     Meanwhile, South Arabia's contact with the Ethiopian
empire of Aksum, with Rome (and its successor, Byzantium),
and with Persia quickened. One concomitant of this was the
spread of the concept of monotheism, introduced by Jewish
immigrants before the dawn of the Christian era and lent
further impetus by Christian missionary activity beginning
in the fourth century. While the myriad tribal deities
were discredited only gradually, the principle that God is
one, and the manner in which He should be worshipped, became
major preoccupations of the last Himyarite dynasty. A
massacre of Christians at Najran by the Judaizing King Dhu
Nuwas precipitated an occupation of Yemen by Aksum, encouraged
by Byzantium. A successor, Abraha, who had embraced Christianity, rebelled successfully against Ethiopian rule. The
country was insufficiently mobilized behind his crusading
policy, however. In the Year of the Elephant (570), when
Abraha was embarked on his storied expedition against the
pagan shrines at Mecca, Himyarite noblemen prevailed upon
Chosroes I of Sassanid Persia to destroy their monarch.
A hastily-assembled army of convicts sufficed to occupy
Yemen and make it a Persian province. Exhausted, however,
by its wars with the Byzantines, Persia lacked the strength
to consolidate its hold over the territory. At the dawn of
Islam Yemen had collapsed into its virtually autonomous
tribal elements. The titular rulers, sons of the Persian
conquerors, had themselves become tantamount to a tribe,
competing on equal terms with the indigenous peoples and
exerting minimal influence beyond the environs of Sanaa,
the capital.

Islamic tradition has held that the people of Yemen were converted to Islam *en masse* during the lifetime of the Prophet Muhammad, who confirmed the Persians in their rule of the country; that al-Aswad Abhala bin Ka'b, of the 'Ans tribe of the Madhhij confederation, set himself up as a rival prophet, seized Sanaa, and expelled Muhammad's agents; that the Persians conspired with chiefs of the Zubaid and Himyar tribes to overthrow al-Aswad but then became the object of a movement by their co-conspirators aimed at freeing Yemen from both Persian rule and that of the nascent Islamic state head-quartered at Medina; and that the country was restored to obedience to Islam by armies sent from Hijaz. Contemporary study of the conflicting early sources treating these events tends to cast doubt on the religious motivations alleged, and on the notion that the revolt in Yemen can properly be in-cluded in the apostasy from Islam that preoccupied Abu Bakr, the first caliph.[1] Neither al-Aswad nor the Zubaid and Himyar chiefs who collaborated briefly with him had been converted to Islam; they were thus not apostates. Their actions can be interpreted more reasonably in terms of an intertribal struggle for supremacy along ancient customary lines, in which some contenders sought outside help against their rivals.

Through the content of Muhammad's revelation and the precedents he set as a ruler, many principles and procedures already solidly rooted in the conduct of public affairs in the Arabian Peninsula were incorporated in the new faith, with some adaptation.[2] In order to mitigate the chaos and suffering attendant upon the perennial feuding, raiding, and warfare among the tribes, pagan Arabia had developed the device of delimiting enclaves, often the site of some natural object believed to possess supernatural properties, where the prohibition against violence was respected by all and where, often at a fixed pilgrimage season, mutually hostile tribesmen could meet, engage in trade, perform religious rites, and negotiate over their differences. Custody of such precincts was vested in recognized clans which con-stituted an aristocracy specialized in the mediation of dis-putes and in the conduct of the cult. In Islam this custom took form in the holiness ascribed to the cities of Mecca and Medina--the *haramain*--and in the revered status of the Prophet's tribe of Quraysh.

When the Abbasid caliphate's control over Yemen relaxed, local authority was assumed by small autonomous states, often at war with each other and all harried by the indiscipline of tribes determined to keep outside authority at arm's length. Descendants of the Prophet gradually settled through-out the area, assumed leadership in religious affairs, and inherited the ancient role of arbitrators. In the northern highlands, where the Zaidi sect of Shia Islam prevailed, the sacred-enclave institution was eradicated as smacking of idolatry, although the political function it served survived in modified form. In present South Yemen the enclaves

(locally called *hawta*) flourished under the management of
the new religious aristocracy. In the south, the Prophet's
posterity relied mainly on their learning in the faith, their
expertise in mediation, and the charisma of their descent
in exerting influence. In the Zaidi north the sayyids became
warriors, propagating their concept of the true faith by the
sword.

Although Islam posited the political unity of all Muslims
and regarded the aim of government as the salvation of men's
souls by enforcing the dictates of Muhammad's revelation and
his example, religion was by no means the sole motivating
factor in the many states that rose and disappeared in medieval
Yemen. Piety and knowledge of the faith, certainly, could be
effective tools in mobilizing men for political ends, as the
Fatimids' agents demonstrated, but the resulting structures
proved fragile. The Sulayhid kingdom (1045-1138) was much
reduced in extent in its later years and troubled by dissidence
led by Shafei religious figures; but its death blow was dealt
by tribal feudatories in whose ambition religion had no part.
Some political entities, such as the Yu'firid state based
on Sanaa (840-1003) and the Hatim sultans who ruled in Sanaa
and Aden in the 11th and 12th centuries, represented successful struggles for tribal supremacy; and the ease with which
their nominal spiritual loyalty shifted among Fatimids,
orthodox caliphs, and Zaidi imams hardly suggests that they
were moved primarily by religious conviction. The pervasiveness of the "warlord" character of Yemeni politics of the
time is aptly illustrated by the boisterous Hamza Sharifs,
who were descendants of an early Zaidi imam but who kept
northern Yemen in turmoil for many decades by a career of
violence and plunder. In the same region a durable and
ultimately successful movement to establish the faith as
the wellspring of political life was nevertheless gestating,
in the form of Zaidism.

THE ZAIDI IMAMATE

At the end of the ninth century no centralized authority
existed in the far north of what is now the Yemen Arab
Republic. Distress prevailed among the tribes around the
town of Saada due to insoluble quarrels among them, aggravated
by a prolonged drouth. The chiefs of two warring clans agreed
to seek an outside mediator, and their choice fell upon
Yahya bin Hussein, of the Rassid clan of sayyids then residing
near Medina. Their envoys prevailed upon him to settle among
them and order their affairs, promising that his guidance
would be followed in all respects. This obscure event,
strikingly reminiscent of pre-Islamic mechanisms for the
resolution of disputes and of the circumstances of the
Prophet's hegira, became the germ of the Zaidi state that
endured well over a thousand years.

Zaidi doctrine, in contrast with other branches of the

Shia, ascribes spiritual and temporal authority--the imamate--
in the Muslim community to any descendant of Ali and Fatima
who is of sound mind and body, learned in the faith, and
willing to enforce by the sword obedience to its commands.[3]
This concept of the imamate is the sole fundamental distinction between Zaidism and Sunni orthodoxy. In theology, Zaidi
theory rejects the idea of a "hidden" imam, any esoteric
interpretation of the scriptures, and the dissimulation of
religious belief--features typical of other Shia branches.
In jurisprudence the Zaidis consider that *ijtihad* remains
permissible, and draw readily upon the four Sunni schools
in deciding points of law.
    The first imam in Yemen, who assumed the title al-Hadi,
made it clear that he proposed to enforce the full gamut of
duties incumbent upon good Muslims as interpreted by Zaidi
theory: prayer, fasting, avoidance of adultery, women's
right to inherit property in prescribed proportions, keeping
the peace within the Muslim community, the bearing of arms
in defense and propagation of the faith, and above all the
payment of the canonical tithes on the produce of the land.
This concept of the purpose of government remained the fixed
orientation of the Yemeni imamate until its extinction in
1970.
    It became immediately apparent that the tribes who invited
al-Hadi into Yemen had a very different view of his mission.
They had sought a charismatic mediator in their quarrels, not
the extinction of their identity and rivalries in a single
theocratic community. Although nominal Muslims, they were
strongly attached to ancient social customs including the
use of spirituous beverages and fornication with both males
and females. They were little inclined to renounce the
lucrative ransoming or plunder of travelers on the roads.
They resented the imposition of taxes, particularly as
al-Hadi's tax-gatherers appear sometimes to have exceeded
the prescribed assessments. Each tribe, moreover, was
accustomed to regulating its internal affairs--marriage,
divorce, inheritance, crimes against person or property,
etc.--by its own customary code of law (*'urf*) differing in
many details from the sharia. The imams never succeeded in
eradicating the tribal codes, and the YAR today, whose
constitution invokes the sharia as the basis of all law,
has been unable to do so among the northern, ostensibly
Zaidi, tribes.[4]
    Naturally enough, the divergence in political outlook
produced tension. The story of al-Hadi's reign is one of
constant armed struggle against sin and rebellion by tribes
who had sworn to obey the imam; of their repentance and
return to obedience; and of intermittent efforts to extend
the nascent state southward. The imam had no resources
beyond the tithes that could be extracted from the mostly
impoverished tribesmen. Operations of large scope were out
of the question for the founder and his early successors.
The state grew very slowly in geographical extent, and even

suffered an extended hiatus during the era of the Sulayhids
and the Hatim sultans (1053-1138) when the imamate had no
incumbent.

Zaidism was preserved during this period of trial by al-
Hadi's posterity and that of other sayyids who followed him
into Yemen. Often a sayyid would settle by invitation in the
territory of a tribe, providing guidance in the faith and
mediating in private or inter-clan disputes, while the tribe
gained a certain prestige from his presence. Over time, many
sayyid families accumulated land and wealth. Marrying almost
exclusively among themselves, they came to constitute an
aristocracy that tended to promote a modicum of political
cohesion in the areas converted to Zaidism. On the other
hand, any sayyid family was in principle capable of producing
an imam; and since primogeniture, however attractive to some
imams,[5] was doctrinally irrelevant, succession disputes became
of common occurrence. Two or more claimants might appear
in widely separated parts of the country, each supported by
a coalition of tribes and religious notables, the issue
being resolved by armed force. Although the majority of
Yemen's 70-odd imams were descendants of al-Hadi, one was
the great-grandson of his brother Abdullah, and ten were
descended from his paternal uncles; a half-dozen were progeny
of Zaid bin Hasan bin Ali bin Abi Talib, and were thus not
Rassids; several, finally, claimed as ancestor not Hasan
bin Ali but his younger brother Hussein, the martyred saint
of "Twelver" Shiism.

Although the imam, once confirmed by the sworn fealty
of leading sayyids, religious scholars, and tribal chiefs,
was acknowledged ultimate spiritual insight, the sayyids
nevertheless monitored the canonical soundness of his acts.
Over time they were seconded in this function by indigenous
Yemenis who acquired competence in the religious sciences
and thus became qualified to serve in administrative
capacities. Eventually they composed a distinct class,
termed qadis, second only to the sayyids in wealth and
political influence. Both aristocracies, but particularly
the qadis, were actively involved in the twenty-year sub-
versive movement that toppled the last Zaidi dynasty, the
Hamid al-Din. The extent to which religious conviction
motivated the dissidents is a rather obscure problem, but
some relevant observations can be set forth.

There is no reason to doubt that the Hamid al-Din
imams, Yahya and Ahmad, whose independent reign spanned the
years 1919-1962, strove to rule by the precepts of the faith.
They endeavored, with very partial success, to keep Yemen
isolated in order to protect their subjects from corrupting
outside influences, through concern for their spiritual
welfare. In practice this tended to contract an already
primitive economy; in order to conduct a central government
and maintain pressure against the British in the *terra
irredenta* of South Yemen, they were compelled to make
regressive tax and other exactions going well beyond the

literal, canonical prescriptions, and this discouraged
production. Their rule was thus harsh, and unresponsive
even to public censure by the ulama. Both imams departed
from Zaidi principle by forcing recognition of their eldest
son as heir apparent to the imamate, thus closing the door
to the ambitions of other, equally qualified sayyid families
and shattering the unity of the royal family itself. The
invidious contrast between the situation of Yemen and the
prosperity and freedom in other countries certainly impressed
itself at all levels of Yemeni society and eroded loyalty to
the concept of divinely-sanctioned rule by a single individual.
    The attitudes of the qadi class in this connection are a
little ambiguous. Qadi Abdul Rahman al-Iryani, a prominent
case in point, became one of Yemen's top jurists under the
old regime, served Imam Ahmad in a post comparable to minister
of justice, served a long prison term for conspiracy against
the Hamid al-Din, and became president of the YAR from 1967
to 1974. The present writer referred to him in a published
work as an "eminent Zaidi jurist." Recently I received a
message from a youthful relative of the former president
challenging this description and asserting that the Iryanis
are not, and never have been, Zaidis. The family are said
to be 14th-century immigrants from the Maghrib who settled
in a village on the border between Zaidi and Shafei territory.
If such a family did in fact harbor for six centuries a secret
rejection of the religious duty of obedience to the imamate,
this would be a remarkable instance of *taqiyya* (dissimulation
of one's true religious beliefs). Other qadis presently
serving in government posts to whom I have put the question
whether they consider themselves Zaidis have given equivocal
replies, but point out that the imamate is the sole distinctive feature of Zaidism. What is clear is that the
Yemeni people of all classes, including the sayyids, have
accommodated themselves without noticeable difficulty to
the end of the imamate, and there is no discernible movement
to restore theocratic rule by the Prophet's descendants.
    Evidence is not lacking of a pronounced shift in the
preoccupations of Yemeni society from spiritual concerns to
those of material well-being during the 1940s and 1950s, and
that this was accompanied by a change in the concept of the
proper locus of government authority. Even the "Party of
God" organized by Muhammad Mahmoud al-Zubayri during the
civil war of the 1960s sought primarily to unite the country
against the Egyptian occupation and other foreign intervention, not to achieve specific religious ends. Even
within the royalist camp attitudes were transformed; Imam
al-Badr's foreign minister formulated proposals for
representative government under a monarchy with consti-
tutionally limited powers, while young royalist officials,
both qadis and sayyids, came close to revolt against the
refusal of the Hamid al-Din princes to delegate what they
considered their proper authority as civil servants.
    The YAR nevertheless reserves an important place for

religion in society and government.   The Constitution
acknowledges the sharia to be the source of all law.
Specialists in the *shari'a* preside over the courts, and the
college of canon law in Sanaa University is among the most
popular departments.   The counsel of the ulama is respect-
fully heard, if not always followed, by the current military
regime.   Continuity is illustrated by the fact that the
grand mufti (a new office under the republic, and a more
typically Sunni than Shiite one), served the *ancien régime*
as chief justice, and was a son-in-law of Imam Ahmad.   As
we have noted, however, *'urf* is still followed by some of
the large northern tribes in preference to the sharia.
There is considerable Yemeni reluctance to bow to Saudi
pressure by applying the full range of canonical punishment
for wrong-doers.   In general, it is difficult to single
out items of current YAR policy clearly based on religious
considerations.

It might be supposed that with the end of the imamate
one major obstacle to national unity in the YAR--the
dichotomy between the Zaidis in the north and the Shafeis
to the south and along the coast--has disappeared.   The
separate identity does in fact persist, but whether it now
revolves around sectarian differences can be questioned.
That it had specific religious overtones in the past is
suggested by an anecdote related of the late Imam Ahmad:
A group of fervently Zaidi notables once denounced the
Shafeis to him for departing from the true faith, and urged
him to move with a strong hand against their waywardness.
The Imam rebuked them by rising and performing a cycle of
prayers according to the Shafei procedures.

Shafeism became nearly universal in its present sector
of Yemen under the Rasulids (1229-ca. 1442 A.D.).   Their
Tahirid successors were destroyed by the Circassian Mamelukes
of Egypt in 1517, but were forced by the Zaidi Imam Sharaf
al-Din to retreat to the Tihama.   The Imam's son Shams
al-Din, appointed to govern the southern highlands from his
seat at Ta'izz, did so so oppressively that the Shafeis
were willing auxiliaries of the Ottoman Turks who invaded
the high Yemen at mid-century.   The Shafei areas were re-
taken by the Qasimi imams who freed Yemen from the Turks
early in the 17th century.   Thenceforth those in authority
over the Shafeis were Zaidis--soldiers, administrators,
and tax-collectors--save for their purely local shaikhs
and ulama.   Furthermore, following an ancient pattern,
Zaidi tribes conducted plundering raids into the south,
despite the imams' occasional efforts to restrain them.[6]
The depredations amounted at times to protracted occupation,
such as that by the Dhu Muhammad and Dhu Hussein branches
of Ghailan in Hujariya, on the present PDRY border.   The
1962 revolution diminished, without erasing, the gap in
status between the two communities, and it appears likely
that the Zaidi reluctance to relinquish the upper hand,
more than sectarian spirit, renders many Shafeis susceptible

to subversion from beyond the border. It is worth noting
that the late President Ibrahim al-Hamdi, the post-revolution
leader with the strongest country-wide appeal, withdrew
Zaidi security forces from the Shafei areas near the frontier,
and endeavored to curb the rapacious conduct of some local
chiefs, many of whom are popularly believed to descend from
Zaidi intruders.

SOUTH YEMEN

     Traditional society in the territory now comprising
South Yemen was organized along lines generally similar to
those in the north, although with even more fragmentation.
The proportion of nomadic population was markedly greater.
The peasant population was differentiated from the warlike
tribes, which was not the case in the Zaidi north. The
rugged terrain and the low productivity of the land seem
to have contributed to a pattern of small tribes, often at
war with their neighbors and recognizing no outside authority
except in those historical junctures where international
commerce was channeled through the area and provided the
resources to support large political units. In such a
society the ancient Arabian phenomenon of the sacred enclave
was a particular necessity, and its management passed into
the hands of the sayyids.[7]
     Sayyids entered South Yemen about the middle of the 10th
century, several decades after the founding of the Zaidi
state in the north. Although most numerous in the eastern
reaches of the Wadi Hadramawt, they settled among tribes
in other areas also, gaining spiritual influence over the
people, asserting the right to counsel the tribal chiefs,
and assuming the function of arbitration in disputes.
In contrast with their Zaidi cousins, the southern sayyids
adhered to Sunni orthodoxy of the Shafei rite. With rare
exceptions,[8] they did not seek to rule directly. They
generally avoided bearing arms; where conflict arose between
them and one or other of the many sultans, emirs, or chiefs
who wielded temporal power, the sayyids could usually rely
upon the military support of the tribes with whom they
had become associated. Beginning in the 15th century
sayyids (as well as commoners) began to emigrate in search
of economic opportunity to the East Indies, Hijaz, and
later East Africa, and many became quite rich. They maintained close contact with the homeland, often returning
there at the close of their careers. Wealth bolstered their
political influence.
     By 1839, the date of the British occupation of Aden,
the prosperity and relative unity South Yemen had known
under the Rasulids, Tahirids, and Ottomans from the 13th
to the 16th centuries were long past.[9] The region was a
mosaic of petty tribal states isolated from world commerce
and barely subsisting on the land's meager produce. The

once flourishing port of Aden was a neglected, ruinous village
of three thousand or so inhabitants.

The stimulus for the British entry stemmed in part
from rivalry with other European powers and in part from
politico-religious events in the Peninsula. The Wahhabi
movement for the reform of Islam overran the holy cities
early in the 19th century and penetrated Yemen's northern
reaches. Muhammad Ali's Egyptian forces pushed the zealots
back from Hijaz, occupied their Nejdi homeland, and pressed
on to the Persian Gulf. With an eye on control of the
coffee trade, the Egyptians seized the North Yemeni Tihama.
Regarding the control of Arabia by a single vigorous power
as a threat to its communications with India, Britain
exerted pressure on the Egyptian ruler to abandon his adventures beyond Suez and forestalled his moves eastward from
the Bab al-Mandab by taking possession of Aden, as a strategic
asset and a potentially lucrative commercial emporium.

In the task of developing sufficiently cooperative relations with the neighboring rulers to ensure the security
of their settlement and its trade with the hinterland, the
British were able to draw on the knowledge and advice of
a member of the 'Aidarus clan of sayyids, resident in Aden.
Other religious figures, however, worked to stir up the
tribesmen against infidel encroachment. Assaults on British
personnel reinforced the reluctance of the Government of
India, directly responsible for Aden, as well as the London
authorities, to assume responsibility beyond the port's
immediate environs, and British influence inland spread
only slowly. After mid-century the rise of the pan-Islamic
movement, espoused by the Ottoman sultans, forced a more
vigorous policy on Britain. The Porte asserted a claim to
sovereignty over the entire Arabian Peninsula. When Ottoman
troops moved into the North Yemen highlands in 1871 they were
in a position to influence the fickle attitudes of the South
Yemeni rulers, and Turkish forces advanced to within twenty
miles of Aden. The British took strong diplomatic action
in 1873, asserting to the Porte their interest in the
independence of the nine-tribe political constellation
centered on the Abdali state, crucial to Aden's security.

Meanwhile, protracted wars had broken out between
Kathiri and Qu'aiti contenders for paramountcy in the Wadi
Hadramawt and the adjacent coastline, an area the British
had previously considered irrelevant to their interests
beyond ensuring that no other outside power acquired influence there. In 1867 Hadrami religious leaders petitioned
the Sharif of Mecca, and through him the Porte, to intervene
to end the conflict. The Turks undertook some desultory
naval activity, and even appointed a local sayyid as their
governor of Hadramawt. The preponderance of local opinion,
however, opposed submission to Ottoman rule and both sides
appealed to Britain to halt Turkish interference. Hadrami
mercenaries who had amassed great wealth in the service of
the Nizam of Hyderabad provided the arms and money that

fueled the civil war, and as leaders of both sides held
senior positions at the Nizam's court, the dispute threatened
India's own domestic tranquility. The fact that the religious
leaders in Hadramawt, with their pan-Islamic and thus pro-
Ottoman leanings, were mainly supporters of the Kathiri
sultan, was among the considerations leading the British to
throw their support to the Qu'aiti sultan, with the result
that by 1881 his forces controlled the coast and much of the
interior. Treaties of 1881 and 1888 formalized a British
protectorate of the Qu'aiti state. This did not, however,
result in an early extension of British presence into the
Hadramawt, where the sayyids' influence promoted a xenophobia
that began to relax only in the 1930s.

The Turkish challenge to the independence of the South
Yemeni states and to British influence was succeeded after
the First World War by that of the Zaidi imams, in whose
claim to sovereignty over all South Arabia dynastic ambition
and the religious spirit of *jihad* were inextricably mingled.
Beginning in the 1880s this pressure induced the South Yemeni
rulers, one by one, to seek British help in preserving their
autonomy. Earlier *ad hoc* agreements on commerce and the slave
trade gave way to treaties of protection, eventually blanketing
the territory. Later, when Britain perceived its duties as
extending to the fields of economic development and the introduction of liberal Western styles of administration, the
agreements came to include advisory treaties by which some
rulers undertook to follow British counsel in the conduct of
their government. Consistently in all these pacts it was
specified that matters related to the Islamic faith were
excluded from the protecting power's purview. (The Colony
of Aden, under direct British rule, was governed from the
first along Western, and purely secular, lines.)

When this elaborate process began no one, Arab or British,
foresaw its ultimately revolutionary consequences for the
future nature of South Yemen's politics. It established by
implication the principle, alien to Islamic theory, that
politics and the faith are separable compartments, and in
the end made the principle reality. The evolution was not
uniform throughout the region, nor did it proceed at the same
pace in all the states, but the overall trend may be briefly
summarized.

Traditionally the rulers were selected from among members
of recognized clans by consensus of the shaikhs of the tribes
composing the state and the most prominent sayyids. The
religious aspect of the process was symbolized in some cases
by the sayyid's investiture of the new ruler with his distinctive turban. The sayyid had unquestioned access to the
ruler to offer advice and advance petitions on behalf of the
citizens. As Aden developed, revenues from road tolls on the
several competing routes to the port became an important
resource for the conduct of government in several states, and
the object of conflict of which the solution was a traditional
function of the sayyids. The security and economic consequences

of the situation engaged the British who, not entirely
realistically, dealt with the rulers from the first as fully
sovereign in their lands. In order to stimulate trade, the
tactic was adopted of encouraging the decrease or elimination
of road taxes, the shortfall in revenue being made up by
British subsidies. A pattern of British intervention arose
where the Aden authorities assisted the rulers in disciplining
their often rebellious tribes and assumed a principal role in
settling their mutual quarrels. Eventually British influence
became decisive in deposing a ruler, in the choice of his
successor, and in the aims and conduct of his government, even
though the protecting power expanded its administrative powers
only slowly and reluctantly while preserving intact the principle that the Protectorate states were independent entities.

     This political transformation, with the accompanying
economic and social change, tended to exclude religion and
its exponents, the sayyids, from the process of government.
With the introduction of Western-type schools, religious
scholars lost their monopoly of education. Civil courts
applying secular codes of law appeared, reducing correspondingly the role of Islamic jurists in settling controversy.
The sayyids generally fought innovation and modernization,
as well as the elevation of tribal chiefs to the highest
level of society they themselves had formerly occupied.
Their ability to resist effectively declined rapidly after
the Second World War when the sources of their wealth dried
up under pressure of nationalism in the Dutch East Indies,
India, and East Africa. Resort to a sayyid for arbitration
of a private dispute began to be a pecuniarily costly
alternative to the civil courts.[10] Sayyids lacking landed
estates found themselves obliged to enter the various
bureaucracies, competing on more or less equal terms with
commoners to whom the new institutions afforded avenues of
upward social mobility and material prosperity previously
impossible to conceive.

     When, in the late 1950s, the full force of Arab national-
ist propaganda from Cairo, Damascus, and Baghdad was focused
against the British position in Aden and the Protectorates,
the mass audience was well conditioned to respond to the
appeal for populist revolution. The religious establishment
was already discredited as a locus of political authority
by its conservatism and by the new tradition of modernizing,
secular government. The existing structure of rule by chiefly
clans, and the South Arabian Federation based on it, were
hopelessly compromised by their dependence on the British,
who could offer no effective ideological riposte to the
nationalists' mass appeal. The structure collapsed even
before the British evacuated the territory in 1967, and the
National Liberation Front proceeded to the organization of its
people on entirely new bases. It is difficult to point to any
social group or ideology around which effective opposition
to its radicalism might now be mobilized.

     The PDRY constitution declares Islam to be the state

religion, and its senior figures lead the prayers on traditional religious holidays. The regime has moved rather
cautiously in revising legislation on such matters as inheritance, marriage, divorce, the status of women, etc.,
traditionally the province of the sharia. In general,
however, religious considerations appear to play a minimal
role in the formulation of either domestic or external
policies. In such cases as PDRY support of Ethiopia
against Somalia, their action in fact appears hostile to the
interests of Islam as perceived by the conservative governments on the Arabian Peninsula. The disestablishment of
Islamic law in the PDRY raises perhaps insuperable problems
for its union with the YAR--a stated primary objective of
both republics, strongly endorsed by the Arab League, and
urged on Sanaa and Aden by Arab leaders of various shades
of opinion.[11]

NOTES

1. Elias Shoufani, *Al-Riddah and the Muslim Conquest of Arabia*
(Toronto: Toronto University Press, 1973), pp. 89-95.
2. A concise description of the process may be found in R. B.
Serjeant's "Historical Review," the opening chapter of *Religion in
the Middle East*, vol. 2, A. J. Arberry, ed. (Cambridge University
Press, 1969), esp. pp. 3-16.
3. The standard Western work on the Zaidiya is Cornelius van
Arendonk, *Les Débuts de l'Imamat Zaidite au Yemen* (Leiden: E. J.
Brill, 1960). See also R. B. Serjeant's "The Zaydis" in Arberry,
op. cit., pp. 285-301; and the present writer's *Yemen: The Politics
of the Yemen Arab Republic* (Boulder: Westview Press, 1978), pp. 79-99.
4. The YAR Grand Mufti, Sayyid Ahmad Muhammad Zabara, asserted
to me with some bitterness that the Shaikhs continue to rule their
tribes according to the *'urf*, in defiance of the central government.
(Conversation on March 3, 1980.)
5. There were exceptions. In 1552 the aged Imam Sharaf al-Din
lost his eyesight and thus, theoretically, his qualification for the
imamate. Recognizing that his own sons were mere warlords motivated
by secular ambition instead of religious principle, he appealed to
the Mu'ayyad clan of sayyids to put forward a claimant to the imamate.
Two successive candidates failed to muster substantial support, and
the Turkish occupation suspended the imamate for a time.
6. See the present writer's *Yemen*, op. cit., pp. 153-154.
7. R. B. Serjeant, *The Saiyids of Hadramawt* (University of London,
School of Oriental and African Studies, 1957).
8. Notably, the Emirate of Baihan, ruled by a sharif (i.e.,
sayyid) family until the 1967 revolution.
9. The process of decline is well analyzed by R. J. Gavin,
Aden under British Rule (London: C. Hurst & Co., 1975), pp. 16-20.
10. Mohamed el Habashi, *Aden: L'Evolution Politique, Economique
et Sociale de l'Arabie du Sud* (Algiers: Société Nationale d'Edition
et de Diffusion, 1966), pp. 401-402.
11. The YAR Grand Mufti, in the conversation mentioned above

(Note 4), expressed the view that the incompatibility between
the two legal systems is the principal obstacle to union.

APPENDIX
A Directory of
Modern Islam

Daniel Pipes

SUNNIS

The overwhelming majority of Muslims--some 93 percent--
adhere to non-sectarian Islam. Known as Sunnis (*sunna* =
"beaten path"), they predominate in nearly all the Muslim
regions. Virtually no communities of sectarian Muslims
live in Morocco, the savannah and desert lands of West
Africa, or in Egypt, Central Arabia, Bengal, China and
Southeast Asia.

In modern times, little distinguishes one Sunni from
another. Until the nineteenth century, the four *madhhab*s
(systems of jurisprudence, usually translated as "law
schools") divided Sunnis and constituted an important part
of their identity, but these have almost disappeared from
the Muslim consciousness. As European influence grew,
Islamic law weakened and its juridical divisions lost most
of their importance.

Sufism

Sufi *tariqa*s, the mystically-oriented brotherhoods,
retain social and political significance in some places;
yet even where strongest, as the Tijaniya is in West Africa
or the Bektashiya in the Balkans, they seldom constitute a
"branch" of Islam (though the Murids of Senegal provide a
striking exception). Instead, they supplement a Muslim's
primary allegiance to Islam with a closer, smaller bond.
The Sanusis of Cyrenaica in Libya had the strongest grip
of any major *tariqa* in modern times, providing both the
Libyan national identity and its ruler, but al-Qadhafi's
government has suppressed it since coming to power in 1969.

Wahhabism

Numerous Sunni reform movements have developed during

the past two hundred and fifty years, starting with Wahhabism.
Its founder, Muhammad ibn 'Abd al-Wahhab (1703-91) rejected
the many accretions Islam had acquired over the centuries and
tried to return to the simple faith of the seventh century.
This singularly stark and harsh vision of Islam grew powerful
in Eastern Arabia and, in a much diluted form, still remains
the ideology of the Saudi government. Wahhabism inspired the
ideology of the Saudi government. Wahhabism inspired innumerable other movements across the Islamic world, from China
and Indonesia to West Africa, some of which, such as the Ansar
(descendants of the Sudanese Mahdi's followers) remain
politically active today).

Ahmadis*

Modern Sunni Islam has spawned only one sect, the *Ahmadis*.
Its founder, Mirza Ghulam Ahmad (c. 1839-1908), an Indian
Muslim, began receiving revelations in 1876, and in 1890 he
claimed to be the *mahdi* (the figure in Islamic eschatology
who initiates the sequence of events which ends the world).
His followers split into two groups after his death. The
Qadyanis remained true to Ahmad's full claim. The *Lahoris*
denied that he had ever thought of himself as a prophet or
mahdi. Ahmadis consider themselves not a sect but regular
Sunni Muslims; this, however, is passionately denied by mainstream Sunnis. The movement has not met with any success in
the old Muslim lands except for Pakistan, but it has found
followings in Indochina and coastal West Africa. Ahmadis
are the only group seriously proselytizing in the Christian
West, where they emphasize the idea that Jesus survived
crucifixion, lived to the age of a hundred and twenty in
Kashmir and now lies entombed in Srinagar. Ahmadis number
between 500,000 and one million. In 1974, the Pakistan
National Assembly ruled that they are not Muslims.

SHI'IS

In the West, Shi'is are occasionally called the Protestants of Islam, an utterly inaccurate description in every
way but one: like Protestants, Shi'is have a tendency toward
schism and toward breaking into smaller and smaller groups
until, finally, some disappear. In short, they share a
problem of authority. Of the many Shi'i differences with
Protestantism (for example, Shi'ism appeared in the first
years of Islam; it does not diverge liturgically in important
ways from Sunnism), the most trenchant is this: while
Protestants split over arguments about truth, Shi'is split
over issues of power. Shi'i groups, that is, began as

---

*The asterisk indicates that a group's adherence to Islam is
 questioned or rejected by mainstream Muslims.

political factions and then developed into religious movements
while Protestant groups did the reverse. In every case where
a new Shi'i group emerged, it had a leader; only secondly did
it also claim a distinct vision of religious truth.

All Shi'is believe in the special role of 'Ali b. Abi
Talib, cousin and son-in-law of the Prophet Muhammad, and of
his descendants, the 'Alids. Although Sunnis share with
Shi'is a natural affection for the House of Muhammad (even
today two Sunni kings, Husayn of Jordan and Hasan of Morocco,
claim Muhammad as an ancestor), they deny 'Ali and the 'Alids
a special place in Islam. Shi'is have always been in the
minority, though they briefly challenged the predominance
of Sunnism in the tenth century. Except for the Zaydis
(see below), Shi'i political psychology is primarily suited
to an opposition role; its tendencies toward secrecy, dissimu-
latin, and martyrdom are hardly appropriate to the religion
of rulers.

Shi'i groups derive their identities from 'Ali's descendants.
The partial genealogy (Fig. A-1, p. 366) outlines their family
relationship.

Zaydis

Zaydis are the most moderate, least sectarian of all
Shi'i groups. They consider Zayd b. 'Ali b. al-Husayn to
have been the fifth *imam* (supreme leader of the Muslim
community in Shi'i terminology). In contrast to other Shi'is,
Zaydis view the 'Alids as earthly leaders without divine
characteristics. Their imam does not differ very greatly
from the Sunnis' caliph. Zaydis have controlled two states,
one long ago by the Caspian Sea, the other in Yemen (from
about 850 until 1962 - except for a three-century hiatus,
1281-1592). Notables selected an imam from among the most
capable of Zayd's descendants, but they often disagreed,
causing repeated splits. The last Yemeni imam was deposed
in 1962, and lives in London, but still retains spiritual
authority for many Yemenis. Zaydis constitute perhaps
slightly over half the population of North Yemen where,
concentrated in the tribes, they have long formed the military
and social (but not economic) elite of the country. They
number about three million.

Twelvers (Ja'faris)

Apart from the Zaydis, all Shi'is believe in a sinless
and infallible imam and are divided into two main groups:
the *Imamis* and the Isma'ilis. More often known as *Twelvers*
(*Ithna'ashariya*) or *Ja'faris*, the Imamis believe in a line
of twelve manifest imams which ended in 874; since that time
imams have been hidden from most of mankind and will become
known to everyone again only at the time of the end of the
world (when they will be called the *mahdi*). In the meantime,
religious leaders (*mujtahids*, led by *marja'-i taqlids* or

Figure A-1. Partial Genealogy of Shi'i Groups

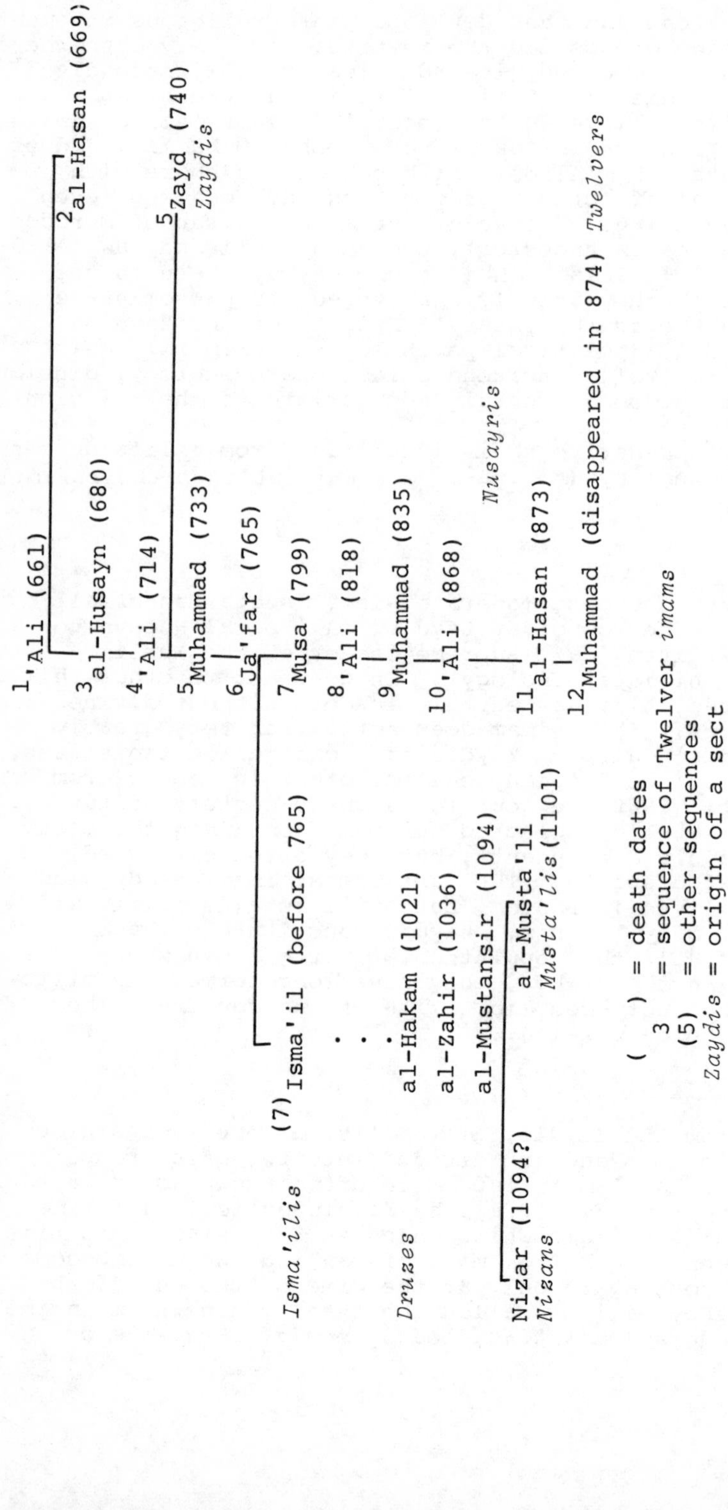

1'Ali (661)

2al-Hasan (669)

3al-Husayn (680)

5Zayd (740)
Zaydis

4'Ali (714)

5Muhammad (733)

6Ja'far (765)

(7)Isma'il (before 765)

7Musa (799)

8'Ali (818)

9Muhammad (835)

Nusayris

10'Ali (868)

11al-Hasan (873)

12Muhammad (disappeared in 874) *Twelvers*

Isma'ilis

al-Hakam (1021)

Druzes

al-Zahir (1036)

al-Mustansir (1094)

al-Musta'li (1101)
Musta'lis

Nizar (1094?)
Nizaris

( ) = death dates
3   = sequence of Twelver *imams*
(5) = other sequences
Zaydis = origin of a sect

*ayatullah*s) interpret the law on behalf of the hidden imam
and direct the community. In contrast to their authority,
which derives from God, that of political rulers is considered religiously irrelevant.

An anti-political attitude of this sort was simple to
maintain so long as Twelvers were out of power, but since the
establishment of the Savafid dynasty, in 1501, Twelver Shi'ism
has been the state religion of Iran. Accustomed to centuries
of opposition, its leaders have not yet defined their position
in a Twelver state ruled by a non-religious leader, and
religious authorities are inclined to take political power
themselves. Outside Iran, Twelvers lack power: in Iraq,
where they make up more than half the population, and in India,
Pakistan, Afghanistan, Kuwait, Bahrain, and Lebanon (in Lebanon
they are called *Mutawalis*). Several of these countries, however, recognize the Shi'i *madhhab*, which diverges little from
the Sunni *madhhab*s [most conspicuously different are the
mention of 'Ali b. Abi Talib in the statement of faith and
recognition of temporary marriage]. Forty million Twelvers
make this by far the largest branch of Shi'ism; of these,
about twenty-five million live in Iran. Because their imams
are hidden, Twelver Shi'is have proved relatively immune to
succession disputes and to schisms.

Two significant Twelver offshoots, lasting to the present
day, are the Nusayris and the Shaykhis-Babis-Baha'is. The
Nusayris*, also known as *Alawis** or *Ansaris**, broke away
from the tenth or eleventh of the twelve imams in about
859. At that time, Ibn Nusayr declared himself the *bab*
("gateway to truth"), the figure who comes right after the
imam in dignity and power. With this authority, Ibn Nusayr
proclaimed new doctrines, notably the incarnation of divinity
in 'Ali; the holy trinity of 'Ali, Muhammad, and Salman al-
Farisi (a freed slave of Muhammad's and the first Persian
convert to Islam); and the soul-less nature of women (leading
to their abominable treatment by Nusayris). The religion
includes many Christian elements, such as the notion of a
trinity and the celebration of Christian festivals.

In modern times, Nusayris live mostly along the coast
of Syria and in nearby regions of Lebanon and Turkey. (The
Qizilbashis in Turkey resemble Nusayris closely.) In Syria,
Nusayris number over half a million and constitute the largest
minority in the country. Between the two world wars the
French authorities in Syria favored this community, granting
it autonomy in an *Etat des Alouites* ('Alawi State) which,
however, did not survive Syrian independence in 1944. With
French encouragement, Nusayris ('Alawis) joined the army in
large numbers and, as a result, today make up a disproportionate element of Syria's officer corps. In addition, they
joined the Ba'th party with enthusiasm; its secular
nationalism de-emphasized the traditional religious differences dividing them from the Muslim majority. Since 1967 the
Ba'th has provided them with a mechanism for ruling Syria;
President Asad and his top officials are mostly 'Alawis.

The other noteworthy Twelver offshoot occurred in the nineteenth century, beginning with the controversial but not clearly irregular teachings of Shaykh Ahmad b. Zayn ad-Din al-Ahsa'i (1753-1826) whose followers became known as *Shaykhis* (they number about 250,000 today). In 1844, exactly one thousand lunar years after the occultation of the twelfth imam in 874, a Persian Shaykhi, Sayyid 'Ali Muhammad (1819-50) claimed to be the *bab*, then the *mahdi*, and finally a prophet in his own right, contradicting the Islamic belief in Muhammad as the final prophet. After 1844, the Bab's doctrines diverged increasingly from those of Islam. In particular, his most sacred writing (the Bayan) abrogated the Qur'an and instituted a large number of new regulations (many, curiously, centering on the number nineteen). Iranian government troops executed him in 1850 as a result of the political unrest caused by his followers, the *Babis**. Violent persecution succeeded, by 1853, in defusing its activism, but not in eliminating the faith.

Two half-brothers succeeded the Bab, Subh-i Azal and Baha'ullah. Subh-i Azal remained true to the Bab's teachings. His followers, known as *Azalis**, number less than 50,000 today. Baha'ullah (1817-90) transformed the Babi doctrine, claiming in 1853 to be the manifestation of God and that his own holiest book (Kitab al-Aqdas) abrogated the Bayan. Living in exile under Ottoman custody, Baha'ullah's outlook and aspirations broadened; with time he developed doctrines attractive to non-Muslims, especially Occidentals. *Baha'ism** advocates pacifism, universal fraternity, racial fusion, and a single universal language. Baha'ism has no cult and became, in effect, a faith for the non-religious. Baha'ullah's descendants have succeeded him, uneventfully, as the sect's leaders until the present day. Baha'is number about a million in Iran, where they have never attained legal recognition and suffer intermitten persecution. Some 10,000 converts in the United States, 3,000 in Uganda, and 1,000 in West Germany provide Baha'ism with important places of refuge outside Iran.

Isma'ilis, or Seveners

Shi'is who believe in Isma'il as the seventh imam are known either as *Isma'ilis* or *Seveners*; they have split the most often and present the most intricate picture. They lived in fairly obscure circumstances from the time of their break with the Twelver Shi'is in about 765 until the Fatimids' stunning capture of Tunisia in 909. Sixty years later, the Fatimids conquered Egypt and moved there, establishing one of the richest and most dynamic polities in medieval Muslim history. One of their kings, al-Hakam (r. 996-1021) behaved in ways so strange that some extremist Isma'ilis thought him divine. Adherents of this new faith, known to the outside world as *Druzes** and to themselves as *Muwahhidun**, withdrew from the community of Islam into the hills of the Levant, espousing a secret doctrine known only to a few initiates.

Druze leaders rose to local political power in the fifteenth
century and still remain an important force in Lebanon.
With populations of about 150,000 in both Lebanon and Syria,
they form a majority in certain small areas. While the Druze
in these two states and in Jordan (where they number 10,000)
have recently de-emphasized their withdrawal from Islam in
order to fit more neatly into the social and political order,
the 35,000 Druze in Israel have openly declared their non-
Islamic sentiments by fighting on the Israeli side since 1948.

Al-Hakam's grandson, al-Mustansir, had a contested
succession. Some Isma'ilis followed his son al-Musta'li.
Others, including the notorious Assassins ("users of hashish,"
a secret order distinguished by its members' blind obedience
to their spiritual leader and their use of murder to eliminate
foes) remained faithful to his son Nizar, even though he died
without an heir. Modern *Nizaris* (known as *Khojas* in India,
Isma'ilis in Syria, and *Muridan-i Agha Khan* in Iran) retain
none of the Assassins' fanaticism or violence but live peacefully as merchants and entrepreneurs, and are distinguished
by their exceptionally developed community consciousness.
In 1834, the Iranian ruler gave their forty-fifth imam the
title "Agha Khan," and the British granted him numerous
privileges when he subsequently took refuge in India. The
Agha Khan is the earthly incarnation of divinity for his
followers, who take his word as law. The current imam,
Karim Khan, succeeded his grandfather in 1957. Two hundred
thousand of his followers live in India and in regions of
Africa to which Indians emigrated (Kenya, Tanzania, South
Africa); about 100,000 are scattered through the Middle East,
in Central Asia, Syria, the al-Hasa province of Saudi Arabia
(near Kuwait) and the Yemen.

The *Musta'lis* splintered into small groups: *Tayyibis*,
Amiris, *Bohoras*, *Da'udis*, *Sulaymanis*, et al. Unable to maintain sectarian cohesion, they have a history of assimilating
with other Muslim groups. To avoid persecution by the Sunnis,
the Musta'lis, like most Shi'is, practice dissimulation but,
lacking clear leadership, some of them forget the pretense
and with time, take the Sunni faith to heart. Highly secretive,
they have prevented most of their religious literature from
being published. Like the Nizaris they are, for the most
part, merchants, mostly the descendants of Indian converts
to Islam in India, Burma, Somalia, Kenya, and Tanzania; and
another branch exists in the Yemen. With their tendency
toward schism and secrecy, the history and distribution of
Musta'lis is poorly known.

Ahl-i Haqq and Yazidis

At the far edge of Shi'ism are two small, barely Islamic
groups. One, the *Ahl-i Haqq** (also known as *'Ali-Illahis**),
definitely sprang from Isma'ili origins, probably in the
fifteenth century. They follow the secret doctrines of Sultan
Suhak, including his immensely complex cosmology and tightly

organized communal life. Ahl-i Haqq are found primarily in
the rural areas of Western Iran and in Syria, Turkey, Central
Asia, and India. Known as *'Alawis** in Turkey, they are frequently confused with Nusayris.

The second group, the *Yazidis**, incorporates Islamic
elements with those of many other religions, especially
Christianity and Zoroastrianism. Its 150,000 or so believers
are almost all Kurds, living in northern Iraq, Syria, and
eastern Turkey. The secret doctrines and endogamous marriages
of the Yazidis have not only helped maintain the community
through centuries of persecution but have also prevented the
outside world from fully understanding the faith's beliefs
and practices.

KHARIJIS

The Ibadis are neither Sunnis nor Shi'is but the only
surviving heirs to a division in Islam once nearly their match
in numbers, the *Kharijis*. When Muslims fought over leadership
of the Islamic community in the decades after Muhammad's
death, the Shi'is insisted that the imam must come from among
'Ali's descendants, the Sunnis allowed the caliph to come from
any branch of Muhammad's tribe, the Quraysh, and the Kharijis
required no descent at all. Conversely, while Shi'is almost
ignored their leader's personal qualitites and Sunnis paid them
only moderate attention, Kharijis insisted that the ruler have
an irreproachable character. They claimed to be ready to
follow a virtuous leader even if he were "an Ethiopian slave
with his nose cut off." Kharijis applied the same severe
standards of morality to ordinary individuals. Anyone guilty
of a major sin was no longer a Muslim in their eyes. Here,
indeed, are the Protestants of Islam, interested in virtue,
not in power or in blood relations.

Khariji groups died out over the centuries, usually in
violent ways. Only the most moderate of them, the *Ibadis*,
have survived to the present. Kharijism has dominated in
Oman (present population 900,000) since 751 and is the state
religion there today. Omanis took Ibadi Islam with them to
Zanzibar in the nineteenth century, where several thousand
Ibadis still live. Another 150,000 are split between isolated
communities in Libya (at Jabal Nafusa), Algeria (in the Mzab
desert region), and Tunisia (on the island of Jarba).

                          * * *

Islamic sects have flourished especially well in a
rectangular area from the eastern Mediterranean shore to
the northwestern border of India. Most sectarians live
within this region; two other clusters live along the southern
coast of Arabia and the western coast of India. Except for
the Zaydis and the Twelvers, no branch has appreciably more
than a million adherents and all of them combined constitute

only a small minority of Muslims.   In contrast to the
emphasis here on schisms and cults, Islam is characterized
by a catholic unity which allows wide varieties of faith
and practice within the Sunni framework.

The Islamic Middle East: An Incomplete Bibliographic Essay

Leonard Librande
Eugene Rothman

Many standard works have been written since the early Arab historians and their later European counterparts wrote about the history of a region known only recently as the Middle East. The former often believed that such history was universal, since the Islamic world was their universe or, at least, the only significant part thereof; the latter felt that their work chronicled the events of the Orient, the East or the 'Hither East' - much of it exotic, curious and other worldly.

Writing about the Middle East has progressed much during this century and particularly since the Second World War. The explosion of knowledge and the expansion of Western awareness of regions outside those with which we are familiar have not left the Middle East untouched and for this students of the region may be grateful.

Early works such as Carl Brockelmann's *History of the Islamic Peoples* have been superseded by massive and incisive studies such as Marshall Hodgson's *The Venture of Islam*, compendia such as *The Cambridge History of Islam*, popular academic works such as Bernard Lewis' *The Arabs in History*, reflections of a lifetime's scholarship such as H.A.R. Gibb's *Studies on Islamic Civilization*, and volumes on specific countries and their evolution such as Bernard Lewis' groundbreaking *The Emergence of Modern Turkey* and Kamal Salibi's *The History of Modern Lebanon*.

However, until recently the Islamic ethos of state and society in the region has been overlooked too frequently. Either it was assumed to be self-evident or it was ignored in numerous studies on the Islamic Middle East. Its recent revival has sparked much self-criticism among specialists. Professor Bernard Lewis, in what has become a benchmark for its far-sighted exposition, wrote in 1976 of the return of Islam. His essay issued a challenge for specialists as well as general observers of the modern and the past:

> If, then, we are to understand anything at all about what
> is happening in the Muslim World at the present time and
> what has happened in the past, there are two essential
> points which need to be grasped. One is the universality
> of religion as a factor in the lives of the Muslim peoples,
> and the other is its centrality.

(In light of recent events, this challenge might just as
easily have been posed to the other religious civilizations of the region.)

With respect to the Islamic Middle East, two questions
at once arise for the reader tempted to reject or accept
this challenge. First, what is intended by "religion"
here? Second, how has and does this "religion" or, more
accurately, religious civilization affect the peoples,
state and society of the Middle East? The responses to
these two crucial questions will undoubtedly be the starting point for some classic work still to be written.

Nevertheless, we already possess a great mass of
published material which can assist our understanding of
at least the outlines of Professor Lewis' challenge and a
few such selections constitute the basis of this incomplete
bibliography - incomplete since much of the work awaits a
generation of scholarship and much already written has
been omitted. This highly selective annotated bibliography
gives illustrations of the kinds of works that might help
the reader formulate some concept of what is intended by
Islam, religion and the Islamic ethos, and provide some
specific instances of their effects on state and society.
The reader wishing to go further is advised to consult
the many excellent bibliographies, such as J.N.D. Pearson's
Index Islamicus, that exist and hope for the best.

ASPECTS OF ISLAM AND ITS IMPACT

Marshall G. S. Hodgson, "The Islamic Vision in Religion
and Civilization," in *The Venture of Islam* (Chicago, 1974),
Vol. I, pp. 71-99.

The three volumes of *The Venture of Islam* are perhaps
the most significant contribution to the study of Islam in
this century. This particular chapter reveals the image of
Muhammad and of the community as the central forces in
Islam and seeks to define what "religion" means for Islam.

Marshall G. S. Hodgson, "The Role of Islam in World History,"
International Journal of Middle Eastern Studies I, 2 (April
1970), pp. 99-123.

This is a summary of some of Hodgson's basic insights. He emphasizes the overriding effect of "religion"

on the classical and medieval society of Islam. The theme
is much expanded in *The Venture of Islam*.

H.A.R. Gibb, "Structure of Religious Thought in Islam,"
The Muslim World (38), pp. 17-28, 113-123, 185-197, 280-291.

Gibb's articles are an ahistorical treatment of the
religious attitudes of Muslims that carefully separates
intellectual and practical attitudes.

H.A.R. Gibb, "An Interpretation of Islamic History,"
Journal of World History 1 (1953), pp. 39-62.

This superb treatment deals with, among other things,
the victory of the Islamic religious institution over other
social traditions.

Ibn Khaldun, "On Dynasties, Royal Authority, The Caliphate...,"
in *The Muqaddimah* (Princeton, 1974), pp. 123-261.

Although the entire book written by a 14th century
scholar merits reading, this chapter discusses the powerful effect of "religious feeling" on "group feeling."

Gustav von Grunebaum, *Unity and Variety in Muslim Civilization* (Chicago, 1956).

This classic work by one of the greatest scholars of
the field identifies a unified community as the central
goal of Muslim civilization.

Maurice Gaudefroy-Demombynes, *Muslim Institutions* (trans.
J. P. MacGregor: London, 1950).

An older but significant work, the study describes
the institutions that sustained a single Muslim community
for centuries. The final chapter takes some first steps
in assessing the present condition of Islam.

Joseph Schacht, "The Nature of Islamic Law," in *An
Introduction to Islamic Law* (Oxford, 1971), pp. 199-211.

This excellent description of the *Shari'a* defines
the scope of the law, its idealistic character, and its
aloofness. Historically, the law has been the major
determinant of the Islamic way of life and has given
"religion" its peculiar orthoprax character.

Majid Khadduri, *The Islamic Law of Nations: Shaybani's
Siyar* (Baltimore, 1966).

This is a useful introduction to the Muslim's theoretical image of himself and non-Muslims. It may be

supplemented by the author's *War and Peace in the Law of Islam.*

W. M. Watt, "Islamic Conceptions of the Holy War," in Thomas Patrick Murphy (ed.), *The Holy War* (Columbus, 1974), pp. 141-156.

Watt here presents a brief description of the ideal image of Holy War and the warrior for the faith. This is part of the self-image of Islam and must be considered.

Gustav von Grunebaum, *Muhammadan Festivals* (New York, 1951).

This excellent book details the major Muslim festivals and, more important, attempts to give the feelings of Muslims towards these events.

THE EVOLUTION OF ISLAMIC SOCIETY

M. A. Shaban, *Islamic History AD 600-750* (Cambridge, 1971).

Shaban's work documents the early shift away from the tribally dominated society of Arabia which coincided with and contributed to the systematic acceptance of Islam as the major force in society.

Gustav von Grunebaum, "Islamic Society and Social-Religious Movements," in *Classical Islam* (London, 1970), pp. 99-113.

This brief chapter gives examples of some of the early religious movements that clashed with local government in Islam and demonstrates how religious ideology was inseparable from social questions.

Jacob Lassner, *The Shaping of Abbasid Rule* (Princeton, 1980).

Lassner's work, undoubtedly the most important on the Abbasids in Western scholarship, studies the transformation of political structures based on tribal and familial relationships to the client structures that ultimately were inherited by the great medieval states of Islam. These new structures supported the caliphate for five centuries as a symbol of the cohesion and stability of the wider Islamic community.

S. D. Goitein, "A Turning Point in the History of the Muslim State," *Islamic Culture* 23 (1949), pp. 120-135.

Ibn al-Muqaffa, a Persian client of the Abbasid caliph al-Mansur, is here seen advising his lord of the enormous power implicit in Islamic belief and practice and of the need for the caliph to direct Islam.

Roy P. Mottahadeh, *Loyalty and Leadership in an Early Islamic Society* (Princeton, 1980).

This study exposes the social networks of Buyid society. Of particular interest are the Introduction which indicates the links between "religion" and "politics" up to the Buyid period and Chapter III where there is a discussion of the *ulama*.

Andrew S. Ehrenkreutz, *Saladin* (Albany, 1972).

This particular biographical study is given as only one example of the type of material available. Saladin here appears as an excellent case-study of the combination of motives that in the West are so easily distinguished as religious and political, but in the East merge readily.

Al-Ghazali, *The Faith and Practice of Al-Ghazali* (Trans. W. M. Watt: London, 1953).

This first work is al-Ghazali's autobiography. In it, his personal and intellectual discomfort at the skepticism bred by philosophy and Isma'ili doctrines and his dissatisfaction with the shortcomings of the legal patterns of Islam are exposed. These lead al-Ghazali to allow a place for the emotion and piety of Sufism which permit medieval Islam to absorb such invaders as the Mongols or converts in China, Africa, Indonesia, etc.

Erwin I. J. Rosenthal, *Political Thought in Medieval Islam* (Cambridge, 1958).

This survey of ideas on government and caliphate, law and religion, attempts to reveal the connection between religion and politics in the medieval age.

Halil Inalcik, *The Ottoman Empire: The Classical Age, 1300-1600* (London, 1973).

This is a study of the origins of the Ottoman Empire which at its height encompassed the entire Middle East and while including significant non-Muslim groups sustained a balanced Islamic state structure.

H.A.R. Gibb and Harold Bowen, *Islamic Society and the West* (Oxford, 1960).

Despite its title, Gibb and Bowen's well-known work is a map that gives the features of Ottoman Islamic society on the eve of Europe's massive entry into the Middle East. It is a detailed study of the theories, structure and nature of the state and society during that period.

THE MODERN DILEMMA

Bernard Lewis, *The Middle East and the West* (London, 1963-4).

Originally a series of lectures, this short work outlines the dilemma of modernity as the influence of the West begins in the nineteenth century to distort the traditional patterns of identity, allegiance and authority in the Islamic Middle East.

W. Polk and Chambers (eds.), *Beginnings of Modernization in the Middle East* (Chicago, 1968).

Faced with the visible superiority of Europe, traditional Middle Eastern rulers such as the Ottoman Sultans Selim III and Mahmud II and Muhammad Ali, Governor of Egypt, attempted in the early nineteenth century to strengthen their medieval societies through technical reforms. Articles by S. J. Shaw, "Some Aspects of the Aims and Achievements of the 19th Century Ottoman Reformers," and F. Steppat, "National Education Projects in Egypt before the British Occupation" show the nature and, at times, impact of these activities.

Helen B. Rivlin, *The Agricultural Policy of Muhammad Ali in Egypt* (Boston, 1961).

Rivlin's excellent work traces the evolution of Muhammad Ali's agricultural reforms and their effect on traditional rural society in Egypt. Many of these policies had a great impact on Egypt's social and economic structure based on earlier medieval forms.

Bernard Lewis, *The Emergence of Modern Turkey* (Oxford, 1968).

This volume on Turkey's transition to a modern secular state remains the major work of its kind. Although some aspects have been expanded by more recent research, its analysis of the processes affecting traditional forms of society is an excellent introduction to the problems of state, society and religion throughout the region.

Wilfred Cantwell Smith, *Islam in Modern History* (Princeton, 1957).

Smith's work deals with the problems of modernization and Islam in the Modern Age. It gives a concise survey of the dilemma of modernity and the modern movements that arose to meet it.

Kenneth Cragg, *Counsels in Contemporary Islam* (Edinburgh, 1965).

This third volume of the *Islamic Surveys* treats the various processes that have affected Islam in the past century and makes some important generalizations regarding the changes of modernization and secularization and the Islamic responses.

J. Spencer Trimingham, "Nineteenth Century Revival Movements," in *The Sufi Orders in Islam* (Oxford, 1973), pp. 105-132.

This chapter catalogues the revival of religious fraternities brought on by the growing dissatisfaction of Muslims with medieval forms and European intrusions. Religious revivalism and fundamentalism are continuing themes that parallel the responses of modernism and secularization.

P. M. Holt, *The Mahdist State in the Sudan, 1881-1898* (Oxford, 1970).

This excellent work by the leading scholar of the modern Sudan describes the history of an Islamic state based on the fulfillment of religious ideals during and after the life of the Mahdi.

Mohammad Ahmad Jamal, *The Intellectual Origins of Egyptian Nationalism* (Oxford, 1968).

Nationalism and patriotism were yet another response to the distortion of patterns of identity in the Islamic Middle East. Jamal traces the evolution of Egyptian national feeling based on its particular heritage and traditional environment.

Sylvia G. Haim, *Arab Nationalism: An Anthology* (Berkeley, 1962).

This anthology brings together excerpts from major primary sources dealing with the broader subject of Arab nationalism. Haim's extensive introduction is an excellent summary of the evolution of Arab nationalism and places it within its cultural perspective.

Albert Hourani, *Arabic Thought in the Liberal Age, 1798-1939* (Oxford, 1962).

The overriding concern of Arab intellectuals throughout the 19th and during the first half of the 20th century was the response to the power and influence of Europe in the Islamic East. Hourani's work surveys the responses

from the early writers such as Shaykh Tahtawi and until
the Second World War.

Nikkie R. Keddie, *An Islamic Response to Imperialism,
Political and Religious Writings of Sayyid Jamal ad-Din
al-Afghani* (Berkeley, 1968).

Jamal ad-Din al-Afghani is one of the most important
intellectual leaders of the Islamic reaction to Europe.
Although there is little doubt of his impact on the Pan-
Islamic movement, there is some question as to the true
nature of his views. Keddie's work is a summary of his
political and religious writings through which he
influenced the struggle against Europe in the late 19th
century.

Malcolm H. Kerr, *Islamic Reform, The Political and Legal
Theories of Muhammad Abduh and Rashid Rida* (Berkeley,
1966).

Al-Afghani's leading disciple was Muhammad Abduh,
later Mufti of Egypt and Rector of al-Azhar University.
Kerr's work outlines the views of Abduh and those of
another Islamic reformer Rashid Rida.

Niyazi Berkes, *The Development of Secularism in Turkey*
(Montreal, 1964).

Although superseded in some respects by more recent
works, this remains an important study of the evolution
of the secularist option adopted by the national state
that replaced the Ottoman Empire.

Nadav Safran, *Egypt in Search of Political Community*
(Boston, 1961).

Safran investigates the accommodation in Egypt between the society's traditional impulses and the development of political community. Within this context he
examines the political culture as it moved from the
nineteenth into the twentieth century.

C. G. Hess and H. L. Bodman, "Confessionalism and Feudality
in Lebanese Politics," *Middle East Journal* 8 (1954),
pp. 10-24.

Where Turkey formally rejected religion as an
organizing principle in the modern age and Egypt attempted
to reconcile at times conflicting approaches in society,
Lebanon tried to maintain a multiconfessional structure
based on the accommodation of different religious
societies. Hess and Bodman's article is an excellent
description of that system before it collapsed.

Richard P. Mitchell, *The Society of the Muslim Brothers* (Oxford, 1969).

Mitchell's book relates the activities and structure of a major force in the Middle East that rejects any compromise with the supremacy of religion as the basis of society.

Erwin I. J. Rosenthal, *Islam in the Modern National State* (Cambridge, 1965).

This work complements the work done in the writer's earlier study of medieval Islam. However, it is not as successful in dealing with the modern Middle East due to the writer's problems with access to sources.

A. M. Lutfiyya and Churchill (eds.), *Readings in Arab Middle Eastern Societies and Cultures* (Paris, 1970).

Articles on the "Family," "The Middle East as a Culture Area," and "The Social Basis of Political Institutions," give the reader an introduction to the approach taken by social anthropologists towards the study of the contemporary Middle East. It is, for all its faults, an increasingly popular methodology adopted by scholars seeking to examine the nexus between state, society and religion.

R. M. Savory (ed.), *Islamic Civilization* (Cambridge, 1976).

This is a more orthodox historical approach to the study of the region. For example, Savory's "Law and Traditional Society" attempts to apply the traditional approaches to the questions under discussion.

Kemal H. Karpat, *Political and Social Thought in the Contemporary Middle East* (New York, 1968).

One of the more interesting aspects of this work is that it enables the reader to gain an insight into what more recent Middle Eastern writers think about religion, state and society and how they would like to direct developments.

About the Editor
and Contributors

Editor

Michael Curtis is Professor of Political Science at
Rutgers University, New Brunswick. He is the author and
editor of over fifteen books on Comparative Politics and
Political Theory, and has also edited and co-edited
several books on the Middle East. Among these are *People
and Politics in the Middle East*, (1971); *Israel, Social
Structure and Change* (with Mordecai S. Chertoff), (1973);
Israel in the Third World (with Susan Aurelia Gitelson),
(1976).

Contributors

Janet Aviad is a member of the Van Leer Institute,
Jerusalem, and lectures in sociology in the School of
Education at the Hebrew University, Jerusalem.

Kevin A. Avruch is Assistant Professor in the Anthropology
Program at George Mason University.

The late Najm A. Bezirgan was Associate Professor of
Middle Eastern Studies and Oriental and African Languages
and Literature at the University of Texas at Austin.
Among other publications, he was the co-author of
Elementary Standard Arabic (1968).

Louis J. Cantori is Chairman of the Department of
Political Science at the University of Maryland, Baltimore
County. His publications include the forthcoming *Political
Mobilization in Pre-Revolutionary Egypt: The Wafd Party*
(1981).

William L. Cleveland is Associate Professor in the Department of History and Associate Dean of Arts at Simon Fraser University. His publications include *The Making of an Arab Nationalist: Ottomanism and Arabism in the Life and Thought of Sati' al Husri* (1971).

R. Hrair Dekmejian is Professor of Political Science at the State University of New York at Binghamton. His publications include *Patterns of Political Leadership: Egypt, Israel, Lebanon* (1976).

Daniel J. Elazar is Professor of Political Science at Temple University, Senator N. M. Paterson Professor of Political Studies at Bar Ilan University, Israel, and Chairman of its Center for Jewish Community Studies.

John P. Entelis is Professor of Political Science at Fordham University. His publications include *Pluralism and Party Transformation in Lebanon* (1974).

Fariborz Ghavidel is an Ed.D. graduate of Oklahoma State University.

Yosef Gotlieb is the Director of the Project for the Study of Middle Eastern Nationalities and Consultant in Middle Eastern and Third World Affairs for the World Jewish Congress.

Emanuel Gutmann is Professor of Political Science at the Hebrew University, Jerusalem. His publications include an essay, with Jacob M. Landau, in *Political Elites in the Middle East*, edited by George Lenczowski, (1975).

Raymond N. Habiby is Professor of Political Science at Oklahoma State University. His publications include a monograph, in Arabic, on *Behaviorism and Management*, prepared for Libya's Qar Yunis University, (1976).

R. Stephen Humphreys is a Visiting Research Fellow at the Institute for Advanced Study at Princeton University. His publications include *From Saladin to the Mongols - The Ayyubids of Damascus, 1193-1260*, (1977).

Aziza Hussein is the Chairwoman of the Cairo Family Planning Association and a prominent Egyptian women's leader.

James P. Jankowski is Professor of History at the University of Colorado at Boulder. His publications include *Egypt's Young Rebels: Young Egypt, 1933-1952* (1975).

Bernard Lewis is Cleveland Dodge Professor of Near Eastern Studies at Princeton University and a long-term member of the School of Historical Studies at the Institute for Advanced Study at Princeton University. Among his many publications is *The Middle East and the West*. He is also the co-editor, with P. M. Holt and Ann K.S. Lambton, of *The Cambridge History of Islam* (1970 and 1977).

Leonard Librande is Assistant Professor of Religion at Carleton University.

George Linabury is Professor of Middle East History at Western Connecticut State College. He has written extensively on the Arabian Peninsula and, in particular, on Yemen and Oman.

The late Mohamed Al-Nowaihi was Professor of Arabic Language and Literature at the American University in Cairo. He was the author of numerous studies.

Daniel Pipes is a member of the Department of History at the University of Chicago. Among his studies is the forthcoming book, *Slave Soldiers and Islam* (1980).

Jeffrey A. Ross is Assistant Professor in the Department of Government at Hamilton College. Among other studies, he is the co-editor, with Ann Baker Cottrell, of *The Mobilization of Collective Identity: Comparative Perspectives* (1980).

Eugene Rothman is Associate Professor of Religion at Carleton University. His forthcoming book is entitled *The Biblical Mosaic*.

Kamal S. Salibi is a member of the Department of History and Archeology at the American University of Beirut. He is the author of *Crossroads to Civil War: Lebanon 1958-1976* (1976).

Roger M. Savory is Professor in the Department of Middle Eastern and Islamic Studies at the University of Toronto. Among his numerous publications is *Introduction to Islamic Civilization* (1976).

Robert M. Stookey is a research associate of the Center for Middle Eastern Studies at the University of Texas at Austin. Among his publications is his translation of Jacques Berque's *Cultural Expression in Arab Society Today* (1978).

Mervin F. Verbit is Associate Professor of Sociology at Brooklyn College and The Graduate School of the City University of New York, and the author of numerous studies.

His contribution to this volume is based on his Dr. Aaron Citron Memorial Lecture (1978).

Gabriel R. Warburg is Professor of Middle East History at the University of Haifa, Israel. His publications include *Islam, Nationalism and Communism in a Traditional Society: The Case of Sudan* (1979).

Index